THE GREAT
ARCHAEOLOGISTS

The modern world's discovery
of ancient civilisations

as originally reported in the pages of

THE ILLUSTRATED
LONDON NEWS

from 1842 to the present day

THE GREAT ARCHAEOLOGISTS

edited by Edward Bacon

BOOK CLUB ASSOCIATES
LONDON

This edition published 1976 by
Book Club Associates
By arrangement with Martin Secker & Warburg Limited

Copyright © 1976 by The Illustrated London
News and Martin Secker & Warburg Limited

Printed in Great Britain by
Jarrold & Sons Ltd, Norwich

Contents

Contents

Contents

Contents

Editor's Note

It has not always been possible to accompany each article here printed with its original illustrations: however, the best, the most important, the most interesting are all reproduced. Cross-references to the illustrations have therefore been introduced into the text: *(Figure 14)*, for example, for black and white illustrations; *(Plate 16, p. 94)*, for example, for colour plates.

The spellings of names have sometimes changed considerably over the years. We have followed the original articles faithfully, although the accepted modern versions of such names are to be found in my (italic) link passages. Thus the reader will follow Catal Huyuk to Chatal Huyuk to Čatal Hüyük; Cnossus to Knossus to Knossos; Nimroud to Nimrud; and find many different transliterations of the Greek word for "Saint": Hagia, Haghia, Agia, Ajia. The index follows the modern versions, but the other spellings are all included and cross-referenced.

E.B.

Acknowledgments

Most of the illustrations have been reproduced direct from *The Illustrated London News*. The publishers wish to thank the following additional sources:

Bayerisches Landesamt für Denkmalpflege, Figure 153; British Museum, courtesy of the Trustees, Plates 18, 22, 24, 29, 30, 33, Figures 79, 115, 128–9, 144–5, 157–8 (now Cyprus Museum); British School of Archaeology in Jerusalem, Plate 40, Figure 165; Chicago, Oriental Institute, Figures 136–8, 141; Peter Clayton, Plates 10 (Herakleion Museum), 25, 26 (Herakleion Museum), 27, 45 (National Museum, Athens); Werner Forman, Plates 8–9 (Hermitage, Leningrad), 16, 38–9 (National Museum of Anthropology, Mexico City); Giraudon, Paris, Plate 34, Figures 160–2 (all Archaeological Museum, Chatillon-sur-Seine); Griffith Institute, Oxford, Figures 86, 88–90, 96–106 (all Cairo Museum); Robert Harding Associates, Plates 19 (National Museum of Pakistan, Karachi), 20 (National Museum of India, New Delhi); Hans Hinz, Basle, Plate 28, Figure 143; Hirmer Verlag, Figure 69; Public Works of Ireland, Figures 202, 205, 207; F. L. Kenett (copyright George Rainbird Ltd), Plates 12, 14–15 (all Cairo Museum); Museum of London, Figure 169; James Mellaart, Plates 49, 51, Figures 181–3, 189–94; Metropolitan Museum of Art (photograph by Egyptian Expedition), Figure 75; Palestine Exploration Fund, Figure 52; Clichés des Musées Nationaux, Paris, Figure 140 (Louvre Museum); Peabody Museum, Harvard University, Plate 31; Josephine Powell, Plates 2 (National Museum, Athens), 46, Figures 60, 61 (Herakleion Museum); Scala, Plates 4, 42–4; Dr. K. St. Joseph, Figure 201; Sussex Archaeological Trust, Plate 50; Lord William Taylour, Figures 203–4; Eileen Tweedy, Plates 1 (collection Edward Bacon), 32, 41 (Archaeological Museum, Plovdiv); Jean Vertut, Plates 5–6.

The publishers wish also to thank Marian Berman who assembled the illustrations, and Cartographic Enterprises who prepared the maps.

Introduction

Although it seems innate in man to be interested in the past and, more particularly, in his own past; although the Babylonian kings preserved memorials of Sumer, and such Roman Emperors as Hadrian were inveterate collectors of splendid antiquities; although history, as an art, stretches back at least to Herodotus, and antiquarianism, as a hobby, at. least to the Renaissance; yet archaeology, as a science, though concerned with the most ancient aspects of humanity, goes back hardly more than a century and a half.

Nearly the whole of this period is covered by the life of *The Illustrated London News*, which began publication in May 1842, when Queen Victoria had reigned but five years, and which still continues at this moment when her great-great-granddaughter has already reigned for nearly twenty-five years.

Since the 1920s the paper has been known, throughout the majority of the world, as one of the few general periodicals which consistently have reported archaeological discoveries as a general thing and not solely when some spectacular discovery momentarily has rivalled a Royal wedding, a revolution, or a war in their claims for popular attention and journalistic newsworthiness. This, then, is and was well enough known; but the writer's researches have revealed to him that since its original publication the paper and its editors have always been concerned with the uncovering of the past as well as with the reporting of the present. The first archaeological item it recorded – Roman remains in the City of London – appeared in the second issue of the paper; as early as 1847, the colossal Assyrian sculptures, discovered by Layard at Nimrud in northern Mesopotamia, and now among the glories of the British Museum, were being recorded in the paper with splendid, accurate and detailed engravings; at one period, for a number of years, a regular feature was "Archaeology of the Month", a full thirteen-inch column of fine print, for the most part of monumental dullness, but still an index of the paper's and the public's close interest in the subject; and throughout Victoria's long reign, in the Edwardian after-glow and the years before the First World War, one can trace the tides, both neap and spring, in the growth of the young science and of the popular interest in the aspects of man's past which were currently being revealed.

In the early years, over a steady groundswell of a somewhat parochial interest in Roman Britain (which still continues), the preoccupation of the archaeologists and their readers lay in "proving the truth of the Bible", principally in Assyria. In 1861 came the discovery of flint tools near Amiens by Boucher de Perthes, a find which can be claimed as the beginning of the study of prehistoric man. The 1870s saw Schliemann's excavations at Mycenae and Troy, which may perhaps be described as "proving the truth of Homer". In the 1880s the interest shifted to Egypt with the discoveries of Maspero and Flinders Petrie; and in the same decade the Incas in Peru and the Mayas in Guatemala drew the archaeologists' attention and the paper's interest.

In 1900 Bruce Ingram (a grandson of the founder of the paper) became editor at the early age of twenty-one, and continued in the editorial chair until his death early in 1963; and his own personal interest in and enthusiasm for archaeological discoveries, sparked by a boyhood visit to Egypt – where he claimed to have stood on the shoulders of Rameses at Abu Simbel – ensured and confirmed the paper's preoccupation with archaeology. These pre-war years of the twentieth century were concerned, primarily, with the amazing discoveries of the Minoan civilisation in Crete by Sir Arthur Evans and other archaeologists at Knossos, Phaistos, Palaikastro, Zakro, Hagia Triada and Gournia, but also with the marvellous Magdalenian rock-paintings of Altamira and south-west France, with the spread of excavation in southern and central America, with rewarding discoveries in Egypt and – to add a note of bathos – the discovery of "Piltdown Man".

This seventy-two-year-long record (1842–1914) was, then, a story of continuous discovery, of rising excitement and interest, a time when a succession of "transformation scenes" was revealing the full splendour of the Egyptians and the Assyrians, disclosing for the first time the unguessed Minoan and Mycenaean origins of Hellas, uncovering the achievements of the early Peruvians and the Mesoamericans, and showing what consummate artists were the Magdalenian prehistoric men of Altamira and south-west France some 18,000 years ago.

But what these seventy-two years had revealed was to seem almost as nothing compared with what the few years between the two great wars were so swiftly to bring to light. It is impossible to turn over the pages of *The Illustrated London News* in the 1920s and 1930s without a sense that the whole world of the past is being newly presented in a brilliant kaleido-

scope of new and newer, more and more brilliant visions – a strange sense that whatever the pace of progress and modern discovery, the past is nevertheless changing far faster, and, as the storm clouds of disaster loom more menacingly over the world of tomorrow, the vision of antiquity grows in brilliance and splendour.

For this was the period of the most dramatic and exciting of all archaeological finds – the discovery of the virtually untouched tomb of the Pharaoh Tutankhamen (as his name was generally spelt in those days). This was a discovery that had everything: a fantastic amount of sheer bullion, vast quantities of works of art and craft of unimaginable richness, beauty, and complexity, funeral goods on an unheard-of scale from ritual pomp to domestic intimacy, and, in the heart of all this opulence and splendour, the untouched mummy of a sickly young king, still in his teens, the symbol of a priestly counter-revolution against the heresies of Akhenaten, who for a few years had violently broken the steady ultra-conservative façade of dynastic Egypt. And furthermore, this burial had taken place at a time when for once the almost unchanging hieratic style of Egyptian art had been affected violently by the new ideas of Akhenaten, and a curiously sophisticated, even decadent, "art nouveau" style shows itself in so many of the treasures of Tutankhamen. *The Illustrated London News* rose to this occasion, and between the discovery, in the last months of 1922, and 1931 published no fewer than twenty-two major features, richly illustrated in colour and black-and-white, on this epoch-making find.

That this was the most amazing discovery of the twenty-one years between the wars can hardly be questioned. But that it was the most important from an archaeological point of view is most certainly open to doubt. It threw a brilliant and piercing light on a few admittedly highly significant years in Egyptian history, it loaded the Cairo Museum with treasures beyond the dreams of avarice and, perhaps most important, it opened the eyes of a vast public to the fascination and glamour of the past. It sensitised them, so to speak, to the other less spectacular but archaeologically more important discoveries which were being made in this remarkable period.

For this was the age when Tell el Amarna, the short-lived capital of Tutankhamen's predecessor, the heretic Akhenaten, was being uncovered; when the revelation of Minoan Crete was being pursued by Sir Arthur Evans and many others; when the Mycenaeans were being brought into the full light of day by Wace at Mycenae, by the Swedes at Dendra, and by Blegen in the Troad and Peloponnese; and when Sir John Marshall, after showing forth Hellenistic India at Taxila, had gone on to excavations at Mohenjo-daro and Harappa to disclose in the hitherto unsuspected Indus Valley civilisation a culture comparable in complexity and significance with the Nile and Mesopotamian nuclear civilisations. Meanwhile, Leonard Woolley at Ur of the Chaldees was revealing the treasures and complexities of Sumer; and this picture of a brilliant and literate Mesopotamian civilisation, then assumed to be the cradle of urban development, was being filled in by the Germans at Warka and by a long series of widely ranging expeditions in the Euphrates–Tigris plain by the Oriental Institute of Chicago under the general direction of Dr. Henry Frankfurt. In Syria the Frenchman Schaeffer found at Ras Shamra the site of ancient Ugarit, a key state in the Egyptian diplomatic correspondence only recently discovered at Tell el Amarna, while in Persia the German Ernst Herzfeld was working among the Achaemenian palaces of Persepolis.

What an age this was! – there seemed no limit to the power and skill of the archaeologists in revealing the past and no limit, likewise, to the riches which lay beneath the soil. World war again intervened and the liberal arts and sciences, as well as the laws, were silent in the clash of arms. But the years since 1945 have been as rich in their way as the years before 1939. Perhaps the finds have not been quite so spectacular, but the commitment has been wider, more archaeologists have been deployed in more fields; skills, methods and techniques have become more refined and the frontiers of knowledge of the past have been pushed further and further back.

A new attitude, too, has come into being. Whereas in the past it sometimes seemed as if archaeologists were concerned primarily in supplying the great museums with spectacular treasures, their objective now is much more clearly concentrated on revealing the nature of man in antiquity, how he lived, what and why he worshipped, what were his thoughts, his objectives, his achievements, what he was like as a man. Where Layard, seeking huge sculptures at Nimrud, had dug mainly along the walls, since this was where one would find major sculpture, Mallowan, re-working the same site, dug more widely and found in wells and shattered storehouses delightful ivories and elaborate furniture which revealed the "brutal and militaristic" Assyrians as connoisseurs of elegant and appealing works of art. Ventris and Chadwick, by "breaking the code" of the Minoan Linear-B script and so revealing that the Mycenaeans spoke an early form of Greek, completely revised the history of Hellas yet again. Technical developments such as Carbon-14 and other sophisticated dating methods have given confirmation to the speculations of the scholar, while such tools as the proton-magnetometer, the use of electrical resistivity methods and the periscope drill have simplified the task of the field archaeologists, and the development and use of the aqualung have taken the archaeologist beneath the waves almost as effectively as the spade and trowel take him below the surface of the earth.

But probably the most fascinating aspects of archaeology in the post-war years are those in which these refined techniques are combined in laying bare that most shadowy of periods in man's past, the time when from being a hunter-gatherer he became a settled farmer and thence began to build communities which developed from villages into towns, and the foundations of urban civilisation were laid. Landmarks of this development duly appeared in the pages of *The Illustrated London News*, and mention can be made of Professor Robert Braidwood's researches among the "First Farmers" of Jarmo in Iraq and allied sites over the border in Iran, of Perrot's work in Israel and Miss Kirkbride's in Jordan and, most notably, of Dr. Kathleen Kenyon's amazing discoveries at Jericho and James Mellaart's neolithic townships at Haçilar and Čatal Hüyük in Anatolia, and, even more recently, of Srejović's discoveries at Lepenski Vir in Yugoslavia.

Looking back, then, over this study of some 130 years of issues of *The Illustrated London News*, it is possible to see an extensive summary of the march of archaeology, a complex science and craft developing, discovering and exploring the whole history of early man, showing what he did, felt, thought, desired and achieved; in short, writing an ever-continuing family history of man – of which the inevitable if not necessarily planned consequence is to reveal the common brotherhood of mankind.

As regards the arrangement of the material to be included in this book, it is possible to argue in favour of different principles. These principles can be summed up as follows: an arrangement purely by date; a division by geographical areas; a division in accordance with cultural groups; or a division along the lines of the work of famous men or specialist organisations – and all have something to be said for them. The writer's decision, however, is for the first of these – the chronological arrangement; and the reasons for this decision are as follows.

As previously stated, this anthology is drawn from the pages of *The Illustrated London News* over a period of more than 130 years, a period which has been shown to coincide with the immense development of the practice and science of archaeology and the consequent public interest in it. Furthermore, it is in the nature of newspaper reports that they are new,

of their time, continuous but often unfinished, and that they are rarely, at any given time, definitive. What they tell is a sort of serial story and it is in this that their drama and interest lie; and this book should, therefore, endeavour to recreate that long serial story which is archaeology since 1842. There are naturally many omissions – strangely enough there was no mention in the paper of General Pitt-Rivers' classic Victorian series of British excavations – but editors are only human and don't know everything and readers, so editors think, are even more human in their apprehension of what is readable.

This anthology, therefore, will proceed year by year (or, in some cases, in groups of years), and will consist of longer or shorter extracts from the more important, striking, or interesting reports. As regards the choice of what constitute the more important, striking, or interesting reports, the onus must lie on the present writer who, like the editors mentioned above, is also human and doesn't know everything but likewise believes that present-day readers, perhaps even more than Victorian readers, have limits to their doggedness.

As regards the writer's qualifications for the task, he has been concerned with the archaeological pages of *The Illustrated London News* for the last thirty years and, most recently, in the course of the background research necessary for the compilation of this book, has been engaged in turning over and studying every page of the paper published in this long tally of years, noting, analysing and recording every archaeological item which has appeared in *The Illustrated London News* since May 1842. Together with the other facts noted, a grading was made of the interest or importance of every item. Those which were of slight or ephemeral interest received no grading; those of slightly greater interest were graded B; those of notable interest A; those of major interest A-plus; and those which were really outstanding A-plus-plus. Before any final decisions were made, these gradings were re-assessed in light of the total picture and some were amended upwards or downwards. The magnitude of this task of selection and rejection may be appreciated after the contemplation of a few statistics.

In the period 1842 to 1921, there appeared 975 archaeological reports of varying length – 111 being of B quality, 221 of A quality and 133 of A-plus (or higher) quality, the remainder being of slight or ephemeral interest. Between 1922 and 1959 there were no fewer than 1,696 items, 293 being of B quality, 812 of A quality and 322 of A-plus (or higher) quality. And between 1960 and the first half of 1970 a further 430 items appeared, making a truly grand total of 3,101 archaeological reports, great and small. With these reports the present writer has been directly concerned since March 1945.

This anthology, then, comprises, in strict order of date, all those items which have been graded A-plus-plus and a number of others of slightly lower grading which were related either to the former or have an important bearing on the news-history of archaeology. But with this last factor in mind – namely that *The Illustrated London News* does in fact represent a news-history of archaeology – all these important items are interspersed with the writer's summaries of what was happening at the same time "in another part of the forest".

Finally, although it is the purpose of an anthology to gather together what is best or most interesting from the material available, sometimes the best must include the most familiar, and there is a danger of overloading such a collection with extracts already well known to the reader. Unexpected or forgotten items enliven the flow perhaps out of proportion to their intrinsic merit. Familiar ones can be all too familiar. To avoid this risk the writer has taken the liberty of compressing innumerable items about Tutankhamen into a précis of events, after the original thrilling first reports – principally because so much has been written, illustrated and seen of Tutankhamen in the last few years. And similarly the paper's reports since 1970 – which are still reasonably familiar to faithful readers of *The Illustrated London News* – have been compressed into a continuous précis.

Since, as has been claimed above, this anthology represents in some sense a news-history of archaeology since 1842, and since all papers or magazines represent, to some degree, the temperaments and intentions of their editors, it may interest the reader to learn who were the editors of *The Illustrated London News* during the 130-odd years concerned. There have been only twelve of them, and two of these occupied the chair for a total of ninety-four years:

From 1842 to 1844, F. W. N. Bayley.
From 1844 to 1852, John Timbs.
From 1852 to 1859, Dr. Charles Mackay, among other things a composer or librettist of convivial songs.
From 1859 to 1891, John Lash Latey.
From 1891 to 1899, Clement K. Shorter.
For a short "holding period", John Latey, son of John Lash Latey.
From 1900 to January 1963, Bruce S. Ingram.
From January 1963 to October 1964, Hugh Ingram.
From November 1964 to March 1966, Timothy Green.
From March 1966 to December 1967, John Kisch.
At the beginning of 1968, a period of six weeks without an editor.
From February 1968 to August 1970, Ian Lyon.
From 1970, James Bishop.

Of these the greatest, not only in length of tenure of office but also in devotion to archaeology, was unquestionably Bruce (later Sir Bruce) Ingram, and his principles were firmly adhered to by his successor (and second cousin) Hugh Ingram; and it was during their two successive consulates that the paper served most generously the cause of archaeology.

XANTHIAN MARBLES.

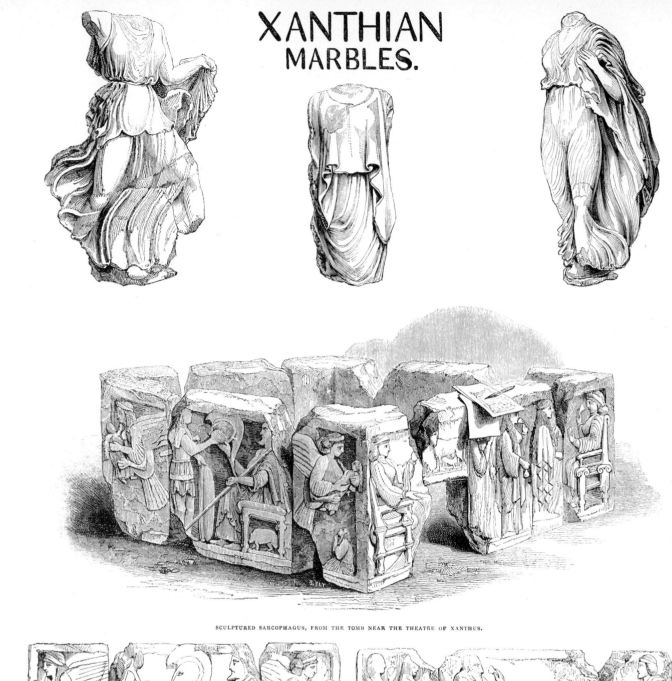

SCULPTURED SARCOPHAGUS, FROM THE TOMB NEAR THE THEATRE OF XANTHUS.

BAS RELIEF ON THE NORTH SIDE OF THE TOMB.

EAST SIDE.

SOUTH SIDE.

WEST SIDE.

1842–46

In these first five years of the paper's existence, there appeared (on May 14, 1842) the very first archaeological item, an unillustrated note on a section of the Roman wall in the City of London; and less than a year later the first illustrated item, a British Museum exhibition of "marbles" sent back from Xanthos in south-west Turkey. During the period there are several reports of Roman remains uncovered during building and sewerage operations in the City, comparable in many ways with the discoveries made in the same area during the rebuilding after the last war. A few minor discoveries of antiquarian rather than archaeological interest are reported; but the most striking features of these years are the reports of annual meetings of the Congress of British Archaeological Societies, of the Society of British Archaeologists and the Archaeological Institute. These were usually sited in some historic town or city and illustrated by the paper with a composite page of engravings of beauty-spots in the neighbourhood, which it was presumed the members would visit. Little of permanent interest was reported.

May 14, 1842

THE WALL OF LONDON

Mr. W. D. Saul, F.S.A., and G.S., at the recent meeting of the Antiquarian Society, communicated an account of his observations upon the foundations of the Roman Wall of London, recently developed at several points, and especially on the site of the French church, in Bull-and-Mouth street, Aldersgate. . . . The wall can thence be traced at intervals to Cripplegate churchyard, where a bastion still remains. . . . It is composed of layers of small rough flints, rough Kentish ragstone (the green sandstone of the geologists) pieces of ferrugineous sandstone irregularly interspersed, two courses of bricks, another layer of ragstone, a double course of tiles and another of ragstone.

February 11, 1843

THE XANTHIAN MARBLES

In the British Museum an exhibition has this week been thrown open to the public of a collection of marbles made in Asia Minor by the celebrated classic traveller Charles Fellowes, and brought to this country at the expense of the Government. We present a selection of them to our readers. They are called popularly the "Xanthian marbles"; but this is not quite correct, as they come from various places besides the ancient capital of Lycia. . . . The bas-reliefs of one of the largest tombs of Xanthus are now in the British Museum. . . . Our engraved perspective view and the separate detailed views of the bas-reliefs on the sides, will make the whole intelligible *(Figure 1)*. The north side is divided into three compartments; in the centre one, a monarch dressed in the double tunic and mantle, bearing the paternal staff – the sceptre of antiquity – is seen, presenting a helmet to a fully accoutred warrior; in the end compartments appear the harpy-like figures, so common in Egyptian sculptures; they are in ascending

17

1 The Xanthian Marbles

positions, and bear in their hands and claws dead human figures, significant, we conjecture, of the entrance of the soul on a happy immortality. The south figure is also disposed in triple tablets. In these the same harpy-like figures occur. In the centre a royal personage is seen, receiving the offerings of a female figure, who presents him with pomegranates and a pigeon. On the east side a venerable king, seated on a throne of state, listens to the address of a child, who presents him with a cock. Behind the chair stand the officers of state, and at the back of the child a man in the act, apparently, of seconding the representations of the supplicant. The western side exhibits two queen-like female figures, seated on thrones, in attitudes of reserved and formal state; between them three heavily draped females, their long hair bound by a tiara, plaited and dishevelled. In front of the former figures a cow suckling a calf appears. The design of these groups, as there is no inscription on the tomb, is not known but their general meaning is obvious. May they not be conjectured to represent the character of the deceased? Do we not see him in the northern sculpture, invested by the king – perhaps his father – with military command? And of the rest, may we not suppose that the southern tablet exhibits his wife, sacrificing, in his absence, and offering to propitiate the favour of the gods, and secure his peace; that in the eastern we see his martial boy, praying that courage, typified by the cock, may be given him on the day of battle; and in the western, that we see his family – his daughters, his wife, his mother – mourning him dead?

April 8, 1843

EXTINCT CITIES OF CENTRAL AMERICA

The political convulsions of Central America, the wars of the Texians, and the recent triumphs of the peoples of Yucatan, Guatemala, Honduras and neighbouring provinces, over the Mexican forces, having invested its "vexed borders" with fresh interest, we have determined on devoting a page to their historic illustrations. . . . Once, however, this beautiful country was the seat of a mighty empire, greatly advanced in the arts and elegancies of life, possessed of a system of religion, and a written language of its own, governed by independent kings, and having at command vast military power and civilised resources. All that now remains of them are the perishing temples, palaces, idols *(Figure 2)*, and altars of the "high places" and a few dispirited Indians, their lineal descendants. . . . The national monuments of their ancestors consist, as far as they have yet been discovered, of the ruins of great palatial cities, built of stone, and usually founded on the site of a hill possessing great military capabilities of defence. The principal of these are

2 Front view of one of the idols of Copen

Quiriga, Copen, Santa de Quiche, Palenque, Uxmal, Chi-Chen, Zayi and Campeachy. . . .

The palaces are built on the same princely scale as those peculiar to the "land of Egypt", but are of an order and style of decoration exclusively their own, and unlike the architecture of any other country. . . . Another remarkable feature in these ruins is the presence of numerous carved pillars, of the average height of twenty-five feet, which still stand erect in the midst of the *débris* of ruined architecture and perished vegetation which imbed their lower portions.

These pillars are square and have bas-reliefs on each of their four sides: on the front, a figure dressed in what we may suppose to be the costume of the country; and on the other sides, rude scroll-like ornaments, which sometimes enclose monograms and other symbols of what Mr. Stephens, in his *Incidents of Travel*, considers to be the language of the people who erected them. In front of these pillars, small richly carved altars have frequently been found.

1847–51

This is, par excellence, *the period of the Assyrian sculptures excavated by Layard and transported to the British Museum and a time of great activity in the Museum; and in 1850 we reported at some length Rawlinson's lecture on the Assyrian inscriptions. Roman villas were found near Chesterfield, Stony Stratford and Pau (in the Pyrenees); and mosaics at Aldborough, Yorks, and Cirencester. The fruitless excavations at Silbury Hill were abandoned. There was a short illustrated article on the paintings in the Ajanta Caves, India; and in 1848 there was "A Grand Antiquarian Banquet" at Newcastle upon Tyne.*

June 26, 1847

THE NIMROUD SCULPTURES

The accounts which have reached this country from time to time of the recent excavations and discoveries amongst the supposed ruins of Nineveh, have excited the curiosity not only of the antiquarian but also of all scriptural students, from the illustration they afford of passages of Holy Writ, of which all material traces appeared to be lost. We are indebted for such remains as have hitherto come to light to the indefatigable labours of M. Botta, the French Consul at Mossal, and to our own countryman, Mr. Layard; and it is no more than justice to the latter to remark that he was the *first* to indicate the probability of these ruins, though his suggestions were so coldly received by our Government that he was left to pursue his researches unaided, excepting by the private resources of Sir Stratford Canning. The French Government, however, with its accustomed liberal sympathy in the cause of science, stepped in and most nobly assisted M. Botta, who was thus enabled to precede Mr. Layard in discoveries of sculptures, etc., etc., at Khorsabad, which have, some time since, been forwarded to

3 The Nimroud sculptures: a lion hunt

Paris. The prompt liberality of our neighbours has, at length, had some effect upon ourselves, as we are informed that some pecuniary assistance has been transmitted to Mr. L., though, certainly, somewhat at the eleventh hour; for he has energetically worked, regardless of obstacles, and succeeded in forwarding to this country some of his important discoveries, which have within the last few days arrived safely at the British Museum. These interesting remains consist of two fragments of a colossal statue of a human-headed bull, and eleven Bassi Relievi, the whole from a vast building upon a mound at Nimroud, on the left bank of the Tigris, about twenty-five miles south of Mossal, and the site, as there is every reason to believe, of the most renowned and ancient city of the Assyrian Empire. . . . The extent and magnificence, however of the two palaces described by Mr. Layard and of that discovered by M. Botta at Khorsabad, as well as the elaborate detail of the sculptures, lead us to the conclusion that they are of such remote antiquity as to afford evidence of that primitive civilisation of the human race, so abundantly proved in the books of the Old Testament. . . .

The Ninth Relievo . . . represents a Bull Hunt. The King is attended by his huntsman, who follows the chariot, riding sideways upon one horse, and leading another richly-caparisoned, with embroidered fringed saddle, necklace and knotted tail, evidently for the King's use in the chase. The King in his chariot, having wounded a bull, seizes him by the horns, and inflicts a deadly wound with one of the daggers that he wears. It is especially remarkable that the King is inserting his dagger precisely between the second and third vertebra, where the spinal cord is most assailable, and that he is doing this carelessly, with his head turned away, with the composure gained by long experience. Another bull, pierced by four arrows, lies upon the ground. The horns of the bulls are peculiarly short and thick, but only one is represented on either. . . . In the usual place is the King's spear, like that carried by the huntsman; it has the addition of a fillet to rouse and frighten the wild beasts . . . the three horses have but six legs shown. The King wears the truncated cap, trilobed ear-rings, bracelets and armlets; in all other respects his dress is the same as before detailed. . . .

The Tenth Relievo represents a Lion Hunt (*Figure 3*). The King in his chariot, drawn by three horses, which the charioteer urges forward to escape a lion which has already placed his claw on the back of the chariot, infuriated at the four arrows which have already taken effect. The King at this juncture aims a deadly wound at the monster, whose tail is admirably indicative of rage and fury. Behind the lion are two of the King's bearded bodyguard, fully armed, and holding their shields and daggers in readiness for defence in the event of the prey escaping the shaft of the King. A wounded lion prowls crouching upon the ground in front – the agony expressed in its action being well contrasted with the fury in the former.

December 16, 1848
THE NIMROUD SCULPTURES LATELY RECEIVED AT THE BRITISH MUSEUM

The fruits of Mr. Layard's excavations which we now have under notice, were sunk in the Jumna during their voyage to England, and are stated to have suffered considerable damage from their submersion; whilst we ourselves can vouch for the irreparable injury to the smaller and more fragile remains – such as glass and ivory – the consequences of careless packing and repacking; nevertheless, enough has been preserved to confirm the interest which already attached to these Scriptural antiquities. . . .

The next relievo *(Figure 4)* is a continuation of the attack and most interestingly indicates that the military operations of this early period closely resemble those of the present day, for the assailants are fighting in ranks under cover of a moveable wicker breastwork, and immediately before the troops is a war-engine on wheels, and covered by a hanging. The engine is impelled against the walls up a levelled roadway on the rocky ascent on which the city is built; and the two spears attached have already effected a breach in a tower, upon the top of which a man stands with hands extended, as if asking for a truce. In front of the walls, and in view of the citizens are three men impaled, as a warning to the besieged; and below, as if fallen from the walls, are a dying man and a headless body, the head having doubtless been removed for the purpose of numbering the slain, as in modern eastern warfare. . . .

The next frieze gives us a novel and most interesting scene – the passage of a river by the army of the Great King and his allies *(Figure 5)*.

4 The Nimroud sculptures: the siege and impalement of prisoners

5 *The Nimroud sculptures: the king crossing the river*

March 31, 1849

Since our article of December 16 last, describing the last collection of Scriptural Antiquities which had then arrived from Nineveh, a farther

6 *The Nimroud obelisk*

portion of the discoveries have reached this country. . . . This fresh importation is likely to stimulate those who are already engaged in researches, as it possesses many points of novelty, and most of the remains are in such

perfect preservation as to satisfy every observer. . . . That which we shall place first in our catalogue, as of great importance to the learned student, is the Slab (size 6 feet 3 inches by 4 feet 8 inches) containing the Inscription, consisting of 22 lines of arrow-head characters, each character being two and a half inches long and most sharply and beautifully engraved. Although we ourselves are unable to construe this inscription, there are so many now engaged in studying this division of cuneiform writing, that we do not hesitate to insert it here, as it will thus meet the eye of many who may not be able to obtain a correct copy of the original without difficulty; and may excite curiosity and induce examination and comparison in others who, perhaps, would never, otherwise, have turned their attention to the subject. We vouch for the perfect accuracy of our copy and merely add that the erasure in the eighth line is no error of ours, but exists in the original; the repetition of the same combination of characters being evidently a mistake, thus erased on revision by the sculptor *(not reproduced here)*. . . .

No. 10 (size 7 feet 3 inches by 3 feet) the King Crossing or Passing down the River *(Figure 5)*. This slab is a continuation of one in the last importation, which we copied for the information of our readers. . . . This fresh frieze

7 *The Nimroud sculptures: a domestic scene*

shows us the King in his fully-equipped war-chariot, which has been placed across the centre of a long boat, with high prow and stern. The vessel is steered by a stalwart naked man, with a long paddle; it is propelled by three rowers; and its progress further accelerated by two men towing on the shore, or in a shallow part of the stream. The King seems magnificently dressed; has three daggers in his girdle, his sword by his side, in his left hand his bow, and in his right two arrows. Before him stands one of his principal beardless officers, pointing with his left hand to the enemy, who, we may imagine, occupy the opposite shore. Behind the King is another Eunuch, in long fringed robes and bearing the usual arms; his left hand holding a bow and his right grasping a mace. Standing in the stern of the vessel is a man who holds the long reins of four horses which are swimming – though the actions of two seem more to resemble galloping and another is starting back. One naked man is swimming, supported by the skin he is inflating.

March 2, 1850

That the interest raised by the exhibition of these remarkable monuments of a remote historic period does not decline, is fully proved by the number of visitors who daily throng the room at the British Museum in which they are deposited. . . .

The Engraving . . . is a faithful delineation of one of the most curious of these Sculptures, representing incidents and occupations of domestic life *(Figure 7)*. The wheel-like figure with serrated projections, on the left of the composition, is supposed to exhibit the ground plan of a circular building, surrounded by embattled turrets, in which various culinary processes are being carried on. Of the two upper subjects in it, that to the left shows a female superintending the boiling of provisions in earthen pots or jars, of various sizes, supported on frames resembling tripods; the females to the right are evidently engaged in grinding corn; the sitting figure is working a hand-mill. Below, two figures are in the act of dressing the carcase of some animal, probably a calf or goat; while, in the opposite compartment, a baker is seen tending his oven. The whole probably represents the kitchen attached to the adjoining pavilion, the entrance to which is between two columns surmounted by ibexes or goats. In front of, or within, the pavilion, is a slave grooming a horse, and a group of those animals are represented loose, some drinking at a tank; they are drawn with great truth and character.

23

In the upper corner, to the right, are two figures dancing, attired in masks resembling the heads of lions or leopards; their performance appears to be directed by an attendant, who is playing on a musical instrument. This group, altogether, bears a remarkable resemblance to the grotesques which are depicted in manuscripts of the Middle Ages. Below these mummers, as they may be called, are four captives who seem to be pinioned, and are being conducted by a soldier towards the entrance of the temple or palace, in the doorway of which an officer stands ready to receive them. . . .

In short, for comparative purposes, independently of their value to the history of art, these Marbles are of the greatest importance; whatever may be their real antiquity, they are probably of an earlier date than the first scintillations of Grecian genius, and, therefore, may be reasonably supposed to have exercised some influence over the conceptions and works of the Ionian colonists at least.

July 27, 1850

THE NIMROUD SCULPTURES AFLOAT

The English public will be rejoiced to hear that the Great Bull and upwards of a hundred tons of sculpture, excavated by our enterprising countryman, Dr. Layard, are now on their way sterling qualities which so strongly characterise her natives – that she is not only distinguished by her arms and commerce, but that she uses these means to extend and disseminate the

8 Shipping the great bull from Nimroud

to England, and may be expected in the course of next September.

It is gratifying that England has not only rendered herself the first of the nations by those wealth, and comfort, and advantages produced by the arts of civilisation, at the same time that she administers happiness and contentment by inculcating the tenets of a pure religion. . . .

The drawing from which the Engraving *(Figure 8)* . . . is taken has been brought over by one of the Messrs. Lynch of Baghdad, who has been with Dr. Layard, exploring the remains of Nineveh. It represents the action of shipping the Great Bull on board the *Apprentice,* at Marghill, on the right bank of the Euphrates, about three miles above the old city of Busrah.

October 26, 1850

THE NIMROUD MAN-BULL

The first of the present series is the Human-headed and Eagle-winged Bull *(Figure 9)*. This animal would seem to bear some analogy to the Egyptian Sphynx, which represents the head of both views perfect, has given the animal five legs. The four seen in the side view show the animal in the act of walking; while to render the representation complete in the front view, he

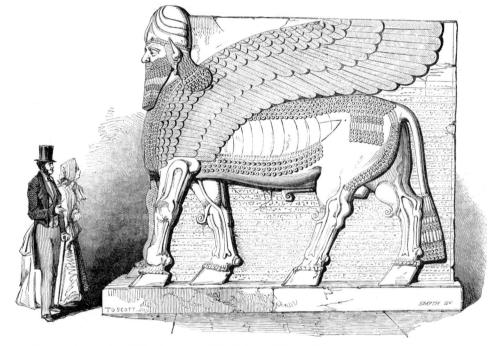

9 Human-headed and Eagle-winged Bull from Nimroud

the King upon the body of a lion and is held by some to be typical of the union of intellectual power with physical strength. . . . The specimen immediately before us is of gypsum, and of colossal dimensions, the slab being ten feet square by two feet in thickness. It was situated at the entrance of a chamber, being built into the side of the door, so that one side and a front view only could be seen by the spectator. Accordingly, the Ninevite sculptor, in order to make has repeated the right foreleg again, but in the act of standing motionless. The countenance is noble and benevolent in expression; the features are of true Persian type; he wears an egg-shaped cap, with three horns, and a cord around the base of it. . . . All the flat surface of the slab is covered with cuneiform inscription; there being twenty-two lines between the forelegs, twenty-one lines in the middle, nineteen lines between the hindlegs and forty-seven lines between the

25

tail and the edge of the slab. The whole of this slab is unbroken, with the exception of the forefeet, which arrived in a former importation, but which are now restored to their proper place.

The second represents the Human-headed and Winged Lion – 9 feet long and the same in height; and in purpose and position the same as the preceding, which, however, it does not quite equal in execution. . . . Upon the flat surface of this slab, as in the last, is a cuneiform inscription; twenty lines being between the forelegs, twenty-six in the middle, eighteen between the hindlegs and seventy-one at the back.

December 21, 1850

THE NIMROUD SCULPTURES AT THE BRITISH MUSEUM

These two slabs *(Figure 10)* are not only interesting because they are of the finest Assyrian sculpture that has yet arrived in this country and because they are in a high state of preservation, but more particularly because they embody a metaphor frequently used in

10 Nimroud sculptures at the British Museum: left *tribute bearers;* right *Assyrian king and sword-bearer*

Psalms, and other of the sacred Books of the Old Testament, expressive of the interference of the Divinity in human affairs. Thus, in the 16th Psalm it is said, "The Lord is the portion of mine inheritance and of *my cup*: thou maintainest my lot." And again in the 23rd Psalm, "Thou preparest a table before me in the presence of mine enemies: thou anointest mine head with oil; *my cup* runneth over."

December 28, 1850

A LETTER TO THE EDITOR

I have no doubt that to many of your readers the question contained in this letter will be nothing new; but as none have given expression to it, I venture to do so. It is stated that the ruins of Nimroud have been buried for a period of not less than 2500 years; now I find in those ruins that the Assyrian Empire, or at least the object of Assyrian worship, is represented by a winged lion or a winged bull; and I have little doubt that the Empire was known in the days of her existence, and in the periods immediately subsequent, under this symbol, since which period in ancient history we do not hear of its use as symbolical in reference either to the Assyrian or any other empire or kingdom. Venice, it is true, has, for a long period, had a winged lion for its symbol; but this does not affect the question. Now I find, in the 7th chapter of the prophecies of Daniel, that the Babylonian Kingdom (which was a part of the Assyrian Empire) was represented under this very figure of a lion with eagle's wings. Might not this be used justly as a strong argument for the antiquity of Daniel's prophecies, and that they were written at a time when the Assyrian Empire was remembered, or the Babylonian Empire (its most important part) was known by this figure. Allow me to refer your readers to the whole of the 7th chapter, and to the 2nd chapter also, in which (under the figure of an image of divers metals) the same successive empires are spoken of. On this point all writers are agreed.

I write only a first impression. (signed) A.M.

1852–56

The principal interest of this period is still Assyrian, with excavations at Nimrud, Nineveh and (Babylonian) at Warka. In 1854 Layard receives the Freedom of the City of London, in the form of a silver-gilt box with "Assyrian" reliefs. Algerian antiquities are exhibited at the Louvre. Mariette excavates the Tombs of Apis at Sakkara. Minor finds are reported of Romano-British and mediaeval antiquities in Great Britain; and a series of excavations are undertaken at Cumae which culminate in the finding of a fine Greek lekythos, of which we published so detailed an engraving that an English pottery firm made and published replicas of it, two of which found their way to the paper's offices in the 1960s and one of which the writer still possesses (see Colour Plate 1, p. 65).

May 29, 1852

NIMROUD ANTIQUITIES

We have selected some fragments of sculpture found by Mr. Layard in a small chamber at the southern extremity of the north-west Palace of the Mound of Nimroud. . . . When the ivories we have delineated *(Figure 11)* were originally discovered by Mr. Layard, owing either to their great antiquity, or, as is more probable, to the conflagration of the roof of the chamber in which they were found, they were in so fragile a condition as to render separation of them from the soil almost impracticable. However, by dint of the utmost perseverance, Mr. Layard succeeded in collecting all possible fragments and in transmitting them to the British Museum, where, by the ingenious process of immersion in boiling isinglass, the animal matter was restored to the mineral structure, and the ivory resumed its natural appearance and solidity.

11 Ivory from Nimroud representing a man with a lotus

November 3, 1855

RECENT DISCOVERIES AT NINEVEH

In 1853 the Assyrian Excavation Fund was established in London for the purpose of prosecuting still further the researches which have conferred such well-deserved honour and fame upon Mr. Layard. The conduct of the expedition was entrusted to Mr. Loftus, who had previously made important discoveries in the rarely visited regions of Lower Chaldaea and Susiana, while attached to General Williams' Commission on the Persian frontier. Mr. Boutcher accompanied him to make drawings of the result of the excavations.

As Mr. Hormuzd Rassam and M. Place were at that time conducting researches in Assyria respectively on behalf of the British and French Museums, the expedition proceeded into Babylonia and commenced its labours at Wurka, Senkereh and the adjacent ruins. . . . At Senkereh (Erech of the Bible, according to Col. Rawlinson) the dedicatory cylinders of Nebuchadnezzar were discovered in the foundations of the Temple of Phara. Here also were

centesimal notation. . . . Meanwhile, in Assyria, on the north side of the mound of Kouyunjik, Mr. Hormuzd Rassam, after more than a year's unsuccessful labour, was rewarded by the discovery of an entirely new palace – that of Assur-bani-pal, the son of Essarhaddon. He had just time to work out what then appeared to be the whole of the palace remaining when the Museum grant terminated, and he then returned to England. . . .

The rest of the valuable collection from Assur-bani-pal's Palace (seventy cases) were placed for the French Government at the disposal of M. Place, the courteous and able conductor of the French researches at Khorsabad. We have to regret that not only they, but

12 Bas-relief discovered at Nineveh showing an Assyrian Queen

found a number of vaults containing stamped and inscribed tablets in clay enclosures (1500 years B.C.) bearing externally the same inscriptions as the enclosures. Another tablet was found with an inscribed list of square roots; confirming, as explained by Col. Rawlinson, the statement of Berosus, that the ancient Babylonians employed a sexagesimal as well as a

nearly the whole of the Assyrian and Babylonian memorials, collected at so great an expense and with such zealous labour for the Louvre, were utterly lost in passing down the Tigris to be shipped at Busrah. . . . The sculptures destined for the British Museum had previously reached Busrah in safety.

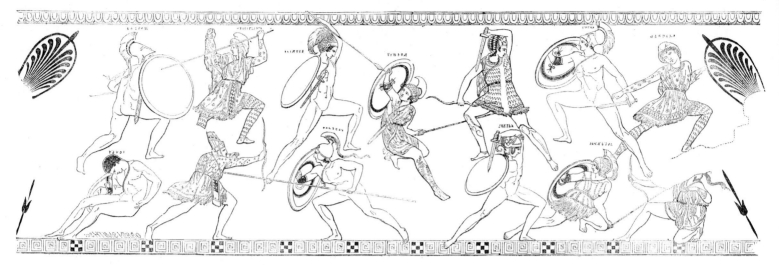

13 Figures upon a vase found at Cumae

February 16, 1856

THE EXCAVATIONS IN CUMAE

(From our own Correspondent)

We are glad to be able to report that his Royal Highness the Count of Syracuse has recommenced the excavations in Cumae. . . . The site chosen for excavation is close to the main road to Licola, and at no great distance from the wall of the city; in short it is in the midst of the Necropolis – a field which has been so fruitful of splendid remains of antiquity within the last three years. The researches of his Royal Highness were not at first attended with any great success, as the tombs into which he entered were found to have been rifled and broken; but, on further investigation, a fragment of a vase struck his attention, by the exquisite delicacy of a figure that was drawn upon it. Would that the other fragments could be found! Orders were issued to sift the earth in the tomb, and the result was that all the pieces were found which compose another beautiful Vase which is the subject of my Illustration *(Figure 13)*. In its form there is nothing either new or remarkably elegant: it is of that class called "Lecythus", of which we find so many in Magna Graecia; but the great merit of this work of art consists in the delicate minuteness and the

wonderful grace which distinguish the design. His Royal Highness has compared it with the splendid collection in the Museum, and is of the opinion that in these respects there is nothing there to equal it. The subject of the design is not uncommon; in fact it is a very favourite one, and frequently found on these fictile vases. It represents the battle between the Greeks and the Amazons, and it is somewhat of a peculiarity that, with the exception of two, where the letters are effaced, every figure has its name above it, yet inscribed so delicately that a glass is required to read them. A glance is sufficient to show the spirit, the ease and elegance which mark the figures. There is nothing stiff or cramped – it is the flexibility of nature we look upon, and we feel almost that the combatants are inspired with life. . . .

We must not conclude this notice without acknowledging the gracious permission which his Royal Highness the Count of Syracuse accorded to us on our application, not only to inspect, but also to make a drawing of, this vase; – indeed, upon all occasions that we have had to request similar favours of his Royal Highness.

we have met with the same courtesy and liberality; showing that the Count of Syracuse is not only a munificent, but enlightened, patron of the arts. We are the more indebted to his Royal Highness on the present occasion, as we shall anticipate a work to be edited by Signor Fiorelli, as also the notice of the Societa Archaeologica. H.W.

1857–61

On the whole a thin period for archaeology in the paper. The principal interest is concentrated on Bodrum (ancient Halicarnassus) where Vice-Consul Newton acquired sculptures from the Tomb of Mausolus (and also from Cnidos) and these were transferred to the British Museum. The British Museum also acquired a number of statues from Cyrene, north Africa, and the Revd. W. Davies reported excavations at Carthage. The landmark of this period was the discussion in 1861 of the flint implements found by Boucher de Perthes – which is the virtual beginning of the study of prehistoric man.

October 24, 1857

SCULPTURES FROM THE TOMB OF MAUSOLUS AT HALICARNASSUS

(From Sketches obligingly communicated by Lieut. Michell, H.M.S. Gorgon)

Halicarnassus, the Royal residence and chief maritime city of ancient Caria, in Asia Minor, will ever be celebrated as the birthplace of Herodotus, and for the magnificent mausoleum known as one of the seven wonders of the world. . . . The interesting ruins existing at Boudroum, and in other parts of Asia Minor, at length aroused sufficient attention to induce our Government to direct an expedition of discovery; and the first result has been the "Gorgon" collection of marbles from Boudroum, which have recently been forwarded from Woolwich Dockyard to the British Museum. . . .

The friezes *(Figure 14)* represent the battles of the Amazons with the Greeks – a favourite subject with the artists of Greece at the best period of art. . . .

14 Part of the friezes from the tomb of Mausolus representing a battle between the Amazons and the Greeks

These sculptures like those of the Elgin Collection, have come to us just as they were dug out of the ruins, without having suffered by passing through the hands of the mender and restorer of sculptures, as have those of the Townley Collection. All that is requisite will be to join the pieces together, and it may be that we shall find some continuation of groups in the frieze – perhaps some corner stone – which may afford assurance that we possess the work of more than one of the celebrated artists to whom the mausoleum is attributed.

January 22, 1859

ARRIVAL OF THE REMAINS OF THE TOMB OF MAUSOLUS AT THE BRITISH MUSEUM

Our engraving *(Figure 15)* not only illustrates an event in the history of English art, but also suggests the necessity which exists for the immediate enlargement of this great national they have, however, crowded all the available space provided within the walls; and the rude hoarding shown in the Engraving is in course of erection along the colonnade of this important

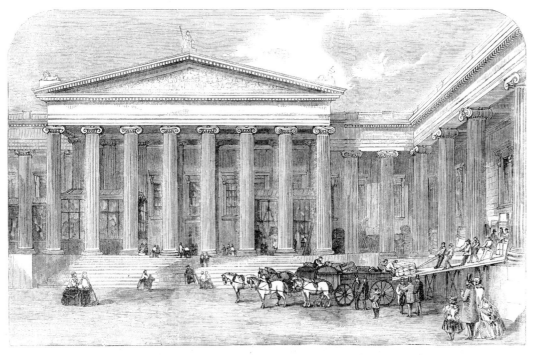

15 *Arrival of the remains of the tomb of Mausolus at the British Museum*

institution. For some time past marbles of the rarest interest, not only from their high artistic merits, but also in consequence of their being examples of the progress of art, have continued to arrive at the British Museum; and so precious have been these additions that we have heard no critic remark that any of them are superfluous; building for the exhibition of this far-famed monument – one of the so-called wonders of the world – which, for architectural design, the excellence of its sculptures, and the interest of its associations, is not surpassed by any of the existing remains of antiquity.

16 Remains of the Roman city Uriconium at Wroxeter

April 16, 1859

EXCAVATIONS AT ROMAN WROXETER

Some excavations have been made at Wroxeter, Shropshire, the site of the Roman Uriconium, of which Mr. J. Wright gives the following account: "Uriconium was one of the earliest Roman cities in Britain, for it is mentioned in 'Ptolemy', and was no doubt a place of importance for it covered a space of ground which . . . is nearly two miles long by one mile in its greatest breadth *(Figure 16)*. . . . About the centre of the area, a large mass of Roman masonry, more than 20 feet high, and of considerable extent, stands above ground, and has from time immemorial been known as the 'Old Wall'. We began digging to the north of this wall, and came upon what appears to have been some large public building. In the middle of it a square enclosure, about 40 feet wide by more than 200 long, was paved with small and narrow red bricks, set very neatly in herring-bone fashion, and would appear, by the number of roof tiles scattered about, to have been at least partially covered. It was, perhaps, a place of public meeting. . . . The excavators came upon the unmistakable remains of rich dwelling-houses. The first of these was a large room, about 35 feet by 25, the hypocaust of which (a very remarkable one) is in good preservation; but the floor has been broken up.

Another hypocaust was found adjoining this to the east, and other apartments of more or less interest have been partially opened to the south of the 'Old Wall'. On Thursday last, when I was present, the workmen came upon a massive flight of stone steps, which led down to a very nicely arched entrance to the hypocausts. In a square space at the foot of these steps rubbish seems to have been thrown by the 'last of the Romans', and a great number of coins, objects of various kinds in bronze, iron, lead, glass, pottery, etc., were found among it. The bottom of this staircase was from 10 to 12 feet below the surface of the soil. . . . Quantities of stucco from the walls show the fresco patterns remarkably fresh, and in tasteful patterns. One piece has a fragment of an inscription in capital letters about two inches high. Quantities of window-glass were strewed about the floors, all rather thick − about the thickness of our common plate-glass, so that the windows of the Roman houses must have been well glazed. . . .

It is the first time we have had the opportunity of ascertaining the character and condition of a Roman town in Britain to any satisfactory extent and the discovery has a similar interest for the history of Roman Britain as that of Pompeii had for Roman Italy."

March 9, 1861

THE DISCOVERIES OF BOUCHER DE PERTHES

A meeting of the Ethnological Society was recently held for the purpose of discussing the subject of the flint instruments found associated with the bones of extinct animals in the "drift". Many archaeologists and geologists were specially invited to take part in the discussion. Mr. Botfield, M.P., the President of the Archaeological Association, took the chair.

The discussion was opened by Mr. Pettigrew, who explained how the subject was originally brought into consideration in this country by the presentation to the Archaeological Association, in 1848, of a number of flint instruments found in the "drift" near Amiens by M. Boucher de Perthes. These implements and a large collection of others, contributed by Dr. Hunt, Mr. Mackie, and Mr. Christie, were displayed on the tables. Mr. Wright said that he considered the flint instruments exhibited were intended for the chase or for domestic use, and not for the purposes of war.

Mr. Evans explained the exact position of the stratum of gravel from which he had extracted some of these implements. It was a stratum of coarse fresh-water gravel, lying on chalk and containing fossil bones of extinct animals, among which was the entire skeleton of an extinct species of rhinoceros. Overlying the gravel was a stratum of sandy marl, containing shells of existing species, and above that was a thin stratum of brick earth. The flint implements were extracted at a depth varying from twenty to thirty feet from the surface, and he felt convinced that the gravel in which they were found had not been disturbed. The same opinion was formed by everyone who had visited the spot, and there seemed to be no doubt whatever that the gravel and the flint instruments were deposited at the same time. It was possible that the animals supposed to have become extinct before man was created might have continued to exist to more recent periods than had been supposed, otherwise it would appear that the implements were fashioned by a race of man that had also become extinct.

Sir Roderick Murchison confirmed Mr.

Evans' view of the great antiquity of the stratum of gravel in which the implements were found, and observed that, without the presence of fossil bones of extinct animals, the surface of the country proved that there must have been an enormous lapse of time since the gravel was deposited. The possibility of the continuance of species of animals supposed to have become extinct, was, he said, rendered probable from the fact that there were now living in a forest in Poland animals which had previously been considered extinct.

In the subsequent discussion, in which Admiral Fitzroy, Mr. Christie, Mr. Pengelly and other gentlemen took part, it was stated that flint implements of the same character as those on the table had been found in various parts of the world, and that they were still used by many savage tribes.

Mr. Botfield, in concluding the proceedings of the meeting, remarked on the circumstance that no bones of man had been discovered accompanying the flint implements, and he expressed his assurance that the cause of religion would have nothing to fear, but everything to hope, from scientific enquiry.

October 19, 1861

SCULPTURES FROM HALICARNASSUS AND CNIDUS

Amongst the most valuable and interesting additions which have been made in our day to the collections of ancient art belonging to this country are unquestionably the sculptured remains, the result of excavations conducted by Mr. C. T. Newton, when Vice-Consul at Mitylene, on the site and in the neighbourhood of the mausoleum at Halicarnassus, now known by the Turkish name of Budrum, in Asia Minor. These works are of the date of the middle of the fourth century before the Christian era – the very best period of Greek art; and their interest and value to the connoisseur and student of art cannot be overrated, being superior to that of many of the collections which now fill the spacious avenues of the British Museum. Unfortunately, however, though they arrived in the course of the years 1857 and 1858, no space has as yet been provided for their display; and they have consequently ever since been huddled away out of sight in a temporary glass shed erected for the purpose under the portico of the building. . . .

We will now speak of a few of the principal remains discovered and transmitted home by Mr. Newton.

Foremost in importance is a noble statue, nearly perfect, though consisting of over fifty fragments, and supposed to be that of King Mausolus. This figure is nearly 10 feet high, is draped in a tunic and *himation*, and stands in a quiescent, dignified attitude. The character of the head is held by some to resemble the ideal portraits of Alexander the Great, on the coins of Lysimachus, and in several extant marble busts. The face is slightly bearded, the features massive and finely formed, and the expression full of majesty, intelligence, and thought. The drapery is admirably composed, and executed in the highest style of the best period of Greek art. The fragments of this statue were found in an excavation beyond the northern boundary of the tomb. Having been executed about the year 350 before Christ, we have in it probably the most ancient example of Greek portrait statuary which has yet been discovered.

Another colossal statue, representing a female standing, has been restored as far as possible,

35

though, unfortunately, still wanting a head. It not improbably formed a companion to the preceding in the same group, in which case it would not be an unreasonable conjecture to assign it as that of Artemesia, the founder of the mausoleum. The cast of the figure is noble and easy; the drapery gracefully, nay, grandly, disposed. From the remains of that portion still visible on the shoulders it appears that the *peplus* or shawl, which forms the only garment superadded to the tunic, was carried over the head like a veil; and this circumstance, according to Mr. Hawkins, in his report to the trustees of the British Museum (to which we are indebted for much of the material of this article), "precludes the possibility of connecting with the body the fine head, of which a photograph was sent over by Mr. Newton, and which has no covering but a cap". . . .

Whilst in this neighbourhood Mr. Newton went over to Cnidus . . . and received information from an intelligent Greek from Calymnos "that he had seen on a promontory a little to the east of Cnidus a colossal marble lion *(Figure 17)*, similar to those found at Budrum, but on a larger scale". Accordingly, this spot was explored, in the first instance by Mr. Pullen, and the noble ruin discovered. Mr. Newton truly describes it as a magnificent example of colossal Greek sculpture, worthy to be compared with the finest remains from Halicarnassus. Its dimensions are 10 feet in length by 6 feet in height from the base to the crown of the head. The body is crouching, the head turned round to the right in the same manner as the lion on many of the Greek coins. It was generally in fine condition; but being found lying on the right side, the left being exposed to the weather, the surface had suffered in some degree, though not to an extent to destroy the main anatomical markings, which retain their original boldness. The entire lion has been sculptured out of one entire block of Parian marble, with the exception of the fore paws, which had been united to the body by a joint, and are lost.

17 Colossal lion sculpture from Cnidus

1862–66

An extremely unfruitful period for archaeology, the only items of interest being the discovery of the House of Cornelius Rufus at Pompeii and a brief note on Copan, central America, with four engravings. But 1865 saw the beginning of a regular feature, "Archaeology of the Month", usually a full 13-inch column of small print, which was kept up until August 1874. This feature is, however, of negligible permanent interest, consisting mainly of reports of meetings and odds and ends of antiquarian interest.

18 General view of the recent excavations at Pompeii

December 31, 1864

POMPEII

During the last three or four years, since the misrule of the Neapolitan Bourbons was superseded by the kingdom of Italy, great progress has been made in the task of bringing to light that abundant store of curious relics of antiquity which had remained for eighteen centuries buried in the ruins of Pompeii.... The Illustrations which we have engraved are selected from a large collection of photographs placed at our disposal by the Revd. James Fletcher, of Newburyport, Massachusetts, author of a treatise on the remains of Pompeii. One of our Engravings presents a general view of the most recent excavations *(Figure 18)*, showing that part of the ancient city which has, within the last year and a half or two years, been laid open by the zeal and energy of the new Administration. . . . The latest discoveries, however, prove that some of the buildings richest in artistic decoration, and otherwise most interesting, are to be found in the quarter which is but now thrown open to modern research. Among these we may particularly notice the house of Cornelius Rufus. The usual features of Roman domestic architecture, as in other mansions of grandees and rich men at Pompeii, may be easily recognised in this example. Here is the *impulvium*, or shallow basin, to catch rain-water, in the centre of the open court around which are disposed the private chambers of the family; the bust of Cornelius Rufus himself, on a pedestal inscribed with his name, is seen beyond. The sculptured griffins, or monsters with ram's horns and claws, are characteristic of the grotesque style of decoration imported into the Roman Empire from its Asiatic conquests. A marble slab laid across here would form a table. The two other Illustrations we present in this Number belong to a higher kind of plastic art. They represent a pair of bronze statuettes, each about two feet in height, which have been found

19 Statuette of Silenus found at Pompeii

in different places among the ruins of the buried city. That of Silenus *(Figure 19)*, bearing a tray on his head, is thought to have been a lampstand. It is remarkable that it shows the serpent and other Egyptian emblems. The figure of Narcissus has been greatly admired for the grace of its proportions and the anatomical correctness of its forms, more especially apparent in the back view.

1867–71

A slightly richer period. An illustrated report on the finding of the Khmer temples at Ongou Wat (now better known as Angkor Wat) in Cambodia; articles on "Druidical Remains" in Brittany and on "Prehistoric remains" in Malta and Gozo (then thought to be Phoenician); and the story of the destruction of the Tol-Maen stone near Falmouth, which led to the setting up of a committee to investigate and preserve prehistoric monuments and so eventually to the formation of the Ancient Monuments branch of what is now the Department of the Environment.

February 1, 1868

ONGOU WAT

Few architectural monuments of a remote antiquity in Asia are more curious than the ruined temples of Cambodia, adjoining Siam. . . . This country was explored and described, eight or nine years ago by the late M. Henri Mouhot, the naturalist; and it has been visited more recently by Mr. J. Thomson, a photographic artist, residing at Bangkok, the capital of Siam. Mr. Thomson, having come home, a year or two since, laid the results of his observations, with a series of photographs, before the Royal Geographical Society, and also before the Geographical and Ethnological Section of the British Association for the Advancement of Science. He gave a particular account of his visit to Ongou Wat; the "Wat" or Buddhist temple at Ongou or Ongcor otherwise called Nakou or Nokhor, the ancient capital of Cambodia, now in ruins. It lies near the head of the great lake, Tonli Sap, through which the Mekon river flows from Cambodia into the Gulf of Siam. The site is almost surrounded by a thickly-grown forest of enormous trees, infested with lions and tigers. . . . "It was with feelings of intense awe", says Mr. Thomson, "that we left the forest path to ascend the worn steps of the outer causeway. . . . We passed through the entrance of the gallery to find a second causeway of greater extent; there we saw the temple in all its magnificence, with its pillared galleries rising tier above tier, and terminating in the great tower. We ascended through sculptured staircases, colonnades, and corridors, crossed over

20 Western colonnade of the temple of Ongou Wat

paved courts having ornamental reservoirs, until we reached the central tower." The rectangular walled enclosure of the temple measures 1080 yards by 1100 yards, and is surrounded by a moat 230 yards wide, which completes an outer rectangle of nearly an

39

English mile each way. . . . The temple itself consists of three enclosures, one within the other, each raised from 15 feet to 20 feet above the level of that outside it, so as to give the whole a pyramidal form. The outer enclosure measures 570 feet by 650 feet. This has three portals on each face, adorned with towers, and externally is surrounded entirely by double open galleries, or verandahs, or, rather, peristyles. . . . Moreover, the walls of the colonnade are sculptured, to the full length of some 2000 feet from top to bottom; and the number of men and animals represented is from 18,000 to 20,000. Numerous female statues appear on the pilasters, but no male. The pillars are very correctly proportioned, and surmounted by a proper architrave, a frieze, which within the temple receives elaborate sculpture, and a cornice, which displays infinite rows and repetitions of seven-headed serpents. In the ancient city of Ongou Thom, situated a little north of Ongou Wat, many of the ruins are supposed to be of superior antiquity to that of Ongou Wat, and in their grotesque sculptures bear more resemblance to the antiquities of Hindostan, Ceylon and Java. These remains of former magnificence show the high state of civilisation the ancient Cambodians had arrived at. Their empire is now an empty name. We have been permitted by Mr. Thomson to engrave two of the views photographed by him, one representing the western façade, another the western colonnade *(Figure 20)* of Ongou Wat. It is, perhaps, needless to remark that the tiger introduced by our draughtsman into one of these scenes does not appear in the photograph; but tigers are said to frequent the neighbourhood of the ruins.

April 10, 1869

THE GREAT TOL-MAEN OF CORNWALL

Our illustration *(Figure 21)* of this great natural and historical curiosity, which has lately been destroyed, will be of interest to many readers.

21 The Tol-Maen or "Main Rock" in Cornwall

The Tolmen, more properly written Tol-Maen, or Hole of Stone, in the ancient Celtic language of West Britain, but usually called the Main Rock, or Men Rock, by modern Cornishmen, stood in the parish of Constantine, half way between Penrhyn and Helston, and 4 miles from Falmouth. It is thus described by Borlase, in his book on the antiquities of Cornwall: "But the most astonishing monument of this kind is in the tenement of 'Men', in the points of two natural rocks, so that a man may creep under the great one and between its supporters through a passage about 3 feet wide and as much high. The longest diameter of this stone is 33 feet, pointing due north and south, 14 feet 6 inches deep, and the breadth in the middle of the surface (where widest) was 18 feet 6 inches from east to west. I measured one half of the circumference, and found it, according to my computation, $48\frac{1}{2}$ feet; so that this stone is 97 feet in circumference, about 60 feet across the middle, and, by the best information I can get, contains at least 750 tons of stone. Getting up by a ladder to view the top of it, we found the surface worked like an imperfect or mutilated honeycomb in basins;

one much larger than the rest was at the south end, about 7 feet long, another at the north end about 5 feet, the rest smaller; seldom more than 1 foot, oftentimes not so much; the sides and shape irregular. Most of these basins discharge into the two principal ones (which lie in the middle of the surface), those only excepted which are near the brim of the stone, and they have little lips or channels which discharge the water they collect over the sides of the Tolmen; and the flat rocks which lie underneath receive the droppings into basins which they have cut into their surfaces.''. . .

Immediately beneath the "tolmen" was a valuable granite quarry, which had been worked to the depth of 40 feet, close up to the bed where the Tol-Maen rested. This has been rented by someone, who, unknown to the proprietor, Mr.

Hosken, had a hole bored underneath the rock and charged, and this, when fired, threw the Tol-Maen off its bed and caused it to roll into the quarry, 40 feet below.

In consequence of Sir John Lubbock's appeal on the destruction of the Tol-Maen, the council of the Ethnological Society have appointed a committee to investigate the prehistoric monuments of these islands, and the measures to be taken for their preservation. It includes Sir John Lubbock, Professor Huxley, Colonel Lane Fox, Mr. Hyde Clarke, Mr. John Evans, Mr. Thomas Wright, Dr. Thurnam, Mr. H. G. Bohn, Mr. Blackmore and Mr. A. W. Franks of the British Museum. It is said that an ancient popular tradition of Cornwall denounces a terrible superhuman vengeance against the destroyer of the Tol-Maen.

April 24, 1869

THE UNDERGROUND SURVEY OF JERUSALEM

22 Wilson's arch, Haram Wall, Jerusalem

The topography of ancient Jerusalem, a subject of profound historical interest, has long been disputed by the learned partisans of different speculative theories, without adding much to our positive knowledge. The labours of Lieutenant Charles Warren, R.E., with the assistance of Sergeant Birtles and one or two other non-commissioned officers, employed during the last two years by the Palestine Exploration Fund, have opened a new series of practical researches, which ought to be well supported by the diplomatic influence of the British Government, and by the pecuniary contributions of those who care either for science or for Scripture. The fund is raised by a society whose objects are the accurate and systematic investigation of the archaeology and topography, the geology and physical geography, and the manners and customs of the Holy Land; with a view to Biblical illustration, but with a view no less to the general interests of historical and scientific inquiry. Its undertaking is therefore one that deserves the aid of persons of the most diverse religious opinions, associating their efforts in the common pursuit of that knowledge which is desired by every intelligent mind. We have great pleasure in recommending this enterprise to the liberality of our readers, and in setting before them a few Illustrations *(e.g., Figure 22)*, furnished by our Special Artist, of some of the underground explorations at Jerusalem, conducted by Lieutenant Warren, the more detailed accounts of which are printed in the society's tracts, with plans and sections of the survey now in progress. . . .

(The rest of the long article is devoted to describing minutely the sites illustrated in the drawings, and the hardships of the party engaged in the exploration – as for example:)

. . . the system of rock-cut passages connected with the Fountain of the Virgin. There is a passage *(Figure 23)* about 1700 feet in length from this intermittent spring to the Pool of Siloam, which has been thoroughly explored by Lieutenant Warren. One of his letters gives an account of the difficulties he met with in this very disagreeable, if not perilous, task. The height of the passage diminishes in going up from Siloam till in some places it is not more

23 *Rock-cut tunnel near the Fountain of the Virgin*

than 16 inches or 20 inches high; so that Lieutenant Warren, Sergeant Birtles, and a fellah, or Arab labourer, with them, were obliged to lie flat on their backs, and crawl along, with the measuring instruments, pencil and note-book, carried in one hand and a lighted candle held in the mouth, through a foul stream of water, sometimes 12 inches deep; they were four hours in making the passage, and might have been drowned by a sudden rising of the water.

1872–76

This period, in which Lieutenant Charles Warren's underground survey of Jerusalem was continued, reached its principal interest in J. T. Wood's excavations of Ephesus. There was a brief note on Mauch's discovery of Ophir (presumably Zimbabwe); and in the December of the last year of the period there was a brief unillustrated note announcing Schliemann's discovery of Royal Tombs at Mycenae.

January 11, 1873
THE OPHIR OF SCRIPTURE

Strange stories have been told of late about the Ophir of Solomon having been discovered. The recently-opened diamond mines of South Africa led to explorations further north, which resulted in the revelation of extensive gold-mines. Mr. Hartley, the lion-hunter, and Mr. Mauch, the German explorer, went further, and made known a more northern auriferous district. It is in the last-discovered gold-field that the real Ophir is supposed to have been seen. . . .

The ruins claimed to mark the position of the Bible Ophir are placed in latitude 20° 15′ south and longitude 31° 40′ east. This is certainly in the interior of Sofala, in Eastern Africa, and easily accessible from the sea.

The story goes that a German missionary was told of great mines there; but, as the natives feared to go as guides, the missionary did not visit the place. Mr. Carl Mauch now reveals it, and has sent down specimens of ancient works, with moulding of cornices, and other architectural forms. Recent examination, however, throws the cold shade of doubt over this pretty romance. A geologist discovers the "mouldings" to be a calcareous deposit upon the shale, and asserts that concretions of a similar kind are common in all gold countries.

(N.B. This is probably the first reference in the West to Zimbabwe.)

March 22, 1873
EPHESUS

(After a summary of the various ancient authorities about the various rebuildings:)
Since May, 1869, when Mr. J. T. Wood discovered the site of the temple among the ruins of that magnificent city, excavations have been diligently continued, under his personal direction, which have gone far to show the exact plan and architectural features. The building is now proved to be octastyle – that is, having eight columns in front. It has eighteen columns at the sides, and the intercolumniations of the latter are chiefly three diameters, making the temple diastyle. The statement of Pliny to its having had one hundred columns (externally) is correct, and twenty-seven of these may have been, as Pliny asserts they were, the contributions of kings. Of the position of the thirty-six *columnae caelatae* (sculptured columns) we shall, no doubt, obtain further proof before the excavations are completed. There may have

been eighteen in front and eighteen in rear. Mr. Wood has found ten or twelve large fragments of these at the western extremity of the building,

some interesting intelligence for our readers. A View of the excavations, shown in our Engraving *(Figure 24)*, is furnished by a sketch from

24 Excavations at Ephesus on the site of the temple of Diana

but no trace of them at the eastern extremity. Allowing for the projection of the sculpture on these columns, which, in the fragments lately found, is as much as 13 inches, the diameter of the columns was about 5 feet 10 inches. The dimensions of the temple given by Pliny – viz. 220 feet by 425 feet, were evidently intended to apply to the raised platform upon which the temple was built. The actual width of the platform, measured at the lowest step, was 238 feet 3½ inches English. The evidence as to its length is not at present so conclusive. The dimensions of the temple itself from plinth to plinth, "out to out", are 163 feet 9½ inches by 308 feet 4 inches. The height of the platform was 9 feet 5¾ inches. The interior appears to have been adorned with two tiers of elliptical columns, Ionic and Corinthian, fragments of these having been found near the walls of the cella. The excavations are now going on with a large number of workmen, and before the termination of the season we hope we shall have

the pencil of Captain S. P. Oliver, R.A., who lately visited the ruins of Ephesus. Some of the

25 Sculptured column from the temple of Diana

portions of sculptured columns *(Figure 25)*, sent home by Mr. Wood, are in the British Museum.

April 3, 1875

EPHESUS

Based largely on the theological and topographical writings of the Revd. W. J. Conybeare and Dean Howson, Mr. Thomas Lewin, the Revd. E. J. Davis and the architect, Mr. E. Falkener

The article is mainly about the life, travels and personality of St. Paul, the point being that, Antiquarian studies in this case . . . cannot be too attentively regarded and scrutinised in every point of view as they constitute the most undeniable witness to the modern world of the faith in Jesus Christ – that is to say, within the scope of historical and literary testimonies.

Of J. T. Wood's researches, the article concludes with:

To that gentleman, who has during twelve years devoted his constant personal labour, and a very large private expenditure of money, to the exploring task, we consider the public greatly indebted. It was in May, 1863, that Mr. Wood began his researches on the spot, braving a most unhealthy climate, and every sort of discomfort. He obtained, a year or two later, the grant of £100 from the trustees of the British Museum, to examine the Odeon or lyric theatre. In February, 1866, he began his exploration of the great theatre, and sent home, in 1868, by H.M.S. *Terrible*, seventy-seven cases of the most valuable relics of sculpture and architecture for our Museum. A year and a half were employed in searching for the true site of the wonderful Temple of Diana. This was discovered, on the last day of 1869, a long distance from the place at which it had been supposed to be, farther up the plain, about half a mile eastward of Mounts Prion and Coressus, and near Ayasolouk. The site, comprising eight acres, was purchased by Mr. Wood, and one third was cleared by him, at a cost of £4000, by April, 1872, disclosing the foundation piers of the temple, with the "drums" or lower cylindrical blocks of its pillars, some of which are now to be seen in Great Russell Street. A grant of £6000 from her Majesty's Government enabled Mr. Wood to go on with his work, employing 300 men till a twelve-month ago. We hope money will soon be forthcoming to finish this noble task. Mr. Wood, during five years, was accompanied by his wife, whose kind care of the work-people did much good.

December 9, 1876

TREASURE TROVE AT MYCENAE

Some remarkable discoveries have been made by Dr. Schliemann at Mycenae, an ancient city in Greece, chiefly among the tombs on the Acropolis.

A correspondent of *The Times* at Argos (from which Mycenae is distant about five miles), telegraphing on November 24, reports:

"In a great circle of parallel slabs beneath the archaic sepulchral stones, considered by Pausanias, following tradition, as the tombs of Atreus, Agamemnon, Cassandra, Eurymedon, and their companions, Dr. Schliemann has discovered immense tombs containing jewellery. He found, yesterday, in one portion of a tomb human bones, male and female, plate, jewellery of pure archaic gold, weighing five kilogrammes, two sceptres with heads of crystal, and chased objects in silver and bronze. It is impossible to describe the rich variety of the treasure."

The same correspondent telegraphs that "Dr. Schliemann has found in the tomb already referred to another great quantity of women's jewellery in gold, and handsomely worked. Immediately after beginning excavations at an adjoining tomb a large head of a cow in silver, with immense horns in pure gold, was found. A large girdle of gold, five gold vases, and immense golden buttons were also found. All these objects were marvellously worked. Among other discoveries are nine silver vases and numerous swords of bronze."

By another telegram we learn that on November 28 "Dr. Schliemann, continuing his researches in the tombs already described, found, yesterday, the following articles of pure gold, splendidly ornamented: A helmet, two diadems, a woman's large comb, a large breastplate, three masks, six vases, two brace-lets, two rings, three brooches, an immense mass of buttons, leaves and other articles, three large girdles, a silver vase, a stag cast in lead, with a mass of swords, daggers, axes, and warriors' knives, all of bronze, with twenty-five flint-headed arrows."

The Times publishes the following telegram from Argos, dated December 2: "In the tomb previously referred to Dr. Schliemann has disovered a large golden mask and an enormous breastplate of gold. He also found the body of a man, wonderfully preserved, especially the face. The head was round, the eyes large, the mouth contained thirty-two fine teeth. There is, however, a difficulty about preserving the remains. There were also found fifteen bronze swords with great golden hilts – a mass of immense golden buttons, splendidly engraved, ornamented the sheaths of the swords; also two great golden goblets, and a great quantity of other objects in gold, articles in earthenware, a carved wooden box, several articles in chased crystal, ten large cooking utensils of bronze, but no traces of anything in iron or glass."

A telegram from Athens to the same journal, dated December 5, states that "Dr. Schliemann has succeeded in preserving the dead body of the man to which reference was made in a previous telegram. There were found on his right three large splendidly ornamented golden goblets, one alabaster goblet, two silver goblets, 134 richly ornamented large golden buttons, four golden sword-handles, eleven bronze swords, and jewels."

1877–81

1877 was especially Schliemann's year, with reports, lectures and copious engravings on the Mycenae finds, and, later in the year, a note on his work in the Troad. This year likewise saw the beginning of Cleopatra's Needle's voyage to England and its abandonment in the Bay of Biscay. The next year saw Cleopatra's Needle rescued, brought to London and erected on the Embankment. Schliemann's operations in the Troad were reported, and also Rassam's discoveries at Balawat in Assyria and his finding of the bronze gates thereof. In 1879, the reporter-artist William Simpson sent back from Afghanistan a number of reports of a somewhat generalised archaeological interest; but the rest of the period was lacking in interest.

February 3, 1877

MYCENAE

A report by Melton Prior

We present this week several views of the ruins of this ancient and famous Greek city, to which attention has lately been called by the excavations there carried on by Dr. Schliemann, with the permission of the King of Greece. Our Special Artist attending the Conference at Constantinople, Mr. Melton Prior, went to Athens and thence to Mycenae, for the express purpose of making these sketches, which will no doubt be interesting to many of our readers *(Figure 26)*.... Its site is about seven miles from Argos, upon a raised recess between two high summits of the mountain range that bounds the east side of the Argolic plain. The Acropolis, the upper city or fortress, of which the entire circuit is yet to be seen was built upon the top of a steep and rugged hill, between two streams; its length is about 400 yards, and its breadth 200 yards. Within this enclosure the ground rises considerably; on the summit are the openings to subterranean chambers, built of large irregular stones lined with plaster. There is a great gate at the north-west angle, and a postern-gate to the north-east. In the great gate, which is called the "Gate of the Lions", the doorway is formed of two massive blocks of stone, with another laid

ANTIQUARIAN DISCOVERIES IN GREECE: OUR ARTIST SKETCHING THE ENTRANCE GATE OF THE ACROPOLIS AT MYCENAE.

26 *"Our artist sketching the entrance gate of the Acropolis at Mycenae"*

47

across them, which upper stone is 15 feet long, 4 feet wide and 6 feet 7 inches high; and above this stands a triangular piece of green limestone, 12 feet long, 10 feet high and 2 feet thick, upon the face of which two lions are sculptured in bas-relief. The lions are represented standing on their hindlegs, one at each side of a round pillar or altar, upon which their forepaws rest; the pillar, which broadens at the top, has a capital decorated with a row of four circles between parallel fillets. Below the mound of the Acropolis, at some little distance towards the modern village of Mycenae, is a series of underground chambers, which has been called the Treasury of Atreus; they are cells of a conical form, the largest about 50 feet in diameter at the floor, and their doorways have Tuscan or Doric half-columns. The Cyclopean architecture of the older ruins of Mycenae differs entirely from what is found in other ancient cities of Greece, and their antiquity is probably much greater.

According to Dr. Schliemann, the walls belong to three distinct periods, the oldest portion being the underlying part, which resembles the architecture of Tiryns. They surrounded the Acropolis, the lower city extending to the south-west, and being still marked by traces of Cyclopean walls and other remains. One of the most curious results of Dr. Schliemann's excavations is the discovery that the city was reinhabited after its capture by the Argives in B.C. 458, although its very site had been so completely forgotten by Strabo's day that he declares no vestiges of it were in existence. The new Mycenae seems to have lasted about two centuries; at all events, the fluted vases found among its rubbish are of the Macedonian era, and come down to the second century B.C. Below the later city lies the ruins of the Mycenae of Homer, and these have already yielded an immense number of objects to Dr. Schliemann's workmen.

It is the opinion of Dr. Schliemann that he has discovered the identical tombs of Atreus and Agamemnon, of Cassandra, another daughter of the last-named King, and of Eurymedon, his charioteer, according to the local tradition which Pausanias has preserved. He has opened five tombs cut in the rock, in which he found two gold cups, a gold diadem, some bronze and crystal vessels, a quantity of fine pottery, knives and lances, and, finally, the bones of a man and a woman, covered with ornaments of pure gold. In another double circular sepulchre, as we learn by a telegram this week, he has found four golden vases, richly ornamented, and two gold signet-rings, one engraved with a palm-tree and seven figures of women. These, and other treasures, belonging to the Greek Government, are to be deposited in a museum at Athens. We hope to give more Illustrations of the subject.

February 24, 1877

THE DISCOVERIES AT MYCENAE

We are indebted to Mr. Marwood Tucker, for some Illustrations, made from recollection, of the interesting exhibition of Dr. Schliemann's Mycenaean antiquities, privately shown to Lord and Lady Salisbury and their party at Athens. All the articles which have been brought from Mycenae are in the custody of the Royal Bank of Greece, and had not previously been exhibited. They covered completely the large table on which they were laid out, the place of honour in the centre being given to the singular and really beautiful cow's head of silver, with golden horns. The object marked No. 1 *(Plate 2, p. 66)* in our Illustration *(Figure 27)* is one of the thin gold masks which had covered the faces of the skeletons in

27 Dr. Schliemann's discoveries at Mycenae

Agamemnon's tomb. These are extremely curious, but, alas! extremely ugly, the features being very coarsely fashioned, with sharp lines and angles, like the face a child might make out of wood with his pocket-knife. If Agamemnon is to be judged by the portrait of him, thus disinterred, he cannot certainly have represented the Greek traditional beauty; and if his brother was like him, it is little to be wondered at that Helen should have preferred Paris.

No. 2 is the finest piece of art in the collection. It is by far the most delicately worked of all the articles now at Athens. The head of the cow, about $4\frac{1}{2}$ or 5 inches long, is of silver, much discoloured, but very carefully modelled and still showing the marks of the finishing-chisel. The horns are nearly 7 inches long and are of

pure gold. As they have become detached from the head at each side of the crest, it can be seen that they are hollow. The head itself is solid.

No. 3 is a tankard of very thin but pure gold, with low repoussé ornament. There are several of these, some with handles, and some without; but all when found were much battered. The one drawn has been in some degree restored to its shape. They are about $3\frac{1}{2}$ inches high and $2\frac{1}{2}$ inches in diameter at the top.

No. 4 is a tazza-shaped goblet of silver, with bands of gold ornament. The silver in this, as in all the other articles discovered, is crusted and discoloured as if by the action of fire, while the gold remains almost as fresh as when first made. The workmanship is very good, except that the handle is roughly fixed on by little pegs or nails.

This goblet is about 8 inches high and 6½ inches of diameter. It is the largest of the objects as yet brought to Athens.

No. 5. Very thin gold ornaments, of different repoussé work. There are many of these, almost identical in shape or pattern, but of various sizes, from 2 feet to 6 inches long and proportionately broad. The larger ones were probably belts; the smaller ones were perhaps frontlets, worn above the forehead. They are, as well as the button next described, almost as thin as gold leaf.

No. 6. Gold buttons or discs, about 2½ inches in diameter, also of poor repoussé work. The skeletons found rested on layers of these singular ornaments, and Dr. Schliemann accounts for their quantity by supposing them to have studded thickly the robes, which would naturally have long since fallen to pieces. *(After this follows a digest of Mr. Thomas Morgan's paper to a meeting of the British Archaeological Association in London, which concludes:)* The strong points of Dr. Schliemann's case were put with much force, and yet with all due candour, before the audience. At the same time, while expressing the greatest admiration of Dr. Schliemann's self-sacrificing devotion to his archaeological enterprises, both in the Troad and Hellas, and recognising fully the great worth (as throwing light on the earliest history of Greece and Asia Minor) of his extraordinary discoveries, the need for caution was not left unmentioned.

March 10, 1877

CLEOPATRA'S NEEDLE

This obelisk of ancient Egypt, which has been left lying so long half buried in the sand at Alexandria, is now about to be made an ornament to the city of London. Its removal has been considered a matter of such great expense that the British Government has not felt justified in undertaking it and, had it not been for the private generosity of Dr. Erasmus Wilson, and the ingenuity of the engineer, it would most likely have remained to form the foundations of the new houses leading to the Alexandria Railway Station. . . .

The consulting engineer is Mr. B. Baker, well known by his connection with the Metropolitan Railway, and the work will be performed by Mr. Dixon.

The removal of this obelisk will be accomplished in the following manner: A wrought-iron cylindrical pontoon, 92 feet long and 15 feet in diameter, tapered at each end to a vertical edge, as shown in the illustration *(Figure 28)*, will be its only support in the water. Its draught is 9 feet, and displacement 270 tons. If completely submerged, its power of flotation is equal to 705 tons, and as the weight of the obelisk is only 150 tons, with 30 tons ballast, it is evident that there is no chance of its foundering. The pontoon is furnished with a series of bulkheads, or diaphragms, which support the obelisk at about every 10 feet, and suitable elastic packing secures it from shocks. The obelisk is 66 feet long over all, and the base (8 feet 6 inches square) will be placed forward, about 20 feet from the prow of the pontoon, thus giving great buoyancy to the forepart, as the apex is close to the stern, which will be furnished with a rudder. On top of the pontoon and near its centre, will be placed a small deck house, with steering-wheel in the forepart and accommodation for three men. There is a long,

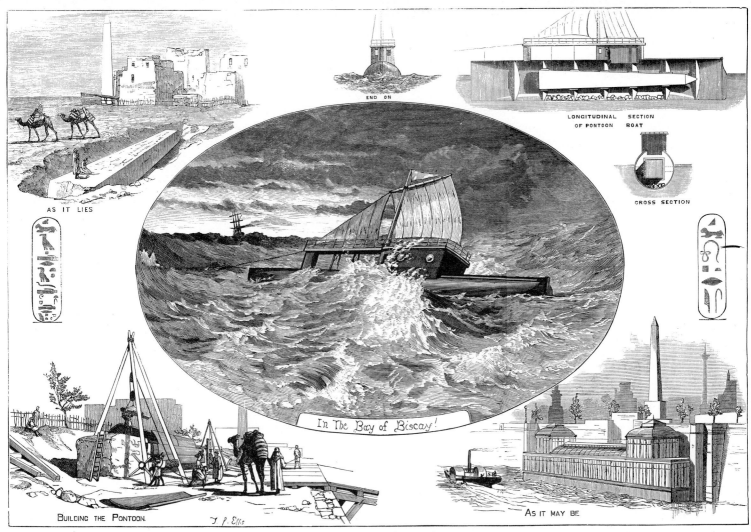

AS IT LIES

END ON

LONGITUDINAL SECTION
OF PONTOON BOAT

CROSS SECTION

In The Bay of Biscay!

BUILDING THE PONTOON

J. P. Ellis

AS IT MAY BE

28 Proposed method for the removal of Cleopatra's Needle from Alexandria

narrow hurricane-deck above the steering-room, and a short mast with two small sails surmounts the whole. . . . The boat will be towed by steamer to London, the sails being merely used for steadying purposes. It is calculated that the roll will not be excessive. . . .

March 24, 1877

DR. SCHLIEMANN'S TREASURES FOUND AT MYCENAE

The arrival of Dr. Schliemann in London, and his address to be delivered here to the Society of Antiquaries, must increase the amount of public interest already felt in his successful explorations of the sites of ancient classic history, or early traditions of romantic events in Greece, celebrated by the epic and tragic poets of that highly gifted nation. Our readers are fully aware of the direct efforts made by the proprietors of this Journal, in the employment successively of two Special Artists on the spot, as well as at Athens, to provide complete and accurate Illustrations of Dr. Schliemann's remarkable discoveries. . . . An exact topographical view of the subject was yet desired. This is now supplied by our well-known artist, Mr. W. Simpson, from whose pencil we have obtained many effective Illustrations, and whose pen, guided by considerable archaeological and ethnological experience, has contributed some notes upon the significance of the recently unearthed memorials of a remote past age. *(Here followed a resumé of Dr. Schliemann's life-story.)*

The objects found by Dr. Schliemann have been more than once on view, in one of the rooms of the National Bank. These precious articles have been placed there for safety, and will remain there in the strong room till a suitable museum can be provided, where they will all be labelled, and will be exposed, in proper cases, for the public to see them. Till this is done, it will only be privileged individuals who will have a chance of getting a peep at what has so long lain quietly under the earth at Mycenae. Mr. Newton, from the British Museum, is expected out here by next French mail, and will no doubt have a special view of all that is important. At present these objects are being photographed, for the purpose of illustrating the work upon which Dr. Schliemann is now employed, relating his discoveries. This is to be published by Mr. Murray, and it is said that £6000 is the sum the publisher has agreed to pay for the copyright. If I mistake not, that is about what Dr. Livingstone received for his *Travels in Africa.*

Two cases of the seventeen at present containing this collection were taken out the other day, and were laid on a table for Admiral Sir James Drummond and the officers of the fleet to look at. These two cases seemed to contain the most valuable of the gold articles, and they are, perhaps, the most important as bearing on the art of the period. The predominating form of ornament is that of a circle, which is filled up in various ways, but most often with radiating lines, each line being connected with a semicircle at the circumference. It might be taken for a subjective

style of representing the petals of a flower. The beautiful cow's head, with golden horns, has one of these circles of gold, about two inches in diameter, attached to the forehead. . . . This particular ornament might be seen on almost every one of the gold objects exhibited. The golden girdle is covered with it; it is upon the gold covering of what have evidently been dagger-sheaths; it figures upon drinking-cups; and there were trays exhibited of circles in gold all impressed with this favourite symbol. . . . One of the symbols which Dr. Schliemann's wonderful discoveries at Troy revealed was that of the swastika, or fylfut, and he has also found it frequent in his late discoveries. . . . It is frequent on the buttons and other objects found at Mycenae; and there is a triple-formed symbol found on the buttons, which one is inclined to believe is only a variety of the Swastika. . . . These buttons are beautifully made, and, although they naturally recall Birmingham to the mind, there is nothing "Brummagem" about them; it is doubtful if that notable Buttonopolis could produce better at the present moment. Although these articles have been called "buttons", it may be doubted if they served the purpose which we associate with such things in the present day. They may have been placed as studs on shields – "on the well-orbed ox-hide shields" – or on such as that of Ajax, which was covered with brass – or, perhaps, upon harness.

The modern theory that the story of the Iliad is nothing more than a myth finds no entrance into the mind of Dr. Schliemann. The golden cups are entirely new in form; the most important of them is not above six inches high, and the single handle at the side suggests that it was a drinking cup. The pouring of wine into cups is often spoken of by Homer; and we have an allusion by Agamemnon himself to his own cup. In the fourth book of the Iliad the son of Atreus says: "The nobles of the Argives mix in their cups the dark red honourable wine; for though the other crested Greeks drink by certain measures, thy cup always stands full, as

29 *Dr. Schliemann's excavations in the Acropolis of Mycenae – general view of the grave circle*

(mine) to me, that thou mayest drink when thy mind desires it." . . . Prominent among the objects exhibited, and perhaps the most interesting in the whole collection of what has turned up at Mycenae is the cow's head with the golden horns. This Dr. Schliemann identifies with Hera, or Juno. She was said to have been born at Argos; hence it is more than probable that she would be a favourite deity in that region. The cow was sacred to her, and was never offered as sacrifice at her temple. This is said to be due to her having assumed the form of that animal. This head which has been found is not so large as that of a cow; its proportion would fit better to that of a human figure, and, if it was not used as a mask, it may have been the head of a statue, supposing, perhaps, the rest of the figure to have been in the form of a woman, to represent the goddess. The head is said to be of silver, but it is now oxidised into a brown coffee-colour. The horns are of gold, still bright; and the nostrils also still retain evidences of gilding. The head is very well executed, and is in itself a good proof of the artistic skill of the time. The only ornament upon it is the gold disc on the forehead, which has already been described. . . .

Dr. Schliemann made a number of experimental borings or shafts all over the Acropolis, and ultimately determined to carry out his operations at the south-west corner, between the Lion Gate and the wall; and here his scent seems to have been on the right track, as the wonderful results have given proof. . . .

On passing the large blocks of the ancient portal, and turning to the right, the first things which we come upon are some old walls laid bare by the recent excavations. As the enclosures formed by these remains present no indication of either doors or windows, the

53

visitor is inclined to believe that they were more likely to have been the houses of the dead than of the living. Some other walls, found at the southeast corner, have been judged by Dr. Schliemann to be the remains of a palace – "A vast Cyclopean house" is his description of it – and the discovery of gold and other valuable articles within these walls he considers as evidence of its having been a regal abode. Supposing it to have been a palace, its close proximity to the Royal tombs would seem to show a custom in early Greece, similar to that mentioned in the Bible, where Manasseh is described, in 2 Chron. xxxiii, 20, as having been buried "in his own house", or, as it is put in 2 Kings xxi, 18, "in the garden of his own house". . . . These tombs are connected with a very remarkable structure, which has been brought to light by Dr. Schliemann's explorations. It is a structure which is entirely new to the students of classical archaeology. No similar construction has yet been found anywhere, in Greece or any other part of the world. . . .

This interesting monument *(Figure 29)* is a circle about 100 feet in diameter. It is composed of two concentric circles of stones, about 3 feet 6 inches apart. As most of these stones are broken or embedded in the earth, it is not easy to give their height; but one or two, which have been left standing, are between 5 feet and 6 feet high, about 2 feet 6 inches wide, and over 4 inches thick. Some of them are now only about a couple of feet above ground; but to what extent they were originally covered below it is now impossible to say. The space between these two circles seems to have been bridged over with slabs of stone, and the upper edges of the stones have all been morticed to receive tenons, which, no doubt, kept the horizontal slabs above in their places. All these stones seem to have been worked tolerably smooth and fitted neatly together; so that the whole, when complete, must have had much the appearance of a circular stone bench. The only break in this circle is at its north side, where there is what now seems a recess; but, as the other extremity is not composed of similar slabs to the rest of the construction, but is, on the contrary, filled up with rude stones and rubbish, it was most probably open, and formed the door of the enclosure. The idea that it was the entrance is strengthened by its being on that side of the circle nearest to the Lion Gate, at which it would be approached by those entering the Acropolis. . . .

It was within this circle that the tombs were discovered by Dr. Schliemann, which yielded such a harvest of ancient treasure of all kinds. Its character as a place of burial may have added to its sanctity as a court of justice; for, in the description of the shield of Achilles, the circle was "sacred", but what made it so is not told.

March 31, 1877

DR. SCHLIEMANN'S LECTURE

On Friday evening last week, a meeting of the Society of Antiquaries was held at its rooms, Burlington-House – Mr. Frederick William Ouvry, president, in the chair. There was a crowded attendance of Fellows and visitors. Among those present were Mr. W. E. Gladstone, M.P., Lord Aberdeen, Sir George Gilbert Scott, the Hon. Spencer Walpole, Mr. Beresford-Hope, M.P., the Revd. Dr. Thompson (Master of Trinity College, Cambridge), Mr. Alfred Tennyson, Professor Leone Levi, Sir Philip Egerton, Earl Stanhope, Professors Colvin and Mahaffy, and Mr. James Spedding.

Mr. Watson, secretary, having read the minutes of the last meeting, which were confirmed, the following gentlemen were admitted members: Lord Houghton, the Revd. Dr. Thompson, the Hon. Spencer Walpole, Lord Acton, the Earl of Aberdeen, and Sir

Philip Egerton. The secretary then said they had arrived at the real business of the meeting. After eight days and nights of incessant travelling, Dr. Schliemann arrived in this country only this morning, with the object of reading his paper before the society on his discoveries at Mycenae. In illustration of these discoveries photographs and plans were exhibited on the walls. Upon the last occasion Dr. Schliemann was present the late president, who then occupied the chair, said he was certain that if the lecturer again visited this country he was sure to have a good reception. The crowded meeting that night verified the late Lord Stanhope's prophecy.

30 Dr. Schliemann giving an account of his discoveries at Mycenae before the Society of Antiquaries

On rising to read his paper the illustrious discoverer *(Figure 30)* was greeted with the heartiest welcome. Dr. Schliemann said that, in his opinion, there was, next to Troy, no Eastern prehistoric city of so high archaeological interest as Mycenae, because, owing to its secluded site in a rugged wilderness, the grandeur and massiveness of the ruins, and its distance from Argos and Nauplia, it has not attracted the modern mason, who found it much easier to cut new blocks from the quarry for his wants than to destroy Mycenae's walls and to carve their enormous and amorphous stones. Hence the conservation of Mycenae's ruins, which can hardly have deteriorated since Pausanias visited them, A.D. 170. At all events, they are far better preserved than those of any one of the Greek cities, the flourishing condition and splendour of whose monuments he describes. His short description (II, 16, 6) of Mycenae runs thus: "Among other remains of the wall is the gate, on which stand lions. They (the wall and the gate) are said to be the work of the Cyclopes, who built the wall for Paetus, in Tiryns. . . . There is a sepulchre of Atreus, with the tombs of Agamemnon's companions, who on their return from Ilium were killed at dinner by Aegisthus. The identity of the sepulchre of Cassandra is called in question by the Lacedaemonians of Amyklae. There is a tomb of Agamemnon and that of his charioteer, Eurymedon. Teledamos and Pelops were deposited in the same sepulchre, for it is said that Cassandra bore these twins, and that, when still little babies, they were slaughtered by Aegisthus, together with their parent. Hellanikos (B.C. 495–411) writes that Pylades, who was married to Electra by the consent of Orestes, had by her two sons, Medon and Strophios. Clytemnestra and Aegisthus were buried at a little distance from the wall, because they were thought unworthy to have their tombs inside of it, where Agamemnon reposed, and those who were slain with him." Pausanias gives no further details, but his short description is of prime interest to science, because it proves that by tradition the great subterranean dome-like buildings had been treasuries, to hoard the wealth of Atreus and his children; it further proves that tradition had handed down the site of the five tombs where Atreus as well as Agamemnon, Cassandra, Eurymedon and their companions, who had been murdered along with them by Aegisthus, lay buried. "But luckily for me", continued Dr. Schliemann, "this passage of Pausanias regarding the site of these tombs had always been misunderstood – nay, misinterpreted – by such eminent scholars as W. M. Leake, Edward Dodwell, Prokesch, and Ernest Curtius, who, with Pausanias in hand, explored the Peloponnese for years, and

31 Interior of the Treasury of Atreus

wrote on it learned works, which will for ever remain celebrated." They had misunderstood their author, because they thought that in speaking of the wall, he meant that of the city, and not the great Acropolis wall, and they, therefore, imagined that he finds the site of the five sepulchres in the lower city, and the site of the tombs of Clytemnestra and Aegisthus outside of it. But that he had the citadel walls only in view he shows by saying that in the wall is the Lions' Gate. True, he afterwards speaks of the ruins of Mycenae, in which he saw the fountain Perseia and the Treasuries of Atreus and his sons, by which latter he can only mean the large Treasury *(Figure 31)*, which is, indeed, in the lower city, and, perhaps, some of the smaller Treasuries. But as further on he again says that the graves of Clytemnestra and Aegisthus are at a little distance outside the walls, because they were thought unworthy to be buried inside of it, where Agamemnon and

his Companions reposed, there cannot be any doubt that he had solely in view the huge Cyclopean walls of the citadel. Having adduced other grounds for his having always understood Pausanias in the sense that the five tombs are in the Acropolis, citing for the fact that such was his opinion in 1869, his work, *Ithaque, le Peloponnese, et Troie*, Dr. Schliemann said that on the strength of it he, three years ago, sunk thirty-four shafts in different parts of the Acropolis to probe the ground and find the spots where he would have to excavate for the tombs. In twenty-eight he found nothing; but the other six, which he sunk in the first western and south-western terrace, gave encouraging results, and particularly those two which he had dug one hundred yards south of the Lions' Gate. For not only there did he strike two Cyclopean house-walls, but he found also there a number of female idols and small cows in terracotta. He therefore began extensive diggings here, but met with serious hindrances, and only at the end of last July did he find it possible to carry out his plans. But going, with Mrs. Schliemann, from Nauplia to Mycenae, they found it impossible to pass Tiryns, the Royal city of Proetus and the birthplace of Hercules, without stopping a week to explore it; its huge Cyclopean walls, deemed by the Greeks themselves the work of the demons, and more stupendous than the Pyramids of Egypt, bound them with a spell the more resistless from the fact that the pickaxe of no explorer had ever touched its virgin soil. There they worked a week with fifty-one labourers, digging a long and large trench, and sinking twenty shafts, 6 feet wide. After further details of the work, Dr. Schliemann said they brought to light Cyclopean house-walls, and in three shafts found Cyclopean water-conduits of a primitive kind, being composed of uncut stones, joined without cement. . . . After mentioning other finds at Tiryns, including coins, Dr. Schliemann continued the account of his excavations at Mycenae, where he gradually increased the number of his workmen to 125, which for four months had been the average. He ordered the workmen near the Lions' Gate to open a passage into the Acropolis, which, when the citadel was taken, had been blocked up by the huge stones hurled by the Mycenae men at the besiegers and by the ruins of houses which had been washed down from the top of the Acropolis, producing a heap of débris much higher than the gate itself. A much larger gang dug 40 feet from the gate trench, 113 feet square. A third party of workmen dug a trench on the south side of the Treasury in the lower city, near the Lions' Gate, in search of the entrance. This Treasury, like that of Atreus, was to turn out subterranean. But either by accident, as some of the inhabitants of the Argolid say, or by the sacrilegious hands of Vely Pasha, son of the notorious Ali Pasha, who is said by others to have tried to force an entrance this way, the upper part of the dome-like vault has been destroyed and the stones had fallen into the interior building, which had by degrees been almost filled with the rubbish. The examination of this Treasury, under Mrs. Schliemann, had been one of the most difficult they had ever made, partly from the nature of the terrain and partly from the obstructiveness of the delegate of the Greek Government, under whose Argus eye all the excavations were conducted. Hence they succeeded only in clearing out the passage of the entrance to the central part of this Treasury. The door has the enormous height of 18 feet 5 inches, and is 8 feet 4 inches broad. On the threshold, which consists of a hard breccia, and which is 2 feet 5 inches broad, was found a very thin round plate of gold. In the entrance also was one of the 4 feet 3 inches high, long-fluted, semi-columns of calcareous stone; one of a pair which stood to the right and left of the entrance. There was also a large fragment of a frieze of blue marble, with an ornamentation of circles and rows of wedge-like signs in form of fish spines; further, an almost entire frieze of white marble, with an ornamentation of beautiful spirals. Nothing further was found in this Treasury, which was evidently empty when the upper walls fell in. There are here no signs of the walls having been lined with brazen plates; it was, besides, less sumptuous, and seems older than the Treasury of Atreus. In the Acropolis Dr. Schliemann had entirely cleared the Lions' Gate, which he went on to describe, discussing also the old question of the symbolism of the lions surmounting the gateway, and of the altar surmounted by a column, on each side of which rest the forepaws of one of the two lions. One theory was that the column related to the solar worship of the Persians; another that the altar is a fire-altar, guarded by the lions; a third that we have here a representation of Apollo Agyieus. Dr. Schliemann was of this last opinion, which he thought was borne out by the Phrygian descent of the Pelopidae. The lion-cult of the Phrygians was well-known. Besides, among the jewels found in the tombs, of which he was to speak afterwards, and especially in the first tomb, this religious lion symbolism reappeared. On two of the repoussé gold plates there found was seen a lion sacrificing a stag to Hera Boopis, who was represented by a large cow's head, with open jaws, just in the act of devouring the sacrifice. On entering the Lions' Gate were seemingly the ancient dwellings of the door-keepers, of whom some account was given. Further on, as at Troy, was quadrangular Cyclopean masonry, marking the site of a second gate of wood. Further on were two small Cyclopean water-conduits; to the right of the entrance-passage were two Cyclopean cisterns. A little further on came to light that large double parallel circle of closely-jointed slanting slabs, which has become so famous during the last three months. Only about one half of it rests on the rock, the other half rests on a 12-foot-high Cyclopean wall, which has been expressly built to support it in the lower part of the Acropolis. The double circle had been originally covered with cross slabs, of which six are still *in situ*. Inside the double slabs was, first, a layer of stones, for the purpose of holding the slabs in their position. The remaining space was filled up with pure earth mixed with long, thin cockles, in the places where the original covering remains in its position, or with débris of houses mixed with countless fragments of archaic pottery wherever the covering was missing. This circumstance could leave no doubt that the cross slabs were removed long before the capture of Mycenae by the Argives (B.C. 468). The entrance to the double circle was from the north side. In the western half of the circle Dr. Schliemann discovered three rows of tomb steles, nine in all, made of calcareous stone. All stood upright; four only which faced the west had sculptures in relief. One stele, precisely that beneath which was found the body with the golden plates representing the lion sacrificing the stag to Hera Boopis, represents a hunting scene. The two next sculptured sepulchral slabs represent each a battle scene. Details of these scenes were given, as well as those presented by the other sculptured tombs, of which Dr. Schliemann's letters in our columns have already given some account. The Mycenae slabs, he said, were unique of their kind. The manner in which they fill up the space not covered with men and animals with a variety of beautiful spiral ornaments reminds us of the principles of the painting on the so-called Orientalising vases. But in the Mycenaean sculptures nowhere do we see a representation of plants, so characteristic of ancient Greek ornamentation of this class. The whole is rather linear ornamentation, representing the forms of the bas-relief. Hereby we have an interesting reference to the epoch in Greek art preceding the time when that art was determined by Oriental influences, an epoch which may approximately be said to reach far back into the Second Millennium B.C. Dr. Schliemann knew of no example in history of an acropolis having served as a burial place save the small building of the Caryatides in the Athenian Acropolis, the traditional sepulchre of Cecrops, first king of Athens. But we now know with certainty that Cecrops is nothing else than Kacyapa, the sun-god, so that the story of Cecrops having been buried in the Acropolis is a pure myth. But here in the Acropolis of Mycenae the tombs are no myth, but a reality. The paper then discussed the question – who were these great personages entombed here, and what were the services rendered by them to Mycenae which deserved such splendid funereal honours. It was argued at length that the inhabitants of these tombs could be none other than the very persons spoken of in the extract Dr. Schliemann had cited at the outset from Pausanias, in spite of the certainty that the traveller of the Antonine age could never have seen the tombs, which were then covered by a 10-foot-thick layer of prehistoric rubbish. No ancient writer mentioned that Mycenae was rebuilt after B.C. 468, and Strabo even said that the site had remained uninhabited ever since its capture; but facts proved that the city had been rebuilt about B.C. 400, and again about B.C. 200. Dr. Schliemann then proceeded to state what he had found below the ruins of the Hellenic city. He spoke of the vast masses of splendidly painted archaic vases. Iron, he remarked, was found in the upper Hellenic city only, and no trace of it in the prehistoric strata. Glass was found now and then in the shape of white beads. Opal glass also occurred as beads or small ornaments. Sometimes wood was found in a state of perfect preservation, as in the board of a box (narthex) on which were carved in bas-relief beautiful spirals. Rock-crystal was frequent, for beads and also for vases. There were also beads of amethyst, onyx, agate, serpentine, and the like, precious stones, with splendid intaglio ornamentation representing men and animals. When, towards the middle of November, he wished to close the excavations, Dr. Schliemann excavated the spots marked by the sepulchral slabs, and found below all of them immense rock-cut tombs, as well as other seemingly much older tombstones, and other very large sepulchres from which the tombstones had disappeared. These tombs and the treasures they contained, consisting of masses of jewels, golden diadems, crowns with foliage, large stars of leaves, girdles, shoulder-belts, breastplates, etc., were described in detail. He argued that as one hundred goldsmiths would need years to prepare such a mass of jewels there must have been goldsmiths in Mycenae from whom such jewels could have been bought ready-made. He spoke of the necklaces, too, and of the golden mask taken from one of the bodies, which must evidently be a portraiture of the deceased. Dr. Schliemann then proceeded to show that in a remote antiquity it was either the custom, or, at least, it was nothing unusual, for living persons to wear masks. That also immortal gods wore masks was proved by the busts of Pallas Athene, of which one copy was in the British Museum and two in Athens. It was also represented on the Corinthian medals. The treasures of Mycenae did not contain an object which represented a trace of Oriental or Egyptian influences, and they proved, therefore, that ages before the epoch of Pericles there existed here a flourishing school of domestic artists, the formation and development of which must have occupied a great number of centuries. They further proved that Homer had lived in Mycenae's golden age, and at or near the time of the tragic event by which the inmates of the five sepulchres lost their lives, because shortly after that event Mycenae by a sudden political catastrophe fell to the condition of a poor, powerless, provincial town, from which it had never again emerged. They had the certainty that Mycenae's flourishing school of art disappeared, together with its wealth; but its artistical genius survived the destruction, and when, in later centuries, circumstances became again favourable for its development it lifted a second time its head to the heavens. In conclusion, he said that if they thought Mrs. Schliemann and he had by their disinterested labours contributed a little to show that Homer did not describe myths, but real events and tangible realities, this would be to them a most flattering acknowledgment and a greater encouragement in the continuation of their works in Troy, which they would resume very soon, for they had the necessary Firman of the Turkish Government in their hands.

After a few remarks from Mr. John Evans, Lord Houghton and Mr. Watson upon the discoveries of Dr. Schliemann. . . . Mr. Gladstone rose to address the meeting, and was loudly cheered. . . . In every respect Dr. Schliemann by his immense labours had gone far beyond expectations. There was one point, however, in which they felt he was not so happy. They had means, when he came back from Ilium, of verifying more or less almost everything he had seen in the way of weapons, utensils, etc., by comparing them with the poems of Homer. It was the standard of an age in which they could carry these remains. . . . Now, thanks to splendid munificence, unwearied perseverance, and discernment they seemed to have attained to a great accession to the antiquarian wealth of the world. They were told there were great men before Agamemnon who remained unknown because they had no sacred poet to sing their praises. Dr. Schliemann's present discoveries seemed to fall between the period of Homeric literature and the classic age of the Greeks. . . . Although the impression given in listening to him was that, for the most part, they were dealing with the remains of a later age than the Dorian Conquest, yet there might be among the objects which he described some which were of greater antiquity even than what were referred to in the poems of Homer. He had seen comments upon some of these discoveries of Dr. Schliemann which had filled him with pain, because they had not been conceived in that spirit of generosity and brotherhood which ought to unite whatever differences of opinion might arise in this inquiry. He was only sorry to say that even in Germany, among that great and learned fraternity, they were not united by that true brotherhood and spirit of generosity in this matter. . . . He would no longer trouble the society, but tender to Dr. Schliemann his most hearty congratulations upon the success of his labours, and express his personal gratitude for the enlargement of knowledge in an age rather degenerate by this noble and high-minded enthusiast.

Professor Sidney Colvin, M.P., and Mr. Lloyd followed with a few remarks, after which the chairman proposed Dr. Schliemann as honorary Fellow of the society, which was carried by acclamation, and the meeting terminated.

April 21, 1877

OUR SPECIAL ARTIST IN GREECE

This issue reproduced a number of drawings by our special artist – of Corinth (Figure 32), Mycenae (an interior), Acrocorinth and Parnassus, and Helicon seen from the Gulf of Corinth.

32 Tomb-hunters in the Isthmus of Corinth

October 27, 1877

CLEOPATRA'S NEEDLE

Our readers last week were informed that the south-west gale of Sunday, the 14th, raging in the Bay of Biscay, as well as in England, compelled the abandonment, early next morning, of Mr. Dixon's ingenious vessel, or iron-plate cylinder, named the Cleopatra, in which the Egyptian obelisk *(Figure 33)* from Alexandria was being towed by the steamer Olga on its voyage to London. It was further stated in our last report that the Cleopatra was afterwards picked up by a steamer, the Fitzmaurice, bound for the Spanish port of Valencia; and we have since learned that the obelisk, in its still floating iron case, is left in safety at Ferrol, whence it will

The circumstance to be most deplored is the drowning of six men belonging to the Olga, who

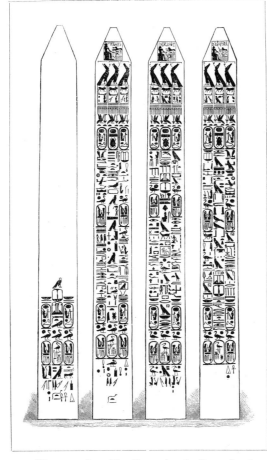

33 Cleopatra's Needle: facsimile of the inscriptions

no doubt soon be brought to its destination; but some delay may arise from the claim of salvage to be paid for its recovery when cast adrift, and apparently in a foundering condition, at sea.

bravely went off to save the men from the Cleopatra and whose boat was swamped during the height of the gale on Sunday week.

December 29, 1877

SCHLIEMANN AND TROY

On former occasions . . . we entered fully into the subject of these excavations. . . . As early as 1870 Dr. Schliemann made some preliminary excavations on the Hill of Hissarlik, an elevated plateau of about eighty feet above the plain of Troy, but he was then forced to suspend his

operations for more than a year, while waiting for the necessary firman from the Turkish Government authorising him to continue the explorations and forcing the proprietors to part with the ground at a lawful price. All through the fine weather of 1872 and 1873 Dr.

61

Schliemann persevered in his labour, which was carried on entirely at his own expense, the Turkish Government even obliging him to pay the salary of the official employed by them to watch his proceedings. During these months Dr. Schliemann discovered the remains of four settlements or cities, one below the other, besides the Greek colony of the time of Alexander the Great. Of this colony he shows, at South Kensington, a very spirited metope of Apollo and four horses, and some small terracotta figures. It is, however, with the four ancient cities, and chiefly with the second from the virgin soil, that we are concerned. Roughly speaking, the two most recent settlements (below the Greek colony) extend from just below the surface to a depth of 23 feet. The third city, which Dr. Schliemann calls Troy proper, Ilium, where he found the so-called Priam treasure, reaches to 33 feet below the surface, and the most ancient to a depth of 50 feet, or in some places to nearly 60 feet. These four cities are separated from each other by layers of ashes and other marks of conflagration.

January 5, 1878

DR. SCHLIEMANN'S EXCAVATIONS IN THE TROAD

In our last week's paper we gave a view of the site of Dr. Schliemann's antiquarian explorations, from 1870 to 1873 inclusive, at the mound or hill of Hissarlik, in the plain of the Troad, which is situated on the north-west coast of Asia Minor, below the entrance to the Dardanelles. The exact site of the famous ancient city of Troy, as our readers know, has been much disputed by historical and classical topographers, but it was somewhere in that limited piece of ground. The different places which have been fixed upon by rival theories and learned opinions, between which we cannot yet pronounce a definitive judgment, are the hills of Bournabashi, with the remains of some old walls at Gergis, at the extremity of those low heights; and the mound of Hissarlik. . . . Our well-known Special Artist, Mr. William Simpson, who is an enthusiastic student of architectural antiquities, has visited the Troad, as well as Mycenae, and in the first-named locality has found cause to dispute the opinion of Dr. Schliemann. We do not wish here to revive the controversy that went on, last July and August, in *Fraser's Magazine* and *The Times*; but as Dr. Schliemann's case rests partly upon his collection of portable relics from the Troad, now on view at the South Kensington Museum *(Figure 35)*, our readers must be warned of the

34 Dr. Schliemann's excavations in the Troad: the so-called Scaean gate and Priam's Palace

conflicting arguments for and against the Hissarlik site of Troy. That this site is to be preferred to Gergis or Bournabashi, is admitted by Mr. Simpson; but he disbelieves the Scaean Gate *(Figure 34)* and Priam's Palace, and the Keep or Great Tower of Ilium, mainly because

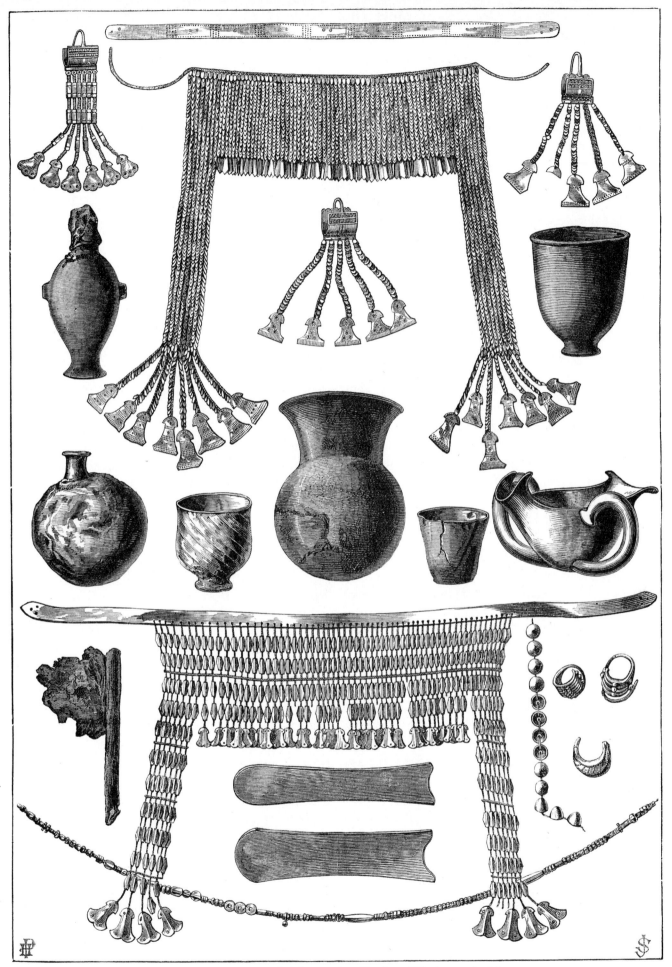

35 *Gold and silver jewellery and vessels from Dr. Schliemann's collection of Trojan antiquities on view at the South Kensington Museum*

he thinks it impossible that the structures to which Dr. Schliemann gives those names can have existed together at one time, and because the style and materials of their building, compared with those of Tiryns and Mycenae, contemporary Greek cities, do not support that identification. . . .

The most valuable treasures were found amidst the calcined remains of a wooden box, or chest, as it seemed in a place 28 feet beneath the present general surface of the ground, but supposed to have been a chamber where the ancient Kings of Troy, and it may be King Priam, had deposited those precious articles for safe keeping. A copper key, presumed to be that of the treasure-chest, lay within two yards of its remains and of its contents, which had escaped destruction by the fire, and are thought to have been accidentally preserved from the clutches of Agamemnon and Achilles, and the other Greek conquerors of Troy, when the city was captured and burnt. Two golden cups, a flask or bottle of gold, half a dozen golden bracelets, two golden diadems and an immense number of tiny golden jewels, besides golden rings and earrings, were crammed into a large silver case or pot, which is eight inches in diameter, and eight or nine inches high. The diadems are furnished with a number of little chains, or pendants, to hang down over the temples and cheeks of the wearer, and each pendant ends with a tiny figure of the owl-faced Pallas, the tutelary goddess of Troy. It can scarcely be doubted that these were worn by royal personages; and Priam and Hecuba may have been accustomed to put them on, when they proceeded to worship at the shrine of the Palladium, while their daughters, Cassandra and others, or Helen, their fatal Greek daughter-in-law, may have been adorned with the multitude of smaller jewels. Let this interesting reflection be cherished, in spite of ungenial scepticism, by the lady visitors to the South Kensington Museum, who will do well to read "the tale of Troy divine", if not in Homer's sonorous Ionic Greek, at least in the graceful English couplets of Alexander Pope, or in the masculine blank verse of the late Earl of Derby. They will like it, we promise them, quite as much as the "Idylls of the King".

January 12, 1878

. . . Dr. Schliemann . . . , in a lecture which he lately delivered upon this subject, attempted to show the grounds for a more precise identification *(of the site of Troy)*. He began by referring to the unanimous opinion of the ancients, including Thucydides and Aristotle, that the Trojan War was historical, and their virtual agreement that Homer's Ilium stood on the site of its Hellenic namesake, which Lysimachus girdled with a great wall nearly five English miles round. Further, that this is marked by the mound now called Hissarlik, was owned on all hands. The Hellenic Ilians, proud of being the successors of Priam's people, showed the ruins of Hector's palace, and of the old Trojan Prytaneum; but, since antiquity had neither archaeologists nor critics, they never used the spade in their researches, or they would have found that, except on Hissarlik, which served Troy as an acropolis, the heaped-up rubbish incrusted but thinly the virgin rock. On this mount, however, which is a solitary calcareous rock, the débris of houses and whole cities piled one upon another is enormous, being from 50 feet to 53 feet deep. The mount, moreover, has bulged eastwards from 260 feet to 270 feet, northward, 130 feet, and about 200 feet to west and south, through the throwing down of rubbish from its steep slopes. All the alternative sites, Bournabashi and others, having been disposed of, Dr. and Mrs. Schliemann went to the Hellenic Ilium, and were astonished to find that one half of Mount Hissarlik consists of made ground, the piled up ruins of layer after layer of houses and streets. Having obtained the necessary firman, Dr. Schliemann went to work. He had formed in his mind the picture of Troy, and his veneration for Homer had made

Plate 1 Facsimile of vase found at Cumae: and inset *base of facsimile of vase found at Cumae*

Plate 2 *Agamemnon's mask found at Mycenae*

Plate 3 Cleopatra's Needle in its proposed position at Westminster

LEIGHTON, BROS.

Plate 4 Fresco in a villa recently excavated near Pompeii: initiation by flagellation

Plate 5 opposite Hind (2 metres 20 long) and a bison painted 25,000 years ago in the Altamira cave

Plate 6 opposite Bison (1 metre 50 long) painted in the Altamira cave

68

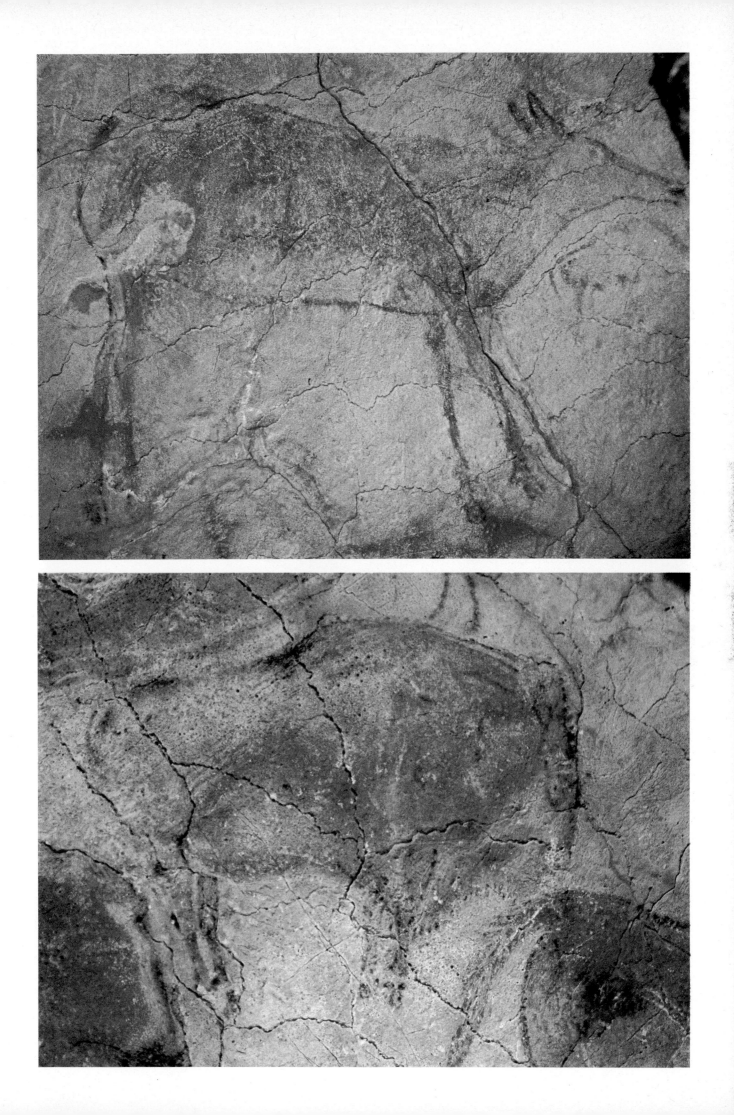

Of a Civilisation whose History is Little Known: A New Type of Peruvian Pottery.

Reproduced from Specimens in the Collection of H. O. Forbes, LL.D., F.R.A.I., F.R.G.S., by his Courtesy.

Plate 7 Peruvian pottery from Nasca

Plate 8 Massive golden comb found in a Scythian king's tomb

Plate 9 Silver vase found in a Scythian king's tomb

him paint it on a gigantic scale. He thought that it extended beyond the city walls of Lysimachus, but his illusions were destroyed by the result of twenty shafts dug on the site of the lower city, because all of them, and even the six shafts sunk close to Hissarlik, produced only fragments of wheel-made Grecian pottery and Hellenic house walls, none of which could claim a higher antiquity than the sixth or seventh century B.C. On the site of Hissarlik, on the contrary, he found Hellenic masonry and fragments of wheel-made Grecian pottery only to an average depth of 6½ feet. Next below he collected seventy hand-made vases and a great many whorls of black or brown terracotta, all of which were perfectly unlike the Hellenic ones. He attributed these to a people who stayed there but a short time. Still deeper, he found a stratum of ashes and rubbish, about 6 feet thick, with masses of hand-made pre-historic vases, and very numerous whorls with incised ornamentation. Again, below this stratum was a whole pre-historic city. In this city he found much more and much better hand-made pottery than in the preceding one, and thousands of terracotta whorls, most of them with a beautiful incised ornamentation; remains of a circuit wall belonging to this city he noticed only on the west side. Below this city, and at an average depth of from 23 feet to 33 feet, he found the calcined remains of an apparently much wealthier city, which evidently had been suddenly destroyed by a tremendous conflagration, of which every stone, every fragment of pottery, and particularly the huge masses of red or yellow ashes bore testimony. This city was encircled by great circuit-walls of larger and smaller stones, in which he brought to light an immense tower and a double gate directed to the south-west. Just on the north-east side of this gate are the ruins of a vast mansion of smaller stones joined with earth, which must have belonged to the Chief or King, for it was the largest building in the town; besides, the other houses consisted of unburnt bricks. There must have existed on the circuit-walls and on the tower, as well as on the gate,

immense wooden fortifications; indeed, all the houses of the city must have had upper stories of wood, for otherwise the masses of wood ashes cannot be explained. This city had evidently suddenly been stormed and destroyed by the enemy; this appears to be proved by the skeletons of men with arms, and by the finding of innumerable beautiful hand-made terracotta vases, with splendidly incised whorls, but particularly by the three treasures, of which the two smaller ones were stolen from Dr. Schliemann by two of his labourers, and they were afterwards seized by the Turkish Government. They are now in the museum at Constantinople; but he had been able to save for himself the third treasure of gold and silver ornaments, goblets and vases, now on view at the South Kensington Museum. This third treasure was found, together with a large number of very primitive battle-axes, lances, daggers, and a shield of bronze, in the ashes on the circuit-wall, close to the mansion of the town's chief or king. All the objects had doubtless been contained in a quadrangular wooden box, of which the ashes had retained the shape; and probably he who endeavoured to save the box was overtaken by fire or the enemy, and was obliged to drop it. The sudden capture and destruction of the city was also proved by the innumerable terracotta vases. He noticed the fact that wherever a vase was broken he found all its fragments together, which could only be explained by the suddenness of the tragic event. Some similarity existed between the various types of the terracotta vases of these pre-historic cities. Nearly all of them were either tripods or had a convex bottom, so that they could not be put down without being leant against other objects. Besides, nearly all of them had on both sides a tubular hole, and in the same direction a hole in the rim and in the lid for being shut and suspended with a string. But there were new types in each city; and it was particularly deserving of attention that the vases were more artistically and far better made in this third city than in the succeeding one; and in this there was again a difference, to the prejudice of

Plate 10 opposite Bull's head libation vessel found in the Little Palace at Knossos

the uppermost pre-historic city, since in this the vases were coarsest. In all the three cities there was an entire absence of colours; the vases had been wrought by hand-polishing to a lustrous surface, and all the ornamentation consists of incised patterns. Identical in all three cities were, further, the goblets in the form of a long and narrow funnel, with two enormous handles, but footless, so that they can be set down on the mouth only. Again in all three cities were found very numerous idols of the Ilian Minerva Glaucopis, the patron deity of Troy, with an owl face, either of marble, or modelled on the sacred vases. Dr. Schliemann observed that this first Trojan city had no walls, and it must have been several times destroyed, so as to form a 20-foot-deep accumulation of rubbish. Homer mentions that Troy had been destroyed by Hercules long before its destruction by the Greeks under Agamemnon, and this legend may refer to the destruction of the first city. But, identical with the Homeric Troy, which was captured by the Greek army, must be the city next in succession from the virgin soil, because here we find the great tower and the huge walls, whose construction Homer attributes to Neptune and Apollo, here we further find the most evident proofs of great wealth and a sudden destruction by the hand of the enemy. The extent of Troy as encompassed by its walls is but very small, and it cannot possibly have contained more than 4000 or 5000 inhabitants; but, small as it was, it was larger than the city of Athens under the Kings, which was confined to the Acropolis until Theseus added the twelve surrounding boroughs to it. At Troy also there must have been straggling suburbs, whence the inhabitants flocked into the Acropolis at the approach of the enemy. . . . Such are the view and opinions of Dr. Schliemann, upon which we cannot pretend to have yet formed a definitive judgment.

January 26, 1878

ARRIVAL OF CLEOPATRA'S NEEDLE

The iron cylinder-vessel Cleopatra, constructed by Mr. John Dixon, civil engineer, to contain the Egyptian obelisk called "Cleopatra's Needle" and to serve for its conveyance from Alexandria to London, arrived safely in the Thames on Monday last. It was towed by a steam tug, in six days, from Ferrol, the Spanish port, on the shore of the Bay of Biscay, where it had been left, as our readers will remember, since October last, after having been cast off in a storm by the Olga, which had brought it from Egypt. The latter part of the voyage has now been successfully accomplished by the aid of the Anglia, a powerful steam-tug belonging to Mr. Watkins, of Lombard-street, which was engaged by Mr. Dixon for this special service. The expenses of bringing the Obelisk to England, it is well known, are defrayed by the splendid liberality of Mr. Erasmus Wilson, the eminent surgeon, to whom some token of Royal favour, or some other public testimonial, should presently be offered. He has received from the Princess of Wales, a gracious message in recognition of his generous gift to the country.

We have to thank both Mr. Dixon and Mr. Watkins for permitting our Special Artist, Mr. J. Wells, to accompany the voyage of the Anglia to and from the port of Ferrol and to make the sketches which furnish our present Illustration *(Figure 36)*. . . .

The controversy about the best site for it in London has not yet been ended. Mr. Erasmus Wilson has proposed the centre of the ornamental garden, adjacent to Old Palace-yard and

36 Cleopatra's Needle. First night out: in the Bay of Biscay

to St. Margaret's-churchyard, Westminister, sometimes called Parliament-square, where a wooden model of the obelisk, equal to it in size, has been erected to show the effect. The view *(Plate 3, p. 67)* presented in the Engraving which forms our Extra Supplement, including portions of the Abbey north front and of the Houses of Parliament, will be acceptable to readers at a distance from London.

February 16, 1878

CLEOPATRA'S NEEDLE

The Cleopatra had her mast unshipped because of the bridges, but Captain Carter displayed the Union Jack, the burgee, and the red ensign. Other vessels joined in a sort of procession, which came up the river with high tide, and reached Westminster Bridge about half-past one in the afternoon. The Cleopatra was moored, or lashed to a dredging-vessel, about one hundred yards above Westminster Bridge, near the Lambeth side, at St. Thomas's Hospital, opposite the Houses of Parliament. Many visitors have been admitted to inspect this curious vessel, and to look at a portion of the surface of the enclosed obelisk, for which purpose an iron plate has been removed from the deck.

August 10, 1878

The Egyptian obelisk called by this name, which Mr. John Dixon, civil engineer, has brought from Alexandria to be erected in London, at the cost of a munificent individual benefactor of the public, Mr. Erasmus Wilson, the eminent surgeon, is now visible to all passers-by on the Thames Embankment, and will soon be reared aloft upon its pedestal, at the riverside steps opposite Adelphi-terrace. . . . *(There follows a description of engineering methods proposed for this purpose.)*

September 21, 1878

The Egyptian obelisk from Alexandria . . . was on Thursday week placed in its due perpendicular attitude, directly over the pedestal, which will now be completed by adding the upper course of masonry *(Figure 37)*. . . . It is stated that Mr. John Dixon, C.E., has expended £5000 over and above the £10,000 liberally bestowed by Mr. Erasmus Wilson, for the cost of bringing Cleopatra's Needle from Egypt, with its detention by the accident in the Bay of Biscay, and finally erecting the obelisk in London. . . . *(There follows a long list of objects placed in two large earthenware jars, in the base below the obelisk, for example a complete set of British coinage, including an Empress of India rupee, bibles in various languages, Bradshaw's railway guide, Mappin's shilling razor, case of cigars, pipes, box of hairpins and sundry articles of female adornment, Alexandra feeding-bottle and children's toys, presented by a lady, photographs of a dozen pretty Englishwomen, presented by Captain Henry Carter. . . .)*

37 Cleopatra's Needle on the Thames Embankment

November 16, 1878

RECENT ASSYRIAN DISCOVERIES BY MR. RASSAM

Some interesting articles in *The Times*, and in several other daily journals, towards the end of last August, described the important discoveries made in the spring of this year by Mr. Hormuzd Rassam at Balawat, nine miles north-east of Nimroud (Kalakh), and fifteen miles from Koyunjik, on the Tigris, the site of ancient Nineveh. Mr. Rassam, a native of that country, but a naturalised British subject, and long in the service of our Foreign office, was the assistant of Sir Austen Henry Layard, now her Majesty's Envoy at Constantinople, in the famous explorations of Nineveh and Nimroud, about thirty years ago, which contributed the first instalment of the Assyrian historical monuments to the British Museum. Since the lamented death of Mr. George Smith, who carried on the work partly for the British Museum, partly at the cost of the proprietors of the *Daily Telegraph*, the Museum authorities have commissioned Mr. Rassam to pursue these researches, from which he has already obtained some valuable results. He came home last summer, bringing some collections which are now in the Museum, and a portion of which, from Balawat, are the subject of our present Illustrations. A lecture explanatory of these sculpture-records of Assyrian history was delivered last week to the Society of Biblical Archaeology, in Conduit-street, by Mr. Theophilus Pinches, the successor of Mr. George Smith at his post in the Oriental Antiquities Department of the British Museum. He described the mound of Balawat as the site of an ancient Assyrian fortress, which had borne a different name before the reign of Assurnazirpal, father of Shalmaneser II, whose reception of tribute from Jehu, King of Israel, is recorded on the famous black obelisk. Though so close to Nineveh, it had been taken and held by the Babylonians during a period of Assyria's political decline, perhaps coincident with the epoch of Hebrew ascendancy. But when Assurnazirpal, a great warrior, came to the throne he recovered the city, and re-named it Imgur-Beli, and built there a temple to the god of war, near the city's north-eastern wall. These facts are recorded on alabaster tablets found by Mr. Rassam in a coffer of the same material near the entrance of the temple itself. As Mr. Pinches remarked, they shed a fresh ray of light on one of the darkest periods of Assyrian history. The mound is nearly rectangular, and its corners are

turned pretty accurately towards the four cardinal points of the compass. The temple ruins lie near the north-eastern edge, where ran the city wall. In the western half of the mound four stone platforms were found marking the sides of an irregular square. While digging round these platforms Mr. Rassam unearthed some pieces of chased bronze, and at length two huge bronze monuments slowly came to view. They were of the strangest shape. Each seemed formed of a centre-piece with seven long arms on either hand, like colossal hat-racks, with which the first published accounts compared them. Even after laying them bare, the energetic excavator had great difficulty in disinterring them, and was mortified at hearing the precious bronzes split and crack as the sun dried up the earth in which they had lain buried during so many centuries. According to the explorer's ground plan, the platforms mark the entrances to the courtyard of a noble palace, having two

38 Recent Assyrian discoveries: bronze sculpted doors from the temple at Balawat, near Nineveh

entrances to the north-east and two others on the north-west. The bronzes arrived at the British Museum at the beginning of August last. There they met with an enthusiastic welcome, and no less naturally called forth much speculation as to their nature and use. To Mr. Ready, the ingenious artificer of the department at the British Museum, whose task it was to see to the cleansing of the fragments, piecing them together and nailing them with the original bronze nails on wood of the same thickness as that which underlay the plates thus fastened, belongs the merit of solving the riddle. He was the first to see that the bronze plates *(Figure 38)* of the larger of the two monuments had formed the coverings of an enormous pair of rectangular folding doors, each about twenty-two feet in height and six feet broad, which had evidently turned on pivots, and were held up at the top by strong rings fixed in the masonry. The body of the doors was of wood three inches thick, as measured by the nails, which are found to be clinched a little more than that distance from the heads, the overplus being just the thickness of the bronze plates themselves, which is about one sixteenth of an inch. Each door revolved on a central post, about a foot in diameter. Each post had a pivot at the bottom. The pivots are at the Museum, but the sockets in which they turned were unfortunately left behind. The bronze plates are about eight feet long. They were nailed horizontally across each door, but, allowing for their extension round the post, the total length across each leaf was but six feet. What is technically termed the "style" of each leaf was also overlaid with a bronze edging, which overlapped the door by about a couple of inches. On the right it is cut plain, but is indented on the side overlapping the back of the doors. The smaller pair of gates is much more decayed than the other. Its designs represent hunting scenes, and it belongs to the same reign as the larger, whose inscriptions are those of Shalmaneser II. The representations on the plates of both pairs are in the repoussé style. Those on the plates of the great gates depict Shalmaneser's battles, sieges, triumphal processions, the tortures inflicted on his prisoners, and his worship of the gods. The bronze plates covering the "styles" of the doors are also engraved with historical inscriptions of which, reserving for another time his account of the extremely numerous and interesting designs chased on the doors themselves, Mr. Pinches gave the general purport. The record on the "styles", he observed, though somewhat fuller than that on the black obelisk, and than the Kurkh and Bull inscriptions, is very carelessly executed, even the chronological order of events having been to some extent inverted. The new document begins with Shalmaneser's Babylonian campaign, when he went to help King Marduku-Suma-Iddin against that Babylonian Monarch's revolted brother. Next, it places his war in the region of Mount Ararat, followed by that against Gozan, and his triumph over Akhuni, King of Borsippa, which paved the way for his conquest of Syria and Palestine. A critical comparison of all the sources proves, however, that the Ararat campaign came first, and then his expeditions against Akhuni and the Babylonian war. In concluding, Mr. Pinches held out the hope of identifying, in his future paper on the bas-reliefs (which greatly exceed in number those in the Nimroud Gallery in the British Museum), some Jewish faces of the ninth century before Christ. It is certain that, as he remarked, this wonderful document cannot fail to be of great use to the ethnologist, as well as to the philologist and the antiquary. *(After a brief reference to George Smith's* History of Assyria:*)* The military expeditions of Shalmaneser II likewise conducted him into Syria, and led to the series of conflicts related in the Second Book of Chronicles, in which Israel and Judah became fatally involved, but at a considerably later period. This circumstance gives a share of Biblical interest to the actions delineated in the bronze sculptures of which we present some Illustrations *(again see Figure 38)*. They show the King with his army on the march; warriors standing in two-horse chariots, like those of

Homer's heroes at the siege of Troy, the horses led by footmen; the King riding on horseback, wearing a loose robe and cap, with attendant eunuchs before and behind him, and men carrying his bows and quivers, wading across the River Tigris. Then, in the piece below, the King appears standing to offer sacrifices upon an altar; the captain of his guard is behind him, with soldiers who are bringing a slaughtered bull and a live ram for the offering. There are four conical stones, the well-known emblems of a common object of Eastern nature-worship; there is a sacred grove of trees, with a lodge or temple in the background, and the guardian priest is talking with the King's herald or secretary, who may perhaps be asking leave to approach or enter the sanctuary. The nethermost scroll would seem to represent the King's servants cutting an inscription on the rock, and lopping a few branches of the trees, to commemorate his visit to the foreign shrine. This was situated, most likely, in Northern Syria, and there would be a motive of policy for thus recording the pious regard of Shalmaneser for the divinities worshipped by the nations over whom his ambition sought to reign.

1882–86

A period of great activity, especially in Egypt, with Maspero's excavations at Luxor and the beginnings of the activities of the Egypt Exploration Fund, and the appearance of such famous names as Amelia B. Edwards, R. Stuart Poole and Flinders Petrie. In addition there was a growth of interest in Peruvian and Colombian antiquities, progress at Pompeii, news of finds in Lake Nemi in central Italy, Schliemann's discovery of the Treasure of Priam and – as a by-product of General Gordon's advance into the Sudan – pictures of the antiquities of Meroe.

February 4, 1882

ROYAL MUMMIES FOUND NEAR THEBES

By Amelia B. Edwards

The recent discovery at Thebes in Upper Egypt has of late been so fully and so frequently discussed in various publications, that it is unnecessary to do more than recapitulate the heads of the story in our present columns. The leading facts are briefly these:

For the last ten years or more it had been suspected that the Theban Arabs (whose main occupation is tomb-pillage and mummy-snatching) had found a royal sepulchre. Objects of great rarity and antiquity were being brought to Europe every season by travellers who purchased them from native dealers living on the spot; and many of these objects were historically traceable to certain royal dynasties which made Thebes their capital city. Some of the travellers were also dealers and resold their purchases to the British Museum and the Louvre. At length suspicion became certainty.

(*An account follows of the proceedings which led to the conducting of Herr Emil Brugsch, Keeper of the Boolak Museum*) to a lonely spot (*Figure 40*) in the most desolate and unfrequented part of the great Necropolis, which extends for between three and four miles along the western bank of the Nile. Hidden behind an angle of limestone cliff, and masked by a huge fragment of fallen rock, he beheld the entrance to a perpendicular shaft descending to a depth of twelve metres. At the bottom of this shaft opened a gallery seventy-four metres in length, leading to a sepulchral vault, measuring seven metres by four. In this gallery and vault were found some thirty-six mummies (*Figure 39*), including more than twenty kings and queens, besides princes, princesses, and high priests; to say nothing of an immense store of sacred vessels, funeral statuettes, alabaster vases, and precious objects in glass, bronze, acacia-wood, etc. In a word, the treasure thus strangely brought to light consisted of some 6000 items, not the least valuable of which were four Royal papyri. Professor Maspero, in his Official Report, warmly eulogises the energy with which Herr Emil Brugsch by the aid of 500 native labourers, exhumed, packed, shipped and brought to Cairo the whole contents of this now famous hiding-place.

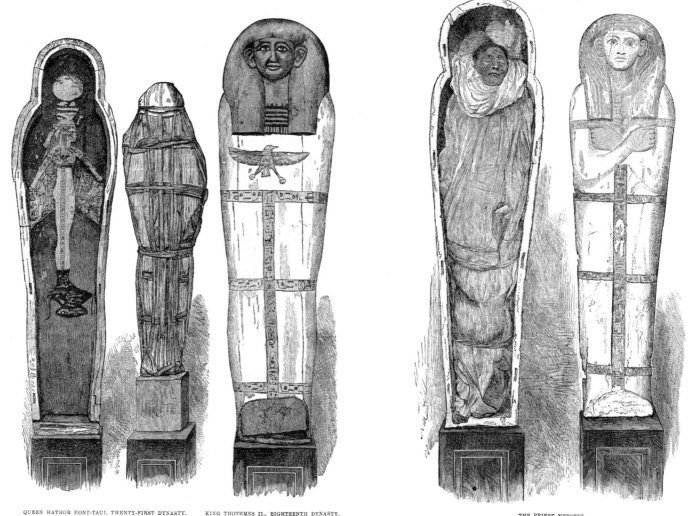

QUEEN HATHOR HONT-TAUI, TWENTY-FIRST DYNASTY. KING THOTHMES II., EIGHTEENTH DYNASTY. THE PRIEST NEBSENI.

39 Royal mummies: Queen Hathor Hont-Taui; King Thotmes II; the Priest Nebseni

40 Deir-el-Bahari, near Thebes, scene of the recent discovery of mummies and sepulchral relics

The following, abridged from Professor Maspero's various reports, is a list of the principal Royal mummies and mummy-cases, chronologically tabulated and classed under the heads of their various dynasties. In some instances the mummy reposes in its original mummy-case, and sometimes in two or three mummy-cases, the whole enclosed in an enormous outer sarcophagus. In others, only the mummy-case is left, the mummy having been destroyed or abstracted. Further, some mummies are found in mummy-cases not their own, or in mummy-cases which have been altered and usurped for their use in ancient times. The presence of a mummy-case, even though empty, is held, however, to indicate the former presence of its original occupant, whose name therefore appears in its proper place in the list:

XVIIth Dynasty – (Approximate date) B.C. 1750 to 1703. King Rasekenen-Taaken, Queen Ansera.

XVIIIth Dynasty – (Approximate date) B.C. 1703 to 1462. King Ahmes Ra-neb-pehti,

Queen Ahmes Nofretari, Queen Aah-hotep, Queen Merit-Amen, Queen Honti-moo-hoo, Prince Se Amen, Princess Set-Amen, King Amen-hotep I, King Thotmes I†, King Thotmes II, King Thotmes III, Queen Sitka.

XIXth Dynasty – (Approximate date) B.C. 1462 to 1288. King Rameses I†, King Seti I, King Rameses II.

XXth Dynasty – Not represented.

XXIst Dynasty – (Approximate date) B.C. 1110 to ?. Queen Notem-Maut, King and High-Priest Pinotem I, King Pinotem II, Prince and High Priest Masahirti, Queen Hathor Hont-Taui, Queen Makara, Queen Isi-em-kheb, Princess Nasi Khonsu, Prince Tat-f-Ankh, Nebseni (a priest), Noi-Shounap (a priest).

The symbol † indicates that the mummy is missing.

Most of the above are now on view in the Eastern Hall of the Boolak Museum, where they are temporarily arranged.

Some few of the Royal mummies were found, however, to be in too dilapidated a state for exhibition. Among those not shown are

81

Thotmes III, Pinotem I and Pinotem II. Of the five thousand nine hundred and odd smaller objects, they are still, for the most part, in the store-houses attached to the museum. The building, meanwhile is being considerably enlarged, in order suitably to accommodate this important accession of antiquities. . . . There can be no doubt that the vault in which these various mummies and funeral treasures were found was the family sepulchre of the Priest-Kings of the XXIst Dynasty. This Dynasty was founded by Her-Hor, High Priest of Amen of the Great Temple of Amen at Thebes, who, towards the close of the XXth Dynasty, at a time the throne of the last Ramessides was tottering to its foundations, either inherited the crown by right of descent, or seized it by force. According to some authorities, Queen Notem-Maut was a Princess of the Rameses blood, and mother of Her-Hor; according to others, she was his wife. In any case, her name is always surrounded by the oval, or cartouche, which is the emblem of Royalty; whereas it was not till he had reigned more than five years that Her-Hor ventured to assume this distinction.

The close of the second Ramesside, or XXth Dynasty, was an epoch of great internal trouble and disorder. During the reigns of the last four or five *rois fainéants* of that line, there had been little security for life and property in Thebes; and organised bands of robbers committed constant depredations in the more retired quarters of the Necropolis; attacking chiefly the tombs of great personages, and venturing even to break open the sepulchres of the Royal Dead. Hence it became the sacred duty of the reigning monarch to take every possible precaution to ensure the mummies of his predecessors against profanation and pillage.

We accordingly find that Her-Hor caused the sepulchres of his predecessors to be periodically visited by a service of regularly appointed Inspectors of Tombs, whose duty it was to report upon the condition of the Royal mummies; to repair their wrappings and mummy-cases when requisite; and, if necessary, to remove them from their own sepulchres into any others which might be deemed more secure. Several of these visits are recorded in the handwriting of the inspectors themselves upon the mummy-cases and bandages of five of the Pharaohs enumerated upon our list; and in most instances the entry is confirmed by the signatures of numerous witnesses. At one time the tomb of Queen Ansera, at another time the tomb of Seti I, at another time the tomb of one of the Amen-hoteps, would seem to have been selected as the chosen hiding-place of several Royal mummies, all of whom had been removed from their own original sepulchres by order of Her-Hor or his successors. The mummy of Rameses II (to whose memory, as the supposed Pharaoh of the oppression of the Hebrews, so strong an interest attaches) appears to have been removed more frequently, and to have suffered more vicissitudes of fortune than any of the others. That his sepulchre in the Valley of the Tombs of the Kings had been violated by robbers can scarcely be doubted, for his original mummy-cases were either destroyed or damaged beyond repair. The very beautiful coffin of carved sycamore wood in which his mummy now reposes, is a new one, made probably during the first years of the reign of Her-Hor, and distinctly appertaining to the style of that period. The coffin of Rameses I is empty and much damaged. The coffin of Thotmes III is greatly injured and the mummy is broken in three pieces. The coffin of Queen Ansera is missing; Queen Ansera herself being found in a coffin originally made for a Lady Raai. The mummy of Thotmes I is also missing. From these and other indications, it may be concluded that the sepulchres of these Sovereigns had been violated before the removal of their relics into the vault of the Her-Hor family. Nor must it be supposed that this conclusion is based upon mere conjecture. The ancient Egyptians were an essentially literary nation. They held the profession of the scribe in the highest honour; and to the successful man of letters the most responsible offices of the State were thrown open. Of their enormous literature, only a very small proportion has survived the wreck of ages; yet even that small proportion numbers many thousands of MSS. of all periods; some in the handwriting called hieratic, others in a later and more abbreviated script known as demotic. These ancient and precious documents, of which the Louvre collection alone contains more than 5000, range over an immense variety of subjects, comprising religious, funereal *(Figure 41)*, mythological, magical, medical, astronomical, geometrical, historical, and moral works; as well as hymns, prayers, tales, poems, aphorisms, private letters, legal draughts and abstracts, inventories, deeds of sale and contract, etc. Now, among the legal papyri preserved to this day, are two which actually relate to the tomb-robberies before mentioned; and one of these, called the "Abbot papyrus", is among the treasures of the British Museum. It was written in the reign of Rameses IX, and it consists of seven pages of hieratic MS., the work of a legal scribe in attendance upon a commission of Tomb Inspectors appointed to inquire into certain depredations which had then lately been committed in the Necropolis of Thebes. The scribe, after duly recording the date, the name of the reigning Pharaoh, and the names of the Commissioners, goes on to make minutes of the proceedings, which extended over four

41 Funeral papyrus of Queen Makara of the XXIst Dynasty found near Thebes

days. Each Royal tomb which was visited, as well as the condition of the tomb and of its occupant, are entered in turn; and among these entries we find mentioned the tombs of two of the Pharaohs whose names appear in our present list – namely, King Rasekenen and King Amen-hotep I. Both came into the first day's round and in the words of the report "were found intact". This was in the sixteenth year of the reign of Rameses IX; and "intact" they would seem to have remained throughout the reigns of the Xth, XIth, XIIth and XIIIth Ramesside Pharaohs, with the last of whom the XXth Dynasty ended.

August 4, 1883

A BURIED CITY OF THE EXODUS

The excavations at Tell-el-Maskhutah . . . have resulted in some of the most interesting and important discoveries that have ever rewarded the labours of archaeologists. The idea of founding an English society for the purpose of exploring the buried cities of the Delta originated with Miss A. B. Edwards, the well-known authoress of *One Thousand Miles up the Nile*, and was carried into effect mainly by her own efforts and the energy and zeal of Mr. Reginald Stuart Poole, aided by the substantial support of Sir Erasmus Wilson; without whose munificent donations the work could never have been accomplished. The "Egypt Exploration

THE·EXCAVATIONS
PITHOM·SUCCOTH

42 *A buried city of the Exodus: Pithom-Succoth*

Fund", thus founded and maintained, was fortunate in securing the co-operation of M. Naville, the distinguished Swiss Egyptologist, who set out for Egypt in January of this year with the object of conducting the explorations contemplated by the society. After a consultation with M. Maspero, the Director of Archaeology in Egypt, who has throughout acted a friendly part towards the society's enterprise, M. Naville decided to begin his campaign by attacking the mounds at Tell-el-Maskhutah, on the Freshwater Canal, a few miles from Ismailia. The mounds of earth here were known to cover some ancient city, for some sphinxes and statues had already been found; but what city it could be, archaeologists were at a loss to determine; though some, with Professor Lepsius at their head, believed it to be none other than the Rameses or "Raamses", which the Children of Israel built for Pharaoh and whence they started on their final Exodus. Any identification, of the sites of the Biblical cities in Egypt was so far merely speculative. . . .

Six weeks of steady digging at Tell-el-Maskhutah, under M. Naville's skilful direction, placed all these speculations in quite a new light. The city under the mound proved to be none other than Pithom *(Figure 42)*, the "store" or "treasure city" which the Children of Israel "built for Pharaoh" (Exod. i, 11). Its character as a store place or granary is seen in its construction; for the greater part of the area is covered with strongly built chambers, without doors, suitable for the storing of grain, which would be introduced through trap-doors in the floor above, of which the ends of the beams are still visible. These curious chambers, unique in their appearance, are constructed of large well-made bricks, sometimes mixed with straw, sometimes without it, dried in the sun, and laid with mortar, with great regularity and precision. The walls are 10 feet thick, and the thickness of the enclosing wall which runs round the whole city is more than 20 feet. In one corner was the temple, dedicated to the god Tum, and hence called Pe-tum, or Pithom, the "Abode of Tum". Only a few statues, groups and tablets (some of which have been presented to the British Museum), remained to testify to its name and purpose; the temple itself was finally destroyed when the Romans turned Pithom into a camp, as shown by the position of the limestone fragments and of the Roman bricks. The statues, however, and especially a large stele, are extremely valuable, since they tell the history of the city during eighteen centuries. From a study of these monuments, M. Naville has learned that Pithom was its sacred, and Thukut (Succoth) its civil, name; that it was founded by Rameses II, restored by Shishak and others of the twenty-second dynasty; was an important place under the Ptolemies, who set up a great stele to commemorate the founding of the city of Arsinoe in the neighbourhood; was called Hero or Heropolis by the Greeks (a name derived from the hieroglyphic *ara*, meaning a "store-house"), and Ero Castra by the Romans, who occupied it at all events as late as A.D. 306. Indications are also found of the position of Pihahiroth, where the Israelites encamped before the passage of the "Reedy Sea", and of Clysma. All these data are directly contradictory to preconceived theories: Pithom, Succoth, Heropolis, Pihahiroth, and Clysma had all been hypothetically placed in totally different positions. The identification of Pithom with Succoth gives us the first absolutely certain point as yet established in the route of the Exodus, and completely overthrows Dr. Brugsch's theory. It is now certain that the Israelites passed along the valley of the Freshwater Canal and not near the Mediterranean and Lake Serbonis. The first definite geographical fact in connection with the sojourn in the Land of Egypt has been established by the excavations at Pithom. The historical identification of Rameses II with Pharaoh the Oppressor also results from the monumental evidence. One short exploration has upset a hundred theories and furnished a wonderful illustration of the historical character of the Book of Exodus.

August 25, 1883

GOLD ORNAMENTS OF THE INCAS OF PERU

We give some illustrations *(Figure 43)* of a very interesting and unique collection of gold ornaments from the "huacas" or graves of the Incas of Peru. They were obtained by Señor Don Leocadio Maria Arango, of Medellia, during a residence of thirty years in that

the Sun-God, was appropriately called "Corieancha", or the "Place of Gold". From Prescott's description it seems to have well merited this name. The interior was like a mine of the precious metal, every part glowing with the most exquisite burnished ornaments, of the

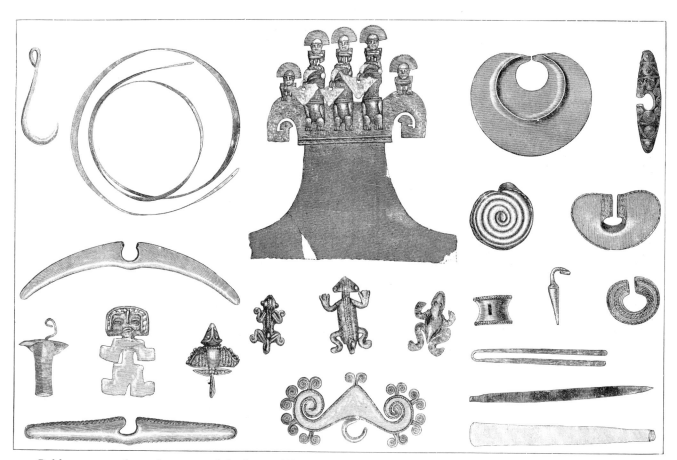

43 Gold ornaments from the graves of the Incas of Peru

country, but have now passed into the collection of Lady Brassey. To readers acquainted with the romantic history of Peru, an inspection of these antiquities will recall the memories of Cuzco, capital of the Incas, the golden City of the Sun, that hallowed spot which surpassed in splendour even the gorgeous fables of the Arabian Nights. Its great edifice, the Temple of

purest gold, whilst the cornices which surrounded the sanctuary were of the same material. Gold, in the figurative language of the people, was the substance of "the tears wept by the Sun". Historical studies find an enticing theme in the wonderful career of this once great and enlightened people.

It seems probable that the ancient Yuncas or

Incas migrated from China or some other parts of eastern Asia; but Manco Capac and his spouse, Mama Ocllo Huaco, centuries afterwards, in the year 1050, founded the Inca Empire proper. Lady Brassey's collection contains objects both from the earlier and the latter period.

November 21, 1885

EXCAVATION OF NAUKRATIS BY FLINDERS PETRIE

By Cecil Smith

It is now two years and more since the Society (*the Egypt Exploration Society*) whose latest success is here recorded first came into existence. The Egypt Exploration Fund was the outcome of a great national want. . . . Chiefly by the energy of the present honorary secretaries of the society, Miss Amelia B. Edwards and Mr. R. Stuart Poole, a band of energetic workers was formed, under the munificent presidency of the late Sir Erasmus Wilson, and including many of the best known English names in archaeology. . . . (*Brief reference to Society's chief excavators, M. Naville and Mr. Flinders Petrie.*) Mr. Petrie, having previously reported on several promising sites, returned to one of these, which has proved to be of a special interest hardly foreseen probably by the originators of the society – he has found Naukratis.

Being offered a Greek statuette by an Arab at the Pyramids, he was, on enquiry, guided to the spot whence it came, and saw the mound . . . strewn with pottery, not of Egyptian but of Greek manufacture. Pursuing his investigations beneath the soil, he has found a large and interesting series of objects, which show that beneath this mountain of sand and mud and rubbish, lay, some 600 years B.C., a flourishing Greek colony. . . .

The site of this colony of Naukratis has long remained uncertain; the shifting character of the Delta coast and the varying statements of ancient authorities have successfully combined to conceal its position; so that even the two latest maps of Kiepert and Smith differ in opinion by a distance of twenty miles. There is, therefore, no *a priori* reason why Mr. Petrie's site of Nebireh, which is nearer the sea than any fixed upon before, and on the opposite bank of the Canopic arm, should not be credited: here he has discovered the undoubted traces of two or more early Greek temples, a palaistra or agora and other extensive remains of a Greek city. Now, Herodotus states expressly that Naukratis was the only early Greek foundation in Egypt; and when we add that inscriptions have been found here bearing the name of the Milesian colony, there can no longer be any reasonable doubt of the identity of Nebireh with Naukratis.

We have called the site Nebireh; but Naukratis is really a mound some 1000 yards long, which has at one end the village of En Nebireh; at the other, that of El Gaief, tenanted by Arabs. . . . The city was never on the river, as had been supposed; but on a canal which has changed but little since the time of Herodotus, who states that it then ran past the Pyramids to Memphis. That this canal was open to sea-going traffic is proved by the quantities of stones with seashells now to be seen in the town, and brought here, no doubt, as ballast. Mr. Petrie has remarked the advantages of such a site over that on the river, whose floods would have paralysed the carrying trade during the three most important months of the year. . . . The explorer has succeeded in tracing the general outline of the ancient town, a plan of which . . . presents in itself marked features of interest. True to the custom obtaining in early Greek towns, we see here the special quarters assigned to the several crafts – the potters, the ironsmelters, the

temenos, identified by a large and very precious series of painted fragments of pottery inscribed with his name; and a temple, of which the drum . . . is a relic. . . .

Passing southward through the agora and the tortuous streets of the city, we come to the traces

44 Antiquities discovered at Naukratis

silversmiths, the scarab factors – each of which probably gave its name to the *deme* or electoral district of the city. . . . We have moreover the sites of several temples; that of Aphrodite and the Dioscuri to the north, or seawards, as befitted those deities of the sea in sea-born Naukratis, "Queen of Ships". Apollo, the great tutelary deity of Milesian Naukratis, has a great

of a gigantic building, the relics of which have puzzled even Mr. Petrie's ingenuity. Conceive a great space, about 220 yards square, enclosed within a colossal wall about the thickness of a London street, of massive masonry, even *now* 30 feet high in parts; within this, again, a mighty structure containing a great number of chambers, on two levels, entered, apparently, from

Plate 11 opposite *Stained with Agamemnon's blood? Bronze daggers from Mycenae*

STAINED WITH AGAMEMNON'S BLOOD? BRONZE DAGGERS FROM MYCENÆ.

By Courtesy of the British School of Archæology at Athens. Copyright Drawings by Piet de Jong, Architect to the School.

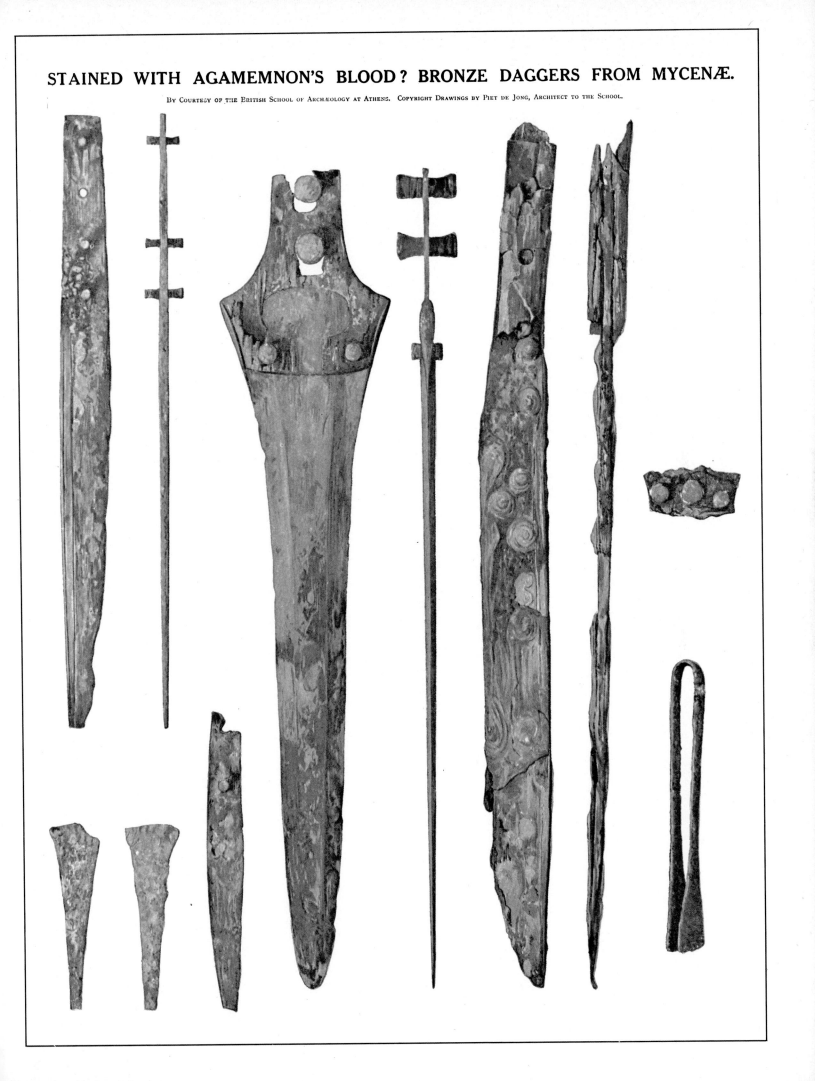

Plate 13 Back panel from Tutankhamen's coronation throne

Plate 12 opposite *The gold portrait mask of the boy-king Tutankhamen*

Plate 14 Tutankhamen's gold perfume box

Plate 15 opposite *A golden statuette of Tutankhamen as Horus the avenger*

Plate 16 The pyramid of Kukulcan, at Chichen Itza, crowned by the temple dedicated to Quetzalcoatl; in front a recumbent statue of the Chacmool and in the near foreground a pillar in the form of a feathered serpent

OUR FIRST GLIMPSE INTO THE WORLD BEYOND AS CONCEIVED BY THE MINOANS.

Plate 17   Restoration of the design from the ring of Nestor: a glimpse into the world beyond as
conceived by the Minoans

Plate 18 Ancient Maya Jade carved plaque found inexplicably in the Toltec capital of Teotihuacan

the top, and reminding us, in this respect, of the store chambers of Pithom and the beehive structure of Orchomenus. Though restored in later times, it is evidently of great antiquity; and we are naturally reminded of the great Pan-Hellenion mentioned in early writers, and erected, probably in troublous times, to serve for the mixed Greek populations the double purpose of treasury and fort.

In looking over the antiquities now exhibited *(Fig. 44, p. 88)*, we see at once just that union of Greek and Egyptian art which we should expect at such a site. Egyptian alabaster statuettes come to us with archaic silver tetradrachms of Athens, and the lotus of old Nile reappears in countless beautiful forms under the magic of Ionian fancy. . . .

Some few objects, it is true, still survive in the collection to tell us of the elder Phoenician inhabitants: the fragment of shell *(No. 32, Fig. 44)* . . . , engraved with a mixed design of Assyrian sacred tree and Egyptian lotus, recalls with certainty the handicraft of these merchant sailors of antiquity. The *tridakna squamosa*, as naturalists tell us, is never found in the Mediterranean, but belongs properly to the Red Sea and Indian Ocean; similar shells, with the same decoration, have come to us from the tombs of Vulci, Nimrud, Kamiros and Bethlehem, sites to which none but Phoenician enterprise can well have brought them. But the objects of purely Phoenician origin are, at Naukratis, as far as Mr. Petrie has yet gone, conspicuous by their scarcity; no doubt that here, as well as elsewhere, the earlier traders found themselves pushed out of the market by the *élan* of Greek enterprise, backed as it was by the Court influence of the time. At any rate from the period of Amasis (530 B.C.) downwards, Naukratis, as the collection shows, was as any other Greek city, save in this – that we have in it an opportunity of observing the beautiful Greek growth of art, fostered by unique circumstances of climate and surroundings; and, as an effect of the wide trade relations which brought the wares of the mother country to the prosperous

colony, we have the further opportunity of comparing Naukratian exotic with its kinsman of Greece. And nowhere is this better exemplified than in the pottery of which Mr. Petrie has made so precious a collection.

Of the many curious inscribed vases, we may mention one which, if Mr. Petrie's tempting attribution is correct, is of the highest importance. Herodotus tells us of a prominent townsman of his, Phanes of Halicarnassus, who played an important part in Egypt under Amasis and Cambyses. "There was among the mercenaries of Amasis a Halicarnassian, by name Phanes, a man of judgment and valiant in conduct. This Phanes, having some quarrel with Amasis, fled by sea from Egypt, wishing to open negotiations with Cambyses. As he was of no small account among the mercenaries, being intimately acquainted with Egypt, Amasis pursued him, making every effort to capture him." Phanes escaped to the court of Cambyses, and became his guide in the invasion of Egypt in the year 527 or 525 B.C. The Greek and Carian mercenaries of Amasis, furious at the desertion of Phanes, slew his sons in camp within sight of their father. Shortly after, a battle took place, in which Amasis was defeated, and Cambyses became master of Egypt.

It would be strange indeed if this were the man whose mighty *krater*, inscribed with his name, is now, in part at least, in this collection. His Egyptian campaign, his connection with Amasis, must have led him to Naukratis; it may even be that, as his vase seems almost too good to have been eliminated in the ordinary course, the Naukratians may have removed his offering in their wrath at his desertion.

It is, in fact, in these remnants of Greek painted ware that the chief interest of the find is centred. We have . . . a great number of pieces, representing almost every fabric of Greek pottery hitherto known, as well as others which are new to us. . . . At a great centre of commercial activity, such as Naukratis was, whose art must have been constantly imparting and receiving external impulses, it is difficult to say what are the distinctive marks of local production. Arranged in chronological order, these fragmentary sherds give us in fact a running commentary on the history of the place; they show us the Greek instinct of art grafting itself upon a foreign stock, its gradual self-assertion, and its final position as an independent growth. Archaeology is the handmaid of history as well as of art, and it is interesting to turn over these tattered pages of an almost forgotten past. Mr. Petrie's antiquities tell us at a glance as much of the political history of this far Greek settlement as they tell us of its private life. We have first the scanty traces of the old Semitic traffickers, as represented by the engraved shell and other kindred objects; the Graeco-Egyptian period under Phil-Hellene Amasis, marked by the Phanes bowl and a large series of little porcelain gods and other objects of Egyptian ritual; the disappearance of Phoenician art as Naukratis became a Greek trading centre; the conquest by Persia, reflected in the corresponding gap in the otherwise continuous series of Greek pottery; the deposit of Ptolemy II . . . which may, as Mr. Petrie thinks, be an alliance coin of Naukratis and Alexandria under the minority of Ptolemy V; and, lastly, as relic of Imperial times, the gold bandeau, with the name of its dedicator or possessor, Tiberius Claudius Artemidorus.

September 11, 1886

PHARAOH'S PALACE AT DAPHNAE (TAHPANHES) IN EGYPT

By Cecil Smith

The Egypt Exploration Fund has not rested content with last year's brilliant discovery of the Greek city of Naukratis, in the Delta.

Last year, it will be remembered, the interest of the excavation centred specially around the Greek problems of art which were thereby solved; in the present exhibition Mr. Petrie, who a third time comes back in triumph, has materials for us all. In his last discovery of Daphnae, which in variety of interest ranks second to none within the present century, Biblical, Egyptian and Greek scholars can all find cause for congratulation.

This time it was not, as before, to a site like Naukratis, hitherto unknown, that he directed his steps. Tell Defenneh has long been recognised by scholars as the site which might cover the remains of the historic fortress of Daphnae. . . . When Mr. Petrie, last spring, brought his Arab diggers to Defenneh, it was not a frowning fortress in a fertile plain that he attacked; fifteen miles of wilderness, where marsh alone varies the monotony of everlasting sand, and where the only shade is that of an occasional telegraph-post, brought his little army to the foot of three mounds, where his tent was pitched near the tamarisk trees. . . .

Behind the tamarisks runs a brackish canal, which broadens higher up into marshy lakes, the only traces now left there of the Pelusiac arm of the Nile; these form two sides of a parallelogram about a mile broad, within which lay the camp and town of Daphnae; and throughout this narrow space the soil is crowded thick with mute witnesses of the teeming life that once must have filled the plain. Towards the centre of this space stands the highest mound of the three, known to local tradition as "El Kasr el Bint el Yahoudi", the "Castle of the Jew's Daughter", a name of special significance, as we shall see; and here Mr. Petrie decided to open the attack *(Figure 45)*. . . .

45 *Pharaoh's Palace of Daphnae in Egypt: view of excavations, looking south-west*

The story of Daphnae is closely interwoven with one of the most interesting chapters of Egyptian history. Herodotus, whose romantic narrative is in the main accepted, tells us of the foundation of the fort under Psamtik I, in B.C. 650. At the death of the Ethiopian King Tihakah, B.C. 666, which left Egypt at the last stage of demoralisation and distress, the country was split up into twelve petty principalities, among whom Psamtik figures in the annals of Assurbanipal as Prince of Memphis and Sais; an oracle had foretold that whichever of the twelve princes should pour a libation "out of a bronze cup" should become King over them all. One day, when all the Princes were sacrificing to the god Ptah, the priest had omitted to bring out the twelfth cup of gold, and when it came to

Psamtik's turn he unthinkingly snatched off his bronze helmet and used that for his libation; seeing that the oracle had thus been fulfilled, the eleven Princes took counsel to put Psamtik to death, but eventually were content to drive him forth into the marshes of the Delta. Here, while brooding over his wrongs, the oracle of Buto told him that "vengeance should come from the sea, on the day that men of bronze should come out thence". Soon after, the arrival of some Carian and Ionian plunderers, clad in bronze cuirasses, explained the mystery; Psamtik took them into his pay, and by their help overcame his eleven rivals. The moment was ripe for ambitious projects; Babylon, which alone was likely to offer an opposition, was fully occupied with an intestine revolt. Assyria's weakness was

Egypt's opportunity, and Psamtik I had leisure to consolidate his sway. The canals and roads, long disused, were reopened; the larger towns, which had one and all suffered at the hands of Assyrian or Ethiopian invaders, were rebuilt and beautified; a fleet of Phoenicians was formed; and an army was prepared for foreign conquest, when an unforeseen calamity changed the course of events.

The Greek mercenaries, who had so greatly helped Psamtik's cause, were rewarded in proportion to their services. The King had founded three forts – namely, Elephantine, for defence against the Ethiopians; Marea, against the Libyans; and Daphnae, against the Arabs and Syrians. The last of these was prepared partly as a Royal residence, partly as a garrison of the King's favourite Greek troops and bodyguard. . . .

The ambitious projects of Psamtik I devolved on his son, Necho, who conquered all Syria, overthrowing Josiah and placing Jehoiakim on the throne of Judaea; as a record of his gratitude to the Greeks who had served in this campaign, he dedicated at the Temple of Apollo, at Miletos, the garment which he had worn. It is doubtless to these same Greeks that Jeremiah refers (xlvi, 9) when he speaks of the "Lydians that handle and bend the bow". Necho died in B.C. 595, and his son Psamtik II, six years later, without effecting anything of importance. But the accession of the ambitious Pharaoh-Hophra was the signal for a general revolt against the Assyrian power; Egypt, Phoenicia and Judaea all rose in arms; and we know from Jeremiah the story of this ill-advised alliance with the "broken reed" of Egypt, which resulted in the overthrow and captivity of Zedekiah. He relates, too, the discords which arose among the remnant of the people left in Jerusalem; and how, fearing the Babylonian wrath, the slayers of Ishmael took the daughters of Zedekiah, and the prophet himself, and carried them "into the land of Egypt, even to Tanpanhes". As to the disasters which the prophet foretold against Egypt at the hand of Nebuchadnezzar, there

seems to be some doubt; it is certain, at any rate, that the Babylonian host reached Egypt. But the Greek fleet of Pharaoh-Hophra gave him the supremacy of the sea, and it seems clear that his enemies experienced a severe check. His tolerance of the hated foreigners – again, probably these Daphnae Greeks – eventually proved his downfall. A large force of native troops had been nearly annihilated in an expedition against Cyrene, and the priests and people affected to believe that their destruction had been fore-arranged; a sedition broke out, and Aahmes was placed on the throne. Too wise to repeat the mistake of his predecessor, this King partly removed the ground of offence in reducing the Greeks in Egypt to a minimum; Naukratis alone was permitted them for trade, and the garrison at Daphnae was removed to the court at Memphis. Last scene of all, before the curtain closes on Daphnae: Herodotus says that in his day the town indeed was in ruins, but the port was held by a garrison of Persians; doubtless, as a military position, it was still kept up for some period: but its raison d'être was gone, and, to all intents, its history ends with the deportation of the Greeks under Aahmes.

Such is, in brief, the outline of the events in which the Kasr must have played a part. Four kings within the century had passed away, and four different races had found a home within its wall. With its brief history before us, we can scarcely imagine a place in ancient history where the *admonitus loci* so strongly appeals to the imagination as here. Its story covers a period of little over a hundred years; and yet, what moving scenes must it not have witnessed! Here must have passed into Asia, the chariots and horsemen of Necho, to return laden with the spoils of Syria and Judaea. Here from his watch-tower on the palace top the Carian sentry of Pharaoh-Hophra must have strained his eyes eastward, looking ever for the cloud of dust and glint of arms which heralded the avenging armies of Nebuchadnezzar. Here Jeremiah may well have foretold the coming of the Babylonian host: "Then came the word of the Lord unto

Jeremiah in Tahpanhes, saying, Take great stones in thine hand, and hide them in mortar in the brickwork which is at the entry of Pharaoh's house in Tahpanhes, in the sight of the men of Judah; and say unto them, 'Thus saith the Lord of Hosts, the God of Israel; behold, I will send and take Nebuchadnezzar, the King of Babylon, my servant, and I will set his throne upon these stones that I have hid; and he shall spread his Royal pavilion over them. And he shall come and shall smite the land of Egypt; such as are for death shall be given to death, and such as are for captivity to captivity, and such as are for the sword to the sword.'" (Chap. xliii, 8–11.)

It is, in truth, this very "house of Pharaoh at Tahpanhes" which Mr. Petrie has found, and where we left him in his (not Royal) "pavilion": and we may now see that his discoveries bear out, in a most striking degree, the relation of history. When, under the energetic spades of the little expedition, the mounds and plain were induced to render up their secrets, it was found that the shapeless mound concealed the remains of a gigantic square keep, with sixteen chambers on each floor, of which naturally only the basement remained nearly intact, the remainder having gone to form the debris of the mound. The Kasr stands in the midst of a courtyard, which again was enclosed within an immense walled area, 2,000 feet by 1,000 feet; the great boundary wall, of which the only trace is now the empty space amid the potsherds . . . within that area which it enclosed, were found remnants of the muniments of war, horses' bits, arrow-heads, weapons and implements in iron, together with all the traces of an iron foundry.

Out in the plain were the traces of a town, with the line of streets and basements of the houses still clearly marked; here were discovered pieces of jewellery and numerous small weights such as goldsmiths would employ; while pottery was scattered broadcast everywhere. As yet no remains of a temple have come to light, though there are walled enclosures within which these may have stood.

The entire character of the remains is, in fact, precisely what we should expect from history: a fortress of great strength and yet on a scale befitting an abode of Kings; a barrack where a great force of soldiery could find quarters; and just so much of a town as would naturally gather round such a nucleus, with industries suitable to its Greek population. In one of the lakes near the town may even be seen the traces of the docks, where, the father of history tells us, the Greek ships were laid up.

If we now turn to the exhibition at Oxford Mansion, we shall find that the date of the Kasr is placed beyond a doubt. Warned by his Naukratis experience, Mr. Petrie searched under the foundations, and discovered at each corner a complete set of foundation deposits. These bring before us, in a most striking degree, the whole ceremony of the dedication. We have models of the objects used in the sacrifice, consisting of Libation-vases, corn-rubbers, and the actual bones of the sacrificial ox; we have models of the bricks employed, specimens of ore, and a series of little tablets in gold, silver, lapis-lazuli, jasper, cornelian, and porcelain; these latter are all engraved with the name and titles of the Royal founder, Psamtik I.

One case in the collection will be viewed with special interest by the curious. In the Egyptian houses, like our own, the basement was apparently consecrated to the domestic offices of the establishment; and Mr. Petrie has even been admitted to the *arcana* of the Royal household; in the pantry of "Pharaoh's chief butler" were numerous jar lids and plaster amphora-stoppers, broken off, no doubt, when the jars were "uncorked" for consumption. According to the general practice, these stoppers were stamped with the Royal names, and we have in consequence a nearly complete series of the Royal names of the very periods of which we have spoken – Psamtik I, Necho, Psamtik II, and Aahmes. Hard by stood the kitchen, doubtless presided over by "Pharaoh's chief baker", with dressers, jars and dishes complete; and near this again a small room, which must have served as a scullery, for it has all the appurtenances of washing up.

Among the other objects found in the palace is a piece of scale-armour, of which only one other piece (now in the British Museum) has ever been discovered; the British Museum piece is on hardened linen, and this may possibly explain a problem which has long puzzled archaeologists: it will be remembered that Aahmes, following the example of Necho, dedicated in a Greek temple his cuirass of linen. Various attempts have been made to explain away this apparent paradox; may it not be that the cuirass of Aahmes was of linen covered with scale-armour? In a hot country like Egypt, the ordinary bronze cuirass would be insupportable; the inventive genius of the Greek mercenaries may well have discovered this substitute, which at once provided for security and ventilation. A cuirass of this description, from its novelty and difficult construction, would thus be an object not unworthy of dedication by an Egyptian King in a temple of the Greeks. . . .

December 11, 1886

SACRED ANTIQUITIES OF THE CHIBCHAS, AT GUATAVITA, COLOMBIA, SOUTH AMERICA

(From the collection of Mr. W. C. Borlase, M.P., lately in the Colonial and Indian Exhibition)

Towards the northern extremity of the Andes mountain range, in South America, the United States of Colombia, one of the most flourishing Spanish Republics, has its capital of Santa Fe de Bogota upon an elevated inland plateau, 8600 feet above the sea-level, which was anciently inhabited by the Chibchas. This nation, who called themselves "Muiscas" or Men *par excellence*, had attained a certain degree of barbaric civilisation previously to the Spanish conquest in the sixteenth century, and knew the art of working gold. They used it for coined money, which the other American races did not, and for personal ornaments; while their most precious offerings to their deities consisted of small golden figures representing men, women, and animals, rites and customs, industries and meteorological calculations. These they deposited in earthen vessels of different forms. Lakes, of which several were considered sacred, in remote defiles of the mountains, were made the receptacles of these treasures. From these lakes they believed that their ancestors sprang, and under the waters, in their fantastic imagi-

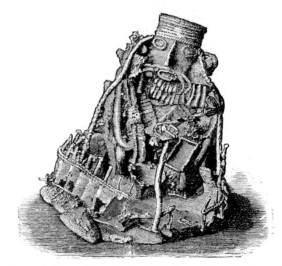

46 Sacred antiquities of the Chibchas: Guesa, the sacrifice to the goddess of the harvest

nation, was the home of their tutelary gods. The lake most celebrated (as the result proved when an attempt was made to drain it) was

47 *Various idols in gold found in the Guacas or sacred graves*

Guatavita, the chief place of worship of the Chibcha nation. The city, which bore the same name, offered a rich booty to the Spanish soldiers. Hernan Perez, who was the first to attempt to drain the lake, found in it a quantity of golden objects. At a later date Antonio Sepulveda made a contract with Philip II, to drain it and found articles valued at 12,000 dollars, besides an emerald of great value. According to the chronicler Zamora, the Chibcha priests, who guarded the temple of Guatavita, taught the people that in the beautiful lake there lived the Cacica, a lady who, flying from the accusations made against her by the Cacique, threw herself, with her daughter, into the lake, and there dwelt in a magnificent palace built in its depths. This belief induced the natives to give her their most precious gifts. They entered the lake on rafts of rushes; and, on reaching the middle, cast in their offerings. Several little rafts in gold and copper, illustrative of the practice, are among the objects recovered. The priests are said to have sacrificed human beings. Besides the lakes, the Guacas, or sacred graves, have always been noted for containing similar relics *(Figure 47)*. Gold and other masks were placed on the faces of the dead; and, as the nations buried the utensils of the deceased by his side, pottery, knives, etc.,

are abundant from the same source. Gold frogs and lizards, supposed to represent the water-god; birds, emblematic of the god of air; and figures of men, to indicate the earth, were common among these people; but the most remarkable among all the gold figures is that of the Guesa *(Figure 46)*. In the city of Hunsa, once every fifteen years, a youth was sacrificed, destined, as they thought, to bear their messages to the moon, the goddess who protected husbandry. The Guesa, as he was called, was born in a town in the plains of San Juan. As a boy he was brought up with great care, and kept in the Temple of the Sun at Iraca until his twelfth year, when he was sent forth, accompanied by guards, to traverse a sacred road along which it was said that the founder of the native civilisation had travelled. This ceremony over, he returned to the temple, where he remained until he was fifteen years old. On the day of the celebration of this human sacrifice, the victim was conducted in procession, accompanied by dancers, and preceded by the priests, or Jeques, adorned with gold ornaments and masks, to a column or pole, to which he was bound by a hempen coil. A shower of arrows was then discharged at him, which put an end to his existence. His blood was caught in sacred vessels, and his heart was torn out and offered to the sun.

1887–91

A quieter period, but still marked by the activities of the Egypt Exploration Fund and the Palestine Exploration Fund (at Lachish). Some notes on Hittite inscriptions; an obituary of J. T. Wood, the excavator of Ephesus; some description of the excavations of Roman Silchester; and in 1891 an obituary and memoir of Schliemann, with notes on, and illustrations of, his discoveries.

September 17, 1887

ENGLISH EXPLORATION IN EGYPT: THE SEASON'S WORK IN THE DELTA
Excavations at Tell-el-Yahoodeyeh, Tukh-el-Karmus, and Tell Basta

By Amelia B. Edwards, Hon. Sec. of the Egypt Exploration Fund

This year the mounds selected for exploration derive their interest . . . from Jewish and classical sources. The story of the one has been known to us for the last eighteen hundred years in the pages of "Josephus"; while the other, dating back to a pen four centuries earlier, forms the subject of one of the most familiar and picturesque descriptions in the history of Herodotus. The local Arabic name of the one is "Tell-el-Yahoodeyeh", "the Mound of the Jews"; the other is "Tell Basta", the "Pa-Bast", or "Abode of Bast", of the ancient Egyptians, the Bubastis of the Greek writers, and the Pi-Beseth of the Bible.

Tell-el-Yahoodeyeh is an extensive mound, distant about 22 miles north-east of Cairo on the Suez line of railway. It was a far more imposing site some thirty or forty years ago than it is now. Then, it was one of the loftiest and most striking mounds in that part of the Delta, with large remains of brick constructions and a massive wall of enclosure. Now it has, for the most part, been dug away almost to the level of the desert sand, and only a few tower-like masses are left standing here and there, like isolated cliffs in a wide field of rubbish. This work of destruction has been done by the fellaheen, who are, unfortunately, but too well acquainted with the value of nitrogenous brick-dust manure, and who are fast destroying the mounds of Lower Egypt. . . .

(Here follows an explanation, based on and supported by quotations from Josephus, of the probable history of the site. Onias, a hereditary High Priest of the Jews, fled, as a child, from Antiochus Epiphanes, King of Syria, in the latter half of the second century B.C., took refuge in Alexandria, and later appealed to Ptolemy Philometer and the Queen Mother, Cleopatra, for permission to fulfil the prophecy of Isaiah that there should be "an altar to the Lord in the midst of the land of Egypt" and to take over a deserted site in the Heliopolitan Nome. Permission was granted and . . .)

Onias was speedily surrounded by a large following of priests and Levites and the city of Onia became the centre of a semi-military colony. This colony was, however, regarded as a quasi-schismatic body by the orthodox Jews of Alexandria, who resented the audacity of Onias in presuming to build an unauthorised temple.

Sometimes persecuted, as under Ptolemy Physcon and Caligula, sometimes tolerated, the Jews of Onia continued to maintain their ground till the time of Titus, when, by Imperial command, the temple was sacked, the gates were closed and the Jews were forcibly expelled: "Insomuch", says Josephus, "that there remained no longer the least trace of any divine worship that had been in that place. Now, the duration of time from the building of this temple till it was shut up again was three hundred and forty-three years." ...

It was in order, therefore, to solve the problem of this mound before every vestige should be destroyed by the native diggers, that Mr. Naville, acting for the Egypt Exploration Fund and accompanied by Mr. F. Llewellyn Griffith, pitched his camp last March at Tell-el-Yahoodeyeh. ...

The object of Mr. Naville's excavations was twofold. He sought (1) to discover the ancient name of the city and temple before the time of its occupation by Onias; and (2) to settle the question whether the later settlement was, or was not, the centre of a Jewish colony. It may as well be said at once that he failed in the one quest and succeeded in the other. *(After failing to find any untouched tomb in one cemetery, they moved on to another.)* Here they found the ground honeycombed with similar tombs; and in one, amid a heap of limestone fragments, were two pieces of a tablet containing part of a much-mutilated epitaph, in metrical and somewhat barbarous Greek, of which only the following was legible: ... "my father, consumed by affliction, to his soul-kindred and friends. But if thou wouldst know how great (were) his faith and grace, come hither and question his son. The invisible. ..."

In the absence of names or date, the only clue to the period of this inscription is found in the words "faith and grace", which were characteristic terms in use by the Alexandrian Jews; and it is likely enough that the epitaph commemorated the martyrdom of a citizen of Onia at the time of the persecution of the Jews by Ptolemy Physcon. Other discoveries followed in quick succession, one tomb after another yielding its funerary tablet. The first names that occurred were those of a mother and daughter, whose bones lay undisturbed in a large recess divided by a brick wall. Over the one was painted in red letters – "Tryphaena, mother"; over the other, "Eiras, daughter"; and under each skull was a brick, by way of pillow. Another tomb, decorated with sculptured ornaments in the Greek style, contained two handsome tablets with the following descriptions in well-cut characters:

"The tenth year, the eleventh of Payni, Glaukias, years 61. Good father. Excellent. Farewell."

"Mikkos, the son of Nethaneus, dear to all. Excellent. Untimely. Farewell. Years 35. The fifteenth year, the fourteenth of Paophi."

Now Eiras is but a Latinised version of Iras; Tryphaena is a name popular in late Ptolemaic times; and Glaukias is distinctly Greek. In these there was nothing remarkable; but when he came to Mikkos and Nethaneus, Mr. Naville at once recognised the presence of Hebraic forms. ... He was not long left in doubt. The next tombs revealed names which were indisputably Hebrew. "Barchias, the son of Barchias", was almost identical with "Barachias". Then came the epitaph of one "Salamis", a name purely Hebrew; and the following, which placed the nationality of the deceased and his neighbours beyond all doubt:

"Eleazar. Untimely. Excellent. Friend to all."

The evidence of these, and some few other inscriptions, was conclusive. Tell-el-Yahoodeyeh was proved to be what local tradition reported – the "Mound of the Jews". That it was also an ancient site sacred to Bast is equally proved by the numbers of little cat-headed statuettes turned up in the course of the excavations. Josephus is thus confirmed as to both statements, and the identification of the city of Onia may be taken as established by plain, circumstantial evidence. ...

Farther out still, in the open desert, yet another cemetery was discovered. Here the dead were buried under isolated tumuli, varying from 4 feet to 12 feet in height. The graves were bedded in sand and basalt chips, built round

48 *English exploration in Egypt: clustered lotus columns, Hypostyle Hall, Great Temple of Bubastis*

with brick walls, and covered in with a rude kind of gable roof, formed of two large stones. In these were found some fifty or sixty coffins of baked clay similar to the "slipper" coffins of Warka in Babylonia. They were baked in one piece, with a large opening above the face, through which the corpse was inserted. A lid moulded in the likeness of a huge face surrounded by a rude imitation of an Egyptian head-dress, fitted this opening and closed in the dead. On some lids the face and head were modelled on a smaller scale, so as to leave space for a pair of attenuated arms crossed upon the breast, like those of the well-known funerary statuettes buried in Egyptian tombs. These coffins were painted with illegible hieroglyphs and figures of Egyptian gods, and are striped with bands of glaring colour in imitation of the outer bandages of a mummy. The corpses inside were, however, not mummified, though beads, bronze arrow-heads, flint implements, and other such trifles ordinarily found in Egyptian graves were buried with them. Two or more large food jars were also found in almost every grave. *(Here follows a description of a short excavation at Tukh-el-Karmus, which was apparently a group of store-chambers.)*

Hearing a rumour of the discovery of some

XVIIIth Dynasty tombs at Tell Basta, Mr. Naville decided to shift camp to that place. . . .

The report touching the so-called XVIIIth Dynasty tombs proved to be false. Some graves had been found; but they were of late date and without interest. . . . (Consequently Mr. Naville decided to follow up the clues in Herodotus' glowing description of the city and temple of Bubastis.) . . . Here, evidently, was a place in which to do little would be to do nothing; so Mr. Naville got together a gang of some two hundred native labourers, and started work in three places at once – i.e. at such distances along the presumed axis of the temple as might be expected to strike the entrance-hall, the central halls and sanctuary. Much to his surprise – for he expected only failure – the three excavations were at once successful. At a comparatively small depth below the surface, the picks of the diggers revealed a vast substratum of red granite blocks, fallen columns, architraves, bas-reliefs and broken statuary. By the end of the first week it became evident the whole temple was there, shattered, overturned, piled block upon block in unimaginable disorder; yet lying as it had fallen, and buried where it lay. Soon, it became possible to determine the character of those parts of the building which were being uncovered. It was oriented, as usual, from east to west; and the westernmost pit laid bare the remains of a structure inscribed with the ovals of Nectanebo I (XXXth Dynasty, B.C. 364). This was clearly the sanctuary. Seeing that it was of comparatively recent date, Mr. Naville abandoned it for the nonce, and concentrated his forces upon the middle and eastern end of the temple. The latter proved to be the Hypostyle Hall *(Figure 48)*, or "Hall of Columns"; while the central pit disclosed the ruins of a splendid hall, in which there were no columns, but the remains of a vast number of statues of all sizes, from miniature to colossal. Though built at different periods, and bearing the names of various Kings, the temple was evidently built throughout of red granite. The columns of the Hypostyle Hall are of the beautiful "clustered lotus" order, with lotus-bud capitals. All are broken; but their glassy surfaces are as lustrous as if they had but yesterday left the hand of the polisher. Though columns and architraves are alike engraved with the names and titles of Rameses II, Mr. Naville does not hesitate to ascribe this part of the building to the Pharaohs of the XIIth Dynasty. The style is the style of the Usertesens and Amenemhats; the inscriptions are evident usurpations. In confirmation of this view, a block engraved with the name of Usertesen III was found in this part of the ruins. The great central hall proved to be the work of Osorkon II, of the XXIInd (Bubastite) Dynasty. This Osorkon was a great-grandson of Shashank, the Biblical Shishak, who was born at Bubastis, and was founder of the Bubastite line; and he is himself supposed to be identical with "Zerakh the Ethiopian", who invaded Judaea in the time of Asa, and was defeated in the valley of Zephathah (2 Chronicles, chap. xiv).

The walls of this hall, to which Mr. Naville has given the name of "The Festive Hall", were apparently lined with a series of enormous tableaux in bas-relief, representing a great religious festival in which Osorkon and Bast and all the gods of Egypt take part. Every block is overthrown, but each is carved with part of the subject. On some are seen processions and dances of priests; on others, scenes of adoration and offering; while Osorkon, always with Bast by his side, is sometimes accompanied by Queen Karoama, his wife. Meanwhile, above the heads, under the feet, and in between these hundreds of figures are graven thousands and tens of thousands of hieroglyphic inscriptions. To turn these blocks – most of which had fallen face downwards – to remove the top ones, to lift out those below, to take paper "squeezes" of the figures and inscriptions with which the face of each was closely covered, was a difficult, but most exciting task. By this time, Mr. Naville's forces were increased to 400; and he could have given employment to half as many more. Count D'Hulst (another officer of the Fund) also

arrived to his assistance, and gave effective help in taking the aforesaid "squeezes". When the whole hall shall have been excavated, and all the bas-reliefs thus reproduced, it is hoped that it may be possible to arrange the squeezes in sequence, and so to restore the order of the subjects and the sense of the inscriptions. Thus far, Mr. Naville has only gathered that the scenes represent a great festival which took place "every fifty years"; but whether Osorkon instituted the festival and thus inaugurated its first celebration, or whether he simply commemorated the splendour with which he kept it when it recurred in due course, it is as yet impossible to discover. That he built, or re-built the Festive Hall in record of the event, and that he peopled it with a vast number of statues executed under preceding reigns, is, however, certain. Of these statues the greater number bear the names and titles of Rameses II. The colossi – some in groups of three, representing Rameses enthroned between two gods – are all broken. Others are single figures, sitting or standing, in black, red, and green granite. The fact that the eyes of some are seven inches in length will give some idea of the magnitude of the scale upon which they were executed. (*There follow descriptions of a head of Rameses II in black granite and a statue of a "Prince of Kush", with battered features.*) . . . The other is a beautiful squatting statue, nearly lifesize, in black granite, very finely worked, and highly polished. It is nearly perfect, only part of the left knee, and a corner of the inscription, which runs in horizontal lines across the front of the legs, being broken away. According to this inscription, we should be looking upon a portrait statue of Prince Menthuherkhopeshef, a son of Rameses II, who is here styled "General of Cavalry of his Father"; but the inscription is a usurpation, recut on the field of a former inscription, which has been erased for the purpose. The statue is in the unmistakable style of the XIIth Dynasty, and the features represent some prince or noble who lived in the time of the builders of the Hypostyle Hall.

September 27, 1890

PALESTINE EXPLORATION DISCOVERIES

In the *Contemporary Review* for September is an article by Professor A. H. Sayce, describing the recent discovery of the sites of Lachish and Eglon, which were towns closely adjacent to each other; Lachish, a strong fortress, is identified with a mound now called Tell-el-Hesy, and he thinks Eglon may probably be found hard by, on Tell-el-Nejileh; but the former is not now considered doubtful. Mr. Flinders Petrie, authorised by a Turkish firman from Constantinople, began digging, on April 14, at Umm-el-Laquis, the name of which had been supposed to refer to Lachish; but he found there only some fragments of Roman pottery. He then transferred his operations to Tell-el-Hesy, six miles from the town of Burer: it is a mound 60 feet high, about 200 feet square, consisting of the accumulated ruins of five or six towns, built successively, one on top of another. The lowest and most ancient, which must have been the Amorite fort or town, constructed at an earlier date than the arrival of the Israelites in Palestine, is surrounded with a wall, 28 feet 6 inches thick, still standing 21 feet high, of clay bricks dried in the sun. Large quantities of Amorite pottery are found in this enclosure. Among the ruins of the old wall are traces of huts, built of stones and clay, which Professor Sayce imagines to have been inhabited by the Israelite garrison after capturing and destroying the Amorite city. The wall may have been 40 feet or 50 feet high; as it is said in Deuteronomy, chap. 1, v. 28, "The cities were great, and fenced up to heaven." A good deal of the thick black Phoenician pottery, reputed to be not older than 1100 B.C., lies above the wall.

Lachish was probably not a place of great importance under the Jewish monarchy, except as a fortress; but there are remains of an upper brick wall, 13 feet thick, along the north and west sides, with a tower at the north-west corner, apparently repaired or rebuilt on three or four occasions, which are pronounced to be of the age of the Kings. To this period is ascribed the date of some stone slabs with sculptured pilasters. . . . This pilaster has a sloping side, based on a low stone cushion, and decorated with a volute at the top, shaped like a ram's horn, executed by masons of the same school with those employed in the building of Solomon's Temple; and one of the slabs bears a graffito of a lion (?), with a line-and-edge ornamentation, ascribed to the reign of Rehoboam. Mr. Petrie had not time, this year, to get into the centre of the mound, and there to search for sculptures or inscriptions. Along with these slabs was a stone with a deep cavetto moulding, similar to that which surmounts ancient Egyptian buildings. . . .

One of the ruins found had doorways of fine white limestone, and among the slabs some of them had a pilaster sculptured on them; these were upside down, showing that they had belonged to some former building. Mr. Petrie ascribes a date of about 1000 B.C. to the structure.

. . . Our explorers have discovered for us the monuments of the Moabites; to a certain extent they have unveiled the hitherto unknown "Kingdom of the Hittites"; and now, for the first time, they have come upon the remains of the Amorites. Having made a beginning, we cannot rest here. More explorations must be looked for.

The capture of Lachish by Sennacherib, King of Assyria, took place in the fourteenth year of Hezekiah's reign in Judah; and Hezekiah is stated, in the second Book of Kings, to have sent a message to the Assyrian monarch at Lachish. Sculptured in bas-relief on the walls of one of the palaces at Babylon, a representation of the taking of Lachish is now at the British Museum, and is equal to such a contemporary pictorial testimony as might have appeared in the *Babylon Illustrated News*. So this old town fell under Assyrian and Babylonian rule; another historical layer of buildings was added to the preceding deposits; and we may look for clay tablets with cuneiform writing, perhaps the official despatches from the Court of the Great King to the Governor of Lachish. In due time, however, came the Macedonian conquests of Western Asia, and a Greek colonial town arose on the site of so many different habitations; the relics of the Grecian settlement being the latest that now appear. The Amorite foundation, of course, is of prehistoric antiquity; that nation seems to have been the most powerful in Syria, conquering many provinces of the Moabite dominion, in the time immediately after Moses bequeathed to Joshua the task of winning the Promised Land.

November 22, 1890

ROMAN SILCHESTER

By Walter Besant

I see a vast area, flat, laid out in fields; and arable land, surrounded by a wall eleven to seventeen feet high. A broad modern road runs through it. A few low mounds rise here and there. You might drive through the road hardly noticing the wall as you enter this area, or as you go out of it. You might look across the flat land to right and left and never dream that, a foot or two below the surface, there lie the foundations and the floors, the tesselated pavements and the hypocausts of a great city, of which not a single tradition or memory survives. This is the ancient Calleva, once capital of the tribe or nation of the Atrebates. . . .

It was a rainy day when my visit was paid to Silchester. Our party consisted of a clergyman, F.S.A.; an archaeologist and artist well known to readers of *The Illustrated London News* for thirty years past; and myself. Most fortunately we found on the spot the hon. sec. of the Antiquaries, and were shown by him all that there is to see. . . . With the friendly aid that we received, we all went away very much wiser, and ready to proclaim, with Rabelais, "that the greatest Treasures and most admirable Things are hidden under ground". (*After a description of how to get to Silchester and the necessity of taking a luncheon basket:*) Archaeology is best followed under a summer sky, with a soft breeze stirring the branches among the ruins, dry fields to walk among, and dry stones to clamber over. The town was built in square blocks – *insulae* – which can be traced when the corn is standing. The excavations *(Figure 49)*, which are now under the direction of the Antiquaries' Society, are conducted block by block. The remains are found very near the surface, and, when they have been laid bare, planned and sketched, are covered up again for preservation. It has been suggested that the ground might be purchased, the whole area uncovered and preserved open, as an example for all to see of a perfect Roman town in ground-plan. This project would be admirable, if the country would also go to the expense of roofing in the whole city with glass, otherwise the frost and rain would very soon – as may be seen by the examples before us – disintegrate the floors and break up the tesselated pavements. It is better to proceed in the way now adopted by the Society – block by block – getting thus, by degrees, a complete plan of the whole.

Besides the discovery of foundations, many things are picked up among the ruins. These are all preserved in a small museum. The cases present the usual objects familiar to all

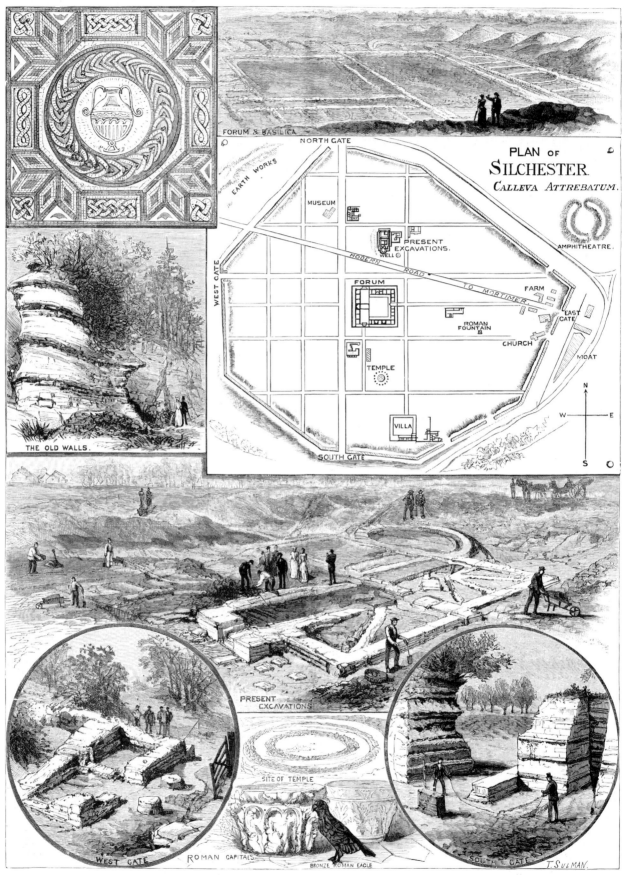

FORUM & BASILICA

NORTH GATE

PLAN OF
SILCHESTER.
CALLEVA ATTREBATUM.

EARTH WORKS

MUSEUM

PRESENT
EXCAVATIONS.
WELL

WEST GATE

MODERN ROAD

TO MORTIMER

AMPHITHEATRE.

FARM

EAST GATE

FORUM

ROMAN
FOUNTAIN

CHURCH

MOAT

TEMPLE

VILLA

SOUTH GATE

N
W   E
S

THE OLD WALLS.

PRESENT
EXCAVATIONS

SITE OF TEMPLE

WEST GATE

ROMAN CAPITALS

BRONZE ROMAN EAGLE

SOUTH GATE

T. SULMAN.

49 *Excavations of the remains of a Roman city at Silchester*

museums of Roman antiquities. There are capitals, pottery of various kinds, implements and tools, weapons, toys, "safety" pins, locks, etc. . . . Here is the foot of a statue, there is a little broken glass; and there are the coins of a great many Roman Emperors, ranging from those of Claudius to those of the last Emperors before the legions were recalled.

The most interesting part of the place is the Forum, which may be completely studied. This is the official centre of the town. Here is the great Basilica, a hall 280 feet long – 40 feet longer than Westminster Hall. It has an apse at one end, and an aisle is clearly marked by the site of pillars. On the west side of it are three great chambers for legal and civic business; on the east side is the Forum with its public office; on the south and on the north, is a row of shops. . . .

A perfect ground-plan of a villa has been laid bare. It shows with what comfort and luxury the better class lived. The tenant of this house, which was probably of one storey only, had a cloister built round three sides of a quadrangle, the fourth remaining open; it enclosed a small garden; but a larger garden lay outside. Behind the cloister he had large rooms for summer and for winter use. Those for the latter were warmed by hot-air pipes connected with great underground stoves, which can be seen. Behind these chambers was another cloister, and at the back were what we call the offices – kitchen, pantry and larder – with, I suppose, sleeping-rooms for some of the household. . . .

Outside, the great wall stretches round the town. It is not quadrangular, like Porchester, nor oval, like Sarum. It is an irregular polygon, following, most likely, the line of the older earthworks of the Atrebates. Its length is 2670 yards, and it encloses an area of 100 acres. These figures mean nothing: say, then, that Silchester is exactly the same size as the City of London. The wall is built without tiles. There is a layer of bonding-stones, then comes mortar, then flints – and so on. When the builders grew tired of flat bonding-stones, they adopted a herring-bone pattern. The gates are recessed for greater protection, so that an enemy would be exposed to weapons in flank. The wall is, indeed, a most beautiful monument. It is overhung with trees, and overgrown with creeping plants. I have walked about it twice – once five or six years ago, when the first glory of the early foliage under the sunshine of a warm May morning gave the monument a frame of exquisite beauty; and once the other day, when the autumn hues lent their splendours of yellow and of red to the grey stones of the wall, and glorified the coppice and undergrowth which fill up the fosse. The rain fell steadily, and the sky was dull, yet the Roman wall lost little of its beauty.

1892–97

A period of few major items, but those, especially Flinders Petrie's finds at Tell el Amarna, Thebes and Deshasheh and M. de Morgan's at Dahshur, of great interest. Notes on the temples of Stonehenge, the Balearics and Malta. An obituary of Sir Henry Layard; and, as a by-product of the Ashanti Wars, articles on "Spoils from Benin" and "Curios from Benin" – the beginning in fact of the growth of interest in West African bronzes.

September 24, 1892

DR. FLINDERS PETRIE'S ANTIQUITIES FROM TELL EL AMARNA

Dr. Flinders Petrie's last excavations in Egypt have resulted in finding an entirely new *couche* of antiquities. It has long been known that Khuenaten had introduced at least one new feature into the worship of the Egyptians. This was the worship of the Aten, or solar disc; which was represented only in his time with rays coming down, each terminating in a hand, to represent the divine power that produces all things for the good of man. Last season Dr. Flinders Petrie explored the "City of Khuenaten", a new city which this Pharaoh built for himself, now known as Tell el Amarna. The strange and interesting results of the explorations show that Khuenaten had introduced many novelties into Egypt in addition to that of a new religion. Among these, it is found that he had brought in a new style of art, not only in sculpture, but in painting and decorative art as well. . . . To anyone acquainted with the rigid rules and formality of Egyptian art, it would be the last thing to expect that those rules had ever been tampered with; but there can be no doubt on this matter after inspecting the ample evidences which Dr. Flinders Petrie has had the good fortune to come upon. One fragment of sculpture, being part of a statue of Nefertiti, the Queen of Khuenaten, is sufficient to show the difference from the usual Egyptian style. A copy of a wall-painting from the palace, with a bull among sedges and the papyrus-plant, and a frightened bird flying away, represents an effort at nature and picturesqueness, which is entirely foreign to Egyptian painting. A rough, unfinished bit of sculpture shows a horse's head, with a touch about it as if it had been done from nature and all conventional rules had been thrown to the winds. Curiously enough, on the other side of this fragment there is a sculptured profile of Khuenaten, done after the Egyptian manner. This may be contrasted with the other representation of him, copied from the cast that was made of him after he died for the use of the sculptors who were making his sarcophagus. Here, in one case, we have a portrait of the man that may be relied upon as if it were a photograph; and all the representations of this Pharaoh agree more or less in giving him a remarkable length of chin. In one of the cases there is a fragment of a painting, and on the part that remains are the two daughters of Khuenaten. The youngest one on the left is Makt-Aten and the other is Merit-Aten; the latter is "chucking" her younger sister under the chin with her hand, by way of chiding her, or in play. Here, again, the painting is not in the usual flat Egyptian style; an effort has been made to produce the effect of roundness to the limbs by means of shading, and with touches on the high lights of a brighter colour. This fragment of

50 *Comic frieze from Dr. Flinders Petrie's Egyptian discoveries*

painting ought to have a special interest in relation to the question of the durability of water-colours, for it belongs to that class of art. 1400 B.C. is the date given to it by Dr. Flinders Petrie, that is over 3000 years ago, and most of the colours appear as sound as when first laid on; the touches with the brush are yet clear and distinct. The question as to how this new style of art reached the Nile Valley will, no doubt, attract the consideration of Egyptologists. Dr. Flinders Petrie thinks it was entirely due to the personality of Khuenaten himself; for the art, as well as the worship of the solar disc, was all swept away by the Pharaohs that followed him. It is only in the mounds of the city that he founded that the remains of this non-Egyptian art have been met with.

October 22, 1892

AN EGYPTIAN DOMESTIC SCENE

By W. M. Flinders Petrie

Although we have been familiar for the last fifty years with the paintings in the tombs and temples of the ancient Egyptians, yet hitherto we have known nothing of the decoration of their houses. Two years ago I found some rough drawings of buildings on the walls of some houses at Kahun, of about 2500 B.C. But they were the more interesting for the architecture than for art. This year, however, a few pieces of wall-painting have come to light in the ruins of the palace of King Khuenaten at Tell el Amarna of about 1400 B.C. These are excellent in quality, and, moreover, belong to that highly interesting outburst of naturalistic art which we have now learned to appreciate in the results of this year. One great wall of the hall of the harem in the palace which contained the great painted pavement was preserved high enough to show the decoration. A dado of striped pattern rose about two-and-a-half feet from the ground; above that was a yellow band with a continuous scene of figures most delicately drawn upon it *(Figure 50)*. The plaster was so powdery that it was impossible to remove it, or even to trace the design; I therefore drew it in colours at once, exactly to the original scale, the painting actually dropping away while I looked at it.

At the left hand we see an open door, showing the limit of the scene in the house: the porter's little window in it is curious. Then comes a servant sweeping up the floor with a brush exactly like those still made from the split fibre of the palm branch. To him enters the steward in haste, with his baton, followed by the cook, who runs with two dishes, hot from the kitchen, on little wooden stands to be placed on the floor. The contrast between the cook and the leisurely house-servant, who follows him, sprinkling the floor with a jar of water, is excellent – the hot haste of the busy cook, wigless and only wearing a kilt; the little pursed-up lips; the spring of the run with bent legs, to avoid shaking the dishes; the evident "go" of the fellow; while the soft pleasant-faced lad, whose only duty is to dawdle about the house and sprinkle floors and do errands, follows in the most leisurely way. We next see the great bowls of grapes covered with garlands which stand near the entrance. By them is the burly porter resting his hands on his staff, to whom a hasty messenger has turned with the news that the master is coming. And just beyond, on the next side of the room, is the chariot seen approaching, which was doubtless followed by a group of the foot-runners and attendants.

We may see here some excellent principles of decoration. The two parts – indoors and outdoors – are separated by turning the corner of the room, being on two adjacent walls. The figures are put at the height of the eye for anyone sitting on a low Egyptian stool. Each figure is a complete study in itself, and yet all are combined so as to tell a continuous story. And the execution is as delicate as it could be (except in the porter and messenger, which are by a far inferior hand), as was suitable for work which stood close to the eye. Probably each figure was a portrait, with that little touch of caricature, which the Egyptians so loved. We may take a lesson from this, as from much else of the varied and beautiful designs which characterise this most interesting period of art.

March 7, 1896

MONSIEUR DE MORGAN'S DISCOVERIES AT DAHSHUR

During the winter of 1893–4 M. de Morgan paid a visit to the stony plateau on the west bank of the Nile, which lies a few hours distant to the south-west of Cairo, where stand the famous pyramids of Dahshur; a little to the north are the pyramids of the Kings of the Fifth and Sixth Dynasties, the "step" pyramid of Sakkara, and other important monuments. The whole district is full of tombs, and all scholars have admitted this fact; yet, strangely enough, no systematic excavations have hitherto been made throughout it. . . . M. de Morgan turned his attention to the southern end, and the results of his labours have fully justified his decision. . . .

51 *M. de Morgan lifting a golden crown from the mummy of Queen Khnemit at Dahshur*

Soon after work was begun at Dahshur fragments of inscriptions of Kings of the Twelfth Dynasty, about 2500 B.C., were found, and these served to indicate the age of the monuments found thereabouts. Further excavations resulted in the discovery of a pit and gallery in which were a number of tombs that showed plainly the marks of the professional robber. From the remains found there it was clear that they had been tenanted by the bodies of Princesses of the Twelfth Dynasty. Close by was a box filled with handsome gold and silver jewellery, and it is thought that the box had escaped the hands of the robbers by accident. It is more probable that these gold and silver ornaments were removed from the mummies by the hands of priests or others who had cause to think that they would be stolen, and that they were hidden in a place where the professional thief, expecting to find nothing, would not seek. . . .

On February 15, 1895, M. de Morgan found an opening (on the west side of the plateau) which led by an inclined plane to a gallery, and believing for several reasons that the tomb there had not been rifled, he removed the covering and laid bare the gallery to the light of day. On the following day, when room had been made to open the sarcophagi which had been placed there, the cover of one was lifted, and, to the great joy of all concerned, it was found to be tenanted by the mummy of the Princess Ha, which was ornamented with most beautiful golden jewellery inlaid with cornelian, turquoise, and lapis-lazuli. The fastenings of the collar and some of the smaller portions of the ornaments had become loose, and had dropped by the side of the mummy into the coffin, but they had been wonderfully preserved by the dry stone chamber in which they were buried, notwithstanding the four thousand years which had passed since they were laid on the dead Princess. In a small vaulted chamber the funeral offerings were found, together with vases of unguents, etc., with which the double of the Princess was intended to delight itself. When the second sarcophagus was opened, it was found to contain the mummy of the Queen Khnemit, who had been buried with most valuable articles of jewellery. Our Illustration *(Figure 51)* shows M. de Morgan in the act of lifting a magnificent golden crown from the head of the mummy of Queen Khnemit. Those who looked on at the removal of the jewellery from a great Queen who had died more than four thousand years ago saw a sight which they will probably never forget. But although the articles of jewellery in the coffin were numerous, and of every sort and kind which are characteristic of the epoch, the "find" which was made in a chamber close by is of greater importance, for here we have examples of the finest possible work of the ancient Egyptian goldsmith. The fine gold of which the crowns, pendants, beads, stars, etc., was made, had been drawn out and worked into cunning patterns and devices, which would not, we think, be easy to imitate. The most beautiful effects are obtained by the inlaying of cornelian, lapis-lazuli, and turquoise, and the patterns, though simple, show a mastery of the ancient craft of ornament which is almost incredible.

52 Painted tombs at Marissa: a hunting scene showing a leopard, horseman, dog and trumpeter

1898–1902

A relatively quiet period, with few archaeological reports. Those worth mentioning include: excavations at Silchester; the suggested sale of Stonehenge; General Sir Charles Wilson's journey (for the Palestine Exploration Fund) through Moab, Edom and Petra; Flinders Petrie's discoveries at Abydos; excavations at Bosco Reale, near Pompeii; fallen monoliths of Stonehenge; some discoveries at Cerigotto, Pompeii and Rome; and discoveries of prehistoric man at Mentone, with photographs by the Prince of Monaco and an article by Dr. Andrew Watson.

1903–5

These are still the early years of Bruce Ingram's sixty-two-year-long editorship and we may imagine him as a very young man, with the joint management of his father and uncle close behind his shoulder, but his confidence in archaeology as a fit subject for the paper is obviously growing. In 1903 a number of minor items are published, of which the most interesting are a piece on the forged Tiara of Saitaphernes and an article on Cretan discoveries by the Italians at Phaistos, written by Professor Federico Halbherr, whose name would become familiar to readers in the next few years. In 1904 there were articles about the Austrian excavations at Ephesus; work at Stonehenge; the examination of Zimbabwe; and the raising of Caligula's galleys from Lake Nemi. 1905 was an even fuller year, the principal items being: Legrain's discovery of 8,500 statues at Luxor; ancient Mexican buildings at Oaxaca; the painted tombs of Marissa in Jordan (Figure 52); Flinders Petrie's discoveries of the Egyptians in Sinai; finds from the Lake Nemi galleys; and excavations at Tepeji Viejo, Mexico, by the Bandolier Expedition of the American Museum of Natural History.

January 14, 1905

THE EXTRAORDINARY FIND OF 8000 HIDDEN STATUES AT KARNAK, UPPER EGYPT

Photographs by the discoverer, M. G. Legrain

For the last nine years the Egyptian Service of Antiquities has been engaged upon some very important works with a view to the restoration of the great Temple of Ammon at Karnak, near Luxor, in Upper Egypt. The director of the works, M. G. Legrain, during the course of his researches, came upon a pit *(Figure 53)* which had been filled with statues and monuments of

53 The hiding place of the hidden statues at Karnak, flooded by infiltration from the Nile

all kinds belonging to the Ptolemaic epoch; thence he has exhumed, up to the present time, eight thousand statues in gilded bronze and more than five hundred in granite, basalt, beryl, limestone, petrified wood, and other materials.

Almost all the discoveries bear historical inscriptions. This find is said to be the most important since Mariette's famous discovery of the Serapeum at Memphis.

July 29, 1905

THE EGYPTIANS IN SINAI

By Professor Flinders Petrie

Far back in prehistoric times the savage who wandered over the wild desert mountains of Sinai picked up little scraps of sky-blue stone which pleased his fancy. These were doubtless preserved by being stuck into holes in his weapons and objects of wood, as the Bedawin do now; and these decorated things were traded over into Egypt. The prehistoric man of Egypt demanded more, and a trade in turquoise sprang up, and provided the turquoise beads which were treasured for necklaces in the Nile Valley about eight thousand years ago. The primitive workers doubtless extracted the stones from the sandstone rock by means of the flint-scrapers, such as are found by hundreds in the old mine-heaps. When Egypt passed into a settled form of unified government, under the dynasties, the early kings would not leave this supply of jewels unclaimed. So in Sinai, as far back as about 4500 B.C., there are figures of the Egyptian king smiting the natives, and of the general who headed the expedition. These are the oldest sculptures known. Several such scenes of triumph were carved by later kings, especially those of the pyramid period, as Seneferu, about 4000 B.C. The ancient Egyptians worked large caves in the sandstone rock, along the lines of the turquoise-beds, to extract the little nodules of brown sand which coat the sought-for stone. They broke up the rock with large hammers of basalt, which are found scattered in all the old mine-heaps. These workings are at about five days' journey from Suez, in the midst of a desert bare of food or water.

In ancient times every place had its deity, and especially such a region as the mines, where all success depended on mysterious chance. If you wished to succeed in your search for these little blue specks among the masses of rock, you must begin by propitiating the goddess of the turquoise. A cave in the top of the rock over the mines was cut out for a shrine and here the goddess Hat-hor of Mafkat (turquoise) was worshipped by all miners who came there. To get the guidance of the goddess, no doubt dreams were the favourite mode, as was commonly the custom in Syria. And accordingly we find dozens of shelters on the top of the hills over the mines, where pilgrim miners might sleep, and where they put up their Bethel stones in token of their vision, as Jacob did. At a later time the Egyptians built cubicles for such dreamers in front of the shrine of the goddess. The Egyptians called her Hat-hor, which is a general name for foreign goddesses. Tall tablets of stone were put up to record the expeditions of the miners who were sent out from Egypt, principally by the kings of about 2500 B.C. This temple is now known as Sarabit el Khadem, or "the heights of the fortress". . . .

Amid the ruins were great numbers of different kinds of offerings to the goddess. Though the existence of the temple had been known long ago and many travellers had visited it, yet it had never been excavated, and even much of the plan of it was unknown. On clearing it, the whole of the walls were found, and the pillars which showed the original height. A group of the early kings who had worked here were commemorated together: Seneferu, Mentuhotep, Amenenhat I and Senusert I (4000 to 2500 B.C.). The heads of the goddess Hat-hor are on the tops of the pillars of about 1500 B.C. About a century later the beautiful statuette of the great Queen Thyi was dedicated here; this gives the best portrait known of her, worked with the greatest delicacy in black steatite. A large number of statuettes and tablets were dedicated by miners and officials, and hundreds of objects in blue glazed ware, bearing the names of the kings from about 1550 to 1150 B.C. Two copper chisels were also found in the temple of about 1200 B.C. And both in the temple and at some of the mines are inscriptions in an unknown writing which was probably one of the forerunners of the Phoenician alphabet.

October 7, 1905

LAKE NEMI'S BURIED GALLEYS

Even in these prosaic days the Lake of Nemi, lying among the Alban Hills, some twenty miles south of Rome, is a place of pilgrimage which few imaginative travellers fail to visit. Here in times past stood the famous Temple of Diana, referred to by Professor Frazer in his "Golden Bough". Julius Caesar erected, or occupied, a beautiful villa on Nemi's banks, and Augustus, Tiberius, and Caligula lived there in their turn, in days when Rome held sway over the greater part of the known world. History preserves faintly some record of the wonderful entertainments that were given in the royal villa, and some years ago the wrecks of two Imperial galleys were located in the bed of the lake. One belonged to Tiberius and the other to Caligula *(Figure 54)*. Their existence there had been known for centuries and many devoted but

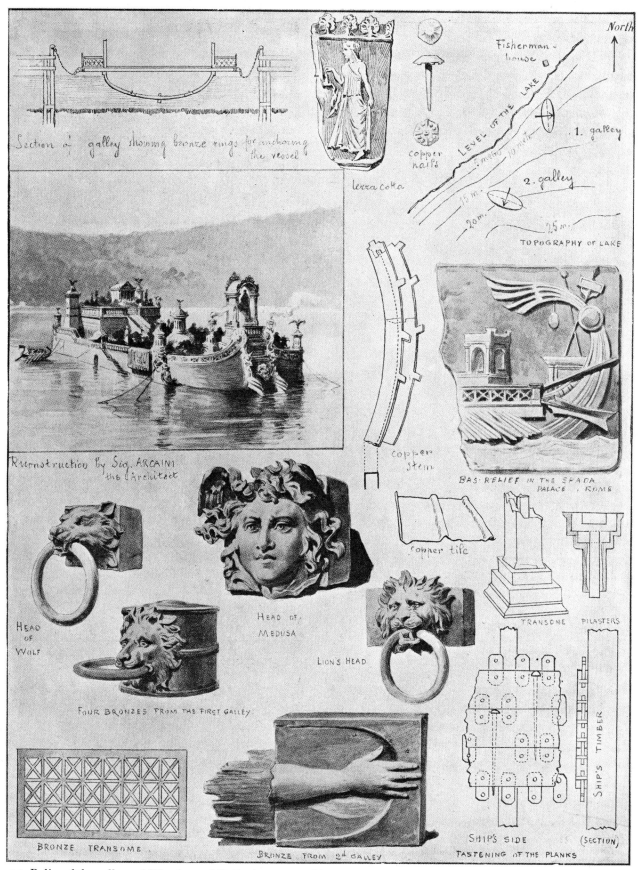

Section of galley showing bronze rings for anchoring the vessel

terra cotta

copper nails

TOPOGRAPHY OF LAKE

North

Fisherman house

LEVEL OF THE LAKE

1. galley

2. galley

Reconstruction by Sig. ARCAINI the Architect

copper stem

BAS-RELIEF IN THE SPADA PALACE, ROME

copper tile

TRANSOME PILASTERS

HEAD OF WOLF

HEAD OF MEDUSA

LION'S HEAD

FOUR BRONZES FROM THE FIRST GALLEY

BRONZE TRANSOME

BRONZE FROM 2nd GALLEY

SHIP'S SIDE (SECTION)

FASTENING OF THE PLANKS

SHIP'S TIMBER

54 *Relics of the galleys of Tiberius and Caligula recovered from the waters of Lake Nemi, and a reconstruction of one of the galleys*

unskilled efforts had been made to raise them. Now the time has come when we may hope to see the wrecks raised successfully, and their beautiful decorations added to the treasures of Italy. Lake Nemi belongs to the famous House of Orsini, whose head has given permission for all necessary steps to be taken.

1906

The first vintage year for archaeology in the new century. In addition to the extracts we give, this year saw as its other highlights: more on the Lake Nemi project; a major piece on the Asklepion of Cos, with a reconstruction drawing by Amedeo Forestier, whose first-class reconstruction drawings became familiar to readers for many years on either side of the First World War; excavations at the Roman site of Newstead near Melrose; a proposal to resume excavations at Herculaneum; and a piece on the cliff-dwellers of Arizona and New Mexico, with a reconstruction drawing by one of the paper's regular artists, Koekkoek, one of many Dutch artists of that name.

Supplement to March 17, 1906

EGYPT'S RICHEST TREASURE TROVE:
Wonderful Discoveries in the Valley of the Kings

By Henry Coply Green

The excavation in the Valley of the Kings, undertaken by Mr. Theodore M. Davis for the benefit of the museum at Cairo, and directed by Mr. Quibell, the Government archaeologist superintending the Theban district, revealed early in February a flight of rock-hewn steps half hidden by ancient debris from the neighbouring tombs of Rameses III and Rameses XII. By the afternoon of the twelfth the overhanging hillside was so far cleared away that one could go safely down the steps to a wall closing the entrance of a corridor leading to an unknown tomb. A break was found in the wall just under the corridor ceiling, and a boy was sent in, who discovered, just inside, a partly gilded chariot-yoke, a scarab, and a slender, long green staff circled with gilding near the top. Now, these things, which no modern thief would have slighted, had clearly been dropped by a robber of long ago when only jewels and solid gold were worth the stealing; and as chippings from the neighbouring tomb had been found on the steps, apparently in the very piles thrown there by the eighteenth dynasty workmen, it seemed certain that this tomb had lain undisturbed through the thirty subsequent centuries. . . .

By nine next morning, when Mr. Davis arrived from his dahabiyeh, only the absence of Mr. Quibell and M. Maspero, official head of all such explorations in Egypt, delayed the final entrance into the tomb.

Mr. Quibell was delayed by official duties.

M. Maspero, however, soon arrived. Joining Mr. Davis, the famous Frenchman, who selected the site for digging, went down the steps and slowly on through the rock-hewn descending corridor. It was barren. No works of funeral art strewed the floor; and the walls, unlike those of other tombs, were bare of both carving and painting. At the end of the corridor, where a second staircase was flanked by shelves, a mere bundle of ancient onions lay on the rock. But on one of the steps, a roll of papyrus met the explorers' eyes. Just beyond it they found a wall plastered with mud and sealed with the priestly seal. This alone separated them from the tomb itself; and the top was so broken that they could peer over into what for centuries on centuries no eye had seen: a confusion of dark forms, shimmering mysteriously here and there with a touch of gold or silver.

Squeezing their way between the wall and the rock ceiling, M. Maspero and Mr. Davis were soon in the midst of such a medley of tomb furniture that, in the glare of their lighted candles, the first effect was one of bewilderment. Gradually, however, one object after another detached itself from the shimmering mass, shining through the cool air, dust-free and golden. Against the wall to the left stood a chair, and beyond it a gilded coffin-cover lay upside down. In it was a conventional mask that gleamed golden through dark veiling; and the mummy whose head this mask had covered lay further off, its body partly encased in gilded open-work. Against the wall to the right leaned two "Osiris beds", flat surfaces on which seed had been sown, which, in sprouting, had outlined the figure of the god. Not far off, along the wall opposite the door, stood a row of boxes, like tiny sentry-boxes, each containing a statuette. In front of these rose, shoulder high, the oblong black mass of a "sledge", the outermost case for a mummy. To the left stood a bed. Nearer again stood a silvered mummy-case; and on this, and on a mummy beyond it, the second in the tomb, a shaft of cold blue light struck down from the outer day.

By daylight, then, mingled with the light of flickering candle-flames, the discoverers examined the second mummy. By candle-light alone they searched the first. Both had been plundered by the thief of long ago. . . . Not a jewel, and only part of one necklace, remained of all those with which the dead must once have been bedecked. But if such trophies were lacking, others of surpassing splendour and significance still packed the tomb-chamber from wall to wall. In the bottom of a mummy-case, from which the thief had removed the cover, he had left a cushion and a graceful alabaster vase. In another mummy-case he had neglected an alabaster jar and the cover of an embroidery-box, which he must have carried across the chamber to a second bed, on which it lay beside a superb gilded chair. Near by, where the floor fell one deep step to a lower level, he had thrown, among a multitude of sealed jars, half of the gilded open-work casing which had encircled one of the mummies. Near these jars again he had propped a coffin-cover against one corner of the tomb. Here, too, he had left a third bed and one of the most important of all finds in the tomb – a chariot, the curving front and wheel-rims of which shone through the darkness golden and scarlet.

Except for its broken pole and the partly bare spokes of its gilded wheels, this chariot was in perfect condition. . . . M. Maspero, baffled by the tomb itself, went back to the mummies of its occupants; and, candle in hand, studied the hieroglyphics on their gleaming mummy-cases. "Tioua", he read after a time; and after further study went on, "Ioua, hereditary prince, chief friend among the friends of the sovereign".

Ioua and Tioua – these were the names of the dead in the tomb; and these dead, as M. Maspero therefore knew, had been the father and mother of Tii, a much-discussed queen of the eighteenth dynasty, whose changing of the national religion had caused such uproar and violence that the burial of her parents in the sacred Valley of the Kings would have had to be hasty and secret. . . .

After such a long burial alabaster is at first curiously fragile, then firm again and strong; and gold leaf is so delicate that it may peel off at a touch. Yet alabaster and gold leaf – cloth, too, and veiling – were almost absolutely uninjured. The graceful alabaster, three beds, three chairs, the mummy cases, came glowing flashing and glittering into the day. A box containing "canopic" jars of alabaster – jars, that is, in which the viscera of the dead are preserved; the little sentry-boxes, each of them holding a *ushapti* figure, or image of a servant for the dead; tarred objects of vague form, recognisable by the archaeologists as the boxes containing mummies of ducks, legs of mutton and other meats; seventy-two sealed jars full of fruits – all these things and more emerged from their long burial as fresh and dustless as when the tomb had first been closed. And as a certain alabaster pitcher appeared, a wasp came buzzing up and sipped what M. Maspero maintained was the still fluid honey poured into it more than three thousand years ago to satisfy the immortally human cravings of Ioua and Tioua. . . .

So a trivial onlooker might have reflected. But when the mummies of Ioua and Tioua were carried up the steps, their faces bare to the sky, their closed eyes warmed by the sunlight, then even a hardened triviality must have failed. Dark and somewhat shrunken as they were, their look compelled awe. So living was it in its stillness, so changeless in its vitality, that death seemed only the sleep of immortality. Each face, as in life, was individual: the woman's delicate, almost wistful; the man's, strong-featured, and keen, with a smile of strange adroitness. . . .

Of the three chairs, one, as M. Maspero said, seemed almost in the style of Louis XVI, and another in the style of the French Empire. All, in fact, were strangely modern; and all were of an elegance or a solidity which ranked two of them among the very few fine specimens in the world, and placed one perhaps second only to the superb chair of Hatshepsah in the British Museum. Finally the chariot, with the flower-like ornaments of its gilded front, with its crimson-rimmed wheels, its pole and its yoke, stood out complete and excelled, if at all, only by the somewhat larger, gaunt car in Florence.

To the non-professional observer, however, intrinsic beauty made a more spontaneous appeal than questions of relative ranking; and beauty abounded both in these and in the rest of the trophies. . . .

The skill through which such strange charm and splendour had been achieved showed itself also in the inlaying of enamel and of semi-precious stones in the vigorously drawn vulture of another superb mummy-case. This skill was evident again in a little embroidery-box, the surfaces of which, tinted with sky-like blue, had been partly covered with gilded plaster bas-reliefs – among them the kneeling Osiris – framed with wood and ivory in a design whose straight brown and white lines bordered and separated alternate gay squares of bright blue and red. A more homely skill appeared in the perfection of many minute implements, models of hoes, water buckets, and tiny yokes to carry them. Finally, in an aspect of startling modernity, this varied Egyptian skill cropped up in the build of a ventilated rush trunk and of a large blue embroidery-box, each of which was upheld not merely at the corners by legs, but at intervening points by wooden rods in the truss-like forms of a steel bridge. . . .

Unlike the vast majority of offerings in Egyptian tombs, many of these were not mere models or symbols of meats, vases, beds and chairs, but the things themselves. In contrast with the few small plaster models found in this tomb, the seventy-two sealed jars were hollow, real, and well-filled with provisions. The vase and the honey-pitcher were equally genuine. While the charming little "Louis XVI" chair was obviously a model lightly built and covered with gilded low reliefs in fragile and thinly gilded plaster, the "Empire" chair with its solid wooden back deeply carved with grotesque gods, was so strongly built that in spite of light gilding, it was almost certainly real. The third chair was doubtful; but the graceful beds must

123

all surely have come from a house of the living. In short, as M. Maspero put it, the find, on the whole, suggested that some store-room crowded with furniture had been emptied into the tomb.

September 22, 1906

THE RECENT WONDERFUL DISCOVERIES IN CRETE

Described by D. G. Hogarth; photographs by the
Cretan Exploration Society

Crete has made no small noise in the world of recent years, and not so much by its modern developments as by its antiquities. Long the least known archaeologically of all the great Mediterranean islands, it was no sooner opened to research by the establishment of autonomy than it proved a veritable mine of things old and strange. Now that the fact is proved, one sees

55 *The so-called throne of Minos at Knossos*

how suitable the island must have been for the evolution of a high civilisation in early times, with its wide plains, high rain-condensing mountains, and long seaboards; the whole set in a singularly favourable geographical position; but no one had more than a dim suspicion of the truth till Mr. Arthur Evans began to lift the veil. Fortunately, more ancient treasures still lay underground in Crete than in any other Greek land. Ever since the Western World began to concern itself about antiquities, this island has been too stormy a spot for treasure-hunters. Christian and Moslem, and even Christians Latin and Orthodox, have fought above the palaces and the graves of more civilised predecessors without being able to spare time or thought to them. Thus the British, Italian, and American scholars, waiting till 1900, had the chance of a century.

They have used it to the full, the British at Knossos, near Candia, in the Cave of Psychro, and at Praesos, Palaikastro and Zakro in Eastern Crete; the Italians at Phaestos and Haghia Triadha in the south centre; and the Americans at Gournia on the Bay of Mirabello. Of most of these explorations and their results, we give some views. Knossos stands first in time and importance. That site had long been in the eye of certain archaeologists, and among them Mr. Arthur Evans, and the latter, enforcing his claim at the right moment, obtained the prize.

There he has laid open a vast Palace, extending over many acres, built and rebuilt in various ages upon a site whose human remains go back at least as far as the earliest Pharaonic dynasties of the Nile. Its intricate corridors and passage-ways probably suggested the idea of labyrinthine complexity to the later Greeks, and we must associate it with the royal dynasty which bore the name of Minos. Its latest remains come down to about 1000 B.C.; its earliest ascend three thousand years into an obscurity that we cannot pierce. The palace ruins as seen from the east across the river are arranged with the royal quarters in the foreground on the facing slope, the throne-room in the centre, and the long rows of magazines behind. The upstanding tower is a modern structure designed to afford a bird's-eye view, and an opportunity of taking general photographs of the site. Individual parts of the palace of particular interest are the stepped area near the main north-west entrance, which probably served as a place where Kings sat in judgment or council, like the stepped dais in an Arab palace at this day, a room with a square central pillar, of which every block bears the sign of the *labrys*, or war-axe, fetish-symbol of the Virgin Mother goddess whom we now know to have presided over the religion of the primitive Aegean lands; the great *megaron*, or hall, with its quadruple door, seen from above; the council chamber, with its bench, frescoed walls, and central throne; the throne *(Figure 55)* itself carved in fine-grained gypsum, with crockets in singularly Gothic style, and once brightly coloured; two magazines with their huge oil-jars and underground treasure cists, receptacles of the tribute to which the still undeciphered clay-tablets found by many hundreds on the site no doubt refer; the outer corridor into which the magazines open; one flight of the grand quadruple staircase which led from the Royal halls to the upper levels of the Palace. A few out of the hundreds of beautiful and curious objects which came to light in the excavation include a statuette of the Great Goddess in native faience, with girdle and tiara

of snakes; a great jar with papyrus reliefs; a group in enamelled terracotta, brilliantly tinted, of a wild she-goat and kids, emblematic of the Great Mother and marvellously true to nature *(Figure 56)*; and, lastly, part of an *intarsia* sea-piece in faience, showing the flying-fish which the Greek sailors know as swallow-fish, cockles and nautilus-shells.

56 Terracotta relief of wild goat and young, Knossos

Among the other British excavations, that at Zakro, a little bay on the south-east of the island, whence the Greek sponge-boats run across to the Cyrenaic fishing-grounds, is represented by a beautiful vase with marine design, the first, and in some ways the finest, of its type found. It belongs to about 1500 B.C. The other specimen of the class was found at the neighbouring site of Palaikastro, where once stood a "Minoan" town, perhaps the chief place of the eastern island, excavated by the British School at Athens. Here the houses are small, and no palace has yet come to light; but in later – i.e. early Greek – times there was a temple here, sacred to the young Zeus, who stood to his Virgin-Mother, Rhea, in the same relation as Attis to Cybele, and Adonis to Astarte. Part of a ritual hymn in his honour has been found engraved on marble. More tombs have been opened at Palaikastro than on any other early Cretan site including one in which the corpse has been buried in a bath-like coffin of painted earthenware. The Italian Mission, under Professor F. Halbherr, has opened out a great palace crowning a bluff near the ancient Phaestos and commanding the broad plain of Messara. In size and interest it is inferior to the Knossian, but in spectacular effect superior, being more easily seen at once, and, in some respects, better preserved. Moreover, it is set in much finer natural surroundings. Its main components are a great central court, on which open the living-rooms; a great stairway to the *megaron*, flanked by a stepped area like that at Knossos; and a western court and plinth of the palace platform. About two miles west of this palace Professor Halbherr hit upon another site of great interest near the little church of the Holy Trinity (Haghia Triadha). Here the remains of a princely villa had been partly preserved by the *talus* of a hill, and the rooms still contained objects of extraordinary value. Two steatite cups, with scenes sculptured in relief, found there rank with the finest "Aegean" art-treasures yet discovered; and a painted sarcophagus, brought to light in a neighbouring cemetery, is a priceless record and monument of the religious beliefs of the early Cretans. The internal frescoes of the villa were also of singular beauty and interest.

A bronze votive shield belonging to a later civilisation, that of the archaic classical period, was found with many other objects in the same metal in a cave on Mount Ida, shown by its rock-cut altar to have been a shrine either of the goddess or her son, or perhaps of the divine pair. This discovery was made before the last revolution, during which these and other precious objects of antiquity were in great danger. The great inscription is part of the famous "Laws of Gortyna", concerning inheritance, land-tenure, marriage, adoption, and dealing to a large extent with women's rights. It was engraved probably in the sixth century B.C., and has a unique philological as well as legal interest. It is still at Gortyna (Haghios Deka), but ought to be moved to a place of greater safety. When discovered, its stones were being used to strengthen the embankment of a mill-race! All these precious things have been left either where they were found or in the museum at Candia, which is now unique among the museums of the world. The island Government, still in its infancy, has made a praise-worthy effort to safeguard and house its treasures, a much more genuine effort than has been made, alas! by the British Administration in Cyprus. But Cretan means are small, and local security is not fully established. The rickety building which serves for the museum at Candia is none too safe; and if a better be not quickly provided, there will be less sympathy for the present policy of confining all antiquities to the island.

1907

A less important year, in which the chief items were the excavation of Geza by the Palestine Exploration Fund; Flinders Petrie's finds near Assiut; and Garstang's discoveries at Abydos in Upper Egypt.

1908

A richer year. The principal item was the discovery of the temple of Artemis Orthia at Sparta by Dawkins and its excavation by the British School at Athens. But other significant features were the excavation of Bismya in Mesopotamia by the American Edgar J. Banks; the discovery of the dead city of Koh-i-Kouadja in Seistan by a French officer, Major H. de Bouillane de Lacoste; the treasure of Bubastis found by Theodore Davis at Thebes; the finding of papyri at Oxyrhynchus; and clay tablets at Nippur in Mesopotamia by a University of Pennsylvania team.

1909

A good year. In addition to Dr. Aurel Stein's discoveries in Chinese Turkestan, other published items included: a discovery of Chimu pottery in the Chimcana valley, Peru by T. Hewitt Myring; the famous discovery of a sunken load of Greek sculpture off Mahdea, Tunis; German excavations at Jericho; the tomb of the engineer Kha found in the Valley of the Queens at Thebes; the jewellery from the tomb of Queen Tanosrit found by Theodore Davis; the threat of demolition of the Byzantine Walls of Constantinople (a fairly regular archaeological threat, this), and the discovery of the "Kensington Stone" in Minnesota.

June 12, 1909

DR. STEIN'S REMARKABLE DISCOVERIES IN CHINESE TURKESTAN

Dr. M. A. Stein, of the Indian Educational Service, who for many years had been at work in India as an Orientalist, scholar and archaeologist, returned to this country early in the year from an extensive journey of exploration in Central Asia, lasting for two years and eight months, undertaken under the auspices of the Indian Government. Its chief object was the discovery and excavation of ancient remains in that great region of innermost Asia known as Chinese Turkestan, which adjoins Tibet from the north. . . .

Among the many ancient sites explored by Dr. Stein in Chinese Turkestan, that of an old settlement situated in the Taklamakan Desert, some eighty miles to the north of the present oasis of Niya, and two long marches beyond the actual end of its river, had a special interest of its own. There, scattered over an extensive area all overrun by dunes, were found numerous groups of ruined houses, remains of orchards, avenues, canals, etc., all abandoned to the desert, as documentary evidence proves, soon after the middle of the third century A.D. . . .

57 *The ruined cave-temples, known as the "Thousand Buddhas", Tun-huang in Chinese Turkestan*

A particularly rich haul rewarded the search in what must have been the residence of an official of some importance. In his office room there lay scattered files of wooden tablets containing letters and miscellaneous records. On scraping the floor there came to light, hidden away below a foundation beam, quite a little archive of perfectly preserved documents on wood, evidently bonds, agreements, and the like, still bearing intact their original string fastenings and clay sealings. The system of wooden stationery used was quite elaborate. For official letters and documents use was made of double oblong tablets, fitted in a very ingenious fashion by which the upper one served as an envelope. For demi-official letters double wedge-shaped tablets were used. In either case a cleverly arranged string-fastening with a clay seal inserted in a socket of the envelope provided an absolute safeguard against unauthorised inspection. The writing and language of these records is early Indian. The system of this wooden stationery is proved by other finds of Dr. Stein to have been of Chinese origin. But most of the clay seal impressions are from classical intaglios showing Heracles, Eros, Pallas Promachos, etc.

From the Lop-nor region Dr. Stein extended in 1907 his explorations eastwards into Kansu, the westernmost province of China proper. In the dreary gravel west of the oasis of Tun-huang, he discovered the remains of a long-forgotten ancient Chinese frontier wall, built at the close of the second century B.C. for the purpose of protecting the direct trade and military route from China into the Tarim Basin against the Huns. There, too, the climate is practically rainless, and among the ruins of the forts, military posts, etc., which Dr. Stein explored along the wall over a distance of some

240 miles, ancient records on wood and silk, remains of arms, implements, etc., had survived in surprising freshness. The contents of this ancient "waste paper" (to use an anachronism) throw curious light on Chinese military administration, and on the daily life led along this most desolate of borders. . . .

58 A group of colossal painted statues in stucco in one of the cave-temples of the "Thousand Buddhas"

Dr. Stein found an important field for antiquarian activity at the hundreds of Buddhist cave-temples, large and small, known as "The Thousand Buddhas" which honeycomb the conglomerate cliffs at the mouth of a barren valley south-east of Tun-huang *(Figure 57)*. These sacred grottoes, notwithstanding their ruinous condition and much damage by iconoclast zeal – and pious restoration – have preserved a great quantity of fine frescoes and stucco sculpture *(Figure 58)* going back to the T'ang dynasty (seventh–ninth century A.D.). Their style shows unmistakably the influence of Graeco-Buddhist art as transplanted from the extreme north-west of India to Central Asia and thence to China.

1910

A year marked by the geographically wide spread of the paper's archaeological interest. In addition to the pieces extracted there were: the "Mirror of Diana" found in Lake Nemi; Gandhara sculptures from India; a temple excavated in Sardinia; a version of the Flood story from a clay tablet found at Nippur, Mesopotamia; excavations by Garstang at Meroe in the Sudan; and Inca and Chimu silver found by T. Hewitt Myring in the Chimcana Valley, Peru.

February 19, 1910

THE EARLIEST SPECIMEN OF EUROPEAN PRINTING:
A Minoan clay disc from Crete, said to be about 4500 years old

Professor Federico Halbherr, of the University of Rome, who has had charge of the Italian archaeological excavations in Crete, has sent us this photograph *(Figure 59)* of a remarkable clay disc found in the Minoan palace at Phaistos, and belonging, he says, to the middle of the third millennium B.C. The inscription contains about 250 hieroglyphic characters, representing arms, implements, ships, human figures, birds, helmeted heads, etc. The hieroglyphics do not belong to any known system, and there is no key at present to their meaning. They were evidently stamped on wet clay, and this represents the first recorded attempt at printing in Europe.

59 *The earliest specimen of European printing: a Minoan clay disc from Crete, said to be about 4500 years old*

August 13, 1910

SIGNS OF A DEAD CIVILISATION:
From "Hundred-Citied" Crete

Mrs. Harriet Boyd Hawes, of Boston, is one of the very few ladies who have organised and conducted archaeological expeditions. For nine years she has been working among the ruined cities of "hundred-citied Crete" and she has made some valuable discoveries including the remains of a city of 3500 years ago. With the exception of the fresco of the wild cat, hunting ducks and the painted coffer, the photographs deal with Mrs. Boyd Hawes' expeditions. In

60 *Remarkable painting unearthed in Crete: on an elaborate coffer designed to hold the bones of the dead*

amplification of the general descriptions already given, we may make the following notes. It is thought that the villa of the Holy Trinity at Phaestus belonged to the heir-apparent of the dynasty.

The octopus was much favoured by designers working on marine subjects. The manner in which it is made to "fit" the vase in this instance *(Figure 61)* is masterly, and the whole thing is a gem of Minoan art. Someone from the little town of Gournia must have visited the capital, Knossus, for its Governor had his house altered that it might resemble the Great Palace at Knossus.

The cone-shaped vessels with a hole in the bottom puzzle archaeologists. They seem too good to have been used for sprinkling the floors. It has been suggested that (like the horn of medieval times) they were vessels that had to be drained at a draught; but the cup-bearer of the King at Knossus (on a fresco) carries one and does not close the hole at the bottom with his finger. The painting on the coffer shows priests and priestesses making offerings *(Figure 60)*.

The discovery of two mugs proves once and for all the accuracy of the theory that the potters of

61 *An octopus design on a vase found in eighty-six pieces*

the time were wont to copy metal vases, for with them was found a silver vase of the same shape. Minoan vases of 2500 B.C. have been found on the site of ancient Troy. The bronze altar-offering designed to represent the sacrifice of an ox was a cheap form of sacrifice: it could be used many times. Crete held high position in prehistoric times and the legends of its power become history in face of such discoveries, which prove an advanced civilisation, a civilisation that culminated in the later Bronze Age (1500–1300 B.C.).

December 17, 1910

THE REMARKABLE VILLA RECENTLY UNEARTHED NEAR POMPEII:
Frescoes of a new character

Reproduced from Notizie degli Scavi di Antichita; published by the Italian Government

Last year excavations on a farm in the immediate neighbourhood of Pompeii brought to light the remains of a fine villa with over twenty rooms and the customary Roman enclosed gardens and open-air courts. This year the removal of volcanic debris hiding the interior walls showed decorative fresco paintings possessing a new character in ancient technique. In the case of certain of these, the artists tried, and with decided success, to imitate architectural features; in other cases, and these are more numerous, the frescoes contain imitations of ancient sculptures. In one of the best examples of the former – that is to say, of the paintings designed to imitate architectural features, it may seem that the representation of the two columns with bases on a projecting ledge at the foot of a wall, is such that the columns appear to be altogether detached from the wall behind them. Even more striking is a second fresco, which shows a door, the upper third of which is filled by a grille, which seems to have true perforations. Another shows a father, a mother, and a son, the last reading from a roll, and a servant taking away a crown of olives in a patera. The fresco illustrated shows an initiation by flagellation, a woman, the richness of whose robes indicates her wealth, stooping to receive the stripes *(Plate 4, p. 68)*. The fresco next to this shows one of the initiated arranging her hair, guided by a mirror held by Cupid.

1911

Again a full year in which the principal interest, apart from the Glastonbury Lake Village, lay in the discovery of Galley Hill Man, with an article by Sir Arthur Keith and a reconstruction by A. Forestier; and Garstang's excavations at Meroe and his presentation to the British Museum of the famous bronze head of Augustus, found there. But the year is chiefly marked by the beginning (on February 11) of an excellent series of articles by D. G. Hogarth. These were called "The Remodelling of History", numbered in all twenty and ended on November 22, 1913. They covered in detail and in broad perspective the latest discoveries in Crete, Greece, the Near East and Mesopotamia.

February 11, 1911

THE REMODELLING OF HISTORY; AND THE REALISATION OF LEGEND:
I – Crete

By D. G. Hogarth

(Mr. David George Hogarth, the distinguished archaeological explorer, geographer and author, became Keeper of the Ashmolean Museum in 1908. He is a Fellow of Magdalen College; a Fellow of the British Academy; F.S.A.; and F.R.G.S. He has made numerous important excavations. From 1897 until 1900 he was Director of the British School at Athens, and he has been Director of the Cretan Exploration Fund since 1899.)

There is a pause in Cretan exploration. Mr. Arthur Evans is going to leave the soil of Cnossus almost undisturbed for a time, while he gets forward with the publication of his amazing discoveries of the last ten years.

The British School at Athens has abandoned the island after exploring the Birth-cave of Zeus on Dicte, and the two towns at Zakro and Palaikastro. The Italians and the Americans have lately been adding to their discoveries in the southern plain and on the Hierapetra isthmus respectively, but working on a smaller scale than when they first uncovered the Palace of Phaestus, the royal villa of Hagia Triada, and the well-preserved town at Gournia. The native Cretan archaeologists use their exceptional opportunities to follow up chance discoveries made by peasants at outlying spots, and have been well rewarded with spoil of late, but they have not added anything novel. In short, the present is a slack time by comparison, and therefore good for taking stock of our gain in historical knowledge.

The gain is, of course, in reasonable probabilities rather than historical certainties. There are no written documents of contemporary times yet known and read which refer to this great prehistoric civilisation in the Aegean, except two or three allusions in hieroglyphic texts to *Keftiu*, who are almost certainly Cretans, and to some other Northern "Peoples of the Sea", when these happened to touch Egypt. The great Aegean Age lay before the period at which either Babylon or Assyria began to concern itself about the West. The Hittite inscriptions, some of which are contemporary with the Late Minoan Age, cannot be read; and the same, unfortunately, has still to be said about the written records of prehistoric Crete itself. Nothing more can be done with the two thousand or more documents in clay found at Cnossus, Hagia Triada, and other Cretan sites, till some key turns up, such as a bilingual text in "Minoan" and some other known script; and it is most improbable that Cretan soil will ever produce such a key. . . .

So on the material monuments we have to rely. They allow us to sketch the bare outlines of political and economic history in Crete before Homer, and to fill in social detail at two great periods. . . . Far back in the local Stone Age, when the historic dynasties of Egypt had not yet entered on their long succession, he [Aegean man] had begun to make vases which, for their fabric and decoration, are to be ranked among products of art; and he must have fared overseas as far as Melos at least (or the ruder Melians must have come to him, which is less likely) for he used obsidian weapons and tools, which Crete does not produce. In the rest of the Aegean area, if the beginnings of civilisation were roughly contemporary, progress was more slow. . . .

The Cretan began to use bronze only a little later than the Egyptian. That he used it at all proves that he was civilised enough in what we call the Early Minoan Age to have commercial relations with alien lands; for neither of the constituents of bronze is found in the natural state in Crete. Cyprus could have sent him copper, but whence his tin came is a mystery. In the Early Minoan Age, contemporary with part of the Old Kingdom in Egypt, we find a high civilisation diffused over Crete, which seems to have developed at several centres, and not to have been dominated by the overlordship of any one city. This was an agricultural age, and it shows evidence of maritime trade, but not of internecine or foreign war. If one city became more rich than others, that appears to have been Phaestus. . . .

Thereafter Cnossus, inhabited and productive in the Neolithic Age, but apparently a poor place in the age succeeding, came to the front, and in the second Middle Minoan period had a royal palace on the Kephala hillock, and a social apparatus of amazing richness and variety. The Twelfth Dynasty was then reigning in Egypt, and both thither, and to the Argolid (as recent excavations at Tiryns prove), to the Cyclades, and to Cyprus, went fine Cretan wares. In this period we find that the earlier civilisation in Eastern Crete has suffered eclipse, and it is a reasonable inference that Cnossus had overrun all the land to east of her, and established overlordship with devastating hand. . . .

Phaestus, however, had her revenge – so at least it appears from the fact that the Middle Minoan Palace at Cnossus was sacked and destroyed, whereas that at Phaestus survived into the succeeding period. . . . But Cnossus also began to recover and it was not long before Phaestus was sacked in her turn, and with her the unhappy East Cretan towns. Cnossus alone shows no signs of sack at the end of the first Late Minoan period, and she was evidently free to advance in wealth and power to her apogee in the second period – the period of the finest existing remains of her Palace. Now she seems to have imposed her own type of culture on all Crete, and not only Crete, but most of the Aegean world. . . .

At its close, Cnossus was devastated by fire and sword; so, also, we find, were all other Cretan towns of the period, so far explored. Yet, the remains of their precedent culture differ, not in character, but only in quality from their remains which belong to the succeeding period, the "third Late Minoan". It has been suggested that the phenomena are only to be explained on the assumption that the invaders who now overran Crete were men who brought a culture like that which they found, and thus no change except a dynastic one ensued. If so, those invaders can hardly have been other than the "Mycenaeans" of the Peloponnese, whose precedent civilisation is seen now to have been so Cretan that it is often supposed they had been subjects of Cnossus. With them, or, at any rate, close in their wake, came also elements from the farther north, forerunners of all the historic Greeks, now beginning to press southward from the Balkan lands; and this slow leakage gathered volume till it became at last a flood, and ended the Bronze Age of Crete for good and all. This final cataclysm seems to have happened some time in the twelfth century B.C., and it was most likely a phase in that same unrest of peoples, which, in the days of Rameses III, carried the Akaiuasha, or Achaeans, to the confines of Egypt. Cnossus now became Achaean, so far, at least, as its rulers went; and Achaean were all its traditions when, two or three generations later, the Aegean world produced its first literary chronicle, the Homeric Epics.

December 2, 1911

NOT THE WOAD-DAUBED SAVAGE OF THE OLD HISTORY-BOOKS: THE CIVILISED ANCIENT BRITON:
The lake village near Glastonbury
By Arthur Bulleid, F.S.A.

The subject of prehistoric archaeology has made such rapid strides during the last fifty years or so that the views we held in our youth of the early inhabitants of the British Isles no longer hold good. Cases of exhibits may be seen in our public museums, showing the state of culture and progress in art during the succeeding Stone, Bronze and early Iron Ages. To the casual observer, however, these relics lack interest, owing to his inability to visualise the everyday life and occupations of the people who made and used them. It is therefore the endeavour of the artist to make the dry bones live by depicting some views and scenes based on the relics found, and other information gained during the investigation of the Glastonbury Lake Village.

The occupations and amusements illustrated *(Figure 62)* in this number are proved by the actual finds. . . . It was an unfortunate circumstance that no actual article of dress or fragment of textile fabric was found; Therefore the artist has taken the responsibility of clothing the inhabitants in the garbs of the

62 Ancient Britons in a hut of the British Lake village. Reconstruction drawing by A. Forestier

contemporary peoples of Ireland and Northern Gaul. . . .

The north central part of Somerset is a low-lying tract of land formerly open to the sea, but in later geological times occupied by a series of shallow meres and broads. It was near the edge of one of these sheets of water that the Glastonbury Lake Village was constructed about two thousand years ago. . . . Speaking generally, lacustrine settlements fall under two main headings: habitations erected on wooden platforms above the surface of the water, supported on piles driven into the bed of the lake; and those on crannogs, or artificial islands, made by heaping timber, clay and stone on the bed of the lake. In the latter the accumulated masses of material were surrounded by a strong stockade. . . .

The Lake Village, which is situated about one mile north of Glastonbury, is in several respects unique. In its construction it resembles the Scotch or Irish crannogs, but in the grouping of the dwellings it is more closely allied to the settlements in the lakes of Switzerland and Southern Europe. . . .

Before the field was disturbed by digging in 1892, the village consisted of some sixty-five to seventy low mounds, grouped with no apparent design and distributed over a space of about three and a half acres. During the examination of the site, the number of mounds was subsequently found to be ninety, the majority of them representing separate dwellings. The foundation of the whole village was made by quantities of timber and brushwood imported from the surrounding swamps; but some willow and alder trees were felled on the actual site, for the stumps and roots were still there. Layers of clay were placed with a certain amount of stone for the floors of the huts. These were circular, from eighteen to thirty-five feet in diameter, the walls composed of wattle and daub, and the roof thatched with reeds supported at or near the centre by an upright post. The clay floors were sometimes covered with planking, a space being left near the centre for a hearth either of baked clay or slabs of stone.

The village was surrounded by a piled stockade, and had its causeway and landing stage for boats. . . . The relics discovered throw considerable light on the life and civilisation of the people, whose artistic qualities were truly wonderful. They were skilled carpenters, and among the many remarkable wooden objects found were ladles, cups, bowls, a ladder and several lathe-turned tubs.

Metal-work was carried on at more than one spot. Crucibles with the bronze still adhering, and the remains of furnaces and tuyères imply smelting. Lead and iron were also worked. Thread was made with whorls of lead and stone, and needles of bone and bronze were used for sewing. Weaving was carried on extensively as evidenced by the number of long-handled combs, shuttle-spools, loomweights, and, above all, by the fragments of the framework of the loom itself. Both wheel and hand-made pottery were manufactured in great quantities, the former ornamented with a profusion of incised designs of rare beauty. They wore rings and brooches of bronze and bracelets of Kimmeridge shale, and decorated their persons with beads of amber, jet and glass. Wheat and peas were found in abundance, as well as two types of querns in which they were ground. Several dice, with a dice-box of bone, found together with a number of small polished pebbles, show that games were not wanting, and the spur of a fighting cock leads us to believe that they indulged in sport like the ancient Gauls.

1912

This was the year of "Piltdown Man" (Figure 63) to which the paper devoted a great deal of space, with articles by a variety of experts. . . .

August 10, 1912

PICTURES PAINTED 25,000 YEARS AGO:
Works by Stone Age artists

[*This article is signed A.F., presumably Amedeo Forestier, the reconstruction artist of the time.*]

The paintings in the Altamira Cave were found by Don Marcelino de Sautuola, a Spanish nobleman, who after a visit to the Paris International Exhibition of 1878, where he had been specially interested by the prehistoric collections resulting from discoveries made in the caves of Southern France, thought of exploring certain caves near his estate at Santander.

While he was occupied in digging in the floor of the cavern of Altamira, his little daughter, tired of watching him unearth bones of extinct animals, flint implements and the usual pal-aeolithic debris, was looking about her, and suddenly cried out, "A bull", pointing at the same time to the roof of the cave, on which her father saw a large painting of a crowd of figures faithfully representing bulls, horses, deer, etc., some of them life-size, in a great variety of movements and attitudes. Don Marcelino brought this discovery before the Archaeological Congress of 1879 and published a full description of it in 1880, but it was received with deep scepticism. It was only in 1905 that the authenticity of the painting was at last recognised, and is now fully admitted.

The authors of these wonderful paintings belonged to the palaeolithic race known as the Aurignacians, who lived during a part of the glacial period – some say between twenty and thirty thousand years ago. The conditions of life being favourable, Europe at that time teeming with game, the Aurignacians experienced no great hardships in procuring food, and found leisure to take advantage of their wonderful artistic gifts, decorating many of their cave dwellings with representations of subjects

63 A reconstruction of the head of the earliest known inhabitant of England – the man of Sussex, later known as the Piltdown Man

which most pleased them – those of useful animals – perhaps acting under some kind of superstition which led them, as a rule, to eschew depicting savage beasts, and only scantily to draw the human form, which they appear to have studied, from the artistic point of view by no means so elaborately as they did the lower animals. The work was admirable, as may be

by M. Emile Cartailhac and Abbé Breuil.

It is now possible to follow the artists at work *(Figure 64)*. The colours they employed were natural oxides, yellow and red ochres, the black oxide of manganese, etc. These colours were ground in mortars and on flat stones, with the aid of granite pestles; examples of those they used have been found. Once ground, the colour

64 A reconstruction drawing by A. Forestier showing Stone Age artists at work in the Altamira cave

judged from the illustrations *(Plates 5 and 6, p. 69)*, which are reproduced from plates in that most valuable volume, *La Caverne d'Altamira*

was mixed with bone-marrow, and preserved in the hollow leg-bones of deer. Crayons were also made of the different colours. The artists also used brushes to spread the tones and blend them in the most perfect fashion, thus obtaining a correct modelling. The burin, or graving tool, was also employed by the Aurignacians, who used it in their best finished work to engrave a deep outline round the figure, as well as certain details. The carving in low relief of the figures lately discovered by Dr. Lalanne suggests the Egyptian intaglio. The palette used for painting was the scapula of some animal; the brushes, one may infer from the Bushmen's practice, were made of feathers, or consisted of the chewed end of a stick. . . .

MM. Breuil and Cartailhac have come to the conclusion that the painted caves must have been sacred spots. The conditions under which the paintings were made were, in most places, painful for the artist, especially in the Altamira Cave, where the roof is so low in some places that the painter could work only in a crouching posture or lying on his back. The merit of the artist was, it is argued, hereby increased, and there is every possibility that only a belief of a religious kind could have incited him. . . .

65 A reconstruction of Halling Man by A. Forestier

1913

"Piltdown Man" still appeared in the paper's pages, also Halling Man from Kent (Figure 65).

December 6, 1913

PERUVIAN POTTERY FROM NASCA

By Henry O. Forbes

The ancient Peruvians, like the ancient Egyptians, appear to have had some settled notion that there existed somewhere beyond their visible horizon "Happy Dwellings" or "Blessed Fields", where the departed resumed their discontinued mundane employment. . . . The corpse, though apparently not embalmed, was in the majority of cases enswathed or mummified. It was bound in a sitting position, the chin upon its knees, then wound round with numerous bandages of different textures and fineness of cloth, within the folds of which, or upon particular bandages, were inserted various metal objects, personal belongings, or textile badges, perhaps representing amulets, supposed to be helpful to the deceased in the other world. The most external covering consisted often of textiles of surprisingly beautiful quality both of cloth and tapestries, the latter brilliantly coloured and in astonishing variety. Over the outermost swathing highly artistic gold and silver ornaments were lavishly displayed in the case of persons of importance. A false head of cloth was usually affixed to the mummy bundle, on which the hair was represented by a wig and the features by a mask of gold, or silver, or of tapestry, or simply depicted on it in coloured ochres. The corpse was, however, not always enswathed: the poor apparently were deposited in their graves quite nude, in the sitting attitude, then covered over with reeds or matting of *Cana brava* before being covered with earth. Alongside his mummy, or nude cadaver, were deposited the deceased's personal treasures and belongings, together with the objects he had used in life – weapons, implements of his craft and pottery vessels in abundance. . . .

It is to these funerary rites of the ancient Peruvians in combination with the arid climate of the region and the preservative nature of its soil, that we are indebted for the many objects of ethnographic interest that have now been recovered. The country became noted for its ceramics soon after its conquest by the Spaniards, and during the interval that has elapsed, it has yielded immense quantities, practically the whole of which have been exhumed from the prehistoric pyramids, graves and caves situated chiefly on the desert belt of the lowlands facing the Pacific ocean. . . .

The type of pottery illustrated on the accompanying plate *(Plate 7, p. 70)* has only comparatively recently become known out of the district of its manufacture. It comes from the burial-grounds around Nasca, inland from the port of Pisco, situated about 150 miles south of Callao. It is at once distinguished by the chasteness of its modelling and its highly artistic polychrome ornamentation. Although the region, including Pisco, Ica, and Nasca, is supposed by some authorities to have possessed a more or less common culture, the potters of both the first-named districts, to my thinking, fall far short of the individuality and artistic gifts of their brethren of Nasca. These Nasca potters were among the best craftsmen of Peru, and the most highly skilled artists who, above others, made things of utility objects of beauty for their own sake. . . .

These Nasca vessels – like all other ancient pottery from Peru – have been produced without the aid of the wheel. The smaller and more moderate-sized pieces have been constructed in sections, for each of which the clay was pressed into a previously prepared and baked mould – the rotund portions in halves, the handles, mouthpieces, spouts and any ornamentation above the surface, separately. These were applied together or affixed when still moist; the lines of junction were then carefully obliterated, and the whole surface smoothed over and burnished with a polished pebble. Larger pieces were built up by clay coils superimposed one upon another, the vessel being shaped and smoothed by hand as the work progressed and finally burnished. The finished pot was set aside to dry; and finally, when decorated, it was submitted to the fire. The extreme grace of form in the examples of this new type . . . is sufficiently obvious from the plate; not less conspicuous are the firm lines of the drawing and the delicacy and harmony of the multifarious tones of the painted decoration. Many of the pieces possess a beautifully glazed surface not easily reproduced on paper.

1914

The year up to the declaration of war was extremely rich, as our extracts show. Other important discoveries included excavations at Taxila in north-west India by Dr. H. J. (later Sir John) Marshall; the discovery of papyri of Sappho at Oxyrhynchus by Grenfell and Hunt; and another article on the discoveries at Meroe by Garstang.

1914–18

Nothing much appeared in the issues of the paper during the war years, but archaeology declined to die completely. In November 1915, French soldiers practising trench-digging on Lemnos found a marble statue of Eros; and in December of the same year, a British Museum relief of Assurbanipal slaying lions was used to illustrate an article on Baghdad as a sporting centre. In May 1916, a large quantity of Roman Samian ware was found in the City of London during excavations for the Phoenix Assurance building; in August of the same year gold, bronze and pottery of the eighth century B.C. were found during trench-digging at Salonika. In November 1916, a tomb was found near Langaza Lake, Salonika by "a well-known English professor of archaeology, now sub-lieutenant in the RNVR", and a little later French trench-diggers found pottery in Macedonia. In August 1917, Australian forces near Shellal, fourteen miles from Gaza, Palestine, found an Early Christian mosaic with a Greek inscription. These items are here recalled not for any intrinsic importance they may have held, but as illustration of editorial determination to get archaeology into the paper against all odds. But the dark days of 1918 were too much, even for archaeology.

January 3, 1914

INTACT AFTER 2000 YEARS:
A Scythian chief's tomb unearthed

By C. Alexis Bobrinskoy

History affords us but limited information concerning the Scythian tribes that inhabited the steppes of Southern Russia many centuries before the birth of Christ. The "father of History" Herodotus tells us of the riches of the Scythian kings, their magnificent funerals and splendid tombs, gorgeously decorated with plate, jewellery, and weapons wrought in gold. These ancient narratives have been fully confirmed by archaeological research pursued in Southern Russia. . . .

The good fortune of opening an intact tomb fell to the lot of the author of these lines in June of this year. The excavation of an enormous tomb, a so-called "kourgane", bearing the name of "Soloha" had been going on for three successive summers under the direction of Professor Wesselowsky, a member of the Russian Imperial Archaeological Commission, in the vicinity of the cataracts of the River Dnieper, in the northern confines of the Tauric government. After strenuous work on the part of Professor Wesselowsky, he succeeded in reaching the great central tomb. I joined him in the autumn of 1912, and we began a careful investigation of the entire subterranean structure, which contained the central sepulchre of the "kourgane".

a date probably not far distant from the time of the interment, the plunderers leaving only some minute articles in gold and bronze and objects which evidently had no value in their eyes, as, for instance, a big bronze utensil, resembling a modern gridiron supported by four small, though massive wheels. . . .

After the disappointment of finding the tomb desecrated, Professor Wesselowsky began to study the high earthen sides of the "kourgane", and soon came to the conclusion that the mound concealed a second lateral tomb. After some months of continuous digging, this supposition proved to be correct, and in June, 1913, in

66 Silver vase from a Scythian king's tomb

The tomb was dug out at a depth of 8 metres (about 26 feet) under the surface of the earth, and this was surmounted by the earthen mass of the "kourgane" attaining the height of more than 10 metres (about 33 feet) above the soil. Unluckily, however, the great central chamber had shared the general fate of most Scythian tombs, and had been entirely plundered at

answer to a second invitation from the explorer, I arrived at Wesselowsky's steppe encampment in the midst of an absolute desert some 10 miles from the nearest dwelling, and we experienced the great satisfaction of opening a Scythian chieftain's, or king's, tomb intact.

To reach this sepulchre we had to explore a great chamber apportioned to the king's horses,

67 *A quiver of wood covered with plaster and silver found in a Scythian king's tomb*

which we found placed in a row, five in number, and arrayed with multitudinous gold and brass ornaments, which formed parts of their harness and bridles. By the side of the horses lay the skeleton remains of a groom, and, at the very entrance of the king's tomb another skeleton, evidently a guard, with bow and arrows. At the feet of the king lay a third man in a coat of mail, with sword and brass arrow-heads.

The remains of the king occupied the centre of a big chamber and were surrounded by various objects and weapons in bronze and iron, such as a coat of mail, two spears, arrows, swords, a big bronze mace with a wooden handle and a splendid bronze helmet. By the king's side lay a big sword in a magnificent gold sheath, with figures of lions, dragons, etc., worked upon it in relief. Round his neck was a heavy gold necklace, and his arms were encircled by numerous gold bracelets. On the right of the king stood five silver vases, some of which were covered with beautiful engravings presenting

scenes of Greek indoor life and of mounted Scythians fighting wild animals *(Figure 66 and Plate 9, p. 71)*. These figures are gilded and attest the skill of some great artist. . . .

Near the king's head, the earthen wall of the tomb contained a special hiding-place, neatly plastered up with clay. In this niche we found two splendid objects, one of which is a massive gold dish (called in Greek "phiale"), richly covered with relief representations of lions and deer. A very faint Greek inscription, running round the edge of the plate, bears the names of Antisthenes and Antilochus. The other article concealed in the niche was a quiver *(Figure 67)* with a great number of fine bronze arrow-heads. The wooden sheath of this quiver was covered with plaster and silver and engraved with a battle scene. This beautiful piece of Greek workmanship has, unfortunately, been totally ruined by the action of time, and it took no end of patience and care to reconstruct the fragments so as to obtain a more or less satisfactory idea of the scene of battle. This picture gives us a most interesting series of figures of bearded Scythians fighting each other.

The same sort of scene, a fight between three warriors, one of whom is on horseback, the others on foot, forms the upper part of a big, massive, golden comb *(Plate 8, p. 71)*, one of the most splendid objects of antique Greek jewellery that exists. This comb lay at the king's right side, near his head. . . . This object is absolutely intact and might have come direct from the artist's workshop. The figures are finished up to the smallest details, so far even as to give each face of the little golden warriors a separate expression. The precision and details of each piece of armour are marvellous. The comb lay on the earthen floor of the tomb, and when we first touched it with our small shovel, the earth that covered the comb easily gave way and the splendid jewel burst upon us in all its glory.

January 24, 1914

REVEALING THE CIVILISATION OF THE HITTITES OF SYRIA:
Excavations at Carchemish

By D. G. Hogarth

Three years ago the Trustees of the British Museum undertook what has proved the largest, and in many respects the most important and fruitful excavation which they have ever promoted. When the enterprise was in its initial stage, in which I myself and Mr. Campbell Thompson conducted it, I wrote in these columns a preliminary notice, giving the history and a description of the site at Jerablus, where the work had been begun, and indulging in a little prophecy of our hopes. Now three years have seen six campaigns in the soil on which there is no reasonable doubt once stood Carchemish, the leading city among the Hittite peoples of Syria. Mr. C. L. Woolley, well known for his Nubian researches, and Mr. T. E. Lawrence, who worked under Mr. Thompson and myself, have been in charge for the most part of this time, carrying on the excavation for a spring season and an autumn season in each year with between two and three hundred men. They have had their difficulties, and even their dangers, for Jerablus lies in a lawless region, among Kurdish tribes excited by recent events in Turkey; but they have faced, and sur-

mounted, them with courage, persistence and signal use of the faculty which so many Britons

68 *A bearded god of Assyro-Hittite style from Carchemish (eighth century* B.C.*?) seated on a base supported by two lions led by an eagle-headed figure*

possess for gaining the confidence of wild fighting folk. . . .

The site consists of what is called a "Royal city"; that is, a strongly fortified enclosure containing palaces and their appurtenances, with a citadel, and an unfortified area inhabited by the commons. It is the first which is being explored. Its ring-wall, which enclosed about half a square mile on the bank of the Euphrates, has been stripped away to build a later town; but the huge mound on which the wall stood still remains, rising from the moat to a height, in places, of nearly fifty feet. Also three gates remain, of which two have been explored. Here, under Hellenistic and Roman structures, the explorers have laid bare remains of Hittite buildings, consisting of flanking towers and successive lion-guarded portals, one within another, divided by open courts, in each of which an enemy, breaking in, would have had to encounter flanking fire. . . . In excavating this gate, the explorers found a fine head of a god or king of the latest Hittite Age, when, in the seventh century, B.C., the lords of Carchemish were Aramaean Semites. . . . The North Gate, of still more elaborate construction and plan, is still under excavation.

Within the walls a large complex of Hittite palatial buildings has been partially cleared, together with a watergate on the river bank which was flanked by great lions in dolerite, inscribed with Hittite hieroglyphic texts. The westernmost member of this complex is a large building entered by a portal from both jambs of which run, as far as the clearance has yet been made, dadoes of sculptured slabs, alternately of black dolerite and white limestone. The finest reliefs, those on the portal itself, show two men, probably two Kings, one being an ally, followed by eight children, of whom the last still totters, holding to a staff, and a baby in the arms of a woman, who leads a pet animal. She should be the Queen, who appears nowhere else in the group. The children throw knuckle-bones or carry whipping-tops according to sex and age. In front of the whole group is a hieroglyphic

69 A human- and lion-headed sphinx with tail ending in a bird's head from a dado of mythological slabs at Carchemish

inscription, the longest known, which, with the legends graven near the head of each member of the group, would tell us who they all were, could we read the script. We can, however, guess safely that it is a royal group of about the ninth century B.C.

The style and execution of these reliefs upset all our previous ideas about the quality of Hittite art; as do also the sculptures which line the opposite side of the portal – royal ministers and servants in whose delineation has been used a grace which is almost Greek. . . . As excavation proceeds, this great series of sculptures will no doubt be found to be prolonged at either end.

From this building a wall, also bearing reliefs along all its length, runs up to a great staircase, which climbs up the face of the Acropolis, and is (or was) lined with sculptures of which some are still in position. To the left is another building of the palatial complex built on the terraced slope. Here was found a small, shrine-like chamber with elaborately inscribed portal, before which stood a great laver, supported, like Solomon's, by two bulls. . . .

On the Acropolis the remains are less well-preserved because in Roman days a great temple was built there, whose foundations almost destroyed the large brick buildings of the Hittites. At the north end, too, Sargon the Assyrian, who captured Carchemish in 717 B.C., built a residence for his officers. . . . But the Acropolis has yielded a most important set of early tombs, with which we can now compare the contents of another cemetery outside the walls.

From Jerablus and its neighbourhood we have a long series of graves which show us the pottery and implements and seals of the Syrian Hittites from about 2000 to about 400 B.C.; and when it is said, in conclusion, that the stratification of the city site gives us orderly evidence from the Neolithic Age to the close of the Bronze Age; that the development of Hittite plastic art can now be studied from its cradle to its grave; that the same is true of the hiero-glyphic script, of which over a hundred new texts have come to light; that we have cuneiform inscriptions already, and may at any moment get a bilingual key to the hieroglyphic puzzles – when so much can be said for three years' work on a part only of this great site, it will be agreed that it is well worth digging completely.

May 30, 1914

"STRABO'S WELL" AND TOMB OF OSIRIS

By Edouard Naville

The excavations made during this winter at Abydos by the Egypt Exploration Fund, under the direction of the present writer, assisted by Professor Whittemore, from Boston, Mr. Wainwright and Mr. Gibson, have given quite unexpected results. They have led to the discovery of a building which at present is unique in its kind, and which probably is one of the most ancient constructions preserved in Egypt: a great pool with porches and the tomb of Osiris. It is situated behind the western wall of the temple built by Seti I, which is the chief attraction at Abydos for travellers. It was entirely subterranean, at a depth of more than thirty feet below the temple, and nothing revealed its existence. . . .

This year's work required a considerable number of men. It was begun with 450; at the end there were 639, four-fifths of whom were boys carrying baskets. The sides of the building had to be traced, and tons of rubbish and loose sand had to be removed from the middle; at the end of eleven weeks the whole structure had been laid bare *(Figure 70)*.

It consists of a rectangle, the inside of which is about a hundred feet long and sixty wide. The two long sides are north and south; east is the side of the temple of Seti; west the doorway with the lintel, fifteen feet long, which had been discovered in 1912. The enclosure wall is twenty feet thick. It consists of two casings: the outer one is limestone rather roughly worked; the inner one is in beautiful masonry of red quartzite sandstone. The joints are very fine; there is only a very thin stratum of mortar, which is hardly perceptible. Here and there the thick knob has been left which was used for moving the stones. The blocks are very large – a length of fifteen feet is by no means rare; and the whole structure has decidedly the character of the primitive constructions which in Greece are called cyclopean, and an Egyptian example of which is at Ghizeh, the so-called temple of the Sphinx.

This colossal character is even more striking in the inner part. It is divided into three naves or aisles of unequal size – the middle one being wider. These naves are separated by two colonnades of square monolithic pillars about fifteen feet high and eight and a half feet square. There are five of them in each colonnade. They supported architraves in proportion with them, their height being more than six feet. These architraves and the enclosure wall supported a ceiling, also of granite monoliths, which was not made of slabs, but of blocks, like the architraves more than six feet thick. It has been calculated that one of the few of them remaining weighs more than thirty tons. Unfortunately, in one corner only has the ceiling been preserved. The whole building has been turned into a quarry, especially the inside, which was entirely granite. Pillars, architraves, ceiling, everything has been broken and split with wedges, traces of which are seen everywhere, in order to make millstones of various sizes. Several of them weighing seven or eight tons, have been left.

The side aisles only, about ten feet wide, had ceilings. It is doubtful whether the middle nave was roofed. It was, perhaps, only covered at the end over the entrance to the "tomb of Osiris".When the work reached the lower layer of the enclosure wall, a very extraordinary discovery was made. In this wall, all round the structure are cells about six feet high and wide, all exactly alike, without any ornament or decoration. They had doors, probably made of wood, with a single leaf; one can see the holes where they turned. Such cells are not seen in any other Egyptian construction.

What was still more surprising is that they do not open on to a floor, but on to a narrow ledge which ran on both sides of the nave. There was no floor in those aisles; under the ledge, which is slightly projecting, the beautiful masonry goes on, and at a depth of twelve feet water was reached. It is at the level of the infiltration water in the cultivated land, though the structure is in the desert. This year the Nile is lower than it is known to have been for more than fifty years.

70 A reconstruction showing the great hall, the pool which is Strabo's well and the "tomb of Osiris"

Were the river at a normal height, the water would reach the ledge, which is below the cultivated land. Thus the two aisles and the two ends of the middle nave form a continuous rectangular pool, the sides of which are very fine masonry on large blocks *(Figure 71)*. . . .

The middle nave is a block of masonry also made of enormous stones, which goes down as deep as the water, and on which rest the pillars of the colonnades. The floor is at the same level as that of the cells and of the ledge. This platform is an island; it could be reached only with a small boat or by a wooden bridge; there is water on the four sides. Even in front of the doorway, there is only the ledge; there is no pathway of any kind leading to it. On both sides – east and west – there are two staircases leading from the platform to the water. The last step is about three feet above the present level of the

147

71 *Cyclopean architecture of Egypt: the huge masonry of Strabo's well*

water. In a normal year the two or three last steps would be covered. . . .

This showed that there was behind the wall something of a funerary character, the tomb of Osiris, perhaps. Osiris, although he was a god, was supposed to have been torn to pieces by his enemy, Set or Typhon, and his limbs had been scattered among the chief cities of Egypt. Abydos being the residence of the god, its share had been the head, which was buried in his tomb. That tomb was very famous, and various excavators have been searching for it for years. When the lower part of the end wall of the nave was cleared, there appeared the door of a cell

quite similar to the other ones. The back wall of this cell had been broken through in order to make an opening, a door which had been blocked afterwards with stones. It gave access to a large subterranean chamber, wider than the whole construction, very well preserved, with a ceiling consisting of two slabs leaning against each other. On the ceiling and on the side walls are funerary representations like those of the tombs of the kings. It is evidently a tomb and the sculptures show it to be what was regarded as the tomb of Osiris. The chamber was quite empty except for a heap of sand in one of the corners. When this had been removed, it was found that the sand came through a hole used by robbers. There was no sarcophagus or object of any kind. It is not to be supposed that anything of that sort can be found in a construction used for centuries as a quarry.

The tomb of Osiris is of a later date than the pool with its cells. . . . As for the pool, it is probably one of the most ancient constructions which have been preserved in Egypt. It is exactly in the style of the so-called temple of the Sphinx, which is a work of the IVth Dynasty, and one of the characteristic features of which is the total absence of any inscription or ornament. But the pool is even more colossal. In the temple of the Sphinx the pillars are 4 feet square; here they are $8\frac{1}{2}$ feet. It is impossible, in spite of the havoc made, not to be struck by the majestic simplicity of the structure, chiefly in the corner where the ceiling has remained.

June 20, 1914

FOUND IN A PLUNDERED PYRAMID:
The treasure of Lahun

By W. M. Flinders Petrie

A tall grey pile of brickwork stands high on the desert edge at the entry to the Fayum, some sixty miles south of Cairo. Here was buried a great sovereign of the land with all his family: two hundred generations of the descendants of his subjects have come and gone since then.

Nearly all the tombs of Egypt were ransacked in early times, probably within fifty or a hundred years of the burial. This King, Senusert II, had no immunity; his pyramid was entered, his sarcophagus broken open; no trace of his burial remained. Likewise the tombs of his family – all were attacked. Five empty tombs stand along the north side of the pyramid, without a bone left in place. When the British School of Archaeology in Egypt began work there last December, a complete clearance was planned out, to lay bare every inch of the site and clean the rock, so that no passages or tombs could remain unsearched. In that clearance the five tombs just named were reopened, and entirely cleaned out. Two of these had not even a coffin left. The others had sarcophagi totally bare; everything seemed to have vanished. In one tomb the wide pit descended by steps in the rock to the depth of about twenty-eight feet, and at the end stood a granite sarcophagus, the lid pushed back as far as it would go, and then bruised and broken away so that a boy could crawl in and destroy the burial. Not a chip of the mummy or its wrappings was left behind. Hours, perhaps days, of work had been spent on thus ransacking the grave. Yet all the time, close by the plunderers' side, was a recess in the tomb which they disregarded. . . .

In the midst of the recess lay the crown; the tall plumes of gold and the three double streamers of gold all lay down flat, with the crown between them. They had evidently been carefully deposited and never disturbed. The crown is a broad band of brilliantly burnished gold, with fifteen beautifully inlaid rosettes of gold around it, and in front of it the royal cobra of gold inlaid, the head of lazuli. This head was missing when the crown first appeared; some days afterwards, in washing the earth from the recess, the head was found. Then one eye was missing. I washed and searched minutely, preserving the smallest specks of precious stone.

Soon a tiny ball of garnet appeared at the bottom of the basinful of mud; this – no larger than a pin's head – was the missing eye. Yet the gold socket of the eye was missing. I remembered having washed out a bead of gold which differed from thousands of others; looking, I found it again, and there was the setting of the eye complete. Above the crown at the back of it stood up double plumes of gold, fitting into a golden flower. At the sides and back hung down broad ties of gold. The whole crown is too large for a modern head, being made to go over the very full Egyptian wig; it is altogether over eighteen inches high.

The next most striking objects are the great collars of gold cowries and gold lion heads. These are ingeniously fastened with one piece in two halves, joining together by a slider, so that the collar has to be much contracted before it can open. Two beautifully wrought pectorals are of gold inlaid with minute pieces of carnelian, turquoise, and lazuli. . . .

A great necklace of long drop-beads must have been worn hanging below the other jewellery. The pendants are of gold, carnelian, lazuli, and amazon stone. From the middle hangs the most splendid scarab known, cut with perfect sharpness in the richest lapis lazuli. . . .

Armlets were worn of gold bars with minute beads of turquoise and carnelian. They were fastened on the arm by sliding a strip of gold, covered with inlays of carnelian, and bearing the name and titles of Amenenhat III. . . .

Four wristlets each have a pair of gold lions, face to face, upon strings of beads of gold, carnelian and turquoise.

The toilet was provided for by a large silver mirror, with a handle of obsidian, and gold head of the goddess Hat-hor; a pair of razors with gold handles; and three jars for ointment made of black obsidian with gold mounting round the base, the brim and the lids.

1919

Only a scatter of minor items, the most important perhaps being the discovery of a hoard of Roman silver at Traprain Law in Scotland.

December 20, 1919

ROCK PAINTINGS OF THE SPANISH LEVANT

By A. Forestier

Some very interesting discoveries made in 1910 by Señor Pascuale Serrano Gomez of rock paintings at El Bosque, in the hilly country north of Alpera, a Spanish town about halfway between Albacete, situated in the plains of La Mancha, and Alicante, on the Mediterranean, throw a fresh light upon the life of prehistoric man in south-western Europe during the Magdalenian period of the Great Ice Age.

These discoveries were carefully investigated by Professor the Abbé Breuil, to whom we are indebted for an exhaustive analysis of the subject published in 1912, with reproductions of his copies of the paintings, in the French periodical *L'Anthropologie*.

The pictures consist of a remarkable painted frieze, in which men and animals are depicted. Other frescoes of a similar character, both in artistic quality and in the indication of the fauna, had already been brought to light at other places in Spain – notably, Cogul and Cretas – and can be related, like the Alpera frescoes, to the Magdalenian art in France. Still, as Professor Breuil observes: "The latter offer a striking difference in the abundance of human representations, very life-like, also in the use of the bow, and even in the attitudes of the figures, to the frescoes of South Africa. These representations are grouped in hunting, or perhaps warlike, scenes." One must notice that the presence of the bow and the dog reveals elements unknown in the French Magdalenian

art, and "one is led to deduce that there existed in the east of Spain during the late Palaeolithic period a Palaeolithic population living also by hunting, but different in some respects from the French tribes, although influenced in a high degree by their art."

Putting aside, however, any question of aesthetics, these unexpected human representations, coupled with what we know from other sources of the industry of the period, permit us now on good authority to reconstitute the life of these Stone Age people, and that is the subject of our endeavour in the drawing reproduced *(Figure 72)*. . . .

These Palaeolithic tribes, when not compelled by the rigour of the climate to find their dwelling in caverns where they obtained protection against both the intense cold and the attacks of ferocious animals, lived under rock shelters on the sides of valleys.

When these shelters, like that at Alpera, happened to be situated near a spring of good water, and commanded a good survey of the country around, they became places of constant habitation, and were occupied in turn by the successive races who dwelt in the land from the remotest antiquity to modern times, and did not fail to make use of these points of vantage. The Magdalenians were living in the course of the last phase of the Ice Age up to its close. . . .

The arts of painting and carving, well known among the kindred tribes on both sides of the

Pyrenees, had spread through the peninsula. The craft in working bone and ivory into implements of war and peace, as well as personal ornaments, had created a flourishing industry, which indeed is typical of the Magdalenian period. . . .

Artistic talent was devoted to the decoration of arms and utensils with beautifully drawn engravings reproducing in a naturalistic manner the animals living at the time. Some of the sculptures are famous for their beauty, as well as for the clever way in which they are adapted to a useful object.

In these, however, the human figure is rarely represented, and it is gratifying to find in the rock paintings of Alpera the long-felt want of adequate images of the Magdalenians made by contemporary artists.

From these pictures, and with the help of previously known materials, it is easy to imagine what life was like under the shelters. Tents made of skins sewn together by the women were erected here. . . . In front of the shelter a broad terrace . . . extended along the valley, forming an excellent ground for exercise and play. There the boys learnt the use and handling of weapons, the children romped about, the men practised their shooting or patiently worked in the making of the numerous articles of their industry.

Some women scraped and stretched the fresh skins; others, with their bone needles and their sinews, could make the tent-coverings, or any garments that were needed. A fire was kept burning in front of the shelter. The game killed by the hunters was cooked on the embers; the bones and antlers, cut, polished, sharpened on sandstone for various purposes, provided easy occupation for young and old members of the tribe. . . .

The sculptor caressed with loving care the polished surface of his ivory handiwork; and the painter profited by whatever light might illuminate the recesses of the shelter to cover its rough walls with marvellous designs depicting episodes of the chase or other incidents, often adding new drawings to some older figures –

indeed, not hesitating to superimpose fresh compositions on some of a greater merit traced there many years before by other artists of the Cromagnon race, once inhabitants of the shelter.

The men would gather on the terrace for the performance of some religious rite before starting on a hunting expedition; or, after their roaming through the forests, would indulge in games, or simply rest in content, watching,

72 Rock-dwellers perform a ceremonial dance at night. A reconstruction drawing by A. Forestier after prehistoric rock paintings

perhaps, some dancing women after a meal of half-roasted meat had been disposed of under the eyes of the chief. Thus life went on at the dawn of human society in south-western Europe many thousand years ago, when the risks of war were few between the sparsely scattered populations, and peace was only disturbed by some occasional domestic quarrels.

1920

In this year, so to speak, archaeology was reborn and, as well as the articles cited, there were three articles by D. G. Hogarth on "Post-war Excavations" at Carchemish, Mycenae and Askalon, and several pieces by the Italian Federico Halbherr on Ostia, Etruscan excavations at Veii, Vetulonia and Castellina (during which the Apollo of Veii was found) and the beginning of the Italian restorations in Rhodes.

September 18, 1920

TEOTIHUACAN

By Señor Manuel Gamino (in charge of excavation); reprinted from the Mexican review Ethnos

A year ago Señor Pastor Rouaix, Secretary of Agriculture and Public Works, visited the explorations which were being carried on in the system of structures which we have called the Temple of the Water God, and when passing near the mounds of the system called La Ciudadela ("The Fort" – now the Temple of Quetzalcoatl) he expressed the wish that the large central mound should be explored.

The system of La Ciudadela consists of a rectangle of approximately 500 metres square, each side being formed by platforms, on three of which there are twelve mounds arranged in series of four, and on the remaining one only three.

The central mound really consisted of two mounds back to back, the higher having a height of 22 metres.

The first part of the exploration consisted in clearing the plateau of the greater mound, various graves and wells being at once discovered. In the former there were found human remains, shells, necklaces, beads, heads of deities and ear ornaments cut and polished in jade, arrows of obsidian, and ritual vases.

We then proceeded to open up near the base of the lower mound, exploration trenches running radially. As a result of this the structure of the mound in question was discovered. It consists of large masses arranged in decreasing order, each being made up of a truncated pyramid, which has superimposed on it a quadrangular prism. All these structures are built of fragments of rock and clay and covered outside with mortar, smoothed and polished,

73 *A reconstruction of the panels of the temple of Quetzalcoatl at Teotihuacan*

and afterwards painted red. The corners of the structures were destroyed, but as the central parts were preserved intact it was easy to effect reconstruction by merely prolonging the slopes, panels, and passages.

The third part of the exploration consisted in cutting a tunnel along the intersection of both mounds. This tunnel brought to light two masses of the western face of the greater mound, which are similar in form to those found on the smaller mound; but they differ very greatly in their structure because they are built of large dressed stones, chiselled in high relief, and painted in several colours.

The decoration of each of these masses consists of large feathered serpents, sculptured in the lower panel, which, between their coils, contain large shells and snails *(Figure 73)*; the heads of these fantastic serpents appear shown in profile ending at the starting point of the flight of steps. In the panel above the slope there are also bodies of serpents, the tails of which terminate in fanciful balls or buttons; while the heads represent two kinds of mythological animals, one of them suggesting the famous Cipactli of the Aztecs, while the other appears to be a mixed representation made up of the owl and the serpent.

December 4, 1920

NEW LIGHT ON THE HOUSE OF ATREUS:
Mycenae

(Photographs and material supplied by courtesy of the British School of Archaeology at Athens)

Forty years ago Schliemann astonished the world with the wonderful treasures he found in the Royal Graves at Mycenae, and was the first to attempt to interpret the gigantic monuments, the marvellous metal-work, and the fine pottery, which are, so to speak, the hieroglyphic archives of prehistoric Greece. Then for fourteen years Professor Tsountas conducted a series of successful campaigns in the palace, houses, and cemeteries of the royal city, and gave us a nearly complete picture of its life. In later years Sir Arthur Evans' discoveries in the palace of Minos at Knossos in Crete have eclipsed even Schliemann's and told us the main source of the culture of Mycenae. Modern archaeological science – for the skilled excavator of today is a scientific observer of ruined walls, broken pottery, and the stratification of the debris of past centuries – has made great progress in its methods of analysing the civilisations of antiquity. . . .

The new excavations at Mycenae undertaken by the British School of Archaeology at Athens aim at tracing the causes of the rise, greatness and decline of the wonderful Mycenaean civilisation immortalised by Homer. The campaign was mainly directed to unravelling the history of the Royal Grave Circle, the famous Lion Gate and the Cyclopean Wall. The six royal graves excavated by Schliemann seem to have formed part of a cemetery *(Figure 74)* that lay on the sloping hillside, just below the earlier town. Later, when the dynasty whose princes were buried there had passed away, and another family, perhaps that of Atreus himself, had established the centre of its dominion at Mycenae, the massive Cyclopean Wall was thrown round the rocky hill so as to ensure the safety of the central tower. Then it was found that the natural line of defence ran through this cemetery; but the royal graves were regarded as sacred because of the semi-divine character of

74 The six royal graves at Mycenae enclosed in a ring of slabs resembling a Druidic circle

their occupants, and so the wall was made to curve outwards to avoid them. They were enclosed with an elaborate ring of slabs somewhat resembling a Druidic circle, and the ground was levelled so as to make an imposing monument to the dead kings where due honours could still be paid to their shades. Other graves, probably non-royal, were opened, and their contents moved elsewhere, perhaps within the circle; one such grave, built in a style similar to the royal graves, was found this year under the floor of a building between the Grave Circle and the Lion Gate, which seems to have been a granary. Nineteen large gold rosettes give some idea of what might have been found and still may be found. Nor is this all: a careful analysis of the broken potsherds – for with such do our trained archaeologists write history when all

other records are lacking – reveal that not only was Mycenae already a flourishing city by 2000 B.C., but some centuries earlier, at the very beginning of the Bronze Age, there was a not inconsiderable settlement here. . . .

South of the Grave Circle, part of a large Mycenaean house, built not long after 1400 B.C., was uncovered. Four rooms and an entrance-porch, which has an outlet for rain-water leading into a main drain running under the house, were cleared, but nothing was found in them except the remains of two large leaden vessels which had stood in one room and had melted in the fire that destroyed the house, and had run over the floor. The stone walls, which still show clearly the positions of the wooden ties to support the superstructure of crude brick, stand even today to a height of five feet;

and their solid construction, together with the unmistakable traces of a staircase, and plentiful fragments of a flat cemented roof, show that it was an important house, and had at least two floors. On the summit of the citadel, part of the palace – perhaps that to which Agamemnon brought home his bride Clytemnestra – was cleared. This, though badly ruined, was, to judge by its painted walls and floors, its spacious court and halls, its staircases and corridors, an elaborate building resembling the palaces of Crete. Other finds, which space prevents us from describing fully, include a bath used as a coffin at a later date; two deep wells, from one of which a clay sealing and three interesting libation vessels in stone were extracted, two being fragments in the shape of bulls' heads; many drains, and many early and important fragments of painted plaster showing a bull-baiting scene and a male and female acrobat. . . .

The dramatic incident of the excavations was the lifting of two of the threshold blocks of the great domed tomb called the treasury of Atreus. This amazing building, one of the wonders of the world, is built on a gigantic scale (for instance, one of the lintel blocks weighs about 120 tons) and so skilfully and so solidly that, even, after the vicissitudes of 3000 years, it is still practically intact. Till the British School re-examined it, this year, all ideas as to the date when it was built were purely hypothetical. In clearing round the threshold some fragments of gold leaf came to light. The Greek archaeological authorities were appealed to for permission to lift one or two of the blocks in the hope that some relics to date the tomb might be found, and they not only granted the permission, but sent Professor Orlandos with skilled masons to do the work. The threshold consists of two big blocks of breccia wedged in tightly across the entrance by two small tapering slabs of soft limestone, and the joints were filled in with yellow clay, which was regularly used by the Mycenaean builders as a cement. The central wedges were loosened and removed, and then the large block of breccia on the south side was lifted. It rested on a bed of stones packed with earth and sunk in a shallow trench cut in the rock, and in the earth were found quantities of gold leaf, bronze nails with fragments of gold-leaf still adhering to them, a few beads of stone and paste, some fragments of ivory, rotten with damp, and, last but not least, some pieces of painted pottery. It is suggested that when the tomb was built the threshold was one of the last portions to be constructed, and then the builders swept into the hollow, together with the earth to pack the stones on which the breccia blocks are set, rubbish that had fallen on the floor from the decoration of the upper part of the dome and entrance. The gold-leaf, bronze nails and ivory could easily be waste material damaged by the decorators. Finally, when complete, the stone threshold, as shown by the bronze nails, still visible in the blocks, was covered with bronze. Bronze thresholds are mentioned by Homer. The fragments of pottery found under the threshold can be dated to the early fourteenth century B.C.

1921

The renaissance of archaeology continued and, as well as the articles cited, other major items included an article on the significance of Tell el Amarna by D. G. Hogarth and on the Egypt Exploration Society's discoveries there by Professor Eric Peet, and a spate of short articles by Professor F. Halbherr on Cyrene, Crete, Caria and Lycia, Rome, and Orvieto.

March 26, 1921

DIGGER'S LUCK:
A Romance of Egyptian excavation
By Ambrose Lansing

In the course of the work of the Egyptian Expedition of the Metropolitan Museum of Art on its concession on the west bank at Thebes, our attention had been drawn to that part of the site south of Deir el Bahari, among the spurs and cliffs of the mountain which separates the Valley of the Kings from the plain. Here, during the troublous times in Egypt, a good deal of plundering had been going on, and in forestalling some of this unauthorised digging I had been fortunate enough to find the burial-place of a young prince of the Eighteenth Dynasty, who had been torn to pieces by ancient tomb-robbers in their search for gold, and had then been re-buried by the priests of the Twenty-first Dynasty. The tomb had been in an almost inaccessible cranny of the cliff wall, and similar clefts in the rock face looked as if they too might contain hidden tombs.

At the beginning of the season of 1919–20, these were thoroughly cleared, but not a trace of occupation was found. A huge tomb of the Eleventh Dynasty – from its size and position evidently that of a high official of the last of the Mentuhoteps – looked as if it might give us a chance of recouping our fortunes. . . .

A few days' work with a big gang of workmen laid bare the platform which had been the forecourt of the tomb. It had originally been in the form of a portico, and the walls had been built of fine imported limestone sculptured in low relief, and painted with a delicacy rarely equalled in Egyptian art. But of this only a few fragments were found, none of them as much as six inches square, and they only resulted in making our disappointment the keener. Two mauls, so rough that, if found in other circumstances, they would have been taken for Palaeolithic implements, suggested the ruthless manner in which the ancient quarrymen had broken up the sculptured blocks for building-stone.

So our hopes were dashed again.

In order to get an adequate plan of the tomb, it was necessary to clear the corridors and the two burial shafts. . . . Conscientiousness was rewarded.

In clearing the fallen rock from the main corridor, a workman dislodged a loose stone from the side near the floor, and the small chip began trickling into a small dark hole. It was the evening of March 17. Burton was in charge of the work, and was called by the excited foreman. The hole was small, and the passage dark, and even matches helped little to show what was hidden within. A hurriedly written note brought Winlock and myself up from the house with an electric torch. Each of us in turn glued his eye and the torch to the hole in the rock. None of us expect ever again to have such a sight appear to us. "The beam of light shone into a little world of four thousand years ago, and I was gazing down into the midst of a myriad of brightly painted little men going this way and that. A tall, slender girl gazed across at me perfectly composed; a gang of little men with sticks in their upraised hands drove spotted oxen; rowers tugged at their oars on a fleet of boats, while one ship seemed foundering right in front of me, with its bow balanced precariously in the air. And all of this busy going and coming was in uncanny silence." (*Figure 75*).

The next three days were the busiest of our several careers. To clear that small chamber of its contents before the change of air loosened the friable shale of the ceiling, and yet not to remove the different objects before all the evidence was recorded and the necessary photographs taken, was a job requiring hard work and nice judgment. But it was done: and just in time, for, soon after we had everything out, the stones began to fall.

The set of models, by far the finest as regards completeness and preservation which have ever been found in Egypt – the two companies of soldiers from Meir are the only ones which compare in workmanship – present a picture of the life of an Egyptian noble and the activities on his estates which volumes of writing could not equal.

In the largest scene he is seated in a portico. Beside him four scribes enumerate and record the herds of cattle being driven before him.

From among these cattle the choicest beeves are selected, and they are shown in the model of a cow stable, some eating from a manger, and others being fed from a pile of green fodder. It is evident that they are being fattened – indeed, the model-maker has given them such proportions that they could not squeeze through the doors of the stable if they tried. A third model in this group is the slaughter-house, where two oxen, bound in the manner in which they are shown in the reliefs, are having their throats cut. A further set of three models gives us a picture of the disposition of the produce of the fields. Sacks of grain are brought to the granary, in the anteroom of which scribes take down the amount coming from each farm, and give credit to the proper person. It is measured out, carried up a flight of steps and dumped into bins. In another model, the baking of bread and cakes is proceeding on one side of a dividing wall, and the brewing of beer on the other. The third shows a weaving establishment with women workers.

75 *Models of Nile craft, with their crews, and an Egyptian granary, as they were left buried about 2000 B.C.*

The most interesting of the house models are two gardens, almost identical. A porch, whose roof is supported by eight brightly-painted columns, looks out on a tank surrounded by seven sycamore trees. In the models, the pool is lined with copper, and may possibly have held water when it was placed in the tomb. These models are especially interesting from an architectural point of view, as few traces of columns from private houses have come down to us.

The noble – he was a prince and chancellor of the kingdom about 2000 B.C., by name Mehenkwetre (an Egyptian equivalent of Heliodorus) – was evidently very fond of boating on the Nile, for no fewer than twelve different boats were found among this collection of models: boats rigged for sailing up stream, and others for paddling or rowing down-stream; comfortable boats, with large cabins and accompanying kitchen tenders, and smaller boats, for afternoon outings on the river.

November 19, 1921

THE BROKEN HILL SKULL

Three articles by William E. Harris, Dr. A. Smith Woodward, L.L.D., F.R.S. and Sir Arthur Keith, M.D., F.R.S., respectively

No little excitement was caused in the far-away mining camp when it was known that a skull had been found *(Figure 76)* in the mine, and many heated discussions took place among the miners, as to whether it was a large ape's skull or that of a human being. The native labourers were not so interested however; so after the native foreman had sent the skull to the "white boss", they went on with their digging, and so broke into pieces what would have been a far more important discovery, that of the complete skeleton of this early ancestor of man. It was after the manager of the property had seen the skull that it was decided to put it aside and make a search for further remains, and so we were able to recover a leg bone, collar bone, portion of a shoulder blade, also portion of the pelvis with coccyx attached, and part of a lower jaw, together with parts of other bones not identified, and most of the pieces of the mineralised cast of the body. The only other large bone found near these human remains was a smashed skull of an animal similar to a lion; also a round stone similar in shape and size to the stones the present-day natives use for various grinding purposes. William E. Harris.

How did the Rhodesian man stand in size of brain? An approximate answer to this question can be given from comparing corresponding outlines of a modern Englishman with the largest headed specimen of Neanderthal race so far discovered in Europe – the specimen from La Chapelle cave, France, elaborately described by Professor Boule of Paris. The profile of each skull has been placed in a corresponding position, and set within a standard frame of the same dimensions. The La Chapelle skull is of remarkable size; it has a brain cavity which measures fully 1600 cubic centimetres, 120 cubic centimetres above the average for modern Englishmen. The roof of the skull will be seen to reach the upper horizontal line of the frame; the forehead projects beyond the front vertical line. The English skull . . . has a brain cavity measuring 1425 cubic centimetres, 65 cubic centimetres short of the average, but in life its owner was known as a clever, notorious rascal. The forehead is seen to fall 15 millimetres short of the anterior vertical line. In its dimensions the newly discovered Rhodesian skull falls between the modern English and the ancient French skulls. The roof of the African fossil skull falls somewhat short of the upper horizontal line, but in length it more than fills the standard frame. Allowing for the thickness of bone and the great projection of the eyebrow ridge, it is clear that this ancient African had a brain which in point of size did not fall greatly short of the average for modern Englishmen. In all Neanderthal skulls, the roof is low-pitched, particularly in the Gibraltar specimen. The Neanderthal people of Europe were not all of the same breed or race; there are several features in which the Gibraltar skull differs from the corresponding kind of skull found in France.

76 *The Broken Hill skull – photographed where it was found*

One infers that the Rhodesian man was much more akin to the Gibraltar breed than to that of France.   Sir Arthur Keith

The new skull from a Rhodesian cave exhibits so many unusual features, and needs so much cleaning before it can be satisfactorily studied, that any account of it must at present be incomplete. It is in a remarkably fresh state of preservation, not at all fossilised, and its substance appears to differ from modern bone only in the loss of its animal matter. The condition alone is insufficient to decide whether it dates back to the Pleistocene period or whether it belongs to a recent century. The associated animal remains at any rate show that the man it represents lived in Rhodesia under circumstances that still existed in that country a few years ago when the white races first arrived there.

The brain-case is that of a very ordinary man, with bone not thicker than that in an average European, and of similar structure. The size of the brain cavity is not yet determined, but it is clearly far above the lower human limit. When seen in side-view, however, the skull has an extraordinary appearance, because the bones of the face are relatively very large, and the upper edges of the eye-sockets are inflated into immense rounded crests, or ridges, which obscure the shape of the forehead and give it a retreating contour. The skull thus approaches that of a great ape, and, when seen in front view, its large, square orbits, with their overhanging ridges, recall those of a gorilla. As readily seen by comparing the photographs, the skull is indeed human, with reminiscences of an ape-like ancestor in its face. The bones of the nose are typically human, but their arrangement shows that it would be broad and flattened.

The skull is seen to be much broken on the right side, but the oval opening (*foramen magnum*) where the spinal cord enters the brain-case, is distinguishable, placed as far forwards as in modern man. This opening makes no approach to the backward position it occupies in the gorilla and other apes, and it shows that the skull would be perfectly poised on an upright trunk. Corresponding with the large size of the face, the palate is enormous for man. It is, however, a typically human palate, beautifully domed and adapted to perfect speech, and bounded by the horseshoe-shaped row of large, though absolutely human, teeth. All the teeth are much worn, and those of the front of the jaw meet their lower opposing teeth edge to edge, as in all the early races. Only one feature is specially noteworthy – the wisdom tooth is much smaller than the other grinders. The whole dentition is remarkable as exhibiting much decay from caries, and the disease has affected the bone round the tooth-sockets, which are partially destroyed in some places. So far as I am aware, this is the only example of caries in the teeth of a prehistoric skull hitherto discovered. . . . The only known skulls which

159

make a really close approach to the Rhodesian fossil are those of the Neanderthal type from caves in Gibraltar, France and Belgium. That from La Chapelle-aux-Saints, as restored by Professor Marcellin Boule, is especially comparable.   A. Smith Woodward

The Rhodesian fossil skull does not represent a type of man which is new to anthropologists; every feature of this skull proclaims the ancient African of whom it formed part to have been first cousin to Neanderthal Man, that peculiar species of humanity which lived in Europe throughout a certain phase of the Ice Age.

The sites at which fossil remains of Neanderthal man have been found in Europe . . . are most numerous in France; but they occur also in Belgium and in the south-western part of Germany. Remains of the Neanderthal type of man have also been found in Jersey, but not hitherto in England, although flint implements and weapons fashioned in his style of workmanship have been found in many localities. Fossil remains of this extinct type of humanity have been found in Croatia to the east of the Adriatic, but none in Italy to the west of that sea. The latest, as well as the earliest, discovery of Neanderthal man was made in the Mediterranean area. The Gibraltar skull, now preserved in the Museum of the Royal College of Surgeons, was found in 1848, when operations were being carried out in Forbes Quarry on the north front of the Rock. It represents the first discovery of the Neanderthal type of man. The latest discovery was made in Malta in 1917, by Mr. Despott, who found two teeth of this peculiar race while excavating the floor of a large cave. Thus the earliest and latest discoveries of Neanderthal man carried his distribution right up to the threshold of Africa. The revelation now made in Northern Rhodesia extends the habitat of this ancient and extinct type of humanity far into Africa, for the site of the Broken Hill Company's works lies 4000 miles from Southern Europe. . . .

December 10, 1921

THE PALACE OF MINOS
By H. R. Hall, D.Litt., F.S.A.

Sir Arthur Evans has published the first volume of his complete publication of his epoch-making discovery of the Palace of Minos at Knossos in Crete, which twenty years ago startled the world with its revelation of an almost unknown early civilisation antedating that of classical Greece by a thousand years, and challenging comparison with that of ancient Greece alike in antiquity and arts. . . .

We shall not find the Cupbearer in this volume, which is but the first of a series of three and deals . . . with the relics of the earlier age that was contemporary with the ancient and middle kingdoms of Egypt, from the earliest times to the end of the period of the Hyksos (B.C. 3500–1580) – in Minoan chronology from the Neolithic to the end of the Middle Minoan period (*circa* 1600 B.C.). . . .

And though we have not yet reached the apogee of Minoan art in this volume, yet we see in it illustrations and descriptions of some of the

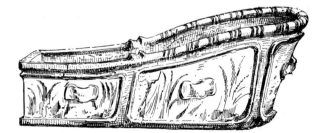

77 *A bath of painted clay (about 4½ feet long) from the palace of Minos*

78 The palace (or "labyrinth") of Minos at Knossos

most extraordinary, probably the most bizarre, productions of the Cretan workers, who at a period contemporary with the Pharaohs of the Twelfth Dynasty were producing pottery of the most startling forms and colours, frescoes of strange naturalism and power, and architecture of the most modern, including sanitary arrangements that were unknown in our day till the middle of the nineteenth century *(Figure 77).* . . .

Not least among the bizarre attractions of the Cretan palace and its architecture and art is the amazing fact that it is veritably a place of which we heard when young readers of the tales of Old Greece, and regarded as no more fact than Hy-Brasil of the Irish or Asgard of the Norse gods. It is the Labyrinth of the Minotaur, to which the tribute of young men and maidens went from Athens to be devoured by the bull-devil;

whence Theseus rescued Ariadne, and from which sailed back the black-sailed galley, which seeing, Aegeus cast himself despairing into the sea. This is the place of the *labrys*, the double axe which was the emblem of its god; here the young men and maidens essayed the death-bringing sport (actual sport it probably was, as were the later Greek games and plays themselves) of leaping over the horns of the bull – to be gored or impaled or saved by their own agility, as the case might be – in the courts of the Labyrinth of Knossos, which Sir Arthur has uncovered, that maze of courts and passages *(Figure 78)* which caused the later Greeks who marvelled at it to give the name of "labyrinth" to any mazy thing, whether building or argument or net or coil of rope.

It is a civilisation that attracts us curiously,

this of the Age of the Heroes in ancient Greece, not only on account of its partial relationship to the later Greek culture of classical days, but from its own strange qualities, half friendly, half repellent. It was an utterly artistic age, a time of aesthetics uncontrolled, very young, with all the qualities of youthful achievement, its brilliancy and its childishness – also probably with its cruelty and its *abandon* to the feeling of the moment. Could we read its records, which we cannot yet do, what might we not learn of its history?

1922

This year ended with three issues in December briefly reporting the discovery of the Tomb of Tutankhamen; and so ushers in the really great period of Illustrated London News *archaeology; but even before this news there were highly important discoveries (as our extracts show) in Crete, Ur of the Chaldees, Taxila in India and Tell el Amarna in Egypt. And in addition to these we published also important articles on Carchemish, Malta, Ostia, and Abydos.*

March 11, 1922

ITALIAN EXCAVATIONS AT GORTYNA, CRETE

By Professor F. Halbherr

Few territories of the ancient Greek world have undergone, in recent years, such deep and extensive archaeological research as Crete. In that island not only the wondrous Minoan palaces and cemeteries of Knossus, Phaestus, Hagia Triada and others have been discovered and thoroughly excavated, but also the Greek and Roman remains, and even the Venetian monuments, all over its area, have been carefully searched and explored. The publication of Sir Arthur Evans' standard work *The Palace of Minos*, and the almost simultaneous issue of Dr. Gerola's new volume on Cretan monuments of the Venetian Age, provide the first and the last chapter of what, shortly, will form a complete illustrated record of the great periods of Cretan history and art.

Like that of the Venetian memorials, the survey of the Roman antiquities has been taken in hand by the Italian Mission. Its first investigations at Lyttus, Hierapytna, Itanus and elsewhere in the eastern region of the island, and at Eleutherna, Lappa, and Polyrrhenia on the western side, have made clear the topography and the aqueduct and road system of those territories in Imperial Roman times, and yielded a great number of inscriptions illustrating the history of Roman administration in the country. But up to the present day they have been confined to the examination of the surface ground only. For systematic diggings and excavations, as was natural, the large town of Gortyna, which was the capital of the province, has been chosen.

The vast area of this city, forming a circle of about two miles in diameter, is completely scattered over with monumental remains of that age. The imposing ruins of theatres, temples, baths, aqueducts, nymphaea and public buildings of every description, still rising in the middle of green cornfields, or emerging from clumps of olive and carob trees, give us an idea of the ancient magnificence of the Roman proconsul, and show how flourishing, not only for the city, but for the island as a whole, was the period of the Roman dominion. . . .

The chief localities partly cleared and partly in course of excavation at the present day are the Agora (market-place), the temple of Pythian Apollo and its surroundings, a Byzantine church built over the ruins of another temple in the same neighbourhood, the Amphitheatre, the Nymphaea, the standing part of the episcopal church of St. Titus, the shrine of the Egyptian divinities and the Roman Governor's palace or Praetorium itself.

The transformation of the Greek agora into a Roman Forum was a gradual process, which commenced in the later Republican times and was accomplished under the Empire. A block of limestone from the entablature of some public building, found in a trench, bears part of a dedicatory inscription to an Emperor, perhaps to Augustus himself. The northern section of the agora, in pre-Roman times, was occupied by a very ancient domed building, on the walls of which the archaic laws of the city were inscribed. It was probably the Prytaneum, or seat of the magistrates of the city fallen in ruins owing to its old age or to one of the earthquakes so frequent in the island, about the first century B.C. It was rebuilt, some years later, by the Romans, to serve as an Odeum, or music-hall; but the code of the ancient laws, or at least that part of it which, according to Strabo, was still in use at the time, was respected and carefully protected under the brick gallery which supported the seats of the auditorium. Less than two centuries later, as shown by a Latin inscription discovered near the place, the building was again in ruins, and was reconstructed a second time by the munificence of the Emperor Trajan, taking the form in which the excavations have found it. Last summer's work resulted in clearing entirely the proscenium and its approaches, as also in defining the plan of both the earliest and the later structures, showing that the foundations of the older building were laid upon a layer of ceramic remains of the geometric style of the eighth century B.C.

With the object of preserving the great inscription, a piece of the original vaulted gallery has been reconstructed, following the plan of Trajan's repairs. The little Odeum – a hundred feet in diameter – appears now as one of the most elegant monuments of Roman Gortyna.

A *stoa*, or portico, with an *exedra*, or semi-circular resting-bench, was built in front of the Odeum, while fountains and statues were dotted about everywhere in the central Forum square and along its eastern side. But great ravages upon these works of art must have been perpetrated by the earlier Byzantines, as almost all the statues representing Pagan deities have been found headless. In its southern and not yet excavated part, near the early Christian church of St. Titus – the first Bishop of Crete, appointed by St. Paul himself – a shrine of Aesculapius must have existed, according to some inscriptions found there in a trial excavation pit, together with a marble torso presenting the features of the god.

The locality of the temples, both in Greek and in Roman times, was the central quarter of the city, which was called the Pythium from the most venerated amongst the Gortynian sanctuaries, that of Pythian Apollo, which was discovered and excavated by the Italian Mission in its first campaigns. Ancient authors mention also the Artemisium, the temple of Jove Hecatombaeus, and that of Latona, the first of which is, perhaps, that converted into a Byzantine church, found on digging some trial trenches in the old olive grove south of the Pythium.

The invasion of foreign cults, which reached the West in Roman Imperial times, affected also the island of Crete, situated as it was halfway between Egypt and the European continent. A recent excavation, which is not yet finished, has brought to light one of these exotic sanctuaries in the same quarter of the Pythium to the north-east. This was dedicated to the Egyptian deities, Isis, Serapis and Anubis, and consisted of a *cella* faced by a great hall with portico. The hall has been only partially explored, while the *cella* is now entirely discovered. Disposed in a row along the back wall of it three fine marble statues were found, almost intact, save the head wanting to one of them – Jove Serapis, with the dog Anubis, three-headed like Cerberus; Isis, with the lunar crescent on her head; and Mercurius, holding his purse in his right hand.

March 18, 1922

A 3300-YEAR-OLD BULL HEAD

By Sir Arthur Evans, reprinted by permission from his article in the Archaeological organ of the Society of Antiquaries

The most remarkable object found in connection with the south-west sanctuary of the "Little Palace" was the rhyton in the form of a bull's head *(Plate 10, p. 72)*. With the exception of the inlays of shell and rock crystal, its material is of black steatite. Its height from the chin to the top of the head is 20 centimetres, so that it may roughly be described as about half the natural dimensions.

The greater part of the head itself was preserved, but a part of the left side and the left eye were wanting, also the horns and ears. The horns . . . were fixed by means of square attachments, secured in each case by a pin inserted from the top of the head by means of a vertical perforation. This method corresponds, in fact with the Minoan system of locking doors . . . by means of a metal pin pushed through a "keyhole" into the wooden bolt. Judging from the small size of the attachments, the material of the horns was probably of wood, and coated with thin gold foil, of which some remains were found in the deposit. But the ears, the sockets for the attachment of which, round in shape, are larger in proportion, were evidently of heavier material, though it is impossible to say whether they were of precious metal – which would account for their disappearance – or of steatite like those from the "Tomb of the Double Axes". In this case, the hole for the projection, by which the ears were attached, went right through the side wall of the rhyton, so that it may have been secured by an internal rivet. . . .

The present example was formed out of two pieces of steatite. The bull's head and neck were wrought out of a solid mass, and set by means of a reveal round the edge into a flat plate forming the base. On the outer surface of this, the artist who executed the work had made – with what object it is difficult to say, perhaps for his own guidance in the work – a little graffito sketch of a bull's head. It is interesting as showing how the horns were intended by him to spring from the head.

Round the nostrils of the animal is a curving inlaid band, consisting of white shell, inserted in a shallow with a rectangular section. The shell used is evidently a large bivalve, and seems to be the tridacna squamosa, which was already imported into Crete from the Persian Gulf at this period.

But the most striking feature of this head was the perfectly preserved right eye. The lens of this consisted of rock crystal, on the slightly hollowed lower surface of which are painted the pupil and iris. The pupil is a brilliant scarlet, the iris black, the rest of the cornea white. The crystal setting is inserted in a border of red stone resembling jasper, which surrounds the white field of the eye like the rims of bloodshot eyelids. To add to the effect, the crystal lens of the eye, both illuminates and magnifies the bright red pupil, and imparts to the whole an almost startling impression of fiery life.

Long hairs are engraved falling about the forehead, brows, and cheeks of the animal, showing that he was of a shaggy breed. Certain incurved, angular designs moreover, on the forehead, the sides of the head, and neck, are evidently intended to indicate coloured patches, resembling those seen on some of the painted designs of bulls. That over the forehead is very symmetrical, and somewhat suggests a Minoan shield. It is possible that it is a religious symbol.

On the face of the bull's-head rhyton from the Tomb of the Double Axe the inlays were of a quatrefoil shape. This suggests the conventional cruciform decoration which stands for spots on some of the cows of the Egyptian Goddess Hathor.

The locks above the forehead and on the protuberance of the head between the horns are of a somewhat schematic nature, and betray derivation from a more naturalistic prototype. Of the character of this prototype, moreover, additional evidence is afforded by the appearance on the ridge between the horns of a raised roundel with revolving rays, repeated in a flatter form between the horns. This ornament is evidently taken over from a metal-work original, the curving rays themselves recalling a similar decoration on the studs of a magnificent "horned" sword from grave 44, at Zafer Papoura, which had probably been coated with gold plate.

A striking parallel to this system of decoration is, in fact, found in the case of a silver "rhyton" from the fourth Shaft Grave at Mycenae, on the forehead was fixed in a similar position a large rosette formed of gold plate. This vessel, formerly supposed to be a kind of votive head with a socket for the reception of a double axe – after an analogy of certain small votive bulls' heads with this symbol – has now been shown by Dr. Karo to be a "rhyton" in shape strikingly resembling the present example, though of slightly smaller dimensions. Further investigation, indeed, revealed the second smaller perforation in the lower lip for the escape of the fluid contents.

April 1, 1922

UR OF THE CHALDEES:
The British Museum Excavations in Babylonia, 1919
By H. R. Hall, D.Litt., F.S.A.

There are now exhibited in the Assyrian galleries of the British Museum some of the results of the excavations at Tell el-Mukayyar (the ancient "Ur of the Chaldees"), Tell Abu Shahrein (the ancient Eridu), and Tell el-Obeid, in Southern Babylonia, carried on by me for the Trustees of the British Museum in 1919. My work began at Ur in February 1919, and the excavations went on until the end of May. At Ur itself the most important result was the excavation of the remains of a building of King Ur-Engur or Ur-Nammu, of the Third Dynasty of Ur, who reigned about 2300 B.C. This residence was named by its builder E-Kharsag, "The House of the Mountain" in Sumerian. It was built of great flat burnt bricks, fourteen inches square, and its walls were five feet thick, showing that the old Babylonians knew how to keep out both the summer heat and the winter cold of Babylonia. Close by were the crude brick walls of a temple, E-Makh, which was sacred to the goddess, Ninsun.

In these buildings little was discovered that dated from the time of the builders. The "palace" was destroyed by fire, perhaps only a century or two after it was built, and traces of the conflagration were everywhere evident. Centuries later, about the eighth century B.C., the site was reoccupied by families of priests of the moon-god, Sin, the deity of Ur, who erected buildings of their own with the old bricks, and left relics in the shape of inscribed tablets and other objects. Burials of this later period were found not far off, the dead being interred in pottery coffins beneath the houses of the living. . . .

At Shahrein, which lies fourteen miles out in the waterless desert ("out in the blue", as they say in "Mespot"), ancient Sumerian houses were found with walls covered with lime-plaster, sometimes adorned with a simple painted decoration of horizontal red, white and black stripes. A section of the rough stone wall of the ancient city was laid bare, and collections made of the remarkably interesting debris that the winter storms have washed out of the lower strata of the soft and easily divided *tell* on to the surrounding desert surface. Similar relics were also found at Tell el-Obeid – flint and chert and obsidian knives, flakes and arrow-heads; celts of jasper and jadeite; mace heads of rough limestone like those of archaic Egypt; fragments of aragonite vases, and small objects of lapis lazuli and shell; innumerable little copper nails, some with gold heads (one nail is of solid gold); sickles (possibly votive, possibly intended for actual use) of hard, vitrified pottery; strange objects, of the same pottery, like bent nails and of unknown use; and, above all, numberless fragments of the remarkable painted pottery vases which recent research has shown to be typical of the ceramic art of this part of the world at the dawn of civilisation, when copper and stone were still used side by side, in the "Chalcolithic" or "Aenolithic" age, which in Babylonia we must date before 3500 B.C. The geometric and naturalistic and somewhat almost "jazz" patterns of this pottery are very remarkable.

The most important of all our discoveries was also made at el-Obeid. The little *tell* is apparently the site of a small shrine of the goddess Damkina, built of burnt bricks of the most archaic type – the "plano-convex" type, as it is called, which is characteristic of early Sumerian building (about 3000 B.C.). Heaped up near the wall of this building, where apparently they had been thrown by a later king who built a platform of his own bricks on the top of them, were remarkable remains of ancient Sumerian art *(Figure 79)* – the rude foreparts and heads of four life-size copper lions, with eyes of red jasper, white shell and blue schist, tongues of red jasper and teeth of shell; two copper panther or cat heads, also life-size; a smaller lion-head; two small copper bulls, about the size of greyhounds; and a great copper relief, 8 feet long by 3 feet 6 inches high, with the figure of Imgig, the lion-headed vulture of the god Ningirsu, holding two stags by their tails. These are finds that are among the most important ever found in Babylonia; unhappily their condition when found was extremely bad, and caused grave doubts whether it would ever be possible to transport them safely to England, where alone they could be given the expert treatment by chemists and metallurgists that might possibly save them for science and for our knowledge of ancient art. The metal was oxidised through and through, so that often little more than a green powder remained of what had originally been a work of copper. But luckily the old metal-workers – who apparently cast the heads of these beasts, though the bodies were hammered – thought it necessary to reinforce them with a filling of clay and bitumen, like the statue of Bel in the Apocrypha, that was "brass without and clay within". This has survived, so that we have the simulacra, so

NOT "FEET OF CLAY"—BUT HEADS: SUMERIAN METHODS OF SCULPTURE.

PHOTOGRAPHS BY DR. H. R. HALL, D.LITT., F.S.A. HEAD OF THE BRITISH MUSEUM ARCHÆOLOGICAL EXPEDITION IN BABYLONIA.

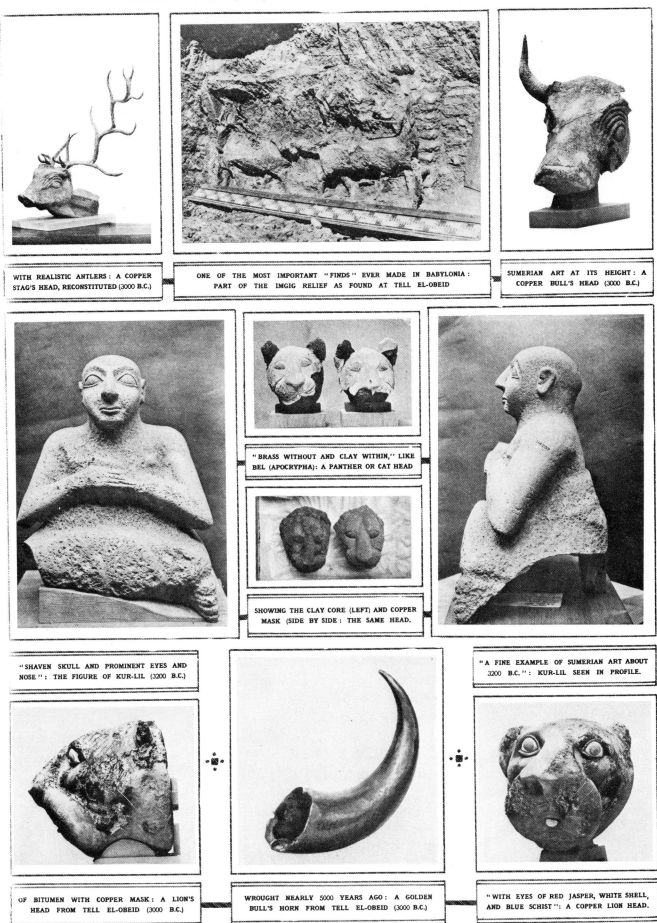

WITH REALISTIC ANTLERS: A COPPER STAG'S HEAD, RECONSTITUTED (3000 B.C.)

ONE OF THE MOST IMPORTANT "FINDS" EVER MADE IN BABYLONIA: PART OF THE IMGIG RELIEF AS FOUND AT TELL EL-OBEID

SUMERIAN ART AT ITS HEIGHT: A COPPER BULL'S HEAD (3000 B.C.)

"BRASS WITHOUT AND CLAY WITHIN," LIKE BEL (APOCRYPHA): A PANTHER OR CAT HEAD

SHOWING THE CLAY CORE (LEFT) AND COPPER MASK (SIDE BY SIDE: THE SAME HEAD.

"SHAVEN SKULL AND PROMINENT EYES AND NOSE": THE FIGURE OF KUR-LIL (3200 B.C.)

"A FINE EXAMPLE OF SUMERIAN ART ABOUT 3200 B.C.": KUR-LIL SEEN IN PROFILE.

OF BITUMEN WITH COPPER MASK: A LION'S HEAD FROM TELL EL-OBEID (3000 B.C.)

WROUGHT NEARLY 5000 YEARS AGO: A GOLDEN BULL'S HORN FROM TELL EL-OBEID (3000 B.C.)

"WITH EYES OF RED JASPER, WHITE SHELL, AND BLUE SCHIST": A COPPER LION HEAD.

79 *Sculptures found in and around the temple at Tell el-Obeid*

to speak of the original heads. They are now exhibited in the British Museum, with the fragments of their copper masks (if they can so be called). Luckily, the cat-heads have retained their copper covering almost intact; and the copper head of one of the stags has been put together, as an earnest of what it is hoped it may be possible to achieve in the case of the Imgig relief. In this case the heads of the stags are far better works of art than their bodies, which are very crudely executed. The heads of the bulls are amongst the finest works of Sumerian art known. The bodies of the beasts were made of copper plates rudely fastened with nails to a wooden core.

Other objects of interest were found with these – a golden bull's horn; mosaic pillars made of tesserae of red and black stone and mother-of-pearl, fastened with copper wire into bitumen laid over a wooden core; and rosettes, for insertion into walls, of pottery with petals of red, white, and black stone.

The early date of these objects would be evident from their style even had we not found with them two inscribed stone statues, of which one is perfect, the other but a torso. The latter has a complete inscription in the most archaic cuneiform characters, recording its dedication by a certain Kur-Lil, Doorkeeper of the Temple of Erech. The perfect figure is a fine example of early Sumerian art of about the time of Ur-Nina, about 3200 B.C., with the shaven skull and prominent eyes and nose characteristic of its style.

May 6, 1922

WORKMEN'S MODEL DWELLINGS OF 3000 YEARS AGO:
Excavations at Tell el-Amarna

By C. Leonard Woolley

Akhenaten, who as a boy ascended the throne of Egypt early in the fourteenth century before Christ, was a religious reformer who tried to impose a new-fangled monotheism upon a country where gods were even more plentiful than usual. Unable, at the old capital, Thebes, to avoid the painful sight of temples and monuments dedicated to the faith he had forsworn, he left it and built for himself a huge new capital on uncontaminated ground at Tell el-Amarna; and here, while the neglected Empire went to rack and ruin, he devoted himself to the worship of the One God symbolised by the disc of the Sun. Only for about twenty years did the dreamer enjoy his retreat; then he died or was killed; his mushroom city was laid under a curse by the priests of the orthodox faith; the Court returned to Thebes; the merchants and the artisans drifted away; and soon over the deserted and plundered houses the wind heaped up the sand which was to preserve them for the spade and camera of the modern archaeologist.

Two miles behind Akhenaten's city, in the cliffs of the high desert, lie the half-finished rock tombs of his courtiers; and in front of the tombs, in a sandy valley, we found the compound where lived the workmen employed in excavating them. It was not the normal Egyptian village, grown up haphazard by degrees, but a settlement built to order on the regular lines of a scheme of model dwellings for the working classes. We know from Theban records that the tomb-quarriers were a rough lot, given to riots and strikes, and so it was perhaps not merely for the convenience of having them close to their job that they were housed, not in Akhetaten itself, but out here in the barren desert, and that the settlement was walled all round and had but two small gates, and that there were sentry-boxes along the road leading to the city. Yet these people, though under a certain discipline, were not slaves, but free Egyptian workmen, who lived with their wives and families, enjoying quite as much comfort as those of their class elsewhere – far more than falls to the lot of the modern Egyptian fellahin.

The compound was an exact square, sub-divided into two unequal parts practically independent of each other. Through it from front to back ran straight narrow streets joined by cross-roads at either end, of which the front one just inside the main gate was almost wide enough to be called a square. All the houses except one, the overseer's, were of the same size and built precisely on the same plan; each had four ground floor rooms, a front hall, a central living-room, a bedroom and another small back room, which was either kitchen or staircase or both, and either in this back room or against the end of the front hall there was a flight of stairs leading up to the roof. In ancient as in modern Egypt the flat roof played an important part in the domestic economy, and though these houses were really built with only one storey, yet, as a great deal of the women's work was done on the roof, most householders would put up there some kind of a shelter, some a mere awning of poles and canvas, some a more permanent structure of wattle and daub, and at least one indulgent husband provided his wife with a regular summer-house, whose walls were gaily painted with papyrus patterns and religious texts.

The front rooms on the ground floor served all sorts of purposes. Here we found remains of the looms on which the women wove while their husbands were out at work; here the men kept their tools – the big wooden mallets, picks, adzes, and paint brushes; or, in their spare time,

80 *Portrait of Mr. Flinders Petrie (see p. 87 and later)*

made stone rings and vases, using a bronze drill worked with a bow. If there was no proper kitchen at the back of the house, then it is in the front room that we find the fireplace and the railed-off patch of smooth floor where the grain was picked over and the dough kneaded for bread-making. Here, too, the animals were brought in at night, for we came upon their tethering-stones let into the floor and the stone troughs for their watering. Donkeys – and most men would own a donkey – were often put at night into the little cupboard under the front stairs; but otherwise – or perhaps that was only in the daytime – might be left tied up in the street. We see outside the front door a brick manger having in one side a recess across which runs a stick embedded in the brickwork; and in one case find the fibre tethering-rope still fast about the stick. Next to the manger, set in a circular stone base, was the great round-bottomed earthenware jar which held the family's water supply, refilled daily by the girls, who carried the water on their heads up from the city wells or from the yet more distant Nile.

The central room was the main room of the house – the "best parlour" – and here custom imposed a respectable uniformity. A post in the middle supported the roof, which was rather higher than that of the rest of the house, so as to allow of little windows near the ceiling to let light in and smoke out. The walls were often faced with plain mud, as in the other rooms; but often, too, they were white-washed, and sometimes even decorated with coloured flower-friezes or figure designs in black and white. Decoration might be a matter of taste, but the general arrangements were quite stereotyped. Along one or two sides ran a low brick divan on which would be spread mats and pillows; here one sat with one's guests to talk or eat, and here at night slept those members of the family who were not provided for elsewhere; in front of this was a round hearth for a charcoal fire, with a hob at one side, where the saucepan was set to keep warm; and against the wall, in a shallow stone bath or over a vase buried rim-deep in the floor, stood a big jar of water for drinking and for the washing of hands. Flat stones, round or oblong, served as tables; and there were semi-circular three-legged stone stools or low wooden chairs with rush seats; beyond this there was no furniture at all. In the bedrooms there was even less; some people boasted a proper bedstead of wood with a cord mattress, but generally one spread one's bedding out on a low brick platform, or, more simply still, on the floor – which is just what one does today.

In the kitchen there was always a bread-oven wherein flat loaves were baked in rough clay platters, a small box-range for charcoal, one or two mud bins, and a railed-off place with a smooth floor into which was let a stone mortar where the wheat was bruised with a long wooden pestle for porridge.

November 11, 1922

WHERE GREEKS ONCE RULED IN INDIA:
Excavations at Taxila

By Sir John Marshall, Director-General of Archaeology in India

Like Bactria, the "Mother of Cities", Taxila is of immemorial antiquity; and in the days of her greatness was a meeting-place of many nations, of strange tongues, and of diverse creeds. The very name of "Taxila" is suggestive, for it is the Graecised form of the Indian "Takshasila", coined first by the soldiers of Alexander the Great, and it seems to conjure up visions of that clash of East and West which recurred time after time in the plains of the Panjab; of the conquering might of Darius, who annexed Taxila to his Persian Empire; of the Macedonian King refreshing his troops in this city ere he set out against the redoubtable Porus; and of Seleucus Nikator thrust back and defeated by the Mauryan Chandragupta. A generation later the pendulum swings back from East to West. Demetrius, the son-in-law of Antiochus the Great, appears on the scene from Bactria; and, after him, a line of Greek Princes who ruled Taxila for more than a century. Then come more invaders from the West – Scythians and Parthians – who counted among their rulers the powerful Azes and Gondophares, familiar from the legends of St. Thomas the Apostle. And following them (in the middle of the first

81 *Greek god Dionysus: a head in silver repoussé. This and other objects found at Taxila illustrate the Greek influence on its art and culture*

brought to the light of day. Curiously enough, among the objects found in its ruins was a broken vase of Greek design with the head of Alexander himself embossed upon its surface; not that it is suggested that this was a relic left behind by one of his soldiers, but it is, at any rate, a significant souvenir of the effect produced by his conquests. The houses of this city are strikingly irregular in plan and built of rough rubble; but they are the earliest examples of their kind that have been unearthed in the Panjab, and their interest is further heightened by some very singular features – notably by the presence of certain altar-like pillars in some of the rooms, the precise purpose of which has yet to be determined; and also of "soak pits" or blind wells for disposing of surplus water and sewage. . . .

century A.D.) the still stranger Kushans. . . . Then, last of all, the White Huns, who rivalled the hordes of Attila himself for cruelty and destruction, and were responsible for the final overthrow of Taxila. In all India there was no city of antiquity, perhaps, which changed hands so many times or experienced greater vicissitudes of fortune – none, certainly, which could boast of the monuments and relics of so many nationalities. . . .

The original city is still buried deep beneath the Bhir Mound, and to what dim and remote past it is to be ascribed the spade has yet to determine. All that we know at present is that it and a second city also built upon its remains, had vanished from the site long ere the armies of Alexander appeared in India, for the city which was standing in the fourth century B.C. is the topmost of the three cities on the Bhir Mound. This is the one which is described by Alexander's historians, and the one which – after two thousand years – is again being

82 *Clay relief baked into terracotta when Huns burnt the Jaulian monastery at Taxila*

The next city, now known as Sirkap, was built by the Bactrian Greeks, a little to the north-east of old Taxila, and on the other side of the Tamra stream. A century later it was destroyed and rebuilt by their successors, the Scythians, and

83 Greek peripteral temple near Taxila

again rebuilt by the Parthians. Little has yet been done to explore the Scythic and Greek strata; but a large area of the Parthian city has been exposed to view, and the visitor can now climb over walls and bastions, walk through its ancient streets, and study the plans and construction of its buildings. One of these, more than three hundred feet in width and depth, and more solidly built than the rest, was probably the palace of the Parthian ruler, and is of special interest for the resemblance it bears to the palace of the Assyrian Sargon at Khorsabad. Of the smaller houses, some belonged, as their contents show, to Jaina occupants; others to Buddhists; others, no doubt, to Fire-worshippers or to Hindus. Though built mainly of rubble, they are stronger and more regularly aligned than the houses in the older city, and are characterised by other striking differences also. One of these is the absence of doorways giving access to the interior on the lowest floor, the reason for this anomaly being that the chambers now visible served as cellars or *tahkhanas*

entered by stairways from above. This peculiarity is alluded to in Philostratus, who remarks that the houses of this city, when viewed from the outside, appeared to possess one storey only, but on entering them you find another series of chambers beneath. Another curious feature of these Parthian houses is the extent of the accommodation provided in them – far greater than any single family could have required. Possibly they served as tenements for several families; but it is more likely that this particular quarter of the city was the University quarter (for Taxila was the greatest University town in ancient India), and that these were the houses of the professors and their pupils, who would certainly need more accommodation than could be found in any ordinary dwelling. . . .

Apart from these excavations within the cities, much has been done also to explore the isolated sites outside the walls. One of these, a lofty mound in a commanding position outside the north gate of Sirkap, has proved to contain a fine Ionic temple built probably for fire-worship *(Figure 83)*. In plan it resembles a Greek peripteral temple, but the usual peristyle is replaced at the sides and back of this temple by a wall pierced with large windows, and, instead of a chamber between the sanctuary and the *opisthodomos*, there is in this temple a solid tower rising like an Assyrian *Ziggurat*, in the middle of the temple. The columns of the front porch are of Ionic design, though not fluted, and they are constructed in all respects like those in Greece or Western Asia. It is not unlikely that this is the temple described by Philostratus where Appollonius and his companion Damis awaited the permission of the Parthian King to enter the city, and where they saw hanging on the walls of the shrine the brazen tablets portraying the battles of Porus and Alexander.

December 9, 1922

THE GREAT "FIND" IN THE VALLEY OF THE KINGS

Last week, Lord Carnarvon *(Figure 84)* and Mr. Howard Carter revealed what has been described as promising "the most sensational Egyptological discovery of the century" – the finding of the complete funeral paraphernalia of King Tutankhamen, of the Eighteenth Dynasty, and other objects of priceless value and the utmost importance. The achievement is the result of nearly sixteen years of patient labour on the part of Lord Carnarvon and his brilliant assistant, Mr. Howard Carter. As *The Times* had it, in a remarkably interesting account: "At last the dogged perseverance of Mr. Carter, his thoroughness, above all his *flair* were rewarded by the discovery, where the royal necropolis of the Theban Empire was situated, directly below the tomb of Rameses VI, of what looked like a *cache*." After covering up the site, he telegraphed to Lord Carnarvon to come out from England. On his arrival, the search was continued. It revealed, as we have said, an unrivalled store of treasures! . . . The great discovery by Lord Carnarvon and Mr. Howard Carter of the complete funeral equipment of the Egyptian King Tutankhamen, has created an immense sensation in the world of archaeology. The chambers were found immediately beneath the tomb of Rameses VI. The contents, which included a royal throne – the first ever discovered – couches, bedsteads, chairs, chariots and alabaster vases, were so numerous and important that the chambers were temporarily walled up again until adequate arrangements

84 The Earl of Carnarvon

could be made for their clearance. A third chamber discovered, but not entered yet, is almost certainly the King's actual tomb. Tutankhamen succeeded the "heretic" Pharaoh, Akhenaten (originally Amenhotep IV) one of whose daughters he married; abandoned the new sun-worship which Akhenaten had introduced; and reverted to the ancient cult of Amen-Ra. None of the new finds has yet been photographed.

December 16, 1922

THE HERETIC PHARAOH'S PRIME MINISTER AND HIS HOUSE:
Another great Egyptian 'find'

By C. Leonard Woolley, formerly Director of the Egypt Exploration Society's Expedition to Tell el-Amarna, and now Director of the British Museum Expedition in Mesopotamia

In *The Illustrated London News* for May 6 last, I described the workmen's dwellings at Tell el-Amarna. At the other end of the social scale came the mansion of the Prime Minister of the Empire, which was discovered by the Egypt Exploration Society last winter in the main city of Akhetaten.

All the wealthier houses stood in their own grounds. A gateway from the road led into a garden round which were ranged blocks of buildings, servants' quarters, stables, granaries, and bread-ovens, and in the middle was a small kiosk, half summer-house and half chapel, and a deep well which was the private water supply. The outbuildings of the Prime Minister's house, which was only found at the close of the season, have not yet been excavated, but the house itself is completely cleared of sand and rubbish.

Like all the rest, it is solidly built of mudbrick on an artificial platform some two feet high, above which the walls were found standing up to six feet. A broad flight of shallow brick steps led up to the front door, on the stone jambs were inscribed the name and titles of the owner. Through a columned lobby and a small second antechamber, one passed into the North Loggia, a long room with a low roof supported by eight wooden columns resting on stone bases, and with big windows looking over the garden, and open in summer to the cool north winds; the walls were white except that the door and window-frames were painted with bands of colour; the floor was painted red and yellow. Small rooms opened out of this at either end; to the east were three chambers, probably bedrooms for guests, and opposite to them a room with cupboards where perhaps was stored the bedding for the guests' use. From the North Loggia three doors led into the main reception-room; a coloured restoration has been made which attempts to show what it looked like when found and before it fell into ruins.

Four columns upheld the lofty roof, and by these was set a portable hearth or brazier; the raised divan was railed in with a low brick screen; the place for ablutions was a raised platform built of and backed with stone slabs, railed round and having a depression in the centre for the great water-jar, painted red and blue, such as we found in many houses. Of course, the movable furniture had all been carried off when the house was deserted, and we have to imagine the carved and gilded chairs, the

X-legged tables, rugs and cushions, which once covered the white-washed floor; but fallen fragments of plaster enabled us to restore faithfully in the drawing the original blue ceiling, the flower friezes high up on the white walls, and the coloured bands round the door frames. Better preserved was the niche, or recess, seen in the south wall; its frame was painted crimson and bore a yellow inscription giving the titles of the Premier, and, in the middle, on a yellow panel set against the red ground, was a picture of the King worshipping the sun's disc and part of the hymn written by Pharaoh in praise of his God. The doorway to the inner reception-room was of stone painted yellow, whereon blue hieroglyphs reiterated the dignities of the owner. The small, stone windows and the green capitals of the columns are restored in our coloured drawing from examples found elsewhere in the town ruins.

Out of the reception-room opened (on the west) a second columned loggia, perhaps a sitting-out place for the colder weather, a flight of brick stairs leading to the upper floor, a bed-room passage, and the inner reception-room (on the south). The latter lay in the centre of the more private part of the mansion; it was flanked by big cupboards wherein one could still trace the wide shelves that had held the household stores, and in the south-east and south-west corners of the building were the bed-rooms of the master and mistress of the house. Each of these has at one end a slightly recessed brick dais, whereon stood the bedstead, and each is provided with its own bath-room and lavatory.

Unluckily these last have been badly ruined, and to illustrate their original character one must turn to other houses; there we see the shallow stone douche-bath, with its overflow basin, the facing of stone slabs that protected the brick wall from wet, and the low platform on which the servant stood to pour water over the crouching bather; while in the lavatory we find, on a raised brick base with central channel, the brick supports for the wooden seat of the earth-closet; certainly no native house in modern Egypt would show so up-to-date a sanitary installation!

The reception-rooms rose to the full height of the house, but over the back rooms there was a second storey, similar in plan, and fallen column-bases prove that on the upper floor there were columned galleries corresponding to the north and west loggias; of the use of these we know nothing, but we must suppose that the whole top storey was reserved for the private needs of the family.

Nekht, the owner of the house, was, according to his inscriptions, originally the Overseer of Public Works, so that probably he was responsible for the erection of most of the royal and state buildings of Akhetaten, perhaps himself the builder. To a King in whose eyes the Empire counted for little and the new capital for everything, this must have made him a very important person; and when, late in Akhenaten's reign, his chief minister fell into disgrace (as is shown by defacement of his memorials), it was only natural that Nekht should step into his shoes, and hardly less natural that in his inscriptions he should give his title of Overseer precedence over the theoretically much more honourable one of Grand Vizier, a subtle flattery of his royal master's wrongheadedness. His next politic act was to elaborate his name to Nekht-pa-Aten, thus identifying himself with the service of Aten, the One God; and he started excavating for himself a tomb alongside those of other courtiers in the cliffs of the sacred valley where alone the soul of the good Aten-worshipper could find peace. But soon Akhenaten died, his new monotheism went out of favour, and his new capital was abandoned and accursed. The Prime Minister was not one to stand out against a popular movement; work on his tomb stopped before the first chamber was fully dug, and his fine house was left to fall to ruin; he must have gone back to Thebes with the rest; and, as there was plenty of work to be done restoring the temples of the old religion, we may imagine him, with his name changed again, back at his old business and doing very well!

85 *An imaginative scene by A. Forestier depicting Tutankhamen, a 3000-year-old Pharoah "coming forth into the day"*

86 *Lady Allenby and Mr. Carter emerging after a visit to Tutankhamen's tomb*

December 16, 1922

TUTANKHAMEN

The offical opening of the tomb, or funeral chambers, of King Tutankhamen, found by the Earl of Carnarvon and Mr. Howard Carter in the Valley of the Kings, took place on November 29. Before the opening, Lord Carnarvon's daughter, Lady Evelyn Herbert, entertained a large party to luncheon in the valley, among the guests being Lady Allenby *(Figure 86)* and the Governor of Kena Province, Abdel Aziz Bey Yehia, who had given invaluable assistance in guarding the treasures. . . .

The Earl of Carnarvon has given a thrilling account (in *The Times*) of the great discovery made by him and Mr. Howard Carter in the Valley of the Kings, near Luxor, and their first entrance into the chambers. "We again reached a sealed door, or wall, bearing the same seals as the former one. . . . I asked Mr. Carter to take out a few stones and have a look in. After a few minutes this was done. He pushed his head partly into the aperture. With the help of a candle, he could dimly discern what was inside. A long silence followed, until I said, I fear in somewhat trembling tones, 'Well, what is it?' 'There are some marvellous objects here', was the welcome reply. Having given up my place to my daughter, I myself went to the hole and I could with difficulty restrain my excitement. . . .

87 *Lord Carnarvon, Lady Evelyn Herbert and Mr. Howard Carter (with candle) making their first inspection of the outer chamber of Tutankhamen's tomb. Drawing by A. Forestier*

We enlarged the hole and Mr. Carter managed to scramble in – the chamber is sunk two feet below the bottom passage – and then, as he moved around with a candle, we knew we had found something absolutely unique and unprecedented.''

December 23, 1922

We despatched Mr. Forestier to Marseilles to meet Lord Carnarvon on his way home, and the latter very kindly supplied the material for the above drawing *(Figure 87)*. He shows his first inspection of the outer chamber of King Tutankhamen's tomb, in company with his daughter, Lady Evelyn Herbert, and his colleague Mr. Howard Carter, the actual discoverer. A glimmer through the side wall on the left indicates the hole by which they clambered in ''by the uncertain light of a candle'', writes Lord Carnarvon in an article, ''a wonderful sight was exposed to our excited eyes. . . . The first thing that one noticed against the wall facing the door were three gigantic carved gilt wood beds, the ends of the beds having carved heads.'' (The drawing shows the middle one, with the head of Typhon, and that on the right, with the head of Hathor, one of whose horns is piercing the planks of another simpler couch piled on top.) ''Beneath the central couch'' (continues Lord Carnarvon) ''were heaped 20 or 30 white wooden boxes containing mummified legs of mutton, ducks, geese, venison, and the like. . . . Beneath another bed (the left-hand one unseen in the background)

88 *The ante-chamber of Tutankhamen's tomb: gilded couches and chariots and a gold and silver throne*

89 *Sealed doorway in the ante-chamber wall believed to conceal King Tutankhamen's mummy: with guardian statues and funerary furniture in position as found*

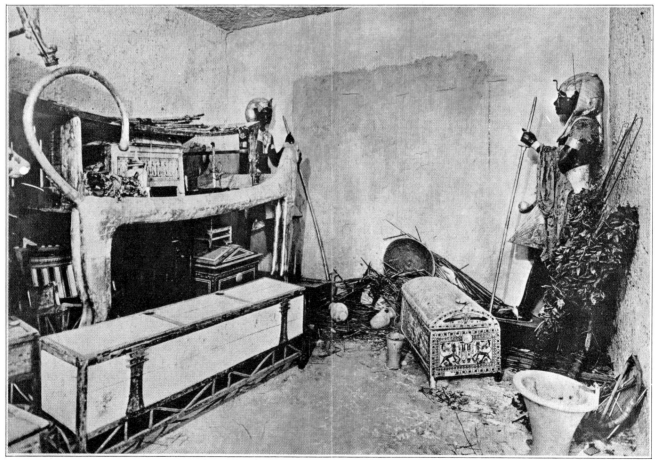

was the throne of the King. . . . We found four chariot bodies in gilt wood inlaid with semi-precious stones. The wheels are in a heap on one side, while the poles are stacked against the wall *(Figure 88)*. . . . At the northern end are two life-other a gilt mace. . . . Between the two statues (we found) a walled and plastered-up entrance. In all probability behind that wall we shall come to the funerary chamber of King Tutan-khamen.'' In front of the couches are some long

90 One of two life-size statues of King Tutankhamen found standing on either side of the sealed door to the tomb

sized portrait statues of the King in bitumenised wood *(Figure 89, and Figure 90 shows one in more detail:)* On his brow is the crown of Egypt; around his neck is the gilt collar, emblem of royalty; he is clad in the 'shenti', a sort of stiff kilt. In one hand he holds a long gilt stick; in the boxes. One, opened by Lord Carnarvon, was full of roses, beautiful but very fragile after their 3000 years' burial. Numerous other boxes, and exquisite alabaster vases, were scattered about the chamber.

1923

Although this year was dominated by Tutankhamen (see below) there were other major discoveries made and reported in the paper's pages. The extracts show what was taking place at Mycenae in Greece and Chichen Itza in Central America, while other important articles covered the Pyramids of Meroe, the find of Roman silver at Traprain Law in Scotland, Ur of the Chaldees and new excavations at Pompeii.

February 24, 1923

THE FIRST UNRIFLED TOMB OF A PHARAOH:
Tutankhamen's sepulchre

By Professor Percy E. Newberry, the famous Egyptologist, Honorary Reader in Egyptian Art, and ex-Professor of Egyptology, at Liverpool University; formerly in charge of the Archaeological Survey of Egypt

The discovery of the Royal Tomb at Thebes is unquestionably the most interesting "find" that has ever been made in Egypt. Never before in the history of archaeological exploration has an unrifled royal tomb been found; it may be said, therefore, that every feature of this wonderful discovery is new. From the other royal sepulchres in the Valley of the Tombs of the Kings much was already known about the funeral paraphernalia of a Pharaoh; but every tomb that had been found up to November of last year had been plundered in ancient times. All the objects brought to light from these rifled sepulchres had been stripped of their gold and other metal coverings, and they had been wilfully smashed to pieces and their fragments scattered about the floors. The chief value, therefore, of Lord Carnarvon's and Mr. Howard Carter's discovery is that it reveals to us a king's tomb, with all its magnificent furniture complete and in position, arranged just as the priests had left it when they sealed up the Pharaoh's sepulchre. That, to the archaeologists, is the most important fact that is revealed by the "find".

The contents of the tomb make us realise the vast amount of wealth that at one period was buried in the subterranean chambers of the desolate Valley of the Tombs of the Kings. Certainly twenty-five monarchs were interred here, and Tutankhamen was one of the least important of them. His funeral furnishings, wonderful as they really are, probably could not have compared with the funeral outfits of such mighty Kings as Thotmes III, Amenhotep III, the "Magnificent", or Rameses "the Great". What a wealth of treasure the huge tomb of Seti I must have contained. . . .

The sarcophagus and the coffin with the body of King Tutankhamen within it have apparently not yet been disclosed, but they are certainly within the great shrine, which is said almost to fill the chamber opened on the 16th inst. This shrine is unique. It seems to be composed of a framework of wood which holds blue-glazed faience tiles within it, and upon these tiles are ornaments and insertions of gold. On one side of this shrine or tabernacle are double doors opening outwards. Inside appears to be a canopy or pall, of some fabric studded with discs of gold. Probably "nested" inside this are three more shrines, and then the sarcophagus. An ancient papyrus, now preserved in the Egyptian Museum at Turin, gives us the plan of

91 Tutankhamen attracts tourists who wait eagerly for the removal of the king himself

the sarcophagus chamber of Rameses IV. The pink granite sarcophagus was enclosed in five shrines, the posts of a canopy being shown between the outer shrine and the next. What the inscriptions on the Tutankhamen shrines tell we have not yet heard. Just within the first tabernacle the explorers found a number of scarabs; these are possibly Tutankhamen's own personal seals, for it was customary to bury personal seals with the deceased. The occurrence of malachite seals is particularly interesting, for no others are known of this material.

In a chamber leading out of the east side of the one containing the tabernacle is the Canopic jar box which Lord Carnarvon describes as "one of the most wondrous objects that has ever been unearthed, either in Egypt or elsewhere". In this box will certainly be found the four Canopic jars which contain the viscera of the Pharaoh, for before a body was embalmed, the viscera,

heart, etc., were taken out of the body, wrapped up in linen bands, and placed in a Canopic jar. Each jar contained a special part of the body, and was placed under the protection of a special deity. . . .

The sledge found near the sarcophagus was undoubtedly the one upon which the coffin of the king was dragged to the Necropolis, and the life-size Jackal Standard must have been the one carried by the Anubis priest in the funeral procession. On the walls of the tombs of the Nobles at Thebes there are many paintings which represent funeral processions, and it would be possible to draw up a catalogue of the objects shown being carried to the tomb by the priests that would tally to some degree with the list of objects brought to light in Tutankhamen's tomb. What the boxes contain no one yet knows, and it is fruitless to conjecture.

March 24, 1923

THE "EGYPT" OF AMERICAN ANTIQUITY:
The great Maya ruins found buried in tropical forests

By Dr. Sylvanus Griswold Morley, of the Carnegie Institution of Washington, the Chief Authority on Maya Hieroglyphics

On the continental bridge, midway between North and South America, there flourished during the first six centuries of the Christian Era the most brilliant aboriginal civilisation of the New World in pre-Columbian times – namely that developed by the Maya Indians of Central America.

The general region occupied by this remarkable people . . . comprises roughly southern Mexico, northern Guatemala, the western edge of the Honduras, and the entire Crown Colony of British Honduras; but the heart, the intellectual and aesthetic centre, the area of maximum development, was what is now the Department or Province of Peten, Guatemala.

Fifteen centuries ago this was probably one of the most densely populated areas on the face of the globe. . . . Now this region, formerly so densely populated, is covered by a vast and uninhabited tropical forest, which has over-

92 A Maya counterpart to the pyramids of Egypt: the chief temple at Chichen Itza

whelmed these cities, literally tearing their temples and palaces block from block with its mighty roots, and reducing these once stately structures to shapeless mounds of fallen stone and earth locked in the embrace of its giant trees.

There are no permanent settlements, and the only people who explore these trackless forests are the chicle-bleeders – who are in search of the gum of the chico-zapote tree; *i.e.* "chicle", from which chewing gum is made – and the archaeologists. Strange bedfellows these, half-castes and scientists, and yet if it were not for the former, the latter could not carry on their investigations in this region.

It is the chicle-bleeder . . . who carries out first notice of the discovery of new ancient cities from time to time as he pushes farther and farther back into the interior in search of chicle. . . .

To stimulate this purely casual and side industry of the chicle-bleeder, the writer has been offering for the past five years rewards of twenty-five dollars each for the location of new ruined sites where there are hieroglyphic monuments, and this expedient has already resulted in the discovery of several large new cities and many smaller ones. . . .

The ancient Maya have been called the "Egyptians of the New World", and not inaptly so, since they excelled all other native American peoples in architecture, sculpture, astronomy, chronology and mathematics; and they were, moreover, the only American aborigines who developed a system of hieroglyphic writing.

In architecture and sculpture they were pre-eminent. They reared great pyramids of stone, sometimes 150 feet in height, and on the lofty summits they built their principal sanctuaries *(Figure 92)*. Arranged around courts and plazas at the bases of these pyramids, were the dwellings of the rulers, priests and nobles, also built of stone and elevated on terraces and platforms. The houses of the humbler folk were made of saplings roofed with palm-thatch, and literally stretched out for miles around these religious and civic centres in every direction.

93 *Seventh-century Maya sculpture: a priest with a small jaguar*

Sculpture was largely confined to the embellishment of large stone monuments which were erected at the ends of successive 1800-day periods called "hotuns", around the principal courts and plazas. The fronts were carved with representations of deities, rulers, and priests *(Figure 93)*, engaged in various ceremonies, the backs and sides being carved with hieroglyphic inscriptions. The façades of the principal buildings *(Figure 94)* were also sculptured with geometric and naturalistic designs, both in stone and stucco, and were then painted in a variety of colours – red, green, blue, yellow, brown, black, and white.

Their knowledge of astronomy was extra-ordinary, equalling if not excelling that of the ancient Egyptians and Babylonians. They devised a mathematical system which employed two different kinds of numbers, the so-called "bar-and-dot" numerals, which may be likened to our own Roman notation, and the "head numerals" (different types of the human head) which may be compared with our Arabic notation.

94 *The façade of a Maya palace at Chichen Itza*

With this numerical system, the Maya recorded the dates of their principal events in a chronology which in some respects was far more accurate than our own, since by means of it they were able to differentiate any given day from every other within a period of more than 370,000 years – a truly amazing feat for any chronological system, ancient or modern. They had reached a conception of zero as a mathematical quantity, and devised three different symbols to express the same – an achievement upon which all higher mathematics necessarily rest – before the birth of Christ, probably half a millennium before its invention in India, and fully a millennium before its introduction into Europe by way of Spain.

But, one may well ask, what has happened to this great civilisation? What calamity so catastrophic as to have caused the utter abandonment of such great centres of population, where such prodigious labours have been freely expended? Why, to-day, does the desolation of a vast luxuriant tropical forest replace these former teeming haunts of men? The answer to this question, while by no means definitely settled, is, in the opinion of many who have studied the matter, including the writer, none other than that same plain homely fact which has stared us all so grimly in the face for the past seven years – namely, the high cost of living.

The Maya civilisation, briefly put, was based upon the cultivation of maize in a region of exceeding fertility; but their system of agriculture, unfortunately for them, was equally destructive. They did not cultivate as we understand the word; there was no turning of the soil, no ploughing, no harrowing, not even hoeing, and they used no fertiliser. Instead, they felled the bush at the end of the rainy season (January or February) and burned it at the end of the dry season (April or May), the maize being planted in holes made by sharply pointed sticks at the time of the first rains in May or June.

The following year any field planted the preceding season was allowed to rest, and another piece of the high bush was felled, burned, and planted; indeed they did not replant a cornfield until it had grown up into woody bush again, a matter of three or four, or even more, years.

Under this system of agriculture, much of the total area available for cultivation must necessarily have lain idle, awaiting the return of sufficient woody growth to warrant felling it again; but even this was not its most serious defect. Repeated burnings such as these encouraged the growth of perennial grasses, and if continued long enough would have transformed, and probably did transform, the whole region from forest into grasslands, open, rolling savannahs; and when, finally, the high bush ceased to exist, agriculture as practised by the ancient Maya came to an end, and the people had to move elsewhere to avoid extinction by starvation.

This is precisely the catastrophe which overtook this highly gifted people in the writer's opinion. By the end of the fifth century after Christ, it seems not improbable that the forest had been largely replaced in the vicinity of the principal cities by grasslands, and that already the problem of finding high bush sufficiently near by was becoming acute. The sixth century probably witnessed the beginning of a great exodus northward into Yucatan, and southwards into the highlands of Guatemala, where in these new environments the Maya experienced a cultural and economic rejuvenation; passed through a Renaissance, only to decline again in the fourteenth and fifteenth centuries, probably because of the very same cause, and finally to fall an easy prey to the shock of the Spanish Conquest in the early decades of the sixteenth century.

March 31, 1923

STAINED WITH AGAMEMNON'S BLOOD?
Bronze daggers from Mycenae

It is not asserted that any of the daggers here illustrated *(Plate 11, p. 89)* was the actual weapon with which Clytemnestra slew her lord, Agamemnon, in his bath. But such a suggestion would not be wholly fantastic or impossible, for the weapons were recently unearthed at Mycenae, where that historic murder was committed, and apparently belong to about the same period (1500 to 1200 B.C.) as the so-called Tombs of Clytemnestra and her paramour, Aegisthus, at Mycenae. These weapons came, however, from another part of the site, the newly discovered Kalkani cemetery, as mentioned by Mr. A. J. B. Wace in his article on another page. "Other treasures", he writes, "include a bronze dagger in excellent condition." Among the objects also are a wood-handled dagger, dagger-points, an ivory-handled knife, and part of a handle.

March 31, 1923

MYCENAE IN TUTANKHAMEN'S TIME:
British excavations
By Alan J. B. Wace, Director of the British School of Archaeology at Athens

The British School at Athens in its third campaign of excavation at Mycenae has been most successful. The palace on the summit of the Citadel has been re-examined and fully planned, with the result that it now appears, in spite of the heavy destruction it has undergone, to have been a large building with several storeys. From the south it is approached by a grand staircase, which was lit by a window, had two flights and three landings, and led up into an antechamber. Thence one could approach either the audience chamber (Room of the Throne) or go straight into the courtyard before the Great Hall. There was another entrance to the north-west, where there was a propylon flanked by a guard-room. This second entrance seems to have led more directly to the store-chambers and the private apartments, among which a tank-bath, lined with red stucco, was discovered. Local rumour declares this to be the scene of the murder of Agamemnon. This palace, built about 1400 B.C. – probably by the king who re-founded Mycenae, built the Lion Gate and the Cyclopean walls, and perhaps, also, the great domed tomb known as the Treasury of Atreus, for himself and his family – lies above the scanty remains of a still earlier palace. This latter was probably the residence of the earlier line of kings, called the Shaft-Grave Dynasty (about 1600 to 1500 B.C.) whose tombs were found by Schliemann in 1876. The later race of kings, the Tholos Tomb Dynasty (1500 to 1200 B.C.), probably were buried in the big domed or Tholos Tombs, built of mighty blocks of stone.

Nine of these tombs are known at Mycenae, and the British School has carefully re-examined them all and prepared careful plans and photographs. One of these tombs, now christened the Tomb of Aegisthus *(Figure 95)*, because it lies by the side of the Tomb of Clytemnestra, had never before been excavated. This is the largest of the first group, and probably was the tomb of one of the earlier kings of the dynasty. Its entrance passage, partly lined with rubble masonry, well packed with tough yellow clay, and partly cut in rock, is over seventy feet long and fifteen feet wide, and is well over twelve feet deep at the deepest point. The doorway was originally constructed of rubble masonry, packed with yellow clay; but at a later date a new façade of ashlar, worked in soft

95 *Digging in the Tomb of Aegisthus at Mycenae*

limestone, was placed in front to make the entrance more imposing, and the joints of this masonry and the older rubble-work were covered with white stucco. The dome itself, of which the peak had collapsed long ago, though it seems to have stood till 200 B.C. at least, was over forty feet in diameter and forty in height. The stone-work of its walls was ingeniously constructed, with an elaborate system of counter-weighting and wedging the stones that inclined inwards to make the dome. This shows that even at this early date Mycenaean engineers and architects had both imagination for drawing plans and the necessary knowledge for making calculations and construction. The dome had long since been plundered, but a quantity of vase-fragments of very good quality, including fragments of a series of large jars of the palace style, were found with some scraps of gold and ivory work.

Other work included the excavation of the fort or signal station on the summit of Mount Hagios Elias (2500 feet) whence the news of the fall of Troy might have been flashed by fire-signal to Mycenae below; and the excavation of a series of tombs in the newly discovered Kalkani cemetery. These tombs proved exceptionally rich, and, as they were all family tombs, had been in use for a long period. In one tomb, No. 529, over eighteen interments were found, dating from just before 1500 B.C. to 1300 B.C., or even later.

One remarkable fact is that the later members of the family, in burying their own dead, seemed to have had no scruples in sweeping aside, or even throwing outside, the bones and other relics of the earlier interments, and removing any valuables of their ancestors' which took their fancy. This accounts for the scarcity of precious objects in the tombs. One tomb, No. 518, had two chambers, the inner a small alcove, or charnel chamber, where the remains of the earlier interments could be swept together; and an outer chamber which had a bench on one side where a lamp was found *in situ*. Probably some kind of memorial rites for the dead were held here, and there are other indications that perhaps a sort of communion with the dead did take place. These sepulchres, with their dark chambers and narrow entrance passages, were perhaps regarded as entrances to the lower world, and would be, naturally, the place which the dead might revisit. It recalls to our mind Ulysses' descent to the lower world and conversation with the dead, as told by Homer.

This tomb, No. 518, yielded a magnificent series of vases, many of them copies in clay of metal originals. There was a splendid string of over 120 amber beads, including a very rare one engraved with the representation of a bull. Some small pieces of gold jewellery were found; a pomegranate bud pendant with delicate granulated work; a bead in the form of a chrysalis; and a gold ring. Six engraved seal stones – one with a very spirited bull-fighting scene, another with a wounded lion biting at a dart buried in its side, a third with a Mycenaean helmet, and three others showing representations of birds and a bull – besides other treasures, including a bronze dagger in excellent condition, and many fragments of ivory inlay from a wooden casket, were unearthed here....

Tomb 526 yielded two Egyptian scarabs of the Eighteenth Dynasty, which confirms the dating of the tombs already determined independently from other sources – perhaps the tomb of Tutankhamen will correspondingly yield some Mycenaean objects, which will give us yet another link in the chronological chain.

Lastly Tomb 523 (1350 to 1250 B.C.) produced a Hittite seal stone in steatite – the first Hittite object found in Greece. This shows that there was contact between Mycenae and the great civilisation of Asia Minor, and is one more piece of evidence that Homer's "Tale of Troy" was based on historical fact.

November 10, 1923

THE MOST BEAUTIFUL TABLEAU EVER FOUND IN EGYPT

We begin here the promised series of reproductions in colour *(pp. 90–93)* of the wonderful examples of ancient Egyptian art found in Tutankhamen's Tomb. As we have already announced, *The Illustrated London News* recently acquired, by arrangement with Mr. Howard Carter (co-discoverer of the tomb with the late Lord Carnarvon) the sole colour rights in everything connected with that epoch-making archaeological event. The autochrome photographs, in natural colours, are taken direct from the originals. To those who have not seen the actual objects, our pages thus afford the only means of appreciating the full glory of the treasures deposited in the tomb over three thousand years ago. Describing the throne panel, Mr. Howard Carter writes, in a note which he has kindly supplied to accompany our reproduction: "The panel is overlaid with heavy sheet gold and richly adorned with glass, faience, and coloured stone inlay. It is the chief glory of the throne, and there can be no hesitation in claiming it to be the most beautiful tableau that has ever been found in Egypt. The scene depicts one of the halls of the palace, a room decorated with flower-garlanded pillars, a frieze of royal cobras, and a dado of conventional 'recessed' panelling. Through a hole in the roof, the sun shoots down his life-giving protective rays. The King himself sits in an unconventional attitude upon a cushioned throne, his arm carelessly across its back. Before him stands the girlish figure of the Queen, putting, apparently, the last touches to his toilet. In one hand she holds a small jar of ointment, and with the other she gently anoints his shoulder, or adds a touch of perfume to his collar." *(Plate 13, p. 91).*

Interest in the treasures of Tutankhamen's Tomb has just been renewed by the resumption of work upon it for the winter season, during which it is expected that the actual mummy of the King will be found within the sarcophagus. The entrance to the tomb was closed last February, when the heavy iron gate, strengthened with great baulks of timber, was shut, and the whole pit containing the steps down to the doorway was filled up with 1700 tons of rock and earth. Eighty Egyptians were employed. Mr. Howard Carter and his assistant, Mr. Callender, with Mr. Harry Burton, the photographer, of the New York Metropolitan Museum, arrived at Luxor on October 17, to resume their activities. The native labourers first spent several days in levelling the ground outside the entrance to the neighbouring Tomb of Seti II, the workshop of the expedition. The arduous task of removing the 1700 tons of rubble from the entrance to Tutankhamen's tomb was completed by October 29, and Mr. Carter arranged to reopen the tomb on November 1, if the electric-light installation was ready by that date. It was pointed out that it would probably take some time to remove the first of the concentric tabernacles enclosing the sarcophagus in the inner sepulchre. The work will be extremely difficult, as there is little more than a foot of space between the shrine and the walls of the sepulchre, and less than three feet between its top and the ceiling. Besides the sepulchre, there are two other chambers still to be cleared of their contents. Of the objects in the ante-chamber, already cleared, perhaps the most wonderful is the King's coronation throne. . . . The entire throne is covered with sheet gold and richly inlaid with polychrome glass, faience and coloured stone. The legs are of feline form, surmounted with lions' heads of chased gold.

96 opposite *Tutankhamen's state chariot showing the head of the god Bes and part of the panel representing the king as a sphinx trampling on his foes*

1923-31

Tutankhamen: this discovery of the incredibly rich and virtually untouched tomb of a young and previously almost unknown Pharaoh was a landmark alike in the history of archaeology and in the development of The Illustrated London News. *In the first instance, it created a new public for archaeology. "King Tut" became a byword and debased Egyptian motifs appeared on every suburban lampshade and the general public became convinced (mistakenly) that this was what archaeology was about. More significantly and, fortunately, more permanently, archaeologists were recognised as important people, their objectives were more widely understood and received far greater support and understanding, and financial aid was much more readily available from public and private sources. As regards* The Illustrated London News, *the effect here was as striking. Here, an exclusivity of reports, shared with the London* Times, *and a national exclusivity of colour illustration of the finds established the paper as the great source of news of Tutankhamen, firmly fixing in the public mind that for popular but informed reports of archaeology* The Illustrated London News *was the* paper. *And, of course, it confirmed Bruce Ingram in his judgment of the part archaeology was to play in the make-up, present and future, of the paper. The public for archaeology now existed; the rôle of the paper was to hold it.*

In this task Tutankhamen played a major part for no less than nine years, in no less than twenty-two major articles, the last of which appeared on May 23, 1931, a great number of colour plates, countless

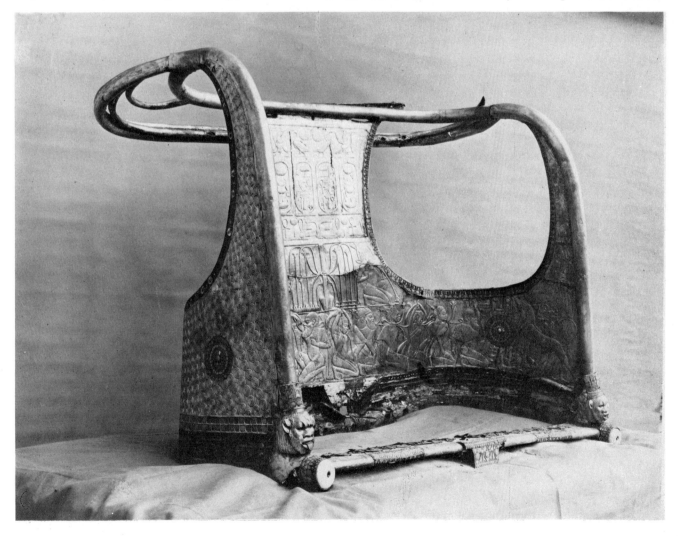

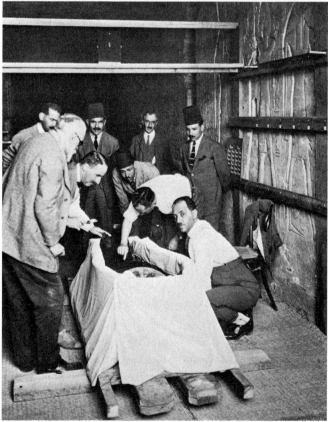

97 above *The great golden coffins of Tutankhamen: Mr. Howard Carter removing the dust of ages from the top of the second coffin lying inside the first*

98 left *Representing Tutankhamen in the form of Osiris; the upper portion of the third and innermost coffin, made of solid gold with precious stones*

99 right *The actual body of Tutankhamen: unwrapping the mummy*

black-and-white illustrations, and innumerable shorter items and cross-references. So great was the public hunger for news about Tutankhamen that much of this was inevitably repetitious, items being reported and described, on discovery, later with official black-and-white photographs, subsequently after restoration, then when published with colour reproductions and, sometimes, later still in the context of the whole discovery. For this reason, therefore, and also because the cream of the Treasures of Tutankhamen have been exhibited in several capitals in recent years with a consequent spate of publications about them, it has been decided to keep only the first dramatic reports of the discovery as extracts; and to compress the rest of the reports into a single narrative précis, as follows.

1923 was the first great Tutankhamen year, with the first photographs of objects in the tomb, a Special Egypt number of the paper (on February 24) – with no fewer than six articles on Pharaonic burials – and on November 23 the first colour plates of details from the coronation throne. 1924 opened with Howard Carter's quarrel with the Egyptian Government and the consequent closing of the tomb, but colour plates were available, and on January 12 appeared three colour plates – a Bes head and panels of the gold state chariot (Figure 96) and royal barges and objects from the outer and second shrines; and in the following week, five colour plates, covering the gold chariot and the first sight of the sarcophagus. 1925 was the year of Howard Carter's lecture on Tutankhamen to the Royal Institution with its account of the opening of the sarcophagus and this we reported with illustrations and colour plates covering the palace lamp, the gold coffin (head and shoulders), alabaster vases, the trumpet and other items. 1926 was a great year for colour. In February we reported the opening of the golden coffins (Figures 97, 98, 101) down to the mummified body, with later the same month a colour plate of the gold portrait mask of the king (Plate 12, p. 90). In July we reported the unwrapping of the mummy (Figures 99, 100), with descriptions of the personal jewellery and the innermost coffin (Figure 98), with colour plates of the gold diadem (Fig. 104, p. 201) and of daggers, including one of iron; and the article accompanying this was a résumé of Howard Carter's work during the last season. Later the same month we published a colour

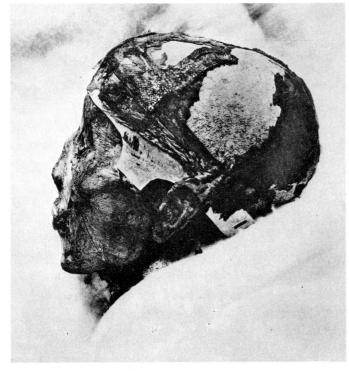

100 Tutankhamen: the face of the young Pharaoh uncovered after 3000 years

101 Showing the collarette of real flowers, the head of the inner gold anthropoid coffin, the inlaid eyes decomposed by the consecration unguents

102 *On guard in Tutankhamen's tomb: the jackal god Anubis*

103 *Canopic shrine guarded by tutelary goddesses in the store chamber of Tutankhamen's tomb*

plate of Tutankhamen's gold coffin. In 1927 there was no slackening in the outpouring of Tutankhamen's treasures. In January the contents of the storechamber were revealed for the first time, with pictures which included the protective goddesses round the Canopic chest (Figure 103), model ships (Fig. 105, p. 202), fans and sceptres. In February came the king's jewellery with an article on the disposition of the jewels in the mummy in accordance with the "Book of the Dead", with two pages of colour illustration. In April still more of the king's gold treasure, including statuettes of the king as Horus (Plate 15, p. 93), orders and collars, a view of the storechamber, an ivory fan, a statuette of the king in gold on a black leopard, a cow goddess with a golden head – with three pages of colour; and in July an article by Howard Carter describing the innermost recess of the tomb with three pages of colour, illustrating such things as slippers, palettes, mirrors, ear-rings and pectorals. The next year, 1928, was the year of the unveiling of the Canopic shrine and the opening of the Canopic chest, followed by colour pages of the funeral fleet of the king. In 1929, between July and October, we published a series of five articles by Howard Carter entitled "New Treasures from Tutankhamen's Tomb", the first being devoted to Royal hat-boxes, shirt-boxes, head-rests and a table-centre of alabaster with a funeral boat; the second to the king's play-box, fire-maker, footstools, gold bed, nursery stool and high-backed chair; the third to wine and unguent jars (Plate 14, p. 92), dalmatics and similar ceremonial robes; the fourth to gaming board and sticks, fans and a sceptre; and the fifth to bows, throwing-sticks, arrows, clubs, falchions, singlesticks and guards and shields. 1930 had nothing on Tutankhamen; but 1931, in May, carried an article on more treasures from the tomb, including a portrait head of the king emerging from a lotus, the ecclesiastical throne, a footstool with "the nine enemies" and statues from the secret recess.

Plate 19 above *The prehistoric civilisation of the Indus: a bearded head with interesting treatment of the hair*

Plate 20 left *Copper statuette of dancing girl found in the Indus valley*

193

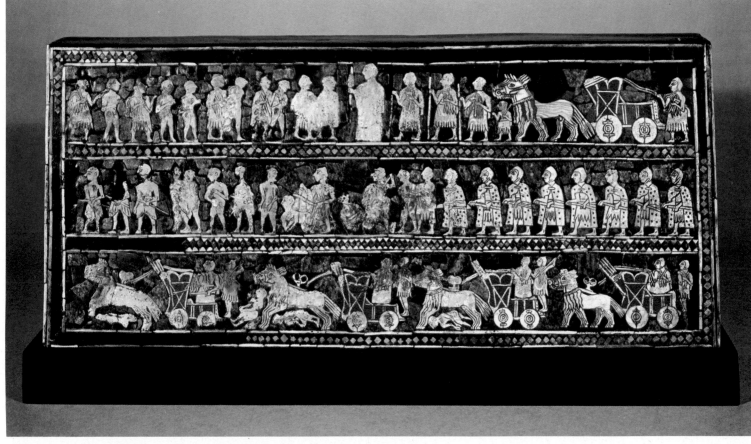

Plate 22 Shell mosaic inlay from Ur showing the Sumerian army

Plate 21 opposite *A bull's head in gold with beard (the*   195
attribute of deity) and hair made of lapis lazuli, discovered
in a king's grave at Ur

196

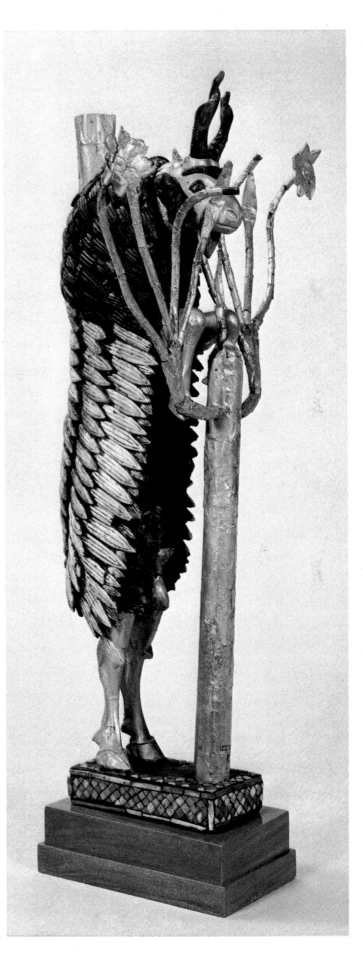

Plate 24 Ram caught in a thicket: a masterpiece of ancient Sumerian art in gold, shell and lapis lazuli found at Ur

Plate 23 opposite Queen Shub-ad's golden head-dress from Ur of the Chaldees reconstructed and placed on a head modelled over the cast of a nearly contemporary female Sumerian skull

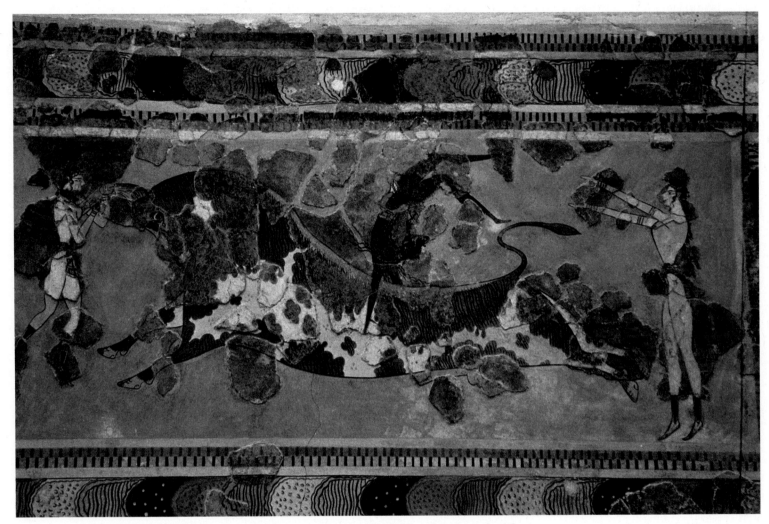

Plate 26 Minoan girls in the bull ring: a restored panel of a wall-painting showing one girl acrobat (left) grasping the horns for a somersault over the bull; another (right) waiting to catch the figure somersaulting on its back

Plate 25 opposite *The great bull relief in its original position above the Sea-Gate at Knossos*

Plate 27 *The throne room at Knossos with the fresco frieze of guardian griffins restored by M. Gilliéron* fils

104 opposite *Tutankhamen's gold diadem*

THE LATEST TUTANKHAMEN DISCOVERIES: A UNIQUE GOLD DIADEM.

PHOTOGRAPHS BY MR. HARRY BURTON, OF THE METROPOLITAN MUSEUM OF ART, NEW YORK. (WORLD COPYRIGHT STRICTLY RESERVED.)

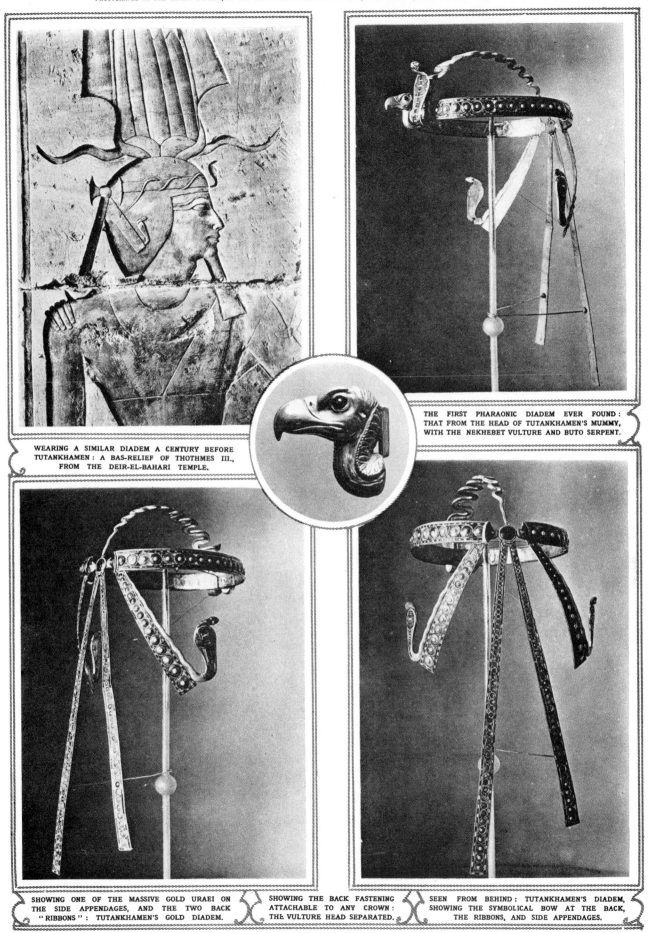

WEARING A SIMILAR DIADEM A CENTURY BEFORE TUTANKHAMEN: A BAS-RELIEF OF THOTHMES III., FROM THE DEIR-EL-BAHARI TEMPLE.

THE FIRST PHARAONIC DIADEM EVER FOUND: THAT FROM THE HEAD OF TUTANKHAMEN'S MUMMY, WITH THE NEKHEBET VULTURE AND BUTO SERPENT.

SHOWING ONE OF THE MASSIVE GOLD URAEI ON THE SIDE APPENDAGES, AND THE TWO BACK "RIBBONS": TUTANKHAMEN'S GOLD DIADEM.

SHOWING THE BACK FASTENING ATTACHABLE TO ANY CROWN: THE VULTURE HEAD SEPARATED.

SEEN FROM BEHIND: TUTANKHAMEN'S DIADEM, SHOWING THE SYMBOLICAL BOW AT THE BACK, THE RIBBONS, AND SIDE APPENDAGES.

105 For Tutankhamen's death voyage: a model ship

106 The cow goddess Meh-urit found in the store chamber of Tutankhamen's tomb

1924

Although Tutankhamen dominated this year, there were also major articles (from which extracts are given) on the first revelation of the Indus Valley civilisation by Sir John Marshall, and on the Ziggurat of Ur (with a coloured reconstruction of this classic "Tower of Babylon"); and other important articles by Dr. Thomas Gann on the Maya cities of Lubaantun and Tuluum.

January 12, 1924

TUTANKHAMEN:
The Sarcophagus revealed

It was announced on January 4 that Mr. Howard Carter had at last been able to open the doors of the remaining three shrines (which are "nested" one within another) and that two bore the seals of the Royal Necropolis. "With the opening of the final door", says the official message, "came an exciting moment, for, as the panels gradually swung outwards, there was revealed to the gaze of the spectators a stone sarcophagus, colossal in size, magnificent in workmanship, and beyond any question intact. . . . Within the first shrine is a second shrine with doors bolted, corded, and sealed with the clay seal of the Royal Necropolis. The seal is intact, just as it was when placed there 3270 years ago. . . . Between the doors of the two shrines lie or stand numbers of beautiful objects. Foremost amongst them is an alabaster vase mounted in silver and gold. There are two 'Hapi' (God of the Nile) figures, one on each side, crowned with the emblems of Upper and Lower Egypt, and holding, one in the right and the other in the left arm, the standards of Upper and Lower Egypt surmounted by Royal Cobras, and bearing the white crown of Upper Egypt and the Red Crown of Lower Egypt. On the lid of the vase is a figure of the goddess Mut in the form of a vulture. The vase is a most exquisite piece of work, the finest yet discovered, but unfortunately its contents, which are of some fatty nature, have caused the neck to burst. Beside it stands a cosmetic vase in calcite, upon the lid of which is a lion with a long red tongue protruding, and the sides of which are decorated. The vase has at either end Hathor columns. Leaning against the north-east corner within the outer shrine are a number of fine gilt staves, a mace, and a Uas sceptre; while at the south-east corner is another stack of royal staves, a mace and a golden bow. Over the inner shrine is a large wooden structure, which supports an enormous linen pall, decorated with innumerable golden rosettes. The structure is bolted and corded, which affords an additional reason for the belief that what lies behind has not been tampered with. The greater portion of the forepart of the pall has fallen, no doubt owing to the weight of the metal rosettes upon it. The interior of the outer shrine is completely gilt, and covered with numerous religious texts. The second shrine is of similar form, and has on the front frieze a great winged solar disc, while on the panels of its doors are representations of King Tutankhamen."

July 26, 1924

A LOST CITY OF AMERICA'S OLDEST CIVILISATION:
"Lubaantun"

By Dr. Thomas Gann, Reader on Central American Archaeology, Liverpool University

The ruined Maya city recently discovered on the Columbia branch of the Rio Grande in the hinterland of British Honduras, near the Guatemala border, is buried in dense, impenetrable bush and the buildings themselves are covered by vegetal mould accumulated over a period of nearly 2000 years, which in many cases gives them the appearance of natural elevations.

The buildings consist of great, stone-faced, terraced pyramids, approached on one side by broad stone stairways. The first structure cleared of bush and humus was a truncated pyramid 90 feet in length by 75 feet in breadth at the base, and 30 feet high. . . . The whole pyramid was completely faced with nicely cut blocks of sandstone and limestone, to the lower surfaces of many of the latter of which a layer of chert $\frac{3}{4}$ inch in thickness, adhered. No mortar or any similar material was used in binding these

107 The great stone stairway leading to the summit of a stone-faced pyramid in "Lubaantun"

stones together, with the result that generations of great trees had torn them apart, so that the greater portion of the west side was in a very poor state of preservation, and only showed the terraced structure in places. It was found that this pyramid had been added to on two separate occasions by building courses of cut stone 3 feet broad round the entire structure, a typically Maya procedure, seen at all their ruined cities over a period of more than 1000 years. . . .

A second pyramid was approached by a great stone stairway . . . from which the bush had to be cleared and the humus removed before it was recognisable as an artificial structure at all (*Figure 107*). . . .

On either side the steps are flanked by a sloping wall of beautifully cut limestone blocks reaching to the front of the extension of the terrace dividing the stairway, from the back of

which another sloping wall reached to the summit of the pyramid, which is quite flat and measures 132 by 36 feet. On it we found an immense uprooted wild cotton-tree, which had brought with it, still firmly gripped in its roots, the squared stones of part of the wall of a chamber contained within the structure of the pyramid.

On a second pyramid we found caved-in, stone-lined chambers, from one of which we endeavoured to clear out the debris of stone and rubbish with which it was filled, but soon had to desist, as the great weight of the stones took the combined exertions of all our labourers to remove through the narrow aperture at the top, and we soon realised that, if we were to do any other work at all in the limited time at our disposal, we must leave these vaults within the pyramids till later. At Uxmal, Copan, and other

Maya cities similar structures have been found within the great stone pyramidal substructures, which had evidently been used as burial-chambers.

The Rio Grande ruins contain a great number of pyramids, and it is highly probable that many, if not all, of them are honeycombed with narrow stone-faced chambers, the tombs of the kings, nobles, and priests of their builders. . . .

Before leaving, we christened the city "Lubaantun" – literally "the place of fallen stones", in the Maya language. This city differs from all other known Maya cities, in that there are no stone palaces and temples standing upon the great pyramidal substructures, and in the entire absence of stone sculptures and of the great monoliths upon which were inscribed the dates of their erection, put up at twenty-year intervals, and later at five-year intervals by the Maya throughout Central America and Yucatan.

It would appear from the absence of stone sculptures, temples and palaces that these ruins ante-date Copan, Quitiga, Uaxactun, and other cities of the Old Empire, the earliest recorded dates at which go back to about the beginning of the Christian Era, for it is almost certain that prior to this Maya dates were recorded on wood, and the earliest temples and palaces constructed of the same material.

Amongst the ruins was found a clay head with typically Maya head-dress and equally typically Archaic face *(Figure 108)*, and it is not improbable that other objects will be found to link up the Maya with the Archaic – the oldest civilisation on the American continent, which flourished from 1000 to 2000 B.C., and of which it is believed that the Maya were an offshoot.

108 Face from the Archaic American civilisation of 2000–1000 B.C. with typical Maya head-dress

In the Rio Grande ruins we have one of the earliest Maya sites, going back to a period prior to any of the ruined cities at present known in Central America.

October 25, 1924

A SECOND "TOWER OF BABEL":
The "House of the Mountain" at Ur

By C. Leonard Woolley, Director of the Joint Expedition of the British Museum and the University Museum, Philadelphia, to Mesopotamia

The Ziggurat of Babylon *(Figure 109)* has been made famous to us by the Biblical story of the Tower of Babel and the confusion of tongues; and it was only one of many, for every great city of ancient Babylonia possessed a similar staged tower, and to-day the ruins of these are the most conspicuous features of the flat Euphrates valley. But though they were so numerous, and though the chief of them had attained such renown, we knew very little about the form and appearance of these gigantic piles. So during last season in Mesopotamia, the Joint Expedition had for its main object the clearing of the Ziggurat of Ur, and for months a gang of about two hundred Arabs was busy carrying off the thousands of tons of broken brick and sand that concealed what was left of the ancient building.

inscriptions, was put up by Ur-Engur, who was King of Ur about 2300 B.C., some three hundred years before Abraham lived here; and the greater part, and the best preserved, of what survives to-day is the work of this early ruler. Whether, as later tradition said, he left the building to be finished by his son Dungi, and

109 Reconstruction of the Ziggurat or "House of the Mountain" at Ur

When we started there was only a mound higher and steeper than the other mounds that mark the site of the city; now there stands up four-square a huge mass of brickwork which may claim to be the most imposing monument in the land.

The normal ziggurat was a rectangular tower built in stages by superimposing a smaller cube upon a larger, so as to give something of the effect of a stepped pyramid; steps or a sloped ramp, led to the summit; and on the flat top of the upmost stage there stood a little shrine dedicated to the patron god of that particular city. At Ur this patron was the Moon God, Nannar, and his temple crowned a rather irregular building whose stages numbered three at one side and four at the other.

The original tower, as we know from

Dungi in turn failed to bring it to completion, so that for 1700 years the chief monument of what had been an imperial city remained an eyesore, we cannot tell; subsequent kings who built much at Ur did not touch the ziggurat, or at most patched the pavement round it; but true it is that when Nabonidus, the last King of Babylon, about 550 B.C. turned his attention to the ancient tower, all the upper stages were in utter ruin, and he could make a clean sweep of these to substitute new work of his own designing. It is the ziggurat in the form which he gave to it that Mr. Newton has succeeded in restoring in the drawing.

The whole structure, except for the shrine on the top, is solid throughout. The core is of mud-brick, the outer walls are kiln-burnt bricks laid in pitch (the "slime" of the writer in Genesis).

These walls are provided with rows of "weeper-holes" to allow any moisture in the core to drain away – otherwise the mud-brick would swell and burst the retaining walls – and are relieved with the shallow panels characteristic of Sumerian architecture. The lower stages were painted black, the top stage was of brick fired a deep red, and the shrine was of bricks covered with a bright blue vitreous glaze.

On three sides buildings, for the most part not yet excavated, came close up to the tower, and it was only the main façade – the north-east – that was really open to view; and this was best seen from the courtyard of a great building that lay at a lower level to the north-east. The wall of the court which acted as the retaining wall of the platform on which the ziggurat stood, was decorated with a row of attached half-columns in white-washed brick. Seen from the court, this columned wall would appear as an intrinsic part of the tower, adding greatly to its height and effect. . . .

When one realises that the lower stage alone (Ur-Engur's work) is a solid mass of brickwork nearly 200 feet long by 150 feet broad and about 50 feet high, and that this is only one of many such towers that dotted all the land, one may well ask whatever induced people to go to all this labour? The explanation seems to be this. The Sumerians, who are the authors of the ziggurats, came into Mesopotamia from somewhere in the north-east, a mountainous country where, like all mountain folk, they had worshipped mountain gods and had built their temples on the hill-tops. When they moved down to the rich newly-formed plains of the river country, they must have been terribly upset to find that there was no hill whereon a temple could be built – and what was the use of a temple on level ground? God would never be at home in a house on the flat. So they set piously to work and built artificial mountains of brick where God might have his seat as of old on the holy hills. Primarily the ziggurat is a hill, yet no ordinary hill, but the throne of God, which is Heaven; so it takes a formal shape, is built up in those ascending stages which compose the upper and the lower heavens, and even its colouring reflects the celestial spheres; yet it remains a hill, as the name "House of the Mountain" clearly shows. And if, as certain inscriptions seem to imply, trees were planted round it, and even set in tubs on its terraces, the man-made ziggurat could not fail to recall to the Sumerian the highlands where once his fathers lived and the true nature of the gods he worshipped, bidding him lift up his eyes to the hills from which came his help.

November 1, 1924

AN UNKNOWN CIVILISATION:
Maya ruins of Yucatan

By Dr. Thomas Gann, Reader in Central American Archaeology, Liverpool University

The Eastern coast of Yucatan, from Cape Catoche to the Chetumal Bay, is perhaps the most desolate and sparsely inhabited stretch of coast along the whole Atlantic seaboard of Central America. A flat expanse of barren land, covered with low scrub and sour grass, it supports now only a scant population of poverty-stricken Indian fishermen; yet at one time it must have been densely populated, for it is covered with the ruins of buildings erected by the ancient Maya inhabitants.

After the conquest of Mayapan, about 1450

A.D., its people were scattered in all directions, and many of them formed settlements along the East Coast, where they developed the curious and characteristic civilisation which lasted for some considerable time after the Spanish Conquest, which in this remote and inaccessible region was never complete.

110 Mayan incense-burner

Practically nothing was known about these ruins till Dr. S. G. Morley of the Carnegie Institution, and the writer visited the whole East Coast, photographing and making plans of all the ruins of which reports were brought in by the Indians.

Tuluum, situated near the centre of the coast line, was undoubtedly the capital city of this civilisation. The first European notice we have of the city is found in the itinerary of Juan de Grijalva's voyage along the coast in 1518, kept by the padre, Juan Diaz, chaplain to the expedition. He writes: "After leaving Cozumel,

we ran along the coast a day and a night, and the next day towards sunset we saw a bourg or village, so large that Seville would not have seemed larger or better; we saw there a very high tower. There was upon the bank a crowd of Indians who carried two standards which they raised and lowered to us as signs to come and join them."

The Spaniards did not go ashore, and so far as we know never set foot on this part of the coast. The fate of the many thousands of Indians who must have occupied Tuluum and its vicinity is completely buried in mystery, as nothing is ever again heard of them, and when in 1842, 324 years after Grijalva's voyage, it was visited by the American explorer Stevens, the site was covered by dense impenetrable bush, amongst which not a single inhabitant was to be found.

The most interesting object at the ruins is a Maya stele, most of the fragments of which were found within one of the temples. (*Here follows a technical description.*) It will be seen, therefore, that Tuluum was occupied by the Maya about the end of the seventh century, and again some 800 years later. Why the first colonists left it, and why it was re-colonised, and what became of the whole dense population which must have occupied not only Tuluum but the entire East Coast, are events completely shrouded in mystery.

The whole group of buildings is surrounded by a great wall, 1500 feet by 600 feet, enclosing an area of approximately 22 acres. The wall varies from 10 to 15 feet in height; the top is level and wide enough for four men to walk abreast, and at the angles square watch-towers look out over the surrounding country. Many of the buildings at Tuluum are decorated inside with beautifully painted, extremely hard stucco, now in a rather poor state of preservation. The colours used are red, black, blue, violet, green and claret. The subjects represented are chiefly elaborately dressed figures of Maya gods with various offerings being made to them. . . .

The ruined city of Chacmool is situated on a

peninsula dividing the San Espiritu from the Ascension Bay. It had never before been visited by Europeans, and the Indian who guided us to it had come across it accidentally when in pursuit of a wounded deer. The architecture is similar to the other East Coast sites – stucco-covered stone buildings standing upon stone-faced pyramids. Here, within a small insignificant temple, we discovered an image of the Chacmool *(Figure 111)*, a gigantic human figure 8 feet high, made of extremely hard cement, reclining upon its back and elbows, the heels drawn up to the buttocks, the forearms and hands extended along the side of the thighs, and the head raised and turned to the right. It was clothed in cotton breast-plate with elaborate collar and maxtli, or apron, falling between the legs, wore sandals, armlets, and wristlets, and was coloured a uniform yellow, over which were painted geometrical devices in red and black.

It was by the merest accident that we discovered this statue, as it was completely buried in the accumulated dirt and rubbish of centuries, through which the tops of the knees projected for a few inches. On removing the debris from round about it, we came upon a shell gorget, two greenstone beads, an earplug, fragments of the bones of a tapir, and a small pottery incense-burner *(Figure 110)*. Some devotee, faithful even after the fall of his god, must have made this little offering before the dirt and debris had begun to accumulate round the statue. This was an extremely important discovery, as these Chacmool figures are purely of Toltec origin, and are found at only one other Maya site – namely, Chichen-Itza *(Plate 16, p. 94)*, where, after its conquest by the Toltecs, their religious and artistic influences were strongly developed. We named the city Chacmool after its tutelary deity.

111   The recumbent statue of the Chacmool

1925

In this year besides the Tutankhamen articles and those (quoted) dealing with Ur and El Obeid, the palaeolithic family tomb of Predmost in Moravia, and Sir Arthur Evans' interpretation of the "Ring of Nestor", there were important items on Lubaantun, Wroxeter, Beth Shan in Palestine and other discoveries by the Czech archaeologist Absolon at Predmost.

April 18, 1925

UR

By Mr. Leonard Woolley

This month we have found, strewn over the floor of a courtyard which we were laboriously clearing, fragments, themselves large enough to be reckoned monuments, of one of the greatest and most splendid works of art in stone that Mesopotamia has yet produced. Last year we laid bare the Ziggurat of Ur, the huge tower of the Moon-god set up by King Ur-Engur about 2300 B.C. Now we have, beautifully carved in relief upon a limestone slab, which when complete was 5 feet across and nearly 15 feet high, the portrait of its builder and his own record of its conception and achievement. In one scene the king receives from his god the order to build the tower; the god holds out to him the rod and line of the architect *(Figure 112)*, the measuring reed and the flaxen line with which Ezekiel, an exile by the waters of Babylon, saw planned out the city and temple of his dreams. In another scene Ur-Engur shows his obedience by appearing before the god carrying all the tools of the mason ready himself to lay the first brick of the Ziggurat. Scenes of sacrifice and of music illustrate the piety and the triumphs of the great founder of the Third Dynasty of Ur. Broken as it is, and in parts much damaged, this stele ranks as one of the two finest works of Sumerian art known, and in dramatic interest is surpassed by none. The discovery was made in the courtyard of E-dub-lal-makh, one of the most important of the

112 Seated figure of the Moon-god, holding out the rod and line of the architect

ancient shrines of Ur *(Figure 113)*. In a previous report *(October 25, 1924)* I described the excavation of its upper levels; now it has been cleared down to the pavements laid by Kuri-galzu, King of Babylon about the sixteenth century B.C., and only the Ziggurat itself is a more imposing ruin.

113 Courtyard of E-dub-lal-makh (the great Ziggurat of Ur in the background) where the stele was found

April 25, 1925

WORSHIP OF THE MOON-GOD AT UR OF THE CHALDEES

By Mr. Leonard Woolley

The Babylonian god was a king, the lord of his city; he controlled its destinies much as did the temporal ruler. Lists of the various functionaries attached to the temple include, besides priests and ministers of state, a choirmaster, a controller of the household, a master of the harem, and directors of livestock, dairy-work, fishing, and donkey-transport. Numbers of women-devotees were attached to the temple and employed in weaving. (*Of the smaller temple of the Moon-god, represented in the picture (Figure 114), Mr. Woolley wrote*) It is immensely old. . . . By the time of Ur-Engur (2300

B.C.) the temple had been completely rebuilt several times, and the building with which Abraham was familiar was perhaps the fifth to occupy the site. . . . The old sanctuary had been strictly private. In the sixth-century reconstruction (by Nebuchadnezzar) there stretched in front of the shrine a large open courtyard. A step, probably once bronze-covered, led up to a smaller court recessed between the newly built wings of the shrine. On this, directly in front of the shrine door, rose a rectangular altar of brick and bitumen, once covered over with metal plates, having in front of it a table for offerings,

114 *Worshipping the Moon-god at Ur. Reconstruction drawing by A. Forestier*

and behind it a low footstool for the ministrant priest. Inside the sanctuary, facing the door, we found the remains of the pedestal on which stood the statue. Clearly the ritual had been changed and a kind of congregational worship had taken the place of, or been added to, the old secret rites.

April 25, 1925

TELL EL OBEID

By Mr. Leonard Woolley

The little temple at Tell el Obeid does not really exist; in fact, of the building proper not a single brick is to-day in its place, and even of the solid platform, on which it stood, the upper part has been overthrown by the hands of man or worn away by the winds and rains of many centuries. To attempt to reconstruct the original appearance of a structure so hopelessly destroyed might well seem rash, fanciful and unscientific.

Yet I claim a very fair degree of truth. When the joint expedition excavated the site, which had already been discovered and partly dug by Dr. H. R. Hall in 1919, the solid brick platform was found standing from two to twelve feet high, its buttressed walls made of kiln-burnt brick below and mud-brick above. From the middle of its south-east face stretched out the mud-brick foundation of the staircase, with the lowest of its great stone treads still *in situ*; and under fifteen feet of debris on the left side of the staircase there lay a mass of remarkable objects which clearly had formed the mural decoration of the fallen shrine. On the other side of the staircase Dr. Hall had found another hoard of architectural remains similar to, though by no means identical with, what we discovered this season. ... Of Dr. Hall's hoard the most important pieces were – the heads and foreparts of four lions made of copper with inlaid eyes and teeth and tongues; fragments of a great copper relief, showing an eagle grasping two stags; of smaller lion and panther heads; of two bulls in the round; of mosaic columns; of wooden columns and beams overlaid with copper; and parts of two limestone statues. On the other side of the stairs we found four copper bulls in the round, of which two could be preserved, two complete mosaic columns, fragments of wooden columns and beams overlaid with copper, twelve more or less complete copper reliefs of cattle and the heads of two more, pieces of a mosaic frieze representing cattle and pastoral scenes, pieces of another mosaic frieze of birds, a quantity of artificial flowers, a carved stone well-head(?) and the inscribed foundation stone of the temple. Of these the reliefs had clearly formed a frieze on the face of the wall, for they were found still fixed to the fallen masses of brickwork by copper hold-fasts; and the same was true of the mosaic friezes. By tracing out carefully the line of fall of the brick masses, the angle at which the objects lay and their distance from the wall, it was not difficult to decide their relative positions on the wall-face; only the exact intervals that separated them were a matter for conjecture. It was also certain that they adorned the temple itself and not the platform. A calculation based on the main stairs, and on a second flight on the S-W side, gave fifteen feet as the approximate height of the platform; and along the top of this, at the foot of the temple wall, there must have run a narrow ledge whereon stood the statues of bulls. Probably this ledge was a double one, and on its lower step

were placed the artificial flowers, so that the bulls seemed to walk in a flowery meadow. Certainly the flowers did stand upright and free, and were not, as we first supposed, rosettes with their long stems embedded in the wall, and only their heads showing. The stone staircase must have led, one supposes, to the temple door, and the objects found on the right of the stairs include just such as best fit the decoration of a door, namely, the foreparts of lions – which, by analogy with later buildings, we can safely put flanking the entrance in the reveals of the door-

115 Hypothetical reconstruction in the British Museum of the interior of the temple at Tell el Obeid

jambs – and the great relief, which almost certainly came from above a lintel. The way in which things had fallen down from above together with the measurements of the things themselves, justified the restoration of a projecting gate-tower with an open porch in front of it, the latter having its columns and roofing-timbers of palm-logs over-laid with sheets of copper, the door of the gate-tower flanked by mosaic columns supporting the great copper relief. The lack on the right-hand side of the stairs of such elements of mural decoration as were common on the other side showed that the temple façade did not extend much, if at all, beyond the doorway. The balustrade wall of the stairs was at first a puzzle; the white-washed floor stretched up to it and ended in a straight line but the mud-brick was of the roughest description, and had no finished face. It must therefore have had some kind of covering now wholly vanished. The discovery all along its face of quantities of small copper nails was tolerably sure proof that this covering was of wood, probably panelled like the main wall, where the brick panelling goes back to a wood original. . . .

What makes this temple and everything found in connection with it of quite extraordinary interest is its great age. From the foundation tablet we learn that it was built in honour of the goddess Nin-Khursag by A-an-ni-pad-da, who was the second king of the First Dynasty of Ur, a dynasty which, until this material proof of its existence came to light, was commonly regarded as mythical. It is too early to fix the king's actual date, for the Babylonian lists of dynasties are not free from error, and other evidence is yet to seek; but his reign certainly falls well within the fourth millennium B.C., and the most conservative estimate would assign to our temple an antiquity of some 5,400 years.

July 18, 1925

THE RING OF NESTOR:
A glimpse into the after-world of prehistoric Greece

By Sir Arthur Evans. Abridged from an article published in the Journal of Hellenic Studies and to be published separately by Macmillans.

Nestor, the Methuselah of the Greeks, whose life extended to three times the span of other mortals, is connected by the Homeric tradition with the western coastland of the Morea. Here, in fact, Dr. Dorpfeld, in pursuing his Homeric investigations on that side in 1907, found a prehistoric acropolis and the remains of three great beehive tombs like those of Mycenae. These remains, which there is every reason to connect with Nestor's seat, lay on a bluff called Kakovatos, overlooking the Pylian Plain.

Dr. Dorpfeld's party came on a gang of peasants who were actually engaged in removing blocks for building material from what remained of the circular wall of the largest of these three great domed chambers, which must have been well-nigh 40 feet in height as well as diameter. This vault – or rather what remains of it – as being somewhat larger than the two

others, has already, owing to Dr. Dorpfeld's discovery, acquired the name of the "Tomb of Nestor". In it was a grave-pit entirely ransacked.

What treasures might not the sepulchral cell have contained had it been found intact! . . .

Recovery of signet-ring
A fortunate chance, due to information kindly supplied me by a friend, put me on the track of another find far surpassing in interest anything that this previous investigation had succeeded in eliciting. It was not only blocks for building material that the peasants had been able to carry off from the tomb before their marauding work was interrupted. My informant had obtained a bad impression of what it was easy to see was a signet-ring *(Figure 116)* of an extraordinary character. The possibility that this might be lost

to science impelled me at once to undertake a special journey to that somewhat inaccessible part of Greece, and I have been able in the end to carry off the precious object itself. The ring . . . is exceptionally massive. It is of solid gold, of about the weight of four sovereigns, and has a hoop of disproportionately small dimensions. It belongs, in fact, to an archaic funereal type of bead-seal, which was originally worn suspended round the neck or wrist.

116 A photograph of the cast of the ring of Nestor

The subject of the "Ring of Nestor"
The ring is remarkable, not only for its massive fabric and old-time Minoan form, but even more for the unrivalled wealth of illustration presented by its intaglio and the deep interest of the subject of its designs *(Plate 17, p. 95)*. The central subject of the ring, with its two arms, might be taken to represent the trunk of a tree with two horizontal branches and spreading roots below. . . . The trunk itself rises from a kind of mound, the incisions on which may be taken as a summary attempt to indicate vegetation. Crouched on the bank, moreover, is an animal, apparently intended for a dog, guarding the base of the tree. . . .

Butterflies and chrysalises: emblems of resurgence
Taking the designs on the intaglio in order . . . we see in the upper left compartment above the bough on that side what are clearly two separate groups. The first of these consists of two female figures, in which the analogy of other scenes enables us to recognise the great Minoan Goddess and a female companion with whom she is often associated. . . .

Fluttering near, and almost settling on her head, are two butterflies, and above them, in turn, two other objects in which, from their form and the associations in which they appear, it seems reasonable to recognise two corresponding chrysalises. . . .

It is noteworthy that the Greek word, *psyche*, a spirit, as transferred to a butterfly, is illustrated by Aristotle, who, in this connection, first described the genesis of the perfect insect from a caterpillar and chrysalis, by the life history of a White butterfly, *Pieris brassicae*, or an allied species. The idea that butterflies are departed spirits is common the world over, but there is evidence that this belief attached itself in a particular way to white butterflies.

There is, however, also abundant evidence that other kinds of butterflies, especially those showing eyes on their wings, were also associated with departed spirits in prehistoric Greece and Crete. . . .

The meeting in the World Beyond
In this compartment we see, in profile, a youth whose long locks fall behind his shoulders and over his breast, girt with the usual Minoan loin-clothing, and with traces of footgear, but otherwise naked, standing in front of a woman with his visible arm half raised as in the act of greeting her. The lady herself raises both hands in a much more accentuated attitude of surprise and delight, as of one who had seen her spouse unexpectedly restored to her.

The attitudes and gestures are so natural and speaking as to admit of one obvious interpretation. We see here, reunited by the life-giving power of the Goddess, symbolised by the chrysalises and butterflies, a young couple whom death had parted, and of whom the female personage was clearly the earlier to reach the Underworld. . . .

The Guardian Lion and the Griffin's Court
On the other side of the upper part of the trunk of the "Tree of the world" from that by which the young couple stand, we see the Lion Guardian of the Underworld, couched on a bench in vigilant repose, and tended by the two little handmaidens of the Goddess.

In the lowest row, which forms a single composition, though divided by the trunk, the young couple reappear in what seems to be a scene of initiation. On the extreme right, in front of a standing figure, in whom we may again recognise the Goddess herself, another of her guardian monsters, a winged griffin of the Minoan type – the incarnation of swiftness and piercing vision – is seated on a kind of throne. In front of him are griffin ladies, two of whom have been deputed to present the young couple at the "Griffin's Court", while one warns off a youth to the left as unworthy of such initiation.

Thus, the entire composition of the designs on this remarkable signet-ring connects itself in a single story, divided, as has been shown, into four successive episodes – the Goddess seated with her companion and her life-giving emblems; the reunited couple; the lion guardian tended by the handmaidens of the divinity; and the "Griffin's Court", representing a ceremony of initiation. It gives us our first real insight into the pre-Hellenic eschatology, and is the first glimpse that we possess into the World Beyond as conceived by the Minoans. . . .

The evident dependence of the intaglio design on a pictorial model, coupled with the singular correspondence shown in the fashion of the dress, as well as the pose and gestures of the figures, with those of the contemporary class of "miniature frescoes", so well illustrated at Knossos, suggested to me the desirability of an attempt to translate back the composition before us into its original form and colouring as a painted panel. Happily, in M. E. Gilliéron *fils*, I had at hand not only a competent artist, but one whose admirable studies of Minoan art in all its branches had thoroughly imbued him with its spirit. M. Gilliéron . . . executed under my superintendence the coloured drawing reproduced *(Plate 17)*. . . . We have here indeed the echo of a Minoan masterpiece, anticipating by over eleven centuries the celebrated painting by Polygnotos of Odysseus in Hades in the Lesche at Delphi.

October 31, 1925

A DISCOVERY AS WONDERFUL AS THAT OF TUTANKHAMEN'S TOMB:
Professor D. K. Absolon's new revelation of prehistoric culture 20,000 years ago

A Prologue by Sir Arthur Keith, F.R.S.

It is my privilege to write a prologue to a wonderful drama of prehistory which the enterprising management of *The Illustrated London News* has secured for its readers. This drama is to have its setting in the very centre of Europe – in the old province of Moravia – now included in Czecho-Slovakia. The chief narrator is to be Dr. D. K. Absolon, the Curator of the Government Museum in Brunn, the capital town of Moravia – the man who has most to do in putting the facts of the story together. The drama or series of discoveries he is to place before the reader is as rich in surprise and as illuminating in its various scenes as that which

Plate 28 Aurochs or extinct wild bull in the grande salle *of the grotto at Lascaux*

Plate 29 A treasure of superb Roman silver turned up by the plough at Mildenhall, Suffolk:
dish and finger bowl

Plate 30 Roman silver covered dish, part of the Mildenhall treasure

Plate 31 The Bonampak murals: detail of a panel in Room I, showing preparations for a ceremony

Plate 32 The Bonampak murals: a panel in Room I, showing part of the ceremony itself

Plate 33 Ivories of unsurpassed magnificence: miniature sculpture of lioness killing an Ethiopian in a field of lotuses

*Plate 34 The great bronze crater found in the tomb of a
Celtic princess at Vix*

was unfolded two years ago in the Valley of the Kings by the discovery of the Tomb of Tutankhamen. In the hands of Mr. Howard Carter that tomb has become a treasury of history; the splendour and perfection of its contents have given a most vivid and intimate picture of the life led in the valley of the Nile fully thirteen centuries before the birth of Christ. The story to be unfolded in these pages is infinitely older. It takes us back at least 15,000 years beyond the time of Tutankhamen. Dr. Absolon is of the opinion that the people and the civilisation he is to describe are twice as old as I have said. Of one thing there can be no doubt: his community of ancient hunters was alive when Glacial conditions prevailed throughout Europe, in all save its southern parts, and when the people of Moravia – in the same latitude as Northern France – lived by hunting the mammoth, the musk-ox, the reindeer, the cave-bear, and carved their daggers from bones (ulnae) cut from the forelimb of the lion. Nor is there any doubt that these ancient hunters of Moravia participated in a culture or manner of living which was prevalent for a long period throughout the central and southern parts of Europe, and which spread into England – the culture and period known as Aurignacian. I am one of those who are penurious of time, and cut estimates down to their lowest limits. Even when all deductions are made, we must suppose that the Aurignacian culture appeared in Europe about 20000 B.C. and came to an end about 15000 B.C.

Never before has so complete a revelation been made of the manner of life led by our forefathers during the Ice Age. In describing their stone implements Dr. Absolon has tens of thousands at his disposal from which to make a selection. The sites on which this community lived and made its hearths abound with the bones and teeth of the mammoth. There was a pile of thirteen tusks, stored for future use; there was a heap of the skulls of wolves, broken open so that their brains might be extracted; everywhere there were bones split open for their marrow. Finished weapons worked in bone and in ivory occur in great numbers; there is an infinite variety of bone utensils and implements for domestic use. They were high artists, those ancient hunters of Central Europe: Dr. Absolon made scores of photographs of their carvings and engravings, of their works of art and of their ornaments, of their idols, toys, and playthings.

Best of all, from my point of view, we know what sort of men, women and children they were who lived in Moravia so long ago. Thanks to Dr. Absolon, the Museum of the Royal College of Surgeons of England was able to acquire accurate casts of the skulls of two members of this ancient community – one of a man, the other of a woman; and also casts taken from the interior of these skulls showing in clear detail the brains which guided their owners through the intricacies of life in these remote times. My interest in these skulls was aroused when I found, primitive and robust as the cranial features of these people were, that in the strictest sense of the term they were true Europeans. They show us the features possessed by our forefathers when they first appeared in Europe. Nothing is more probable than that the blood of some of them is still flowing in living veins – particularly in the veins of men who now live in the northern and western parts of Europe. After all, 800 generations will carry the ancestry of any one of us as far back as the Aurignacian period. . . .

But it was not until last year (1924) that the extent of the ancient settlement and the perfection of its preservation became known. The loess deposits contain earth which is valuable for brickmaking, and Moravia, like every other country in Europe, is in need of houses. A brick-making company, in 1924, dug wide trenches or pits across these deposits, which extended beyond the cliff. These trenches laid bare the hearths round which the ancient hunters had squatted and celebrated their feasts. . . . It was a charnel house of the great animals of the Glacial period. Such was

Plate 35 opposite *Earliest human portrait in the history of man*

the profusion of implements in stone and bone, of domestic utensils, of ornaments and objects of art, that the Government took over the right of exploiting the site on behalf of its Museum in Brunn, and to rescue a unique record of prehistory for the benefit of science. . . .

Although it is only now that the importance of the discovery at Predmost is being realised, skulls and skeletons of the ancient hunters

twelve of them were adults, eight of them were children of varying ages. With the remains of one child lay a beautiful necklace; beside another was the skull of an Arctic fox. In the contemporary cave-burials in the South of France, bodies were interred singly, except in the case of the mother and son, in the deepest layer of the Grimaldi Cave near Mentone. But at Predmost they had a family tomb. In this

117 Dr. Absolon photographing an unusually complete skeleton of an Ice-Age man found at Predmost in Moravia

have been known for some years, although no adequate account has ever been published of them. In 1894 Professor Maska laid bare, in the deposits at the foot of the rock shelter at Predmost, a tomb of a most remarkable kind. It contained the remains of twenty individuals;

tomb we must infer, from the disordered state of many of the skeletons, that burials were made from time to time. And it was a remarkable tomb – oval, or boatlike in shape, being 13 feet long and 7½ feet wide. One side of the tomb had its wall formed by the shoulder-blades of the mammoth, set upright and forming a row or palisade; the opposite side of the tomb was held up by a row of lower jaws from the same great animal. Over the tomb, and covering the human remains, was a layer of stones 16 inches in thickness – clearly a protection against wolf and hyena. All was sealed deeply down in the loess which continued to gather after Predmost was deserted.

They were large-headed and big-brained people, these ancient hunters of Moravia. . . . If the part of the skull (of a man found in the tomb) containing the brain is fitted within a framework of lines which is designed to take the same part of the skull of an average modern Englishman, it will be seen that, as regards length, the skull of the ancient hunter exceeds the length of the frame by 13 millimetres, being thus fully half an inch longer than the average English skull. The excess in length is largely due to the great development of the bony ridges over the orbits. The vault of the skull rises somewhat higher than in English skulls, and its width is also greater, being 146 millimetres. The width of the skull is 72 per cent of the total length – showing us we are dealing with a race of long-headed, or dolichocephalic people. The brain-containing capacity of the skull is 1578 cubic centimetres – 100 cubic centimetres above the average for modern Englishmen. The cast taken from the interior of the skull reveals a complex and voluminous brain – its total length being 188 millimetres – a striking amount. We need not wonder at the big-brainedness of these ancient hunters when we look at their handiwork, and realise the difficult and dangerous problems they had to solve.

To find a living race with facial features as robustly developed as in this ancient hunter we have to go to Tierra del Fuego, in the furthest limit of South America; but we must not suppose that a resemblance in robustness of facial development indicates a racial affinity between living Fuegian and extinct Moravian. The ancient Moravian hunter, in all the features of his skull and face, was a true European, but

one of the most primitive yet discovered.

The peculiarity of this ancient hunter's face lies in the extent of its forward projection. . . . Yet, owing to the forward position of the forehead, there is no evident muzzle – no prognathism or projection of the jaws. In this the men of Predmost resemble their contemporaries of France – the Cromagnon people. For, although the Predmost men were not tall, as the Cromagnons were, yet there can be no doubt they were racial cousins; both represent ancestral states of the men of Europe.

We have only to look at the skull of one of the Predmost women – perhaps she was wife or daughter of the man whose features have just been described – to realise that we are dealing with people of a true European type. A duplicate of the woman's skull might easily be found among the living inhabitants of Scandinavia and of Britain. . . .

Her face was regularly formed; it shows none of the robust and primitive features seen in the man's face. We need not be surprised to find this marked sexual differentiation in a primitive people: in all races of mankind the woman tends much more than the man to retain the features of childhood and youth. Amongst the Cromagnon people we find the same sharp separation of the sexes: the male has been awarded the brutal features and the fighting spirit. Amongst the Cromagnon people only the men were tall; the women were of medium stature – often they were really short. Woman's features point the direction in which evolution moves.

Professor Absolon's lengthy articles were published in the issues of 7 November, 14 November and 21 November. All were headlined – a topical spirit – as A DISCOVERY AS WONDERFUL AS THAT OF TUTANKHAMEN'S TOMB – in a mood more of hope than accuracy.

1926

Archaeology was now on a flood tide, and besides the Tutankhamen articles and others on the Indus Valley and the Maya civilisation, there were important articles on Ur, Pompeii, Jerash in Jordan, Dendra and Asine in Greece, Hittite Kultepe in Anatolia and Taxila in north-west India.

February 27, 1926

MOHENJO-DARO

By Sir John Marshall, Kt., C.I.E., Litt.D., Director-General of Archaeology in India

At the moment of writing I am starting on the systematic excavation of Mohenjo-daro with 800 labourers, five officers besides myself, and an adequate number of technical assistants. Later on, our operations will be extended over the Punjab, Western Rajputana, and Baluchistan, and this will embrace a general survey of the remains of this remarkable civilisation, as well as the excavation of other important sites. But at the outset it has seemed advisable to concentrate our available resources on one site only, so that we may get from it a more comprehensive and detailed picture of Indo-Sumerian culture than we could by dividing up our forces, and so that our officers and staffs may at the same time profit to the full by mutual co-operation in the first difficult stages of unveiling an entirely unknown civilisation. . . .

From these and other researches it has now become evident that this Indus civilisation must have developed and flourished in Western India for untold centuries, and that it extended over an immense area including Sind, much of the Punjab, Baluchistan and probably Rajputana and countries even further to the east. Baluchistan is likely to prove a specially fertile field, inasmuch as it was the connecting link by land between the Indus region and Seistan, Persia, and Mesopotamia, in all of which countries remains have been found analogous to those uncovered at Harappa and Mohenjo-daro. The term "Indo-Sumerian" let it be said, has been provisionally adopted merely as indicating the close cultural connection between this prehistoric civilisation of the Indus and that of Sumer, not as implying that the peoples of these two regions were of the same stock or spoke the same language.

To the archaeologist the site of Mohenjo-daro is one of the most fascinating that can well be imagined. The outskirts of the old city are now buried beneath the deep alluvial soil of the surrounding plains, deposited by the annual flooding of the Indus during the long ages before the modern embankment was constructed. The central part of the city, which was higher than its outskirts, still covers an area of about a square mile, and takes the form of rolling mounds of brick debris some thirty feet in height, dominated by a higher mound at its north-west corner. This higher mound, which is capped by a Buddhist *stupa* of a later date, appears to conceal the remains of the principal temple of Indo-Sumerian times, which thus occupied the same position in relation to the rest of the city as the principal temples of Sumer and Babylonia did. . . .

Some of these buildings, with unusually thick walls and small sanctuary-like chambers, are evidently temples. But the majority appear to

The drainage system, in particular, is extraordinarily well developed. Every street and alley-way and passage seems to have had its own covered conduits of finely chiselled brick, laid with a precision that could hardly be improved on. . . . The use of lime-mortar appears to have been unknown at this period in India, and, in any case, there is no limestone in the neighbourhood of Mohenjo-daro from which lime could be burnt; nor is there in Sind any bitumen such as is used as a cementing agent in Mesopotamia. It was for this reason that the joints of the brick-work laid in the water channels had to be so finely worked.

The usual method of disposing of the dead seems to have been by cremation, and a large cremation-urn used for the purpose was found in one of the houses – a wide-bodied jar in which a few fragments of bone were placed along with a number of medium-sized and miniature pottery vessels. Many examples of these cinerary urns have been found both at Mohenjo-daro *(Figure 118)* and at Harappa, and at the latter site burial structures of brick like the modern Hindu Samadhi have also been found. On the other hand, bones have been discovered in what appear to have been graves formed in the solid brick-work of the walls or beneath the threshold of doors. In the latter case it is tempting to see in these remains evidence of human sacrifice, the victim being intended to act as a guardian spirit of the house; but the evidence is too slender at present to be reliable.

Among the smaller antiquities found by Mr. Dikshit, the most interesting perhaps are the engraved seals with pictographic legends *(Figure 119)*, of which he has obtained a remarkably fine series, numbering 146 in all. The most beautiful of them is the one bearing the effigy of a Brahmani bull, which in the stylish treatment of the dewlap, the modelling of the muscles, and the slenderness of the hoofs, recalls the best glyptic efforts of Mycenaean Greece. Another interesting specimen depicts a *pipal* tree *(Ficus religiosa)*, the Indian "tree of life", with twin heads of some horned animal,

118 A broken cinerary urn at Mohenjo-daro

be ordinary dwelling-houses or shops, which for the most part are divided into good-sized rooms, furnished with their own wells and bathrooms, floored over with brick, and provided with covered drains connecting with larger drains in the side streets. The existence of these roomy and well-built houses, and the relatively high degree of luxury denoted by their elaborate system of drainage, as well as by the character of many of the smaller antiquities found within, seem to betoken a social condition of the people much in advance of what was then prevailing in Mesopotamia or Egypt. Not that anything is likely to be found at Mohenjo-daro as magnificent as the royal tombs or temples of early Egypt. That would be too much to hope for, especially at a spot where little or no stone is available for building. But, so far as the writer is aware, neither Egypt nor Sumer has yielded anything at all comparable to the average type of citizen's house now being unearthed in Sind.

119 Indo-Sumerian seals with pictographic inscriptions found at Mohenjo-daro

real or fabulous, springing from its stem; others represent elephants, tigers, or rhinoceros, with a trough, as a rule, placed beneath their heads; others, again, are engraved with pictographic legends only. Buried beneath the floors of the houses Mr. Dikshit found a number of copper vessels and utensils, including a curved saw; and in one of the larger vessels he recovered a valuable collection of jewellery. . . . They comprise gold and silver bangles, ear-ornaments, gold netting needles, charms and two particularly handsome necklaces or girdles (*kanchi*) made of tubular beads of carnelian, with terminals and smaller beads of copper gilt. . . .

Of the character of other objects of bone, ivory, shell, terracotta and the like which Mr. Dikshit found in the houses, some idea can be obtained by the samples reproduced. . . . What is particularly striking and not a little anomalous about these finds is the great disparity in the quality of their technique. Rough flakes of chert, for example, which served as knives and scrapers, have been found in hundreds all over the site, and these utensils are as crude as such objects could well-nigh be. But mingled with them, and contrasting strangely with their primitive appearance, are finely made objects of gold and blue faience and exquisitely engraved seals, such as could only have been turned out by people possessed of marked artistic ability as well as great technical skill.

March 6, 1926

MOHENJO-DARO

By Sir John Marshall, Kt., C.I.E., Litt.D., Director-General of Archaeology in India

Last summer an expedition under Mr. H. Hargreaves was dispatched to Baluchistan in order to examine afresh certain mounds at a spot called Nal, in the Jhalawan District, from which, over twenty years ago, I secured some unique specimens of early painted pottery. The result of Mr. Hargreaves' expedition has been the discovery of a number of burials and other remains of the Chalcolithic Age, closely related to what we are finding in the Indus Valley, and the recovery of a fine series of painted wares, copper and stone implements, and so on. . . . Preliminary excavations have been made at both Harappa and Mohenjo-daro: at the former by Mr. Daya Ram Sahni, at the latter by Mr. K. N. Dikshit; and the results obtained are full of interest and promise. . . .

As already stated the common practice at Mohenjo-daro and Harappa appears to have been to cremate the dead and place some fragments of the bones in a cinerary jar or a small brick structure. But at Nal, in Baluchistan, Mr. Hargreaves discovered a burial-ground of this same Chalcolithic Age in which two different forms of burial are exhibited. In one the corpse was laid entire in a shallow grave of unburnt brick; in the other the skull and a few of the bigger bones only were laid directly in the ground, along with numerous earthenware vases, copper implements, beads, grindstones and other small objects, the body having presumably been exposed to the vultures, and such of the bones as were left subsequently collected and buried. The painted earthenware vessels found in the latter class of graves constitute a remarkably fine series, most of them being superior in fabric and design to the potteries found on the city sites, to which, however, they are closely akin.

The houses, temples, and antiquities unearthed by Mr. Sahni at Harappa are, for the most part, analogous to, though less well preserved than, those of Mohenjo-daro; but there is one vast structure of brick at Harappa, which has no counterpart at the latter site. It consists of two series of solidly-built brick walls, laid parallel to one another, with a broad aisle of 24 feet down the centre. Up to the present, twenty of these parallel walls have been exhumed – namely, fourteen on the east of the central aisle and six on the west. They have a uniform length of nearly 52 feet, but they differ in thickness. The stouter kind are 9 feet thick at the base, and these are placed at regular intervals of 17 feet. So that, had it not been for the thinner walls intervening between them, it might reasonably have been inferred that they belonged to a series of long, narrow, halls. As it is, the intervening walls leave no more than corridors between, the purpose of which it is difficult to surmise.

Though much damaged on the surface by the depredations of railway contractors and the neighbouring villagers, who for generations have quarried from it a never-ending supply of well-burnt brick, Harappa has the advantage over Mohenjo-daro in that its mounds are much loftier and more extensive, while the subsoil water has not risen so near the surface of the surrounding plains as at the other sites. This being so, it is probable that we shall be able to work back here to an even more remote age than at Mohenjo-daro. . . .

How long were the periods of time that elapsed here or at Mohenjo-daro between the destruction of each city and the erection of its successor, it is not possible to surmise; nor is it likely that we shall ever be able to form an accurate estimate, unless we are lucky enough to establish some definite synchronisms between India and Sumer, or some other country where more or less reliable chronological data are available. But no one who is familiar with the exploration of prehistoric sites can doubt that the vast remains which lie buried at Harappa and Mohenjo-daro represent the growth of thousands of years anterior to the date when the last of these Indo-Sumerian cities was built. That that date is to be placed in the third millennium B.C. appears more and more certain as the digging proceeds, the new finds showing ever closer affinities with the Sumerian antiquities of Mesopotamia; and this date, which was arrived at on the strength of internal evidence, has now been strikingly corroborated by the discovery, which Mr. Mackay has made at Kish in Mesopotamia, of one of our typical seals of this period underneath the foundations of a building of the time of Hammurabi (*circa* 2100 B.C.). . . .

Postscript

Since writing the above, and before I have been able to post it, many new finds of great interest have been unearthed at Mohenjo-daro. Among them I select three for special notice. One is a small tablet of blue faience depicting a figure – probably a deity – seated cross-legged on a throne, and to the right and left of him a kneeling devotee with a snake (Naga) behind; while on the back of the tablet is an inscription in Indo-Sumerian pictographs. . . .

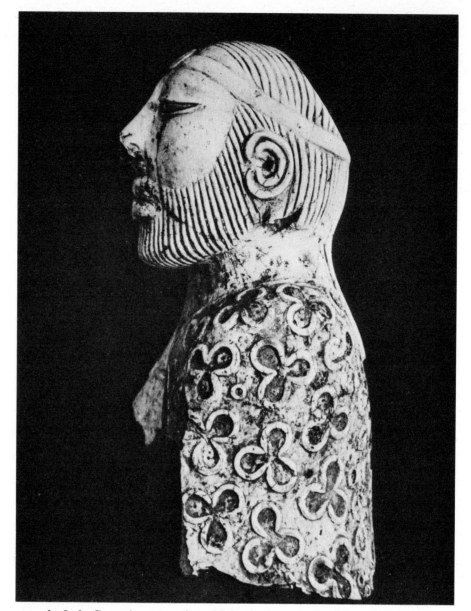

120 An Indo-Sumerian statue from Mohenjo-daro, made of limestone

A second find of exceptional value is that of a silver vase containing a variety of gold jewellery and a number of square and round silver pieces – probably coins, one of which is inscribed with a few characters in the cuneiform script of Babylonia. Assuming that cuneiform was understood and used on the banks of the Indus, the likelihood of unearthing other records in this script and discovering in them a key to the language of the people is obviously not an altogether remote one.

But the most striking find made in the last few days is that of two statues of bearded men, one carved out of alabaster, the other of limestone *(Figure 120)*, finished with a veneer of fine white paste, its eyes inlaid with shell, and the patterning on its robe picked out in red ochre. Both of these statues portray a type of man as unlike the modern Sindhi as the ancient Sumerian was unlike the present-day inhabitant of Southern Mesopotamia – a type with low receding forehead, prominent nose, thick lips (the upper shaved) and narrow oblique eyes.

1927

This was the year when Leonard Woolley's discoveries at Ur in southern Mesopotamia began to challenge even Tutankhamen in public interest, with such gold treasures as a gold dagger and the gold wig of Mes-Kalam-Dug. The Harvard-Boston expedition discovered the Tomb of Hetepheres, mother of Cheops, at Giza; and there were some new discoveries at Pompeii.

March 12, 1927

THE 5000-YEARS "MYSTERY" TOMB OF HETEPHERES:
The mother of Cheops

One of the chief archaeological events in Egypt, since the Tomb of Tutankhamen (18th Dynasty, about 1350 B.C.) came to light, was the discovery at Giza, near the Pyramids, of the secret burial place of Queen Hetepheres, mother of Cheops (Khufu), builder of the Great Pyramid that bears his name. This discovery is the result of several years' research by the Joint Expedition of Harvard University and the Boston Museum of Fine Arts, directed by Mr. George A. Reisner, who has recently contributed to *The Times* a full and deeply interesting account of the work. Hetepheres was the wife of Sneferuw, the first Pharaoh of Dynasty IV, who reigned about 3000 B.C., father of Cheops and ancestor of the Kings who built the Pyramids. The Queen's sepulchre is therefore nearly 5000 years old. "This intact tomb", writes Dr. Reisner in his first article, "presented for the first time in the history of Egyptian excavation an opportunity of studying the burial of a great personage of an early period, 1500 years older than the royal tombs of the New Kingdom. Looking in from a small opening, the excavators had seen a beautiful alabaster sarcophagus with its lid in place. Partly on the sarcophagus and partly fallen behind it lay about twenty gold-cased poles and beams of a large canopy. On the western edge of the sarcophagus were spread several sheets of gold inlaid with faience, and

on the floor was a confused mass of gold-cased furniture." The tomb was a secret one, at the bottom of a shaft nearly 100 feet deep, the mouth of which was discovered through a photographer observing a patch of plaster on a rock-scrap. The shaft had been filled up with masonry, which all had to be removed. About 30 feet down a niche was found in the side of the shaft, and thought at first to be the tomb, but proved to be a sacrificial offering consisting of the skull and three legs of a bull, wrapped in a mat, two beer-jars, and some charcoal. The digging went on. At 98 feet was found "the only intact tomb discovered at that time (March 8, 1925) of a royal personage before Dynasty XII". The identification of the tomb as that of Hetepheres was proved by inscriptions. Dr. Reisner became convinced that the deposit was a re-burial. "The original tomb of Queen Hetepheres", he says, "was without doubt made by her husband, Sneferuw, beside his pyramid at Dahsur. She outlived her husband and was buried by her son, Cheops. The condition of the contents of the Giza tomb proves that thieves had broken into the Dahsur tomb. When the royal police discovered this fact, he ordered the body, brought to Giza, to be placed in a secret tomb." It is a small chamber (10 feet by 15 feet) cut, like the shaft, in the solid rock. A few days ago (March 3) the sarcophagus

233

was at last opened, but proved to be empty – a great disappointment. Dr. Reisner, however, still hoped to find the mummy, believing that Cheops had hidden it, as an extra precaution against robbers, instead of placing it in the sarcophagus. The next step in the search was to open a concealed recess which had been discovered on the west wall of the chamber.

March 26, 1927

Objects of extraordinary interest, as illustrating life in Egypt about 3000 B.C., were found in the tomb of Queen Hetepheres. . . . "A group of eight small toilet jars of fine alabaster", writes Dr. Reisner, "had contained the traditional perfumed ointments. . . . The box lay in decay on the floor, but the measurements were fixed at about 26 centimetres long by 14 centimetres wide and 13 centimetres high. A mass of inlays lay under and over parts of a bed, cased in heavy sheets of gold." Picturing the scene at the closing of the tomb 5000 years ago, Dr. Reisner says:"The masons were ordered out, and apparently left in haste, dropping some of their tools on the floor. It may be suspected that they were all executed on coming out. . . . We found three great heavy tools of copper of two forms . . .

one like a stone punch and the other perhaps a crushing tool, both hitherto unknown in ancient Egypt. . . . Seven implements (two of solid gold and five of copper) consisted of a round-topped oblong plate, to the square bottom of which a tag of the same metal was welded and inserted in a wooden handle. One side of the plate had been whetted to a sharp cutting edge . . . and no doubt the seven implements are razors. Another smaller implement likewise found in seven examples (three of solid gold and four of copper) was of rectangular form, with all four sides whetted to sharp edges. One face was flat and the other raised in panel form. . . . A perfect little wine-cup of polished gold had re-curved rim and long open spout. Two other small gold cups were found and a copper ewer and basin for washing the mouth and hands after a meal. . . . On the sarcophagus were remains of a dismantled baldachin, or canopy, with golden poles and two inscribed jambs; also fragments of gold sheeting, with faience inlay, from a box for the canopy curtains. The inlay work has been pieced together, and a model of the baldachin made. . . . The inlay design included the vulture Nekheber, goddess of Upper Egypt, a seated figure of Sneferuw, his cartouches and a representation of Wazit, goddess of Lower Egypt."

November 26, 1927

A MIRACLE OF GOLD-WORK 5500 YEARS OLD:
The Ur dagger, the gem of the "dagger grave" at Ur – lately a source of new discoveries

A new season of excavations began last month at Ur of the Chaldees, the city of Abraham, and work was resumed at the "dagger grave" (named after the beautiful weapon found there). Further diggings soon revealed new treasures, including hundreds of gold beads and pendants.

Describing the dagger and sheath in all its colourful beauty as "the season's crowning reward", Mr. Woolley writes: "The hilt is of one piece of deep-blue lapis lazuli studded with gold; the blade is of burnished gold. The sheath is of solid gold, the front entirely covered with an intricate design in filigree. It is in perfect condition. Produced at any date, it would have been a marvel of design and workmanship. It is astonishing indeed when we realise that it was actually made nearly 5500 years ago and is one of the oldest-known examples of the goldsmith's art." The handle, it may be noted, is pierced with a hole for a gold ring.

December 17, 1927

THE "GOLD WIG" OF MES-KALAM-DUG:
A wonderful discovery in a royal grave at Ur, rivalling the gold mask of Tutankhamen, and some 2000 years earlier.

By Mr. Leonard Woolley, Director of the excavations at Ur-of-the-Chaldees

In the coffin itself were placed the more personal possessions of the dead prince. One of the latter is perhaps the most remarkable object that has yet been found in the land of Sumer, a great wig of hammered and engraved gold *(Figure 121)*. It is life-size, meant to be worn – the holes round the rim are for fixing the wadded lining, of which traces were found inside – and was perhaps a helmet, perhaps a ceremonial head-dress. The workmanship is admirable and reflects the greatest credit on the goldsmiths of the fourth millennium B.C. . . . This technical skill at so early a date is far more important than the mere richness of the material. Specially noticeable is the faultless regularity of the fine wavy lines engraved on the wig.

Even the most optimistic of us had hardly ventured to hope that we should ever find at Ur the grave of one of the kings. Now good fortune has given us the undisturbed grave of one who, if he was not a king, was certainly a prince of the royal house. . . . The grave was much the same as others of its time in the cemetery, only rather larger; what distinguished it was the extraordinary richness of its contents. The body lay in a wooden coffin set against one side of the grave-shaft; the free space round three sides was crowded with offerings, and in the coffin were the more personal possessions of the dead prince. One is the remarkable great wig of hammered and engraved gold. . . . Not less perfect is the fluted gold bowl found outside the coffin, the richness of whose decoration contrasted strongly with the simplicity of the drinking bowls and of the lamp, also of gold, found inside with the body; but these atoned for their plainness by the fact that each was inscribed with the name of the owner, Meskalam-dug, "the good hero of the land". Even his weapons were of gold, or of electrum, an alloy of gold and silver, harder and more serviceable; the dagger which hung from his silver belt was a blade of bright gold and a hilt of gold and silver; even the humble whetstone was of blue lapis lazuli on a gold ring. For artistic workmanship perhaps the finest thing is a tiny gold figure of a monkey forming the head of a pin; last year we found miniature figures which astonished us by the delicacy of their modelling, but none equalled this tiny squatting beast only five-eighths of an inch high. This technical skill at this date – the grave must go back to nearly 3500 B.C. – is more significant than the great richness of the material. The . . . real value of the metal is that it preserves, as silver never does and copper seldom, the full quality of the

121 The "gold wig" of Mes-kalam-dug

artistic work. . . . The faultless regularity of the fine lines engraved on the gold wig, the feeling for form in the monkey's figure and attitude, the balance of design in the fluted bowl, enable us to judge better the less well-preserved objects in silver and copper. There was a tall silver vase precisely like those which, on early stone reliefs, priests use for pouring libations, and there were silver bowls and fluted copper vessels and many spears stuck upright at the grave's head and foot. These weapons were reversed, point downwards in the ground as troops reverse arms at a modern funeral; but one, with copper blade and shaft mounted with gold jointed to imitate bamboo, stood right way up. It was this that led us down through the earth to the prince's grave.

1928

A great year for Tutankhamen, Ur and Mohenjo-daro and the Indus Valley civilisation, and Mycenaean bronzes from Dendra. This was, incidentally, the year in which human sacrifice was added to gold treasure among the public attractions of Ur. Among other published items of major interest were Etruscan and Greek vases from Spina in the Po Estuary; a star map of 3,400 years ago found in the Tomb of Senmut near Hatshepsut's temple; important Swedish excavations in Cyprus at Soli, Lapithos, Vouni and Dali; discoveries at Coclé in Panama (with two pages in colour) and a report of the discovery by fishermen at Artemision of the famous bronze of Poseidon (or Zeus) which is now so fine a feature of the Athens Museum.

January 7, 1928

A NEW CHAPTER IN ARCHAEOLOGY:
The prehistoric civilisation of the Indus

By Sir John Marshall, C.I.E., Litt.D., F.S.A., Director-General of Archaeology in India

During the last few months many enquiries have been addressed to me from Europe and America about our recent archaeological discoveries in India, and particularly about the results of our work among prehistoric remains in the Indus Valley and the Punjab. The points on which information has been chiefly sought are the nature of the finds made at Mohenjo-daro and Harappa; the extent and age and character of the culture revealed; its relationship with other known cultures of the Chalcolithic epoch in Asia and Europe; and the race and language and religion of the people who developed it, as well as the mode of their daily life. Many of the questions put to me can be answered but very vaguely at present; others are not yet susceptible of being answered at all; for we are still at the beginning of our labours, and there is much spade-work to be done and many more sites to be explored before we can hope to find the solution of the problems before us. So far, however, as far as answers are possible, and so far as they can be given within the narrow compass of these articles, I will endeavour to supply them.

The remains now laid bare at Mohenjo-daro cover an area of more than thirteen acres, and belong to the three latest cities on the site. The best-built structures are those of the third city; the poorest, of the first. All, however, are built of well-burnt brick, usually laid in mud, but occasionally in gypsum (plaster of Paris) mortar with foundations and in-fillings of sun-dried brick. Of the various groups of buildings that have been exposed, the most striking are focussed round about a lofty eminence near the north-west corner of the city, which in after times was crowned with a Buddhist stupa. Beneath this stupa there are reasons for believing that the chief temple of the city is located, and it is probable that the structures grouped around it are all of a religious or quasi-religious character. Outstanding among them is an imposing edifice containing a large bath or tank *(Figure 122)*, which may be assumed to have been used either for ablution purposes in connection with the neighbouring temple, or possibly as a reservoir for sacred fish, crocodiles or the like. Sacred tanks for both purposes have

122 The Great Bath at Mohenjo-daro possibly used for temple ablutions or as a reservoir for sacred fish or crocodiles

long been a familiar feature in India, and it is likely that they were already in use during the Chalcolithic Age. The reservoir itself is 39 feet in length by 23 feet in breadth, and is sunk 8 feet below the floor level. On the four sides is a boldly fenestrated corridor, with a platform in front and halls or small chambers behind. The outer wall, which is more than 6 feet in thickness, with a pronounced batter on the outside, was pierced by two large entrances on the south and smaller ones on the east and north. Of the chambers ranged along the east side of the building, the middle one is occupied by a large well, from which the bath could be fed. At either end of the bath is a descending flight of steps, with a shallow landing at their foot. Like

the bathroom floors of the private houses, the floor is laid in finely-jointed brick-on-edge, and remarkable care and ingenuity has been exercised in the construction of the surrounding walls. These walls, which are nearly 10 feet in thickness, are made in three sections, the inner and outer of burnt brick, the in-filling between them of sun-dried brick; but in order to make them completely watertight, the brick-work has been laid in gypsum mortar, and the back of the inner wall coated with an inch-thick layer of bitumen. Bitumen was also used for bedding the wooden planks with which the steps were lined. The practice of employing this material as a cementing and waterproofing agent was, of course, widespread in Mesopotamia; but it does not therefore follow that the architects of Mohenjo-daro learnt the use of it from that quarter, since bitumen was also obtainable in the Suleiman Range, as well as further west in Baluchistan. Another feature of special interest in connection with this bath is a great covered drain over 6 feet in height, and furnished with a corbelled vaulted roof by which the water was conducted outside the city. . . .

Apart from the above, the remains brought to light at Mohenjo-daro are for the most part private dwelling-houses or shops, which tend to confirm more and more our earlier impression that the amenities of life enjoyed by the average citizen at Mohenjo-daro were far in advance of anything to be found at that time in Babylonia or on the banks of the Nile. At Ur, in Sumer, it is true, Mr. Woolley has recently unearthed a group of houses which afford a most interesting parallel with those at Mohenjo-daro, and supply still another proof of a close cultural connection between Southern Mesopotamia and Sind. But even at Ur the houses are by no means equal in point of construction to those at Mohenjo-daro, nor are they provided with a system of drainage (*Figure 123*) at all comparable with that found at the latter site – a system by which the sewage was carried by drains into street tanks and thence removed by scavengers.

At Harappa, which is 450 miles up country from Mohenjo-daro, Mr. Vat's excavations have now been carried to a greater depth than previously and a number of antiquities have been recovered of an earlier type than those found at Mohenjo-daro. Among these may be mentioned a copper vessel containing a collection of copper weapons and implements – namely, a mace-head, two double axes, seven daggers, two lance-heads, sixteen spear-heads, twenty-one celts, one saw, two choppers and thirteen chisels. . . . Two of the daggers and two of the celts bear inscriptions in the pictographic script. The same early stratum yielded more than 150 seals and terracotta sealings, the majority of which are smaller in size and different in shape from those discovered in the upper strata. One of the most striking of these seals depicts a procession of seven men wearing kilts and helmets and marching in line from right to left. On another is a man attacking a tiger from a *machan*; while a third portrays a man carrying a standard (which was no doubt an object of cult worship) being a wicker manger identical with those from which many of the

123 Drainage on modern lines in a house at Mohenjo-daro, showing a vertical drain pipe

animals on the seals are feeding. A unique object found in this low stratum was a model in copper of a two-wheeled cart with a gabled roof, and driver seated in front. This, possibly, is the oldest known example of a wheeled vehicle, older even than the stele fragment with the picture of a chariot recently found by Mr. Woolley at Ur, which in its turn antedates by a thousand years the use of the wheel in Egypt. . . .

Chronology

The date of the buildings described is determined within tolerably narrow limits by the discovery at Susa and several sites in Mesopotamia of typical Indian seals inscribed with Indian pictographic legends, in positions which leave no doubt that they belonged to the period before Sargon I – that is before about 2700 B.C. On another seal of the same pattern recently unearthed at Ur, the legend is in cuneiform characters of about 2700 B.C. It may be inferred, therefore, that this class of Indian seal is to be assigned to the first half of the third millennium B.C. or earlier; and inasmuch as seals of this class are associated with the three uppermost cities at Mohenjo-daro, we may confidently fix the date of these cities between 3500 and 2500 B.C. . . . Taking everything into consideration, a period of six centuries may reasonably be allowed for the rise and fall of the three cities, and we shall probably not be far wrong if we provisionally assign the first city to about 2700 B.C., the second city to about 3000 B.C. and the third to about 3300 B.C. The uppermost cities of Harappa are approximately contemporary while the lower ones, with the more primitive type of seals and other antiquities mentioned above, are referable to an earlier period.

Races

Of what race or races were the authors of this Indus culture? And what was their religion? In the present state of our knowledge only the vaguest answers to either question can be returned. As might have been expected, nearly all the skeletal remains found at Mohenjo-daro appertain to a dolichocephalic people, who may reasonably be assumed to have belonged to the great long-headed race of Southern Asia and Europe to which the name of "Mediterranean" is commonly applied, but which, besides the Mediterraneans, comprised also the pre-Aryan Dravidians of India, as well as many other peoples. The only skull approximating to a brachycephalic type is from the fractional burial . . . and this appears to exhibit the same racial characteristics as the marble and alabaster statues from Mohenjo-daro, which are pronouncedly brachycephalic. . . .

Weaving and dress

Numerous spindle whorls in the debris of the houses attest the practice of spinning and weaving, and scraps of a fine woven cotton material have also been found. . . .

124 Terracotta figurine from the Indus Valley of a woman with elaborate headdress and necklaces

Male attire among the upper classes consisted of two garments: a skirt or kilt fastened round the waist, like the primitive Sumerian skirt, and a plain or patterned shawl which was drawn over the left and under the right shoulder, so as to leave the right arm free. Men *(Plate 19, p. 193)* wore short beards and whiskers, with the upper lip sometimes shaven, as in Sumer, sometimes not. Their hair was taken back from the forehead and coiled in a knot at the back of the head with a filet to support it. The one and only head of a female statue that we possess shows the hair falling loose behind; but whether this was the prevailing fashion or not is questionable. Among the lower classes, men apparently went naked and women with a narrow loin-cloth only; though there is one statuette of a dancing girl *(Plate 20, p. 193)* without even this garment. Ornaments were freely worn by all classes alike, necklaces *(Figure 124)* and finger-rings by both men and women; earrings, bangles, girdles, and anklets by the latter only.

Domesticated animals
Among the domesticated animals were: the humped Indian long-horned bull (*Bos Indicus*) – of which, to judge by the frequency of the remains, large herds must have been maintained; the buffalo (*Bos bubalus*), a short-horned bull, the sheep, pig (*Sus cristatus*), dog, horse and elephant. No trace has been found of either the camel or the cat. The horse in the Indus Valley was the small *Equus caballus*, near akin to the Indian country-bred. Of dogs there are two very distinct breeds: one, the *Canis familiaris*, closely related to the common pariah, and the other remarkably like our present-day mastiff. . . .

Wild animals
The remains of wild animals are few, but among those frequently depicted on the seal-stones are the tiger, elephant, and rhinoceros, the presence of which may be taken as an indication that the climate was damper and the vegetation more dense than at present. The lion, which prefers arid and sparsely covered country, does not occur.

January 14, 1928

A NEW CHAPTER IN ARCHAEOLOGY:
The Prehistoric Civilisation of the Indus
By Sir John Marshall, C.I.E., Litt.D., F.S.A., Director-General of Archaeology in India

Agriculture
Big cities with teeming populations like Harappa and Mohenjo-daro could never have existed save in an agricultural country which was producing its own food on a large scale. Though little has yet been discovered of the processes of agriculture and irrigation then in vogue, it is worthy of remark that the specimens of wheat found in Mohenjo-daro resemble the common variety grown in the Punjab to-day. Touching this question of agriculture, it is also noteworthy that there are strong reasons for inferring (a) that the rainfall in Sind and the Western Punjab was then substantially heavier than it is now; (b) that Sind was then watered by two large rivers instead of one, and as a consequence was at once more fertile and less subject to violent inundations. . . .

Food
Besides bread and milk, the food of the Indus people appears to have included beef, mutton, and pork, the flesh of turtles, tortoises, and gharial, fresh fish from the Indus and dried fish imported from the sea-coast. Evidence of these various articles of diet is furnished by bones – sometimes in half-burnt condition – found among the houses. . . .

Personal ornaments
The ornaments of the rich were of silver and gold, or copper plated with gold, of blue faience,

ivory, carnelian, jadeite, and multicoloured stones of various kinds. For the poor, they were mainly of shell or terracotta. Many examples of both kinds have been recovered. Especially striking are the girdles of carnelian and gilded copper, and some of the small objects, e.g. earrings and "netting" needles of pure gold, the surface of which is polished to a degree that would do credit to a present-day jeweller.

Metals

Besides gold and silver, the Indus people were familiar with copper, tin, and lead. Copper they used freely for weapons, implements, and domestic utensils, daggers, knives, hatchets, sickles, celts, chisels, vessels, figurines, and personal ornaments, amulets, wire, and so on. Most of these objects were wrought by hammering but examples of cast copper are not unknown. Copper was easily obtainable – on the west from Baluchistan, on the east from Rajputana, and on the north from Afghanistan. Tin was more difficult to get, and was probably imported from Khorasan, or through Sumer from further west. It is found, not as a pure metal, but alloyed with copper to form bronze, which was used mainly for tools requiring a hard cutting edge – namely, razors, chisels, celts, and saws, but also for vessels, statuettes, bangles, beads, buttons, and other ornaments. The bronze is of a high grade, containing from 6 to 12 per cent of tin; but, in spite of its advantage over copper being well recognised, the number of bronze objects is comparatively small, doubtless owing to the difficulty and cost of procuring tin.

Weapons and knives

The paucity of weapons at both Harappa and Mohenjo-daro is surprising, the only ones yet found being a few mace-heads, axes, daggers, arrow-heads and possibly spear-heads. It looks as if these cities were but little acquainted with warfare! While copper was used, and used freely, for all sorts of utensils, knives made from flakes of chert were also common, and show,

like the stone maces and celts, that the influence of the Neolithic age had not entirely passed away. . . .

Pottery

Common domestic vessels were of earthenware. Their great variety of shapes – each evolved for some particular purpose – evidences a long period of antecedent development, though it is curious how few of the vases are provided with handles. Most of the pottery is plain, undecorated red ware, but painted ware is by no means uncommon. As a rule the designs are painted in black, on a darkish red slip, and consist of geometric and foliate devices with occasional figures of animals. . . .

Writing

The presence of inscribed seals, sealings and other objects in almost every building is sufficient indication that the occupants must have been familiar with the art of writing, and it may be inferred that it was employed for business and other purposes, though what materials took the place of the clay commonly used for writing on in Mesopotamia is not known. . . .

Inscribed seals

The seals, of which nearly a thousand have been recovered, were worn by a cord round the neck or wrist, and were used probably for sealing parcels, merchandise, and so on, just as they were used in historical times in India. It is not improbable, also, that they may have served as amulets, and that the animals engraved on them may have had some religious significance. . . .

Art

The art of the Indus is distinct from that of any neighbouring country, notwithstanding the elements in common between them. The best of the figures on the engraved seals – notably the humped Indian bulls and short-horn cattle – are distinguished by a breadth of treatment and a feeling for line and form unequalled in the

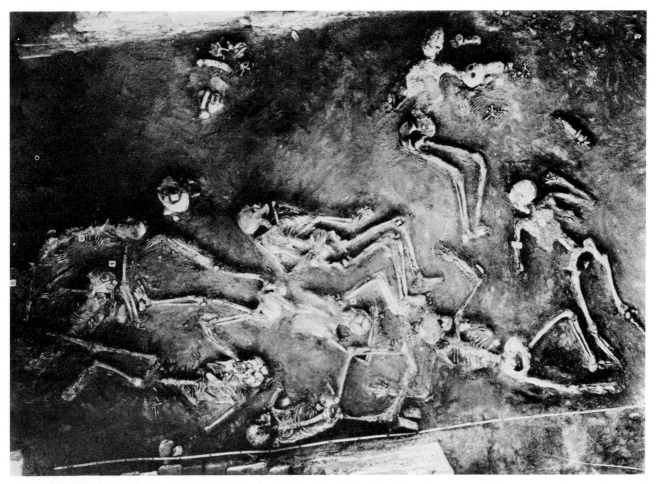

125 Five victims of some tragedy, affording no evidence of ordinary burial customs among the ancient Indians

contemporary glyptic art of Elam or Meso-potamia or Egypt. The modelling, too, in the faience of the miniature rams, monkeys, dogs and squirrels is of a very high order – far in advance of what we should expect in the fourth and third millenniums B.C. Contrasted with these, the few examples we possess of human figures, whether executed in marble, stone, clay, or bronze, are strangely uncouth, and suggest that, for some reason or other, the artists could have relatively little experience in delineating the human form. . . . There is not one of them, however, comparable to the best of the Sumerian portrait figures.

Disposal of the dead

Two large groups of skeletons have been found in Mohenjo-daro; one group inside a house, the other in a street. All of these, however, appear to have been the victims of some tragedy – murder, perhaps, or pestilence – and afford no evidence as to how the dead were ordinarily disposed of *(Figure 125)*. Only one indisputable example of inhumation during the Chalcolithic age has been found at Mohenjo-daro. This is a "fractional" burial of the same type as those found at Nal in Baluchistan and at Musyan in Western Persia, the distinctive feature of such burials being that only a fraction of the skeleton was buried, together with an assortment of earthenware vases and other small objects personal to the dead – the corpse having been either exposed to the vultures or (which is less likely) subjected to a previous burial. . . .

That cremation was also practised is proved by the presence at Harappa of small brick structures somewhat like Hindu *samadhis*, containing cinerary remains, as well as of a platform covered with ashes and half-charred bones, which is thought to be a cremation platform. . . .

Religion

That there were some features in common between the religious cults of the Indus and Mesopotamian peoples may be inferred from several figures closely resembling the Babylonian Eabani, which are engraved on seals and copper pieces. The numerous terracotta figurines, moreover, which portray a nude female crowned with elaborate headdress and bedecked with ornaments can hardly fail to be identified with the figures of the mother goddess familiar in Mesopotamia and countries further to the west.

On the other hand there is a certain amount of evidence pointing to a connection with pre-Dynastic Egypt. Thus, on one of the faience sealings is a row of four standards borne aloft by men, each of which supports a totem figure remarkably like the well-known totem standards of the Egyptian nomes. The resemblance, indeed, is so striking that it might almost be supposed that this particular sealing was an import from Egypt, were it not that it is inscribed on the reverse with an Indian pictographic legend. Moreover, that totems played an important part in the religion of the "Indus" people seems evident from the statues and other representations of a strange composite animal, partly ram, partly bull, and partly elephant, as well as from a multitude of other animals – real or fabulous – engraved on the seals, among which attention may be drawn especially to a pair of ass-headed creatures like those depicted on a well-known Mycenaean gem from Vaphio in Greece.

If, however, the above elements are suggestive of parallels with the West, there are other elements which are characteristically and exclusively Indian. Thus, one of the sealings depicts a figure sitting cross-legged with snake-hooded Nagas worshipping on either side, just as they are portrayed worshipping the Buddha three thousand years later. Then there are certain curious rings and phallus-like objects – the latter somewhat resembling in form the so-called chessmen pillars of Assam, the religious character of which can hardly be doubted, though symbolic meaning has not yet been established. A great variety of both classes of objects has been found at Harappa and Mohenjo-daro.

March 3, 1928

UR

By Mr. C. Leonard Woolley. Reproduced from his article in The Times

Among the remarkable new discoveries made at Ur . . . one of the most important was that of a queen's tomb, intact and full of rich treasure. Describing it recently . . . he [Mr. C. Leonard Woolley] says: "At one end of the chamber were piled the offerings, once set on wooden shelves, now fallen in heaps on the ground and covered with wreckage; at the other end, on a wooden bier at the head and foot of which were crouched the bodies of attendants lay the bones of the Queen Shub-ad. Her headdress, worn originally over a great wig, was a marvellous sight as it was laboriously disengaged from stones and earth. Coil after coil of broad gold ribbon surrounded the hair; above these, across the forehead, ran a frontlet of lapis and carnelian beads from which hung heavy rings of gold; higher up was a wreath of big gold mulberry leaves hanging from another string of beads, and above this another wreath of leaves like willow-leaves with large gold flowers between, their petals inlaid with lapis and white shell. Under the edge of the ribbons hung enormous gold earrings; towering over the top of the head was a golden ornament like a Spanish comb, shaped like a hand with seven fingers, each finger ending in a golden flower. The cloak was fastened on the right shoulder with three gold pins with lapis heads, and by the fastening were worn amulets – two gold fish and one of lapis, a lapis figure of a reclining calf, and a little group in gold of two antelopes. By the side of the bier was a second crown. Against a background of minute gold and lapis beads sewn on to a leather fillet were gold ornaments of a remarkable sort:

besides conventional palmettes and flowers there were ears of corn, clusters of pomegranates, the fruit and leaves rendered with absolute realism, and pairs of little animals, stags and rams, antelopes and bearded bulls. The tomb produced three gold bowls, two of them plain, one decorated with fluting and engraved patterns; a gold strainer, a pair of cockleshells in gold and another in silver, containing toilet paints; ten gold finger-rings, more earrings, quantities of beads, a set of eighteen fluted silver tumblers, many silver bowls, two of them fitted with drinking-tubes of gold and of lapis lazuli; the head of a bull in silver, silver lamps, thirty or more vases of alabaster and steatite, a copper brazier supported on bulls' feet, and a mass of copper vessels, about 150 objects in all."

June 9, 1928

NEW LIGHT ON HOMERIC GREECE: DENDRA TREASURES:

Exquisite gold-work; a cenotaph with a unique hoard of bronzes and a "table of sacrifice"

By A. J. B. Wace, from material supplied by Professor Persson, Head of the Swedish Archaeological Expedition in Greece

The Swedish archaeological expedition to Greece, under the patronage of H.R.H. the Crown Prince of Sweden, has followed up the great success of 1926, when Professor Persson, in conjunction with Dr. Bertos, the Greek Inspector of Antiquities, opened an unplundered beehive tomb at Dendra. This village lies in the shadow of the citadel of Midea, the third after Mycenae and Tiryns of the great prehistoric fortresses of Argolis, and the tombs found probably formed part of the cemeteries of Midea.

The first work of the season was devoted to cleaning and studying the rich finds from the beehive tomb, which brought out interesting details. The order of the burials and the ritual followed seems clear. The princess, who wore a necklace of gold rosettes, was buried first. Later came the king and queen, at opposite ends of a long grave, with their feet turned towards one another. By the king were his weapons, his gold and silver bowls, with his signets; by the queen who wore a necklace of gold beads with an ivy-leaf design, her treasures. Between them lay other objects, including a fine lamp and an ostrich egg once ornamented with gold, silver, and faience. At the king's feet lay some weapons in disorder, and other funeral offerings. It seems that, when the royal pair were interred with their more permanent possessions, the perishable objects were laid upon a wooden frame placed over a small pit alongside. Fire was set to this, and, as it died down, the relatives filed by, pouring, in the Homeric fashion, libations to quench the fire and throwing at the king's feet a choice dagger or some other valued object as a last offering.

Specially noticeable are the gold plates which covered the hilts and pommels of the king's swords, and the gold studs edged with filigree work in which each small grain was soldered on separately. On one of the king's gold rings, with an oval-shaped bezel, are seen at the bottom two recumbent quadrupeds "affronted". On the line above them two horned animals stand on curious objects which appear to consist of a triple band of snakes. . . . Three of the royal signets found in the famous octopus cup which lay on the king's breast are of exceptional size, being over an inch and a half in diameter. One shows two recumbent oxen and two scenes with lions pulling down bulls. Some suggest that since the lion was the badge of Mycenae, and the bull that of Crete, there may be some allusions in the choice of subject. The spirit and refinement of the work are amazing. Other ornaments discovered are small decorative pieces of glass for the purpose of necklaces and borders.

In 1927 work was resumed in the cemetery at Dendra. Two rock-cut chambers of the usual type contained the funeral offerings expected in ordinary graves of the later Bronze Age in the thirteenth century B.C. The third tomb was soon found to be unusual in size and contents, and therefore important. The tomb chamber, hewn out of solid rock at a depth of seventeen feet from the surface, is approached by an entrance passage six feet wide, driven straight into the hillside for a distance of sixty feet. At the doorway of the tomb, this passage, or "dromos", was completely obstructed by a heap of great stones torn down from the wall which closed the door. Buried beneath them lay the skeleton of a woman, who had with her a few ornaments, a long bronze pin, two spindle whorls, and some moulded plaques of glass once covered with thin gold leaf. Robbers who broke through the wall in the doorway had presumably found these and abandoned them when they discovered they were not solid gold. This entry by plunderers occurred in the Mycenaean epoch, but fortunately their efforts were in vain, because, before they broke in, a large section of the rock roof of the tomb chamber had fallen in and covered the floor with debris to a depth of four and a half feet.

When the excavators cleared away the wall which blocked the doorway and was still standing to a height of five feet, there appeared two large stone slabs fitted in with smaller stones, and making a sill in the floor. They seemed to roof a grave-pit, and, in order to avoid too much excitement in the village, which had a lively recollection of the golden treasures of the year before, it was decided to lift the slabs during the midday siesta with the assistance of two trusted workmen only. When the stones were turned over, the pit, nearly five feet long, three feet deep and about one and a half feet broad, showed a magnificent sight. It was almost filled with a splendid series of thirty-three bronze vessels and implements, all showing rich patination, and lying just as they were placed many centuries ago. There are six jugs, seven bowls (one with wishbone handles like that of the queen's gold cup found the previous year), four tripods, five lamps, four mirrors, two knives, two razors, a spear-head, a sword, and a six-pronged fish-spear.

It is undoubtedly one of the most beautiful and one of the richest finds of bronzes of the Mycenaean period that has ever been made in Greece, and several are ornamented with finely incised patterns, floral, marine and geometric. Remarkable, indeed unique in Greece, is the fact that the original wooden handles are still attached to the implements. Though much shrivelled, and showing no sign of decoration, the wood swelled out when soaked with a special preservative solution, and carved relief stood out again as if by magic. A mirror-handle . . . shows two female figures, one holding a mirror and the other a branch, a motive similar to that on a carved ivory mirror-handle from the Tomb of Clytemnestra at Mycenae. In one of the lamps a large piece of textile is preserved.

When the chamber was cleared a low hearth or altar, built of small stones and plaster, was found against the inner wall, on which were smoke marks and holes for the insertion of metal objects. On and around it were traces of charcoal, which was also found in great quantities on the left of the door, where there seems to have been another fire. The tomb yielded seven vessels of stone, three lamps of steatite, and four vases of alabaster, one perhaps Egyptian. There were several small objects of gold, some in the shape of shells with delicate filigree-work; quantities of embossed glass plaques of unusual size, several of which still retain a coating of thin gold leaf; a seal stone, many pieces of boar's tusk from a leather helmet, and a broken bronze sword with hundreds of small glass beads that had decorated its hilt. Thousands of other small glass beads of various colours lay close together in a mass, and were removed as they lay in great flakes of earth. They show a bead pattern worked in colour, probably the remains of a beaded garment. This is a new feature of Mycenaean art. One of the two pits in the floor was empty. The other held bones of animals, oxen, sheep, or goats, with a few small objects, a badly preserved silver cup, a seal stone, an ivory flower, and a bronze sacrificial knife.

Most surprising of all, no human bones of any kind were found in the tomb, and this presents a problem. Here is a tomb, large and well-furnished, but apparently a cenotaph only. The explanation is to be sought in some worked fragments of soft stone found among the debris which covered the floor. These, fifty in all, were carefully numbered and removed from the chamber, and, after forming a giant puzzle for the excavators, who spent many hours in endeavouring to fit them together, proved to make up four separate slabs. The first, about six feet long by three feet wide, has square sinkings at each corner within a raised edge, and seems to have been a table for sacrifices, since there is a notch on each side to bind the victim in place. . . . The sinkings in the corner would collect the blood, and in one there is a stain as if of clotted gore. The second, somewhat smaller, is smooth on one side, and has a number of cup marks scattered all over the other. The last two, the largest of which is nearly four feet long by two broad, have small head-like projections at one end, and cup-marks and grooves which call to mind the cresset or menhir stones of Nordic religions, while in shape they resemble some Trojan idols.

Their presence in the tomb – for we must regard this as a tomb of about 1300 B.C. – and some Homeric references suggest a reasonable explanation for the absence of human remains. Athena, when Telemachus departs in search of his father, tells him to raise up a mound for him, if dead, and to make the proper offerings. Achilles built such a cenotaph for Patroclus at Troy and Menelaus for Agamemnon in Egypt. In the Odyssey, when Odysseus (Ulysses) goes to the Underworld, he entices the shades by the blood of the victims he sacrifices. If, then, this tomb was made for some great man who had perished at sea or abroad, his relatives would wish to call home his wandering and restless spirit, so that it should be at peace and not harm them, and they not be blamed for failing to pay due rites to the dead, and also that the dead hero might be at hand to help in time of danger. Then, as the soul could not rest while the body was unburied, the menhir stones in rough human shape would suggest the lost body, and the sacrifices would call the spirit to rest in comfort in its own land and among its own kin surrounded with all proper rites and honours.

June 23, 1928

WHOLESALE HUMAN SACRIFICE AT UR:

A revelation of unrecorded barbarities practised at royal burials 5000 years ago

By C. Leonard Woolley, Director of the Joint Expedition of the British Museum and the Museum of the University of Pennsylvania to Mesopotamia

No less remarkable than the objects found last winter in the royal graves at Ur was the discovery of the rites of human sacrifice which accompanied the burial of a king. In all the literature of Babylonia there is no hint of any such custom as having been practised at any time; long before the historic period from which our written records date it had been discontinued and the memory of it either forgotten or carefully concealed by writers grown ashamed of the barbarities of an earlier day. But now we have definite proof that in the fourth millennium before Christ the Sumerian king went to his tomb in company with a whole following of soldiers, courtiers and women, who, like the vases of food and drink, the weapons and the tools set in his grave, should minister to his needs and pleasures in another world.

Mr. Forestier's double-page drawing *(Figure 126)* is a reconstruction, as faithful as may be, of the scene in the shaft of the king's grave just before the sacrifice took place: it is based upon the actual plan of the grave, with the exact position of every body marked, and upon the objects found with those bodies, while details of costume have been reproduced from contemporary designs in carving or mosaic-work. The view is taken from one corner of the rectangular pit. In the background is seen the tomb-chamber built of stone and brick, its vaulted roof rounded off by half-domes at either end, its walls smoothly plastered, its arched doorway sealed with masonry. On the left is the sloped approach which led from the ground surface to the bottom of the grave-shaft. The earth sides of the shaft itself are hidden by matting;

above, it is open to the sun; the whole area is crowded with the victims dedicated to the dead king's majesty. After the victims fell (as shown in Mr. Forestier's other drawing) *(Figure 127)* reed matting was spread all over the bodies, earth was thrown in, and the pit filled up.

At the foot of the slope stand the six soldiers of the guard wearing copper helmets and great cloaks of heavy felt. Their bones, their helmets, and their spears were found there lying in order; the dress, cloaks, and kilts are copied from a remarkable mosaic found in another tomb. . . . Then just inside the shaft proper, standing as they had been backed down the slope, come two wagons, clumsy four-wheeled affairs each drawn by three oxen. The grooms stand at the beasts' heads; the driver of one wagon is in his place, that of the other stands beside the wheels. Of the wooden wagons little was found, for wood can not long endure in the soil of Ur, and, as a rule, no more can be traced than a black film such as might be left by a fire lit against the face of an earth cutting. But we could make out and even photograph the outlines of the wheels and axle-trees; the design of the wagons is taken from the same mosaic as supplied the details of the soldiers' dress. The oxen wore wide collars of silver decorated with patterns in repoussé-work, and had large silver rings in their nostrils; on the reins were strung beads of silver and lapis lazuli, and they passed through rein-rings of silver surmounted by a "mascot" in the form of a bull; these can be seen in the drawing attached to the poles of the cars.

Against the end of the masonry chamber stand nine ladies of the Court, wearing elaborate

126 *An Ur king's harem, servants and bodyguard ready to be sacrificed to form his retinue in the next world. Reconstruction drawing by A. Forestier*

head-dresses of stone beads and gold; round the forehead was a wreath of beads and gold leaves which held up the veil; in the ears were grotesquely large ear-rings of gold in the form of crescent moons. The hair was bound in a hair-net of gold ribbon, and above the head was a sort of Spanish comb ornament in silver, its points decorated with flower rosettes whose petals were inlaid with red, white, blue, and gold. In front of these was a mixed crowd of people, men and women, less richly dressed, the subordinate attendants of the Court. Along the walls of the narrow passage leading to the chamber door were two rows of servants, women on the left, on the right men wearing head-bands of beads and silver chains, and carrying daggers at their belts. Altogether there were fifty-nine persons crowd-ed into the narrow space of the tomb shaft. Two other objects which figure in the recon-struction call for attention. Set above the fallen bodies of the Court women against the chamber

wall was a statue of a bull, its body of wood hopelessly decayed, its head of copper; and against the left side of the shaft, also set above the bones of the victims, a second bull figure (*Plate 21, p. 194*), but in this case the head was of lapis lazuli and gold. This head, found crushed and shapeless, has now been re-stored.... Of the wooden body only the barest outline could be traced, and it seems to have been very sketchily modelled, the legs in low relief against a solid block, the tail rising straight and stiff in the air. Possibly it was not really a statue as such, but a harp, different in type from the harp found in the queen's grave, but resembling one drawn on a fine shell-relief which adorned the front of the bull's body; the "tail" in that case would have been the support for the horizontal beam from which the strings came down to the back of the bull figure.

We do not know how the sacrifice of all these human victims was carried out. Whether they body of the statue was of wood; the head of lapis lazuli and gold *(Plate 21)*. The technique of its manufacture is interesting. The head, all except the ears and horns, was hammered up from a sheet of thin gold and set over a wooden core; the horns and ears made separately, were fixed to this. Under the chin, a deep cut was made in the wood, the edges of the gold being bent down into the cut, and here was inserted the beard: the base of this was a wooden board on which the tresses, cut from lapis lazuli, were set in bitumen, while the back and sides of the board were concealed by a plate of thin silver seamed by silver nails. The upper part of the woodwork went right up into the wood of the head, and was made fast to it by copper nails driven through the crown. The gold did not cover the crown at all; here the wooden core, left exposed, was coated with bitumen, and into the bitumen were laid the lapis lazuli locks of hair, each lock separately carved. The eyes, of white shell with lapis pupils enclosed in eye-sockets of lapis, were secured by copper bolts to the wood core of the head; a strip of gold, nailed on behind the horns, completed the neck, and a narrow band of mosaic in shell and lapis formed a collar to mark the distinction between the metal head and the wooden body. A row of engraved shell plaques ornamented the front of the figure, set between the legs just below the level of the beard.

127 Fifty-nine people – men and women – along with six oxen, sacrificed at Ur at a royal burial. Reconstruction drawing by A. Forestier

all were really marshalled in order and cut down where they stood, as must have been the case with the oxen, or whether they were slaughtered apart and then laid in the grave, the evidence does not definitely show; but, on the whole, the former theory seems the most probable and Mr. Forestier's reconstruction must represent very faithfully the scene in the tomb shaft a few moments before the ritual murder was performed, and the victims were stretched out in the places where we found their mouldering skeletons more than five thousand years later.

The golden bull's head from Ur

This is the head of a bull statue found standing in the shaft of the king's grave over the bodies of the human beings sacrificed in his honour. The

The bearded bull has now become for us a commonplace of early Sumerian art. The bull as the symbol of strength, is the natural victim for sacrifice to the gods, and may itself stand for the god. By the addition of a beard, the regular attribute of deity, the sacrificial animal may be in some measure identified with the god to whom it is offered, may become "the great Bull of Heaven"; certainly with this curious appanage the bull acquires an extra religious significance which makes it a favourite subject for amulets and for sculpture. It is possible that this gold-headed bull was not really an independent figure, but was part of a harp; if so, the instrument differs in type from that found by us in the queen's grave, but might agree with one represented on one of the shell plaques inset in the breast of the animal.

The shell mosaics

The object here illustrated *(Plate 22, p. 195)* is an elaborate example of inlay-work in shell, lapis lazuli and pink limestone. The two large plaques were set back to back at a slight angle with triangular pieces between their ends, and the whole may have been mounted on a pole so as to be carried as a standard. It was found beside the shoulder of a man buried in a side-chamber of the oldest of the royal tombs. Though the wooden framework had entirely perished, and the bitumen in which the mosaic was set had been reduced to powder, the *tesserae* had for the most part not shifted from their position, and, though much labour had to be spent on straightening and levelling the face of the mosaic, this could be done without disturbing the fragments of inlay, and what is shown here is not a reconstruction, but the original mosaic. Some of the border has been restored, but the figures are in their original places, and neither they nor their background have been scattered and re-assembled: only the triangular ends had been seriously broken up by the pressure of the forty feet of soil under which they lay, and have had to be reconstructed; but we have, almost intact, the whole composition as it was worked out by the craftsmen of 3500 B.C. On one panel is seen the royal family at feast: in the top row the king and his court sit and eat; in the lower rows servants bring the materials for the feast – sheep and oxen, goats, fish and bundles of unrecognisable objects. On the other panel is a war scene. In the bottom row are the chariots, four-wheeled cars, each drawn by four asses, and containing a driver and a fighting man; they advance over the fallen bodies of their foes. In the middle row, on the left, is the phalanx of heavy-armed troops, the men wearing copper helmets and heavy cloaks of felt, armed with short stabbing-spears; in front of then the light-armed skirmishers are already engaged with the enemy. In the middle of the top row stands the king, with his family and his empty chariot behind him, and before him prisoners, driven in under guard that he may decide their fate. Here we have a contemporary picture of the Sumerian army in its various branches. As a work of art it is unparalleled; as a historic document, invaluable.

QUEEN SHUB-AD'S 5000-YEAR-OLD HEAD-DRESS:
An Ur treasure

By Mr. C. Leonard Woolley

It was found on the queen's skull inside the stone-built tomb-chamber. Though crushed by stones and earth, every one of its component parts kept its position in the soil, and their order could be noted with such accuracy that a reconstruction was comparatively simple *(Plate 23, p. 196)*. The gold ribbon, the basis of the whole, retained its oval form, and, for the purposes of removal from the soil, the different strands were fixed by strips of glued paper twisted between them. This gave the outline of the wig. A new wig was made, of these measurements, and dressed in the style illustrated by early Sumerian sculpture, and, when the ribbon was laid over this and the bands which held it were undone, the strands fell naturally into position. The head has been modelled by Mrs. Woolley, over a cast of a nearly contemporary female Sumerian skull, the features being added in wax over the bony structure. Thus was produced a face which, while in no sense a portrait of Queen Shub-ad, must approximate closely to the physical type of the period.

1929

The year, especially, of the Death-pit of Ur, and the discovery of the statues of the Ram caught in a thicket and the series of Sumerian harps. In addition there were three long articles by the Czech, Dr. K. Absolon, on the mammoth-hunters of Moravia, and the palaeolithic statuette usually called the "Venus of Vestoniće".

January 26, 1929

SUMERIAN ART AND HUMAN SACRIFICE:
Archaeological riches of the Ur "Death-pit" containing 74 skeletons, mostly of women

By C. Leonard Woolley, Director of the Joint Expedition of the British Museum and the University of Pennsylvania Museum to Mesopotamia

The new discoveries at Ur, while they are of the same general nature as those of last winter, do not lack the element of novelty. The outstanding feature of last season was the unearthing of the royal graves, with their stone-built chambers and their outer courts crowded with the bodies of human victims. At the present stage of this year's work we have not laid bare any one royal grave in its entirety, but we have found the domed chamber of one with its roof and door intact, and of another we have just finished clearing the outer pit, with really astonishing results *(Figure 128)*. The pit, about twenty-five feet square, contained the remains of no fewer than seventy-four persons, chiefly women,

victims in the wholesale sacrifice which celebrated the funeral of the King.

There were very few of the victims who were not wearing gold ornaments, while many of them were most elaborately adorned, and the ground was thickly covered with gold ribbons, gold leaves from the wreaths, beads of gold and lapis lazuli and carnelian, and the inlaid flowers of the tall hair-combs. . . . What the sight must have been when these glittering things lay, not on the brown soil amongst crumbling bones, but on a carpet of white and coloured draperies (we could distinguish white stuffs and coats dyed scarlet), it is difficult to imagine.

In one place four harps were piled together.

One of these was a brilliant thing, its sounding-box decorated with inlay, its uprights covered with mosaic and gold, its top beam of silver, while from the front of it projected the magnificent gold head of a bearded bull *(Figure 129)*. Two other harps were entirely of silver; one is decorated with a silver cow's head, and it is curious to observe how the shape of the sounding-box recalls in a highly stylised form the body of the animal; the second has the silver statue of a stag standing on a sort of boat. The harps are not only splendid examples of Sumerian art; they are of exceptional interest as illustrating the musical instruments of the fourth millennium before Christ, and by their very diversity they may well enable us to learn something of the nature of the music itself.

In another corner of the pit lay two statues of rams *(Plate 24, p. 197)*, perhaps the most remarkable things that our work at Ur has yet produced. They are of gold, lapis lazuli, and white shell over a wooden core. The core has decayed and the weight of the soil has crushed the bodies, so that only after they have been treated in the museum laboratories will they be seen as they originally were; but, despite all this distortion, the sight of them as they emerged from the earth was one to reward us for any amount of work.

128 Excavating the Death-pit at Ur

In each case the ram is shown standing up on its hindlegs, its forelegs caught in a thicket whose golden stems and flowers rise on each side of the beast's head. The eyes, horns, and shoulder locks of the ram are of blue lapis, the head and legs of gold, the fleece of shell, each lock carved separately and inlaid, and the body of silver. No such monument of Sumerian craftsmanship had ever before come into our hands.

September 21, 1929

DIFFICULTIES OF SCIENTIFIC TREASURE HUNTING:
Retrieving works of ancient art crushed in the soil at Ur

By C. Leonard Woolley, Director of the Joint Expedition of the British Museum and the Pennsylvania University Museum to Mesopotamia

Few people looking at the objects from Ur exhibited in the British Museum would realise the amount of actual labour which is required for their discovery. It is perfectly true that things may be found close to the surface, rewarding almost the first turn of the spade; but generally such would be objects divorced from their proper setting and brought by accident into a level with which they have no historical connection, or else they must belong to the very latest period in the city's existence. But the tombs which have yielded our greatest treasures lie deep down, and to find them we have had to excavate a pit which now measures more than fifty yards across, and anything up to forty feet in depth; and, since graves may occur at any level, and isolated objects from plundered graves may lie anywhere in the tight-packed earth, work has to go forward cautiously, and the digging out of so many thousand of tons of soil has been a slow and a toilsome business.

129 Fragile remains of the gold harp and one of the silver harps as they were found in the soil at Ur

The great death-pit in which were found the harps and the statues illustrated *(see previous article)* was originally open to the sky, and, when the earth was thrown back into it, after the ceremonies of the king's funeral were complete, there was nothing except a shroud of reed-matting to protect the delicate offerings deposited there from the soil. When we dug it out, it was not surprising to find that everything was crushed, the skulls of the women victims grotesquely flattened and distorted, their big earrings of hollow gold squeezed flat, the lyres and statues reduced to mere silhouettes of themselves. The treasures of a rock-cut tomb

may be discovered looking almost uncannily new, but those which, as at Ur, have lain for five thousand years and more under thirty feet of soil are only too often in a sorry state; however much labour has gone to the finding of them, yet, great as that is, it may cost almost as much again to remove them from the earth and to prepare them for exhibition.

The splendid lyre . . . was one of four which had been piled one on another at the bottom of the death-pit; of the others, two were of wood plated with silver, and one of wood decorated with a copper statue of a stag. As the mats spread over the offerings decayed, the earth settled down and surrounded the objects, which were thus brought into direct contact with the damp and acid-impregnated soil. Gradually the wood likewise decayed and vanished altogether, and the earth above pressed down to fill the gap. In the case of the other lyres, the thin silver plate which covered the wood had also decayed, and now cracked and gave way until the edges buckled out and the two sides touched each other; the gold lyre collapsed in the same way, and where the instruments overlapped they were crushed right through each other, twisted and warped and almost inextricably mixed.

We were working with knives, clearing away the last four or five inches of earth that covered one of the silver lyres, when, with a lump of the hard soil, there came away a few triangular pieces of shell and lapis lazuli inlay, which had been lying on the top of the rotten silver; following these up we found one of the uprights of the gold lyre. Work of this sort needs the greatest care. The *tesserae* belonging to the upper face of the woodwork have fallen through on to those of the lower face, and those of the edges may still be standing upright in the ground, or may have fallen with them in disorder. Thanks to the earth which surrounds it, the mosaic may have kept its position fairly well on the whole, but, as it is now necessary to remove that earth, and as the bitumen into which the *tesserae* were originally fixed has turned to powder, it is extremely difficult not to disturb the little squares and triangles; there is nothing to hold them in place, and the only thing to which they are inclined to stick is just that earth which one is trying to remove. Lying on one's face, one uses the knife-edge to break up the earth coating into dust light enough to be blown away; but one too quick movement of the hand, or one too violent breath, may scatter the *tesserae*, which, for the reconstruction of the object, it is essential to keep in their position; yet, if the cleaning be not thoroughly done, the next stages of the work cannot be successful. The uprights with their heavier mosaic, were a less tiresome problem than the sounding-board, for here the *tesserae*, being merely let into the border of the woodwork, instead of casing it entirely, could slip sideways as well as collapse inwards, and the lines were more difficult to follow; further, a silver bar from one of the other lyres had fallen across it, and had broken away most of the front end. It was just as we nearly despaired of completing it that we found the great gold bull's head with its shell plaques giving definitely the front edge of the instrument.

When all was clear, photographs were taken of the lyre, and scale drawings were made; these showed the mosaic as it lay, and in addition there were many measurements checking all the irregularities, so that, by striking a balance, the original dimensions could be arrived at with accuracy. Now the lyre was ready for removal. For this, boiling paraffin wax was poured over the mosaic, and strips of muslin dipped in hot wax were laid along and pressed on to it. In this way the decoration of the sounding-box was turned into a solid mass which could be lifted up by means of the muslin and a board slipped under it, and it was then fixed to the board with wax so as to keep it in shape, while sticks were waxed to each of the uprights, and they also were lifted each as a whole. The gold head and the shell plaques were lifted separately, the latter, too, being waxed together and backed with muslin. In the British Museum, a new lyre body was made in solid walnut wood according to the measurements taken of the mosaic in the field, and the *tesserae* were transferred to this from the strips of waxed muslin, each piece being removed and cleaned and refixed in its original position on the new background: in a few places, where the design had been broken, it was completed with the *tesserae* which had been found loose in the earth; but for the greater part of the decoration we have not merely a copy of the original pattern, but an exact reproduction of it with the individual pieces of lapis lazuli, red stone, and shell in their original places. The only doubtful point is the length of the legs. Here there was no mosaic to guide us, and it may well be that the legs were rather longer than they have been made in the restoration; but otherwise the fitting of the mosaic proved the accuracy of our field measurements, and the new lyre must be, within an eighth of an inch, a replica of the old.

The importance of employing methods of this sort is shown by the following. On the side of the lyre which lay downwards in the soil, and was therefore not seen by us until the work of restoration was in progress, there is in the middle of the lower edge of the sounding-box a sudden interruption of the pattern of the mosaic. For half the width of the band there are short vertical rods of red and white, and below these a gap indicating a hole through the wood: either this was an air-hole to increase the tone of the box, or it was for a pedal: had the *tesserae* not been waxed together and lifted as a continuous strip, the existence of this interesting feature could never have been guessed. I should explain that the strings were all at the back end of the instrument; they were attached above to that part of the cross-beam which was not plated with silver, and below were fixed into the side of the sounding-box about two-thirds of the way down, passing over a bridge. Of the latter, and of the actual attachment of the strings, the decay of the wood has destroyed all traces. The gold bull's head is perhaps the finest work of art yet found in the cemetery. The right side of it was absolutely intact; the left side was crushed, and has been pressed out so far as it was possible to do this without cracking the metal.

Work on the "Ram Caught in a Thicket" *(Plate 24)* was of a rather different sort. Of the twin statues, one . . . had been pressed absolutely flat; the other was broken into several pieces and distorted, but luckily one side of its body had not been crushed, and preserved the original curve and fullness. Here again wax and muslin had to be used to keep the object together. The head and legs of the figure had been carved in wood and plated with very thin gold-leaf, the ears and lapis horns and eyes being fixed by copper rivets going right through the wood of the head. The finished limbs were morticed into a rough wooden body, which was then rounded off with plaster-of-Paris and coated with bitumen, and into the bitumen were fixed the separate *tesserae* of white shell and lapis which make up the fleece; the belly was of silver plate laid over the wood. The tree was of wood covered with gold-foil, which was used double for the leaves and flowers; the base was of wood covered with pink and white mosaic above, and its edges were plated with silver. All the wood had disappeared; the plaster was in powder or in shapeless lumps, and the bitumen also powdered; the gold-foil of the face was broken into eighteen pieces, all flattened and folded together, and the hollow tubes of the legs were split and bent; the branches of the tree fortunately kept their shape remarkably well. The silver-work was completely decayed, and only the wax prevented it from falling into dust.

In the field the figure was waxed and covered with muslin on the outside to keep it together. In the laboratory the earth and plaster and bitumen dust was cleaned out from the inside, and the inner face of the *tesserae* of the fleece exposed, and wax and muslin were applied to the inside. The head and legs were taken off, the outer muslin removed, and by applying gentle heat I was able to press out the crushed flank of the animal until it matched the intact flank, without dislodging the shell and lapis locks of hair from the interior skin of waxed muslin. By inserting fine tools down the tubes of the legs it was possible to straighten these and to press out the crushed metal; then copper wires were put down them, and a mixture of hot wax and bitumen poured in to solidify them. The head presented greater difficulties. Each tiny fragment of gold-foil had to be heated and pressed out to its original curve and strengthened from the back, and then the broken edges had to be fitted together in such a way that the curves of the surfaces were continuous, and a fresh backing applied to fasten the two bits together. It was a jigsaw puzzle in three dimensions, but at last all the pieces were joined up, and to my no small surprise, the result was a ram's head, with no more than a pardonable distortion, the work of the Sumerian craftsman. The head and body were filled in with plastic wood into which the wires of the legs were fixed. Since the decay of the silver had left no guide for the under-part of the body, this was left unmodelled, and was painted with a mixture of aluminium and silver chloride to give something of the effect of the metal. The trunk of the tree was made to measure in wood, and into it were fixed copper wires bent to the curve of the original branches, and broken bits of gold tubing were removed from the block of earth and waxed one by one, and transferred to this new core; and finally beast and tree were mounted on the reconstructed wooden base.

1930

In this year begins a pattern which continued until the outbreak of the Second World War. There is a diminution in what might be called real headline archaeological news stories, but an increase in the number of archaeological reports of major interest to archaeologists and to the new public which the paper was winning round to an interest in the subject. Another factor was the realisation by archaeologists that The Illustrated London News *now provided them with an international "shop window" for their activities. 1930, accordingly, was marked by one important article by Sir Arthur Evans on Knossos, and a number of interesting reports on, for example: the bird-woman sculptures of Ur, rock art in Rhodesia (with three colour pages), the German expedition at Warka in Iraq, a bronze helmet discovered at Corinth, an Aegean-type site at Vinca near Belgrade, Tell Halaf in Iraq, Ras Shamra (later to be identified with Ugarit) in Syria, a Viking ship found at Oseberg in Norway, excavations of the Gila Valley culture in Arizona, and of Maya remains at Uxmal in Yucatan.*

September 13, 1930

"CROWNING RESULTS" OF RESTORATION WORK AT KNOSSOS:
Griffin frescoes of the throne room and wonderful painted stucco reliefs of bull-hunting on the northern portico

By Sir Arthur Evans

My present theme must confine itself to the original objective of the campaign, and what may be regarded as the crowning results of the work of reconstitution and restoration within the interior of the great building. . . .

Of the northern entrance passage, with its porticos – originally on both sides – adorned with painted friezes in relief depicting bull-hunting scenes, some account will be found in the third volume of my "Palace" book, now issued. The western terrace of this, the masonry of which rises in places nine courses, has been largely preserved, in contrast to the other, of which only the back wall and the lower part of the supporting bastions have escaped those who found it a convenient quarry. After the cessation of the palace as a palace – about 1400 B.C. – the surface of the ascending entrance passage, still used by later squatters, continuously rose, and it was on a level at least as late as the settlement of

the Achaeans on the neighbouring town site – a level only a little below the terrace flat of the portico – that were found the noble remains of the painted stucco reliefs and, with them, the base of one of its supporting columns. The fact to which all this points, that some part of these fine compositions still clung to the back wall of the gallery above the Sea-Gate of Knossos *(Plate 25, p. 198)* at the coming of the Greeks, may itself have a real significance in relation to the origin of the legends that here grew up of the bull-headed monster within the Labyrinth and the fate of the captive children.

The existing remains – doubtless a mere fraction of the whole – show that these compositions included, besides the coursing bulls, "cowboys" *(Plate 26, p. 199)* of both sexes and the rocks and olive trees amidst which the scene was set. The most magnificent fragment *(Figure 130)* here found was the head of a huge bull of the Urus breed. The whole is instinct with fiery life. The eyeball, between the red lines of the lids, is exceedingly prominent, the upstanding ear marks intense excitement; the tongue protrudes, the hot breath seems to blow through the nostrils. The folds of the dewlap show that the head was in a lowered position – it is that of a bull coursing wildly. . . .

130 "The most magnificent fragment" of a painted frieze at Knossos, restored by M. E. Gilliéron fils

The fact that the head and apparently part of the flank as well as a forefoot of the coursing bull have been preserved, besides very full remains of the neighbouring olive tree, with indications of a conventional rock border, suggested to me the possibility of restoring at least the section of the great painted frieze in the original position on the back wall of the portico. Thanks to the able work of reconstruction executed for me by Mr. Piet de Jong, the Architect of the British School, the back wall of the gallery has now been raised to its original height, and part of the roof and entablature, with three of the supporting columns, restored. . . . Behind this the raising of the back wall has, at the same time, much improved the appearance of the north-west entrance porch on that side.

For the very considerable and at the same time delicate task of restoring a section of the painted stucco reliefs themselves, I was happily able to enlist the services of Monsieur E. Gilliéron *fils*, whose technical ability and power of entering into the very spirit of Minoan works of art have won a general recognition. On the basis of the existing remains (now preserved in the Museum of Candia) and by the aid of very careful casts, the forepart of the charging bull was successfully grouped with the olive tree, which, as its angular cutting above and on the right side shows, formed the end of the composition. The execution of the foliage itself shows a remarkable resourcefulness, combined with a close observation of nature, on the part of the Minoan artist. The sprays are in each case given relief by oval bases of the plaster, following the ramification of the stems, while the varied colours of the leaves – black, white and red – recalls the characteristic foliage of the olive tree, in which the dark brown upper surface of the leaves, relieved by glimpses of their silvery undersides, is further varied by the prolonged attachment of others, gold and bright reddish-brown. The border below illustrates the curious convention by which rocks – in this case, conglomerate, with red-bordered pebbles – are shown in section. The descending waved indication of the upper landscape, seen to the left of the field above, is an insertion warranted by the analogy of other fresco backgrounds. These artificial features, while giving a quite individual effect to the restored design . . . only serve to accentuate the noble relief of the forepart of the bull itself, which on its own lines may compare with the work of any later age. . . .

Finally Monsieur Gilliéron has completed the entire series of guardian griffins *(Plate 27, p. 200)*, two facing the throne and two the doorway of a shrine beyond, of which, in all cases, parts of the original have been preserved.

. . . The result is to bring home in a singular degree the time when the last of the Priest-Kings seems to have used this chamber, with its surrounding benches, for lustral rites and the holding of consistories. Alabaster ointment-vases of elegant design – to be used, no doubt, in one of these functions – were found ranged on the pavement, and had actually been in the course of being replenished from a large oil-jar, laid on its side, when, with dramatic sudden-ness, the stroke of Fate fell, and for some three-and-half millennia the whole lay buried not more than a dozen feet beneath the surface of the ground.

1931

The last article on Tutankhamen and Sir Arthur Evans' discovery of a Royal tomb near Knossos. But also, at an important level: excavations of Royal tombs at Ur, a patrician's treasure chest found at Pompeii, Garstang's excavations at Jericho, and Doro Levi's on Lemnos; in Corinth a Roman villa with earlier Greek mosaics was found, the Ras Shamra excavations were continued, and work began on the Heraeum at Perachora in the Isthmus of Corinth. In Central America there were reports on the Toltec sites of Calixtlahuacan and Teotihuacan.

September 26, 1931

THE MAGIC CLUE OF A ROYAL SIGNET-RING: CRETAN TRADITIONS COME TRUE:

By Sir Arthur Evans, D.Litt., F.R.S., F.S.A.

Throughout the whole story of discovery that has shown Crete to have been the scene of a civilisation far anterior to the Greek, nothing has been more striking than the confirmation thus brought to light of the early traditions preserved by the Sicilian historian, Diodorus. We know that one of his authorities was the Cretan prophet, Epimenides of Knossos, also spoken of as a "divine" (*theologos*) in the same sense as the writer of Revelations who may truly be said to have had one foot in an earlier world. Epimenides had composed a long epic on "Minos and Rhadamanthos", and, though writing in Greek at the end of the seventh century B.C., may well have been acquainted with sagas in the older tongue – still spoken in a large part of Crete to a much later date.

The statement that the Phoenicians had not invented letters, but had only adapted an existing (Cretan) system, had never received serious consideration till over a thousand clay documents in an advanced linear script came to light in the palace archives at Knossos. What more signal confirmation, again, could be imagined of the claims put forward for the religious indebtedness of Greece in her most

259

holy places to Minoan Crete than the emergence from beneath the inner sanctuary of the Delphian Apollo of a ritual vessel, the double of which was found in the treasury of the central shrine in the same Minoan palace?

131   The seal of a royal signet ring found near Knossos

From the same records we learn that the last Minos, pursuing the runaway Daedalus to Sicily, had taken refuge with the native king, Cocalus, the story of whose treachery in pushing him into a bath of boiling hot water may itself have originated from the bath-like form of common Late Minoan clay coffins. . . .

The whole course of the excavations at Knossos has emphasised the fact that the "House of Minos" was a sanctuary quite as much as a palace. It was, in fact, the home of a succession of priest-kings. It was natural, then, to suppose that the burial-place of these might also conform to the old tradition, and, in the course of the early explorations, I had myself been inspired by the hope of finding such a "temple-tomb". But the only tomb discovered which had a claim to be called "royal" – that brought out at Isopata, at some distance from the palace on a height overlooking the harbour-town – though of considerable architectural interest, was still simply a burial-vault. It was of a corbelled type, representing a development of an earlier indigenous form, and may have been that traditionally connected with the warrior-prince, Idomeneus, who was said to have led

eighty ships – the largest contingent – to the siege of Troy.

The work on the palace site itself, however, being concluded, I decided to have one more try for a tomb of the priest-kings in the area more immediately surrounding it. Happily, there was a clue ready to hand. A few years since, a small boy working in his father's vineyard – lying in a hollow between two rocky promontories of the hillside immediately south of the palace, at about a kilometre's distance – had picked up a massive gold signet-ring, the exceptional importance of which was at once apparent. Though the ring itself has since been spirited away by irresponsible hands, and according to one account actually lost, it had been possible for me to obtain an exact replica of it *(Figure 131)*. . . .

Briefly, it represents the advent of the great Minoan Goddess to a rock-set sanctuary from another lying beyond an arm of the sea. She is seated, richly robed, receiving refreshment contained in a flask held out to her by a male attendant, which he seems to have filled with the juice of a sacred tree, while a small handmaiden descends towards her from the sky. The actual passage of the Goddess, in a monster-headed boat containing her small shrine, over the conventionally rendered waves must be taken as a separate scene. By the shrine that seems to have been her starting-point sits another female figure, wholly nude, who pulls down towards the Goddess, with a gesture of obeisance, a branch of another sacred tree. The abnormal weight of the ring and the microscopic character of the engraving recall the signet-ring found in the great beehive tomb of "Nestor's Pylos" (and named after him). That this came too from a royal interment, as doubtless also the great signet-ring from Mycenae, was a natural conclusion. In all three the subjects might be described as chapters of religious history.

As a hunting-ground, this vineyard and bordering olive-grove where the ring was found was peculiarly favourable, since the detritus at the foot of the steeps on either side might, as in

*132 The temple-tomb at Knossos: a general view from the north-east showing (*left foreground*) part of the roof-terrace of the pavilion, the court for funeral sports, the entrance to the basement chambers and (*top background*) steps to the upper columnar sanctuary with the "horns of consecration"*

similar cases, conceal the entrance of rock tombs. Trenching round, we hit on a series of small graves of this kind, much disturbed, but containing remains of painted clay vessels and jewellery of better style than might have been expected from the size of the vaults. In one of these was a great variety of bead types of different shapes and materials, including, together with many glass imitations of a class of amethyst beads characteristic of the Egyptian Middle Kingdom, a whole series of elegant gold forms. One of these represents a couchant calf, another a Nilotic papyrus spray. The discovery of such a collection among the fragments left by plunderers of a small and inconspicuous interment throws a fresh light on the comparative well-being reached by even the smaller burghers of "broad Knossos" in the great days of Minoan culture. But a much more important discovery awaited us. The owner of the vineyard pointed out a spot, about thirty paces north of the finding-place of the signet, where, in the course of tillage, he had struck some large blocks of masonry, and here, on digging down, we found ourselves in a square chamber with massive walls descending further and further below the surface of the slope. The lower part of this, when excavated after weeks of labour, proved to be a pillar crypt with sacred double axes finely inscribed on each of its blocks. The piers of this had supported colossal beams, the sockets of which, as well as the cross-beams above, were so well preserved as to make possible their restoration in ferro-concrete. The

261

two pillars, according to the usual practice, had, in the chamber above, supported two corresponding columns, and, at a level answering to its original floor, remains appeared of a limestone cult object, well known as "horns of consecration", and examples of which, indeed, are to be seen on the shrine and altar of the Goddess on the signet-ring.

Here then, above ground, had stood a small bi-columnar temple, clearly visible from the southern terrace of the palace on the hill opposite. Except the lower part of its west wall, where it backed the rocky steep, little of this was actually preserved, and all that can be learnt of its inner decoration was supplied by a small fragment or so of red-faced stucco.

But this upper structure proved to be the outstanding feature of a much larger sanctuary building *(Figure 132)*, set in a long cutting running into the soft rock of the slope. This was approached by a low entrance passage giving on to a two-columned pavilion designed, it may be supposed, for memorial feasts. It faced a small massively-paved area, adapted for the funeral sports, and with roof terraces on either side for spectators. From this a door, between two pylons carved with trident signs, gave access to the basement system, consisting of a hall with a staircase that led to the roof terrace, and beyond it the pillar crypt above mentioned, the excavation of which revealed a feature of yet more thrilling interest. In its western, or inner, side an opening appeared in the masonry of a passage running into the cut face of the cliff. Finally, there was disclosed the doorway of a chamber excavated in the rock, the roof of which – in spite of a central pillar that had originally supported massive cross-beams – was in too dangerous a state to allow of its being cleared from below. It was necessary to resort to the laborious process of sinking a large shaft from above, some 20 feet down through the overlying limestone.

That it was indeed a sepulchral vault was sufficiently shown by a small burial-pit in the right-hand corner, in which were the relics of a later interment of a prince found worthy of a prolonged posthumous cult. But the earlier interments – contained, we may believe, in chests against the back wall, and going back, as the ceramic remains indicate, to the beginning of the sixteenth century B.C. – had been removed, apparently at the time of a great seismic catastrophe to which the ruin of the upper shrine seems to have been due. The chamber itself was of imposing effect, its wall lined with gypsum slabs and pilasters, and the central pillar of the same material glistening white in its original state. To add to the effect, the rock ceiling – squares of which were visible between the beams – had been tinted with the brilliant Egyptian blue, or *kyanos*, so that the dead beneath the vault might not be without the illusion of the sky above. Remains of the cypress beams also showed traces of having been covered with painted decoration. A still more vivid touch for the benefit of the departed was supplied by an incense vessel, of the date of the latest interment, adorned with foliage and alternating bands in partly unfixed colours on the terracotta ground – blue, yellow, and vermilion red. It was a funereal object, never meant for use. . . .

For the successive phases in the history of the building, the ceramic evidence afforded clear definitions. In the original state it was a temple-tomb, vindicating ancient traditions. Its arrangement, indeed, shows a very perfect combination of that dual conception. The bi-columnar shrine above was approached by an upper entrance leading from a roof terrace. A lower entrance led to the pavilion well and entrance-hall, already described, and thence, through the pillar crypt, to the sepulchral chamber itself. So well preserved were the details that the system by which the different compartments were secured could be followed out. A bronze locking-pin – the key of a primitive lock – was also found.

The earthquake that ruined the upper sanctuary seems to correspond with one that caused much damage to the palace towards the close of the first Late Minoan period, about 1520 B.C. Rearrangements were then made, by which compartments of the two-pillared crypt were walled off for private interments. These, however, cease at the time when the available space was practically exhausted, about the end of the concluding Late Minoan phase. The approach to the sepulchral chamber itself was still left open for cult purposes, and, about the date of the final overthrow of the palace, it was reopened for the burial in a corner pit of one who may well have been the latest scion of the House of Minos. At a still later date, approaching the close of the Minoan Age, this grave too was rifled, and objects in precious metals carried off, though ... a series of interesting relics were left to posterity, including a fine alabaster vessel and a globular flask in the late "palace style". If a skull and additional bones, found immediately outside the entrance passage, belong, as seems almost certain, to this grave, the personage here interred was an elderly man – although of athletic training – who combined as was fitting, proto-Armenoid and Mediterranean ancestral features.

1932

As well as the astonishing "Archaic Congregation" on Ajia Irini in Cyprus, there were reports of: Ras Shamra in Syria; the Royal buildings of Tell el Amarna; a tomb at Monte Alban, Mexico; the extraordinary "X-group" finds in Nubia; work on the Agora, Athens; the discovery of Mount Carmel Man by Dorothy Garrod, with a note by Sir Arthur Keith; Italian excavations on Rhodes by Professor Jacopi; and the beginning of the great series of excavations by the Oriental Institute of Chicago University in the Middle and Near East, under the general direction of Professor Henry Frankfurt, in this year at Tell Asmar, Khafaje and Khorsabad. And there were several reports from Guatemala, notably at Piedra Negras.

September 24, 1932

A CYPRIOTE MYSTERY:
A unique discovery of archaic sculpture on the site of a sacred enclosure

By Dr. Einar Gjerstad, Leader of the Swedish Archaeological Expedition to Cyprus

Ajia Irini is a small village in the western part of the north coast of Cyprus. The village priest, Papa Prokopios, while digging in a field belonging to the church, chanced to unearth the upper part of a terracotta statue and some smaller terracotta sculptures. He brought these finds to the Cyprus Museum. In this way the site became known and could be scientifically

A TERRA-COTTA "CONGREGATION" OF OVER TWO THOUSAND YEARS AGO RANGED BEFORE AN ALTAR.

Photographs by Courtesy of Dr. Einar Gjerstad, Leader of the Swedish Archæological Expedition in Cyprus. (See his Illustrated Article on Page 454, and Photographs on Pages 455 and 456.)

133 Votive sculptures ranged around the altar in a sacred enclosure in Cyprus

examined. Through the courtesy of Sir Ronald Storrs (at that time Governor of Cyprus), the Inspector of Antiquities and the Cyprus Museum authorities, the Swedish Archaeological Expedition which had been working in Cyprus since 1927, was entrusted with the excavation.

From the priest's find of the votive terracotta sculptures, it was evident that the site contained remains of a cult-place, and the excavations proved that the history of the cult dated back to the end of the Bronze Age, about 1200 B.C. At that time the cult-place consisted of an open area, with a row of houses built round it. Most of the rooms of these houses served as store-rooms

and living-rooms for the priests. In two of the rooms, which were the proper cult-rooms, remains of the sacral requisites were found: a couple of stone sacrificial and libation tables, some cult axes of the same material, carbonised stones of olives, which were once brought as votive offerings, a terracotta votive statuette of a bull, and several terracotta libation vases. The cult performed here . . . was a typical "house-cult" and a cult of fertility whose god was thought of in the shape of a bull.

At the beginning of the Iron Age, about 1000 B.C., the character of the cult-place was entirely changed. The houses that surrounded the open space in the middle were covered with debris of earth, forming an encircling wall, and inside this wall a small, low altar was built of rough stones as a central point of the sacred open, but enclosed, area: the temenos. This change must be understood in connection with the great historical events and disturbing migrations of peoples (colonisation by the Greeks) through which Cyprus passed from the Bronze Age to the Iron Age. But in spite of this change of the cult-place, it seems that the cult itself remained practically unaltered: the God was still thought of in the shape of a bull, as is shown by votive statuettes of bulls which we found in the temenos. This cult-place of the early Iron Age dates from about 1000 B.C. to 700 B.C. – i.e., the so-called Geometrical Period.

About 700 B.C. there was another change in the temenos, but not so radical. The earth-wall was still in use, but a new altar, in the shape of a square pillar, was built instead of the old one. Among the votive offerings found in this new temenos were some terracotta statuettes representing men and minotaurs – i.e., half-man and half-bull. Both in the cult and in the art the idea of man begins to appear.

About 600 B.C. or some decades earlier, there is a third, and more thorough, change of the temenos, which at that time was considerably enlarged: the earth-wall was demolished, and a new encircling wall of rough stones was erected around the new temenos. The pillar-altar of the earlier period was preserved. Close to the altar two small rectangular rooms were found. The walls, of rough stones, are preserved up to a height of about one metre above the floor-level of the temenos. There is nothing to indicate that they had been higher, and there were no traces of upper brick walls or the like. It is necessary, therefore, to suppose that these rooms had no roofs. What were they used for? It was observed during the excavations that the earth inside these rooms was dark, mouldy, of a composition quite different from that of the debris outside. Now it is an interesting fact that in representations of Minoan cult-places engraved on seals, which show great similarities to that of

Ajia Irini, there is an enclosure with two sacred trees depicted close to the altar. It seems, therefore, most probable that two sacred trees had been planted within these enclosures in Ajia Irini; and that, would, of course, explain the difference in the composition of the earths within and without these enclosures.

This temenos dates from the early Archaic Period (*circa* 600–525 B.C.). Among the rich votive offerings, sculptures are most numerous and important. They are nearly all of terracotta, and vary in size from statuettes of about 20 centimetres in height to life-size statues. Some

134 Terracotta warrior: head of one of the life-size statues found at Ajia Irini in Cyprus

2000 sculptures were found, all of them approximately *in situ*: a unique discovery. They had been placed round the altar in a wide semi-circle, and arranged in concentric rows, so that the statuettes were placed nearest the altar, the smaller statues behind the statuettes, and the life-size statues farther back, forming the background of the mass of sculptures. Apart from the sculptures, the votive offerings consisted of scarab-seals, metal objects, and terracotta vases, etc. Who was the God to whom all these votive offerings were made? We do not know his name, as no inscriptions were found. Furthermore, no cult-statue representing the God existed; the cult was aniconic, without images. The character and nature of the God, however, are clear. The cult-object was an oval stone found close to the altar, where it had been placed. It is well known that the stone played an important part in the cult of fertility; the trees associated with the God, and the fact that he was conceived in the shape of a bull, which was a representative of the power of fertility in the belief of many peoples – all these conditions point in the same direction; *viz.*, that he was a God of Fertility.

At about 525 B.C. the temenos was partly destroyed by the flood of heavy winter rains, which covered it with sand and gravel, and half-buried the votive sculptures. After this catastrophe the temenos was again brought into use. The floor-level was only raised up to the level of the overlying sand, and the earlier statues were left where they stood, buried in the sand up to the knees or the waist. The pious people did not dare to touch them. On the raised floor-level new votive sculptures were placed in a manner similar to that adopted for the earlier ones. This temenos dates from the late Archaic Period (*circa* 525–450 B.C.), when it was completely destroyed by another winter flood, which buried it with sand and gravel. After this new catastrophe it was not restored to its former condition, but abandoned.

135 Chariot with warriors: a votive offering found at Ajia Irini in Cyprus

1933

The outstanding item of this year was a series on Dr. Ernst Herzfeld's excavations at Persepolis (which included some colour transcripts). But the year was also marked by what might almost be described as a "posthumous" item on Tutankhamen, the re-erection in the Cairo Museum of the four "nested" shrines; continued discoveries at Ras Shamra in Syria and the "X-group" cemeteries near Abu Simbel; portraits of Akhenaten and Nefertiti were found at Tell el Amarna; the Oriental Institute reported on work at Tell Asmar, Khafaje and Gerwan in Iraq; there were reports too on Dura-Europos and the Athens Agora; Bishop White described work at Old Loyang, China, and Christian mosaics were discovered in St. Sophia, Istanbul. There was also an article on Tal Arpachijah near Nineveh, by M. E. L. Mallowan, the first of many which he was to contribute to The Illustrated London News.

March 25, 1933

"THE MAGNIFICENT DISCOVERY" AT PERSEPOLIS:

Stairway sculptures that will take rank among the greatest works of art surviving from Antiquity

By Professor Ernst Herzfeld, Field Director of the University of Chicago Oriental Institute Expedition to Persia. Photos by courtesy of Professor James Henry Breasted, Director of the Institute

In full recognition of the necessity of preserving the magnificent monuments of Persia's great past at Persepolis, the Persian Government granted the authorisation to undertake this work to the Oriental Institute of the University of Chicago. The work began less than two years ago, in the spring of 1931. The benevolent interest of the Government found its expresssion in the visit of H.I.M. the Shah of Persia on October 28, 1932, and, after inspecting the work, he expressed his appreciation and thanked the Field Director for the real cultural work done by the Chicago Oriental Institute.

The work at Persepolis has followed a triple aim: (1) Examination by excavation of the whole terrace, on which stand the palaces of Darius, Xerxes and Artaxerxes. (2) Reconstruction of one of the palaces as a specimen of old Achaemenian architecture. For this purpose the Hareem of Xerxes has been chosen, on account of its excellent preservation and its favourable situation on the terrace. The reconstruction is now finished, except some interior work still to be done. (3) Preservation of the buildings and sculptures on the terrace, to be largely effected by reopening the ancient subterranean drainage system, and protection against damage by rain, frost, and man.

Under the accumulations which cover the platform, much more plentiful remains of architecture and sculpture were buried and preserved than were expected by anyone. These accumulations have been produced in the course of twenty-five centuries by the decay of the walls of sun-dried brick, which were of far larger bulk and extent than is commonly supposed, and therefore produced, when they fell, an enormous volume of debris. Furthermore,

136 The newly discovered stairway in front of the Apadana or audience hall of Darius at Persepolis

the level of the front part of the terrace is lower, and extends farther, than was heretofore realised. The first huge building, the great audience hall (Apadana) stands on a platform raised about 3 metres (nearly 10 feet) above the level; this height is gained by a great monumental stairway *(Figure 136)*, and it has proved to be covered all over with sculptures. In the same way, the still higher level of the smaller palaces, serving purposes of daily use, is accessible only by a double staircase (the tripylon stairway) leading up about 5 metres (about 16 feet) and likewise covered with sculptures *(Figure 137)*. It is these two impressive groups of relief sculptures which were so unexpectedly disclosed by the recent discovery of the two great stairways.

Every line that stands against the sky, whether parapet of steps or upper margin of walls, is surmounted by a long line of crenellations, an old scheme long employed in the Assyrian art of fortification, which already in Assyrian architecture had become a mere decorative element, and survives in Mahommedan architecture all over the East. The triangles produced by the ascending flight of steps and the level of the ground are always decorated with the figure of a lion attacking a bull, the lion's head – an old Sumerian heritage – being represented in front view. This group may be called the "arms" of Achaemenian Persia, a symbol of astrological meaning which originated in Babylonia. The modern Persian "lion and sun" are not older than the late mediaeval epoch, but are, nevertheless, another example of an astrological symbol of Babylonian origin.

The newly discovered staircase in front of the great audience hall, called "Apadana" by convention and in analogy to the name used at Susa for a building of similar description but almost completely destroyed, has a length of 90 metres (about 292 feet) with sculptures on three of its walls. On the main front outside, to the left on the *southern* wing, is the picture of a great tribute procession *(Figure 138)*, showing repre-

sentatives of twenty-eight nations of the empire, alternately introduced by a Persian or a Median *"introducteur des ambassadeurs"*, who might be called a "gentleman usher" – they bring their gifts to the Noruz or New Year's festival, on March 21. The procession is arranged in three rows, and the representatives of each nation occupy a field of their own, framed by cypresses,

137 Crowned human-headed bull from the tripylon staircase at Persepolis

the typical tree of Southern Persia. On the right or *northern* wing of the staircase the palace guards are to be seen, partly "at arms", partly as spectators in various positions and gestures, apparently conversing with each other. The regiments of guards consist of Persians, Medians, and Susians, and were called the "Ten Thousand Immortals", their number being always kept up. At the end of the first row of

138. *Sculptures on the Apadana stairway at Persepolis: tribute bearers from three of the twenty-eight nations subject to Darius*

these guards two chariots are conducted, with their horses. According to Herodotus, these were the chariots of the god, Ahuramazda, and that of the king, each drawn by eight white stallions from the famous breeding-farm at Nisaia in Media, near modern Kirmanshah. The grooms also lead a riding-horse for the king, and other servants bear his camp-stool.

The twenty-eight nations represent the twenty satrapies of old Iran, including a vast territory extending from Farghana in the north-east to Abyssinia in the south-west, and from the Balkans in the north-west to Sind in the south-east. Some of the large satrapies are represented by more than one nation. Although no inscriptions indicate their names, they may be identified by a comparison with the figures of men supporting the king's throne on the royal tombs, where the names indicating the nationalities of these men were added by the ancient Persian sculptor. A few of them, such as the Syrians, Phoenicians, and Cilicians may be determined by a kind of interpolation and comparison with representations on foreign monuments. The usual gifts they bear are horses, camels, or bulls of special breeding, and beautiful enough to win a prize at a "live-stock" show, or rarer animals such as a lioness with her cubs, an antelope, a giraffe, the last ones being brought by Abyssinians and the people of Punt, which is the frankincense country on the Straits of Aden. Besides animals, every nation was accustomed to present specimens of the national costume of each, and, furthermore, vessels, probably containing something gold, or actually made of gold, and rendered with great care and skill by the Achaemenian artist.

Neither the idea of the subject nor the principles of the entire composition in long rows of strongly architectural rhythm, nor the details of the single groups with their ceremonial seriousness reveal any trace of Greek influence on this art, as is often supposed and discussed. The art of Persepolis may better be characterised as a late manifestation of ceremonial character, a sort of "Empire" of the art of the Ancient East. The glory of Persepolis went up in the flames of the incendiary fire started by Alexander the Great.

1934

In this year the work at Ras Shamra and Tell Asmar increased in importance and in each case was illustrated in colour. Other important items were: the stairway at Persepolis; a Bronze Age gold collar found in Co. Clare, Ireland, and gold treasure at Coclé, Panama; Oriental Institute reports from Khafaje and Khorsabad; more from Bishop White on Honan, China; excavations by the French at Mari, which might be described as the westernmost Mesopotamian city; a Mithraic shrine at Dura-Europos; prehistoric rock-art in the Libyan desert; and Peruvian excavations at Cuzco.

March 3, 1934

AN ANCIENT SYRIAN KINGDOM AND ITS GOLD:

Rich discoveries during the fifth season at Ras Shamra (ancient Ugarit), including two exquisitely wrought gold vessels of the fourteenth century B.C.

By Professor Claude F. A. Schaeffer

(This is a report on the fifth season, previous reports having appeared in 1929, 1930, 1931, 1932 and 1933.) The site was "the capital of one of the kingdoms of ancient Syria, not far from the deserted bay of Minet-el-Beida on the Syrian coast, 15 kilometres north of Latakia".

Situated on the nearest point of the Syrian coast opposite Cyprus, which can be seen on clear days, Ras Shamra became a real international port. At a period when iron was still reserved for jewellery, the indispensable Cyprian copper was conveyed by caravan from Ras Shamra to the interior of Syria and Mesopotamia, in exchange for Asiatic produce exported from Ras Shamra to Cyprus, Mycenaean Greece and Egypt. A celebrated temple existed at Ras Shamra, where learned priests noted on large tablets, in alphabetic cuneiform script invented by them, the traditions and myths of their ancestors – documents of inestimable historic value, revealing an archaic Phoenician literature which, ever since Ernest Renan's researches, was believed to have been irretrievably lost. And just as that great historian of religion had anticipated, it is in these ancient Phoenician traditions that we find one of the sources of the most famous of all human writings – the Old Testament.

. . . South of the library we discovered the ruins of a great temple, whose walls had been partly removed during the construction of the buildings of the fourteenth and thirteenth centuries B.C. Here we found, among other votive offerings, a statuette of a high Egyptian dignitary, sent by one of the XIIth Dynasty Pharaohs, probably Amenemhat III, to the court of the King of Ras Shamra. The ambassador, by name Senousrit-Ankh, is represented seated between his wife and his daughter. This precious monument, with other Egyptian statuettes previously discovered at Ras Shamra, proves the activity of Egyptian diplomacy in Syria ever since the Middle Empire. The Pharaohs wanted to establish – marching with the Eastern frontier of Egypt – a vast Asiatic empire which would form a buffer against the barbaric nations of the north menacing their realm.

Under these monuments of the second level at Ras Shamra, dating from about 2000 B.C., we now discovered, beyond doubt, the existence of a third town buried in the depths of the mound. It shows traces of a culture totally different from that of the two towns whose ruins are contained in the upper strata. At the period of this town of the third stratum, the Phoenicians had apparently not yet occupied the coast of Northern Syria, and its civilisation seems to have been closely related to the great centre of culture in Mesopotamia. Indeed the fine pottery with geometrical paintings in brownish black and red on a grey-green ground, characteristic of the third stratum of Ras Shamra, shows a surprising likeness to ceramics found on archaeological sites in Iraq and Persia (Susa, Tepe Giyan, Tepe Moussian, and Tello) dating from the third and even the fourth millennium B.C.

South of the library we discovered also three important burial vaults of rectangular plan, with corbelled roofs and approached by a *dromos* (corridor) with a stairway leading down to it. They were further provided with a complete system of stone conduits, wells, and jars, to ensure a supply of fresh water for the persons buried in these vaults. As in the Mycenaean tombs discovered by us in the necropolis of Minet-el-Beida, the wells of the tombs of Ras Shamra are accessible from the interior of the vault by a window inserted in the body of the wall. Over the vaults was formerly a building, above ground, used for funeral ceremonies.

The remains of the contents of these tombs, pillaged many centuries ago – Mycenaean pottery, faience, glass, alabaster, and some small jewels in gold which escaped the robbers – give one an idea of their original riches, which is further emphasised by the dimensions and the fine architecture of these vaults, recalling in many respects the famous tombs of Mycenae and Crete. There is no doubt that the personages buried in these tombs according to Mycenaean traditions were not of Semitic origin. They must have belonged to the race of those conquerors who came by sea to take possession of the Syrian coasts during the great Achaean expansion, whose forerunners are mentioned in the letters of Tell-el-Amarna and the Hittite archives of Boghaz-Heui, dating from the end of the fifteenth and the beginning of the fourteenth centuries B.C.

Patient and systematic research enabled us to rescue fragments of several new tablets abandoned after the destruction of the library. Among them there is a treatise on the diseases or malformation of horses and the appropriate remedies. M. Charles Virolleaud, the translator of the alphabetic tablets of Ras Shamra, whom I asked to examine these new tablets as well, informed me that amongst the commonest remedies was the *debelat*, a kind of cake made of figs. It is the same remedy which, according to the Second Book of Kings, chapter 20, verse 7, the Prophet Isaiah prescribed for King Hezekiah when he was suffering from an ulcer.

I must point out another important point of contact between the Ras Shamra tablets and the Old Testament. Among fragments of Accadian and Sumerian tablets discovered during this fifth season, there is a tablet of accounts. The well-known expert on cuneiform writing, M. François Thureau-Dangin, to whom I entrusted it for deciphering, found it to be an enumeration of quantities of wool due to a merchant from several purveyors. The enumeration is made in talents of 3000 shekels. Thus there was current at Ras Shamra, not the Babylonian talent worth 3600 shekels, but the talent used by the Hebrews in the Tabernacle accounts, a fact which confirms the statements in Exodus.

Ugarit was the capital and port of a kingdom in North Syria, which played an important part in the history of the ancient East. . . . In all these popular accounts a characteristic feature is the reputed wealth in gold of the town buried in the depth of the Ras Shamra mound. . . . We found these vessels amid a network of trenches made during former excavations, not far from a temple, on the clearance of which we had been engaged for several seasons. The hiding-place, when discovered, was in the actual soil, and at a shallow depth. It contained a bowl (or cup), and a patera, both of gold in a very good state of preservation.

The bowl, which was intact, is shaped like a round skull-cap, and is 17 centimetres in diameter. It is completely covered with reliefs in repoussé, retouched or finished with delicate engraving *(Figure 139)*. The principal theme of decoration, that nearest to the cup's edge, shows, between two friezes of spirals engraved in Mycenaean style, a succession of animals and human figures. The most important *motif* is a lion-hunt. The beast is seen near a dead stag, evidently used as a bait, and attacked by two hunters, one of whom thrusts a spear into the lion's chest, and the other a dagger into his flank. Among astral rosettes, birds and stylised branches indicate that the action is taking place in a forest. Other lions are seen attacking antelopes or wild bulls, whose terror and agony are most realistically represented. Among these

140 Golden patera from Ras Shamra

139 Repoussé decoration on the golden bowl found at Ras Shamra

real animals there are fantastic creatures – a griffin, a winged lion with horns like a bull, and a sphinx with outspread wings which is approaching a stylised shrub that represents, no doubt, the Sacred Tree.

The gold patera (or plate), 19 centimetres in diameter, has vertical edges like Egyptian dishes of the XVIIIth Dynasty period *(Figure 140)*.

On the flat surface round the umbilical centre, four vigorous ibexes, supporting on their horns the solar disc, move round in a majestic circle. In the next band of decoration we see a superb composition of most alluring beauty. A hunter standing on a chariot drawn by two fiery stallions draws with vigour a great bow. He is about to let fly an arrow at an ibex, rising in a superb leap, and a wild bull, both fleeing before him. The bull covers the retreat of a cow (recognised by her udders) and a calf running, head down, beside its mother. In front of the cow another bull is taking the offensive by dashing furiously at the back of the chariot, behind which runs a big hound.

We have here the work of a very remarkable artist. The modelling of the bulls and the attitudes of these great beasts, the line of the ibex in its flying leap, and the mad motion animating the whole scene, rival the best work that has come down to us from the ancient East.

Of local origin, without a doubt, and of somewhat composite style, betraying considerable debt to the art of neighbouring countries, especially Cyprus, Mycenae, Egypt and Assyria, the cup and patera of Ras Shamra can be dated to about the fourteenth century B.C. They are, therefore, amongst the oldest and most beautiful of historic metal vessels of Phoenician origin. They do great credit to the genius of the Syrian artists and jewellers, who, though less original, were nevertheless capable of producing true works of art.

As to the purpose of these precious receptacles, it was undoubtedly religious, for a text on the Ras Shamra tablets mention the gold bowl and patera as objects reserved for the service of the gods.

May 19, 1934

A GREAT DISCOVERY OF SUMERIAN SCULPTURE:

A unique hoard of statues, 5000 years old, found at Tell Asmar

By Dr. Henry Frankfort, Director of the Iraq Expedition of the Oriental Institute of the University of Chicago

(Mr. Seton Lloyd was again in immediate charge of the work at the temple, and Dr. Thorkild Jacobsen of that at the private houses.)

The work of our expedition during the past winter at Tell Asmar, 50 miles N.E. of Baghdad, has been attended by extraordinary good fortune. It has now been established that the temple of Ab-u . . . was used continuously from about 3000 B.C. until the end of Sargon of Akkad's Dynasty – about 2350. Consequently, objects hidden in the lower layers were well out of the reach of robbers and marauders such as normally ransack deserted buildings or ruins left after a destructive war. Neither desertion nor destruction overtook our temple before the comparatively recent date given above – and by then the unparalleled objects described in this article were covered by not less than six metres of earth *(Figure 141)*.

Underneath the temple . . . (were) . . . the walls of an earlier stage of its history, built on a different alignment. . . . We may recall here that a hoard of copper vases, some of them inscribed, and identical in shape with the gold and silver specimens from the tombs at Ur, revealed the dedication of the temple to Ab-u, the "Lord of Vegetation", who is none other, in fact, than Tammuz. It would be more correct to call him "Lord of Fertility", or, rather, "Lord of vital energy", since his emblems include plants, flowers, and corn, as well as animals, especially goats, gazelles, and ibexes. Another mythical emblem, the lion-headed eagle, Imgi, characterises the Lord of Life as the vanquisher of chaos and death; in this aspect – namely, as victor – the god is shown on a cylinder seal, discovered and published last year, destroying a seven-headed Hydra; and evidence has been collected . . . which establishes the linear descent of the Greek Herakles from the Sumerian god whose temple we are excavating.

The older structures . . . are also built of plano-convex bricks, but belong to an earlier part of the Early Dynastic Period than has yet been explored elsewhere. They correspond in fact with the accumulation at Ur of the rubbish heaps into which the famous tombs were afterwards dug. . . .

Let us now consider the arrangement of the earlier temple. . . . The ground plan of the temple is almost square, and tallies in general lay-out with that of private houses of the period – it is, in fact, the "house of the gods". One

141 Temple of Tell Asmar where the hoard of statues was discovered

enters by a lobby, which contains the stairs leading to the roof, and which adjoins a small square room floored with baked bricks covered with bitumen, and provided with a square sink in one corner. Here the worshipper performed his ritual ablutions. Beyond this is a large central room; grouped around it are three sanctuaries. A path lined with bitumen led across the floor of the central room to a shrine appearing in the middle, while another shrine, with four short pillars in front of the pedestal stood on the right. A third shrine existed on the near side of the central room. The shrines do not differ from those in use down to Akkadian times. They contain at one end of a long narrow room a pedestal about six feet square and four high, upon which, above a narrow brick ledge, would have been placed the statue of the god. In details, however, the three shrines show some differences. In the far sanctuary a hearth seems to have been placed before the pedestal and a bitumen-lined drain fitted to its side, presumably to draw off libations. In the nearer shrine a row of square brick bases, two standing free and two against the walls, were placed in front of the pedestal as if to support statues or a screen. . . . The general character of the shrines is clear, and is corroborated by the extraordinary objects found in them.

The objects were neatly packed together and evidently buried with some care beneath the floor on either side of the pedestal for the god's statue. It is clear that this happened each time that the temple fabric was overhauled and repaired. On those occasions a new floor of stamped earth, from 4 to 20 inches above the

142 The Lord of Life and the Great Mother-Goddess found at Tell Asmar

level of the previous one, was put down, and votive offerings, temple furniture and similar objects which were damaged or no longer required, but which could not be thrown away, since they had once been consecrated, were collected and buried beneath this new floor. The objects thus discovered are of a most extraordinary nature. Those found in the far shrine . . . suggest that the Great Mother-Goddess was worshipped in this particular shrine; they included, for instance, such an essentially feminine object as a copper mirror. There was also found there a necklace of very large serpentine and alabaster beads, together with

some stone stamp seals; and a unique pectoral of green stone, engraved with a male figure surrounded by dogs and snakes. The style of engraving is entirely un-Babylonian, but recalls work of the Persian highlanders, whose snow-capped mountains are visible from Tell Asmar on a clear day. It is interesting to note that the dogs seem to be Salukis (or Persian greyhounds), such as are still used for hunting gazelles. Beside this was an ivory image of the lion-headed eagle Imgi taking wing, symbol of the Lord of Fertility. With the figure of Imgi was a small violin-shaped figurine of the Mother-Goddess, of the type known in the Cyclades early in the third millennium B.C., a most unexpected object to find in Mesopotamia. But no doubt Transcaucasia and Anatolia are the original homeland of this type of mother-goddess statuette, and its occurrence at Tell Asmar proves that relations were kept up between our region and the mountains in the far north. Other objects include exquisite human figures cut out of mother-of-pearl and shell, and used as inlays in plaques of schist, into which they were fastened with bitumen, thus acquiring a dull dark background which set off the delicacy of colour and carving to the best advantage. The hair of the figures was also picked out with bitumen. . . .

Nothing had prepared us, however, for the revelation in the second shrine of our temple of a group of no fewer than twelve complete statues, all in an unparalleled state of preservation, ranging in height from 12 to 30 inches. The most serious damage was only that of cracks due to the pressure of earth, which in the course of five millennia had piled above the spot where they lay packed together, so closely that this pressure had actually caused an impression of part of a marble statue to be left on the skirt of a softer statue (made of alabaster) below it. Here, for the first time, we obtained an impression of the polychrome effect of Sumerian sculpture. The faces were strongly set off by the black hair, to which bituminous paint was still adhering. The men wore long locks, hanging before the shoulders, and long wavy beards, cut square at the ends. The eyes were inlaid, the eyeballs being made of shell and the pupils of bitumen or lapis lazuli. The variety in the statues is extraordinary, and it is not only caused by the diversity of subject; it is true that one represents a woman with elaborately plaited coiffure; and another a priest with shaven head and face. But most striking is the difference of sculptural achievement between the various members of the group. In some the attitude of prayer and humility is magnificently expressed; in others the stone-cutter seems barely able to render the proportions of the human body. There is a striking absence of that tradition of the workshops which in Egypt gives a character of competency even to mediocre work. . . .

Three statues render superhuman beings, each without parallel among known Babylonian works of art. The smallest of the three is an incomplete figure of golden alabaster, anciently repaired after it had been broken in the middle. It represents a bearded man with a large head-dress, hollowed out like the head of a modern candlestick. It obviously formed a piece of temple furniture, and, as in the case of the three copper statues found some years ago at Khafaje, it seems that a mythical and not a human figure was thought appropriate to serve the god. Our figure kneels on both knees and is naked except for a girdle. An important detail, which we could not observe with precision in the case of the Khafaje statues because of the corrosion of the metal, is now clear: the Sumerians, in contrast with the Egyptians and with the Semites, did not practise circumcision.

The other two statues are equally unusual and are the first Sumerian cult-statues ever found *(Figure 142)*. One represents the Great Mother-Goddess; a miniature figure of her son is let into the base. The other actually renders the Lord of Life, to whom temples were dedicated here through many centuries: his emblems are engraved on the base of the statue: we see two ibexes and plants, symmetrically arranged, and between them the lion-headed eagle, Imgi; here also, amongst all the known representations, he is shown as not attacking the animals above which he hovers, since, they, like himself, signify the god. This is the meaning, for instance, of the antelope and flowering twig incised in the exceptionally fine seal of serpentine cut in the shape of a lion's head. The hands of the god and goddess, like those of some of the worshippers, hold a cup. Thus they are depicted as though partaking of a feast, which is often represented on plaques and on cylinder seals of later periods, and is elaborately described in the texts of Gudea and other rulers, a feast following the connubium of god and goddess which ensures the fertility of crops and herds during the twelve months to follow, and which is therefore the most important event of the religious year.

1935

A relatively quiet year; but even so we were reporting excavations at Vounous and Enkomi in Cyprus; Cham sculptures found in Annam; Bronze Age pottery in Jericho; Ptolemaic frescoes at Hermopolis, Egypt; and continued work at Dura-Europos, Mari, Syria, the Athens Agora; and the Chicago Oriental Institute excavations at Tell Asmar and Khafaje.

1936

Among the more interesting items reported were: the discovery of a new beehive tomb at Berbati, near Mycenae; excavations at Ras Shamra (Ugarit) and Mari; American excavations of an Indus Valley civilisation site at Chanhudaro; the extension of the activities of the Chicago Oriental Institute to include Megiddo (Palestine), Ishcali, Tell Asmar, Khafaje and a new Sumerian site at Tell Agrab; and excavation of a Maya site near Guatemala City.

1937

A somewhat similar year to the last, with important articles: on Ras Shamra; the Maya site of Chichenitza in Yucatan; the mammoth-hunters' site at Vestoniće, Moravia; continued excavations at Mari; Oriental Institute excavations at Megiddo in Palestine and Tell Agrab in Iraq; and in Mexico, work at Malinalco and Calixtlahuaca.

1938

The major reports of this year were: an article by M. E. L. Mallowan on excavations at Brak in Syria; one by W. B. Emery on early tombs at Sakkara, Egypt; a gold treasure found at Illimo, Peru; and a duck-billed god at Calixtlahuaca, Mexico; the Oriental Institute excavations at Khafaje; and from Olympia, Greece, Emil Kunze's excavation of the stadium and find of bronzes.

1939

In what remained of uneasy peace, archaeology was still busy; and we published reports of the rock-art of Hoggar, Syria; the discovery of thirteen Ife bronzes in Nigeria; Mallowan's excavations at Brak, Syria; Blegen's discovery of Linear-B tablets at Nestor's Palace, Pylos; the discovery of the ship grave of Sutton Hoo in East Anglia; a report by Sir Leonard Woolley on the Hittite site of Alalakh, Syria, to which he had moved after his work at Ur; and the discovery by A. J. B. Wace at Mycenae of an ivory of a woman and a boy.

1940–44

As might be expected, archaeology took a back seat during the war years and only a few items found their way into the paper. In 1940 there appeared an article by Professor C. F. A. Schaeffer (then serving with the Free French Navy) on the royal stables of Ras Shamra (Ugarit); and another by Professor L. Montet on the Treasures of the Tomb of Psusennes at Tanis, in Egypt. In 1941 there was nothing; in 1942 this illustrated report on the cave paintings discovered at Lascaux; in 1943 a note by Professor Froelich Rainey on Ipiutak culture discovered in the Bering Straits; and in 1944, nothing.

February 28, 1942

LASCAUX DISCOVERED

In the French region of La Dordogne on September 12, 1940, on the estate of the Comtesse de Rochefoucauld, four young men chasing a wounded bird they had shot discovered a hole in the limestone rock, concealed beneath bushes and shrubs. A terrier accompanying them had dug his way down, and stones thrown by one of the party rolled down the incline and, striking an obstacle, rebounded with a loud echo far below in what was undoubtedly a cavern. Forcing their way with difficulty through the narrow opening, filled with debris, the men eventually found themselves in a great cave which when lighted, revealed to their astonished eyes numbers of prehistoric beasts in blacks, browns, yellows, and reds, painted on the ceiling and walls, and as fresh as though painted yesterday. At first their report was received with scepticism, but a month later the Abbé Breuil, the great expert on prehistory, and other well-known French archaeologists, saw revealed before them the most marvellously executed paintings and engravings of extinct wild beasts, besides horses and ponies, many superimposed on earlier designs, and belonging to an epoch estimated at some 20,000 years ago.

This remarkable portrait of a plunging aurochs, or extinct wild ox *(Plate 28, p. 217)*, in the grotto of Lascaux, near Montignac, in the Dordogne, France, measures 16 feet 5 inches,

and was found at the end of a long grotto, where the ceiling and walls are covered with designs. It is the largest and best-preserved of a group of five bulls, although it will be observed that the limestone has flaked off from its neck, shoulders, and chest. Drawn in black, it plunges ahead of the others – short-horned bulls painted in red. Not the least interesting aspect of this remarkable find at Lascaux is that it was successively inhabited by two distinct schools of prehistoric animal painters, for in many instances the later work has been superimposed on the earlier and, it might be said, more artistic Aurignacian work. Another notable aspect of this cavern is that the great thickness of limestone, and its outer covering of clay, have kept out the damp, although minute particles of lime have during the ages formed tiny crystals, which have acted as a protection to the frescoes and, indeed, have glazed them with a thin veneer. When a light is thrown on the paintings, a thousand tiny facets glitter and reflect the lustre of the pure colourings in red, brown, yellow and black. Who were these artists, and what object had they in decorating this grotto – and others in the same region – in this manner? Many believe that such caves were used for ancient religious ceremonies. The races concerned are firstly the Aurignacians – so-called from races in the Aurignac, Pyrenees, also called Crô-Magnon – a race of square-jawed

143 Cave painting from Lascaux: a huntsman who has wounded a bison with his spear is himself charged down by his victim. The bird is perhaps a funeral emblem

giants of Neanderthal type. They were extremely artistic and their animal portraits included both the mammoth and reindeer (not found at Lascaux) and are believed to have existed towards the end of the Glacial period, estimated by geologists at *circa* 25000 B.C. After a rise in temperature, followed by another partial glaciation, the Magdalenians appeared approximately some 6000 years afterwards, and it is the Magdalenians who are thought to have superimposed their pictures here on the former Aurignacian designs.

1945

This was the year the writer joined the staff of The Illustrated London News *and subject to the overriding decisions and personality of the Editor gradually assumed responsibility of the archaeological items in the paper. It was, however, a quiet year. Archaeology in the field had really not yet had time or opportunity to get started; and the more notable articles published – concerning principally Hittite and pre-Hittite remains, work at Alaca Huyuk in Anatolia, and Toltec remains and colossal statuary at Tula in Mexico – were of material in stock for which no space had been available during the war years.*

1946

As well as the discovery of the outstanding hoard of Roman silver at Mildenhall in Suffolk, this was a year in which we published an article by Dr. R. E. M. (later Sir Mortimer) Wheeler on excavations at Harappa, which revealed the existence of fortifications, thus undermining an earlier held conviction that the Indus Valley civilisation had existed in conditions of unparalleled peace; mosaics were discovered at Low Ham, Somerset; and the Czech, Dr. K. Absolon, published his findings on the burial of a Hallstatt Age king in the Býči Skala cave in Moravia. This last confirmed the writer in his belief that there is nothing the general archaeological public enjoy more than gold treasure combined with human sacrifice. The article included a reconstruction drawing of positively surrealist brilliance, showing the dead king enthroned, in all his panoply, in a cave, and surrounded with the slaughtered bodies of horses, cattle and pigs and lusciously beautiful young girls. The publisher was so impressed by this that he had a huge photographic enlargement made and placed this in a shop window below the editorial offices. Throughout the week that this was exhibited, the pavement outside was impassable with the press of fascinated office-workers.

June 29, 1946

A TREASURE OF SUPERB ROMAN SILVER TURNED UP BY THE PLOUGH

While ploughing in a field at West Row, Mildenhall, Suffolk, Mr. Sidney Ford turned up with the plough a bright piece of metal. Freeing it from the earth, he discovered it to be a massive tray about 2 feet to 2 feet 6 inches in diameter and bearing beautiful designs in relief. It appeared to be silver and of the most exquisite craftsmanship. He thereupon investigated the neighbourhood of his find with a spade and eventually unearthed another thirty-three pieces (*Plates 29 and 30, pp. 218–9*), including another large tray, two small trays of exquisite design, dishes, a dish with a cover, goblets, finger-bowls, spoons and a pair of handles,

144 Roman silver turned up by a plough at Mildenhall, Suffolk

which might possibly have come from a piece of furniture. The spoons, which number eight, are of great interest and striking design. Some bear inscriptions, and it has been suggested that they may prove to be individual spoons for different members of a family or household. Some specimens have been submitted to the British Museum and, together with photographs, suggested the probability that they were late Roman silver, possibly of the third century A.D. They are described as of extremely fine quality and the find is regarded as one of great importance. The items of the treasure have been placed in safe custody, pending the findings of an inquest to decide whether the silver is treasure-trove or not. If treasure-trove, it may be retained for the Crown or a museum, in which case the finder (by a regulation in force since 1931) is paid the full market value.

145 Roman silver side dish

282

October 19, 1946

HOW A KING WAS BURIED 2500 YEARS AGO:

The ghastly climax to a royal funeral in prehistoric Moravia

The ghastly yet magnificent sacrifice which we describe here is without parallel in the prehistory of Czechoslovakia, and can only be compared with the Death Pits of Ur (described in detail in our issue of June 23, 1928) and the North China royal funerals of about 600 B.C. (described in our issue of November 3, 1934). The event is almost exactly contemporary with the North China Funeral, though separated by so many thousand miles. Our report is based on the notes and discoveries of the famous Czech archaeologist, so well known to our readers for his remarkable prehistoric discoveries in Moravia, Dr. K. Absolon, who has been continuing, expanding and systematising the discoveries of his grandfather, Dr. Wankel, sometimes described as "the father of Moravian prehistory" and who died in 1897. These discoveries have been made in the district north-east of Brno, in Czechoslovakia, in a deep cave called Býči Skála, "the Bull Rock", to which an age-old tradition of horror has always been attached. In brief, these discoveries comprise a palaeolithic site in the depth of the cave, a smithy of about 600 B.C. in which was found a cast-iron ring which revolutionises previous theories as to the date of the invention of casting iron; and also in the forepart of the cave the profuse and illuminating remains of a kingly funeral sacrifice of the Hallstatt Period (600 B.C.). . . . Concerning the event itself and the incidents leading up to its ghastly climax, Dr. Absolon writes: "Let us follow Wankel in reconstructing this event. A long and solemn procession wends its way through the lonely valley. It moves slowly on the rough path until it reaches the opening of the cave. It is a funeral procession. Two horses draw a wooden chariot ornamented with sheets of bronze and iron. A corpse lies in state on the carriage. Armed men follow and among them many women and girls, young and beautiful, dressed in precious garments garnished with coloured beads of glass and amber. On their arms and legs they wear rings, and many a jewel of gold or bronze sparkles on them. Their garments are held together by fibulae and their long hair by gold fillets. Sadly they tread their way. They are followed by a crowd of people, carrying grain in sacrificial vessels and driving cattle for the pyre of the beloved chieftain. These offerings are meant as symbols of farming and cattle-raising. The procession halts in front of the cave. A pyre is erected in the front chamber, illuminated by the dim light filtering into it. The chariot with the corpse is put on the pyre and fire is applied to it. The fire crackles and flares up, throwing a blinding light into the back of the chamber. It reveals a scene horrible beyond description. The women and servants are driven into the cave, robbed of their jewels and killed. Some women have their hands chopped off, others their heads broken. There is no pause in the killing until all the victims are dead. At the altar a priest, assisted by the bravest of the comrades-in-arms of the dead king, performs a bloody ceremony. Horses and other domestic animals are killed and cut into pieces which are thrown all over the floor of the chamber. The vessels with the offerings are put into a heap over which charred grain is strewn. Then the funeral feast takes place. After this the crowd rolls big stones over the corpses and the entire floor of the cave to protect the holy place from desecration. . . . The memory of the dreadful event lingered among the population of the neighbourhood for centuries, and it was left to the spade of the modern explorer to unravel the mystery of the cave."

1947

In addition to the articles quoted, there were important articles on Eridu (perhaps the oldest city of Sumer) by Seton Lloyd; and a Roman parade helmet found at Worthing in Norfolk.

April 12, 1947

THE WALL-PAINTINGS OF THE LASCAUX CAVES

By Alan Houghton Brodrick

The discovery of painted caves is always a matter of chance, since, for the pictures to have been preserved, the caverns must have been sealed up for ages. So, in September 1940, when we were still fighting the Battle of Britain and the Germans had subjugated France, four lads set out one morning from the little town of Montignac, on the Vézère River, in southwestern France. They had with them a couple of guns and a dog and made their way up on to the rising ground to the south of the river. This plateau of springy turf is set with clumps of trees and scored, here and there, with vineyards. While in one of the thickets the boys found they had lost their dog. Their whistles and calls were answered by a muffled bark coming out of a small hole torn in the ground by an uprooted fir-tree. The lads chucked in a stone, which rattled down and then fell with a dull plop. The leader of the boys, a youth named Ravidat, decided to go after the dog.

When the hole had been enlarged they slithered in. The drop was not very great, and the roofs of the caves may not be much more than 20 feet below the level of the earth.

The lads were standing in a large cavern, one side of which opened into darkness. They had only a few matches with them but, advancing into the gloom, they saw that they were in a larger cave, roughly oval in shape, whose walls were covered with great paintings of beasts.

The youths went back to Montignac, manufactured a torch out of a bicycle pump, and for five days kept their own counsel while thoroughly exploring the caverns. At last they told their schoolmaster, M. Laval, of their discovery, and he informed the Abbé Breuil, the eminent prehistorian, who had retired to Les Eyzies (the prehistoric site on the Vézère, some twelve miles or so downstream from Montignac) before the German advance.

During the war the French Fine-Arts department took over the site of Lascaux, closed the place to the public, and erected a stout masonry wall between the outer cave and the main hall, thus protecting the paintings from the deterioration which has overtaken other Palaeolithic cave-pictures.

From the floor-level of this "apse" gapes a hole down into a winding passage some 25 feet below the floor of the "apse". In this sunken passage (whose farther end seems to lead into a cave with a collapsed roof) is only one painting, but it is, perhaps, the most remarkable of all the Vézère Valley cave pictures (*Figure 143, p. 280*).

On a convex and rather irregular rock-face is spread a scene so drawn that you cannot view the whole of it from any one angle. The picture is not very large, about 3 feet high by 6 feet long. To your right is a rufous bison, his flanks transpierced by a javelin whose head lies broken off near him. His belly has been ripped open and his guts sag down bloodily. His head is drawn in and his horns are lowered as though to gore the prone figure of a man before him. This figure is highly stylised (naturalistically drawn human figures are unknown in French Palaeolithic art) – it is mere outline. On his head the man wears a bird-mask. Nearer to you than the man is a bird on a pole, while, to the left, is a wicked-looking woolly rhinoceros. It is clear what has happened. The hunter has wounded the bison. The bison has killed the man. The rhinoceros has torn open the bison. The man is dead, the bison is dying. The rhinoceros is ambling off, while the bird surveys the tragedy from its pole.

There are, it is true, among the French cave-paintings, some scenes apparently depicting ritual or even "magic", but little or nothing which we can call anecdote or "history", but this picture of the hunter, the bison, the bird and the rhinoceros is a flash-back to an incident of Stone Age life. It is the earliest "problem picture" we have. The Abbé Breuil has ventured the guess that possibly the hunter was interred near this "votive" painting.

June 28, 1947
BONAMPAK: A NEW MAYA SITE

An expedition, sponsored and financed by the United Fruit Company, authorised by the Mexican Government, supervised by the Carnegie Institute of Washington and led by Mr. Giles Greville Healey, has recently discovered at Bonampak, in Chiapas State, in Southeastern Mexico, eleven hitherto unknown Mayan temples dating from the Mayan Old Empire. Highlights of the discovery include some 1200 square feet of brilliant and excellently preserved mural paintings, three remarkable carved *stelae*, or record stones, and two elaborately carved altar stones.

August 9, 1947

Since recording in *The Illustrated London News* of June 28 this year the amazing discovery of the ancient Mayan capital of Bonampak by Mr. Giles G. Healey, further information and photographs have come to hand. . . .

An expedition of seven archaeologists, financed by the United Fruit Company under Mr. Healey's leadership and supervised by the Carnegie Institution, was sent to the site in February this year to appraise the find, and returned in May with a mass of material. In the Bonampak area Mr. Healey has located forty-eight building sites, and a number of carved *stelae* or recording stones *(Figure 146)*. The most important find is undoubtedly the painted murals which demonstrate the skill of the Mayan artists of over 1200 years ago. These murals, which feature bright blues, ochres, reds

146 One of the carved stelae *or recording stones found at Bonampak*

and greens, and in terms of colour-quality show strong resemblance to Persian art of a far later era, prove a degree of skill which transcends all commonly-known primitive art. Three rooms of one of the Bonampak temples are painted from floor to sharply angled ceilings with life-size figures of warriors in full regalia, including feather plumes, sceptres and handsome togas into which are woven numerous astronomical symbols. Magnificently dressed and bejewelled kings or priests are depicted receiving gifts from the warriors, some of whom are accompanied by musicians. The Mayas of 1200 to 1500 years ago are shown as being a handsome, strong-featured and robust people. The costumes worn by the priests, or kings, are made of jaguar or deer skin, richly ornamented with jade and inlay work. The cloths are apparently made of cotton and are coloured red on white, dark green on brown, and dark brown on white. The sashes are usually bright red. Apparently the newly discovered frescoes are painted with both mineral and vegetable dyes on a sort of plaster or stucco superimposed on hard limestone.

October 25, 1947

THE TOMB OF YARIM-LIM:
A Hittite king's four-thousand-year-old mausoleum

By Sir Leonard Woolley, Director of the Excavations at Alalakh, 1937–39 and 1946–47

In our last season at Atchana we have traced the history of the city of Alalakh back to its beginnings, and a trial dig on a little neighbouring mound called Tell esh Sheikh has told us something of what the Amk plain was like before Alalakh was founded. Tell esh Sheikh belongs to the "Chalcolithic" Age when copper was beginning to be worked but was still a rarity, and stone was the material for ordinary tools and weapons. . . .

We found, though we could not fully excavate, a royal tomb of the eighteenth century B.C. Attached to the palace of King Yarim-Lim was a chapel, sacked and burnt by the rebellious populace, which contained numerous objects, including the wonderfully fine stone portrait-head of a king, probably Yarim-Lim himself *(Figure 147)*. Believing it to be a funerary chapel, I dug down under the floor and found the walls of a burnt building filled with and enveloped in a solid mass of mud brickwork. The brickwork continued below its floor for 10 feet, relieved only by a few small gold objects placed between the courses. Then came the beams and planks of the roof of a building, but the same mud brick came under the roof and against the outer face of its fire-blackened walls; on the floor of the building was a layer of mixed soil containing quantities of potsherds which we knew to be more than a thousand years earlier than the tomb we sought. Still we dug down. The building rested directly on another, an almost solid cube, a "mastaba", as it would have been called in Egypt, with a fore-court and entrance-passage, built of mud bricks, but resting on a pavement of burnt tiles. Below the tiles was a square brick-lined shaft packed with sand and stones, great blocks of which the biggest weighed nearly three tons, then mixed earth, then a mud-brick blocking, then sand, another blocking and sand again. But by now we were digging 14 feet below water-level, the sides of the shaft, mere mud, fell in constantly, work became really dangerous, and when our pumps broke and no others could be obtained, we were scarcely sorry to close the season, although the cremation-urn of King Yarim-Lim probably lay only a few feet further down.

147 Portrait head of Yarim-Lim

But if we failed to open the tomb, we have learnt a great deal about the burial rites of a Hittite king.

First men dug a rectangular pit about 60 feet wide and 150 feet long, going down in steps to a depth of 30 feet. In the bottom of it was dug the well-like shaft perhaps 20 feet deep for the cinerary urn. They filled this in, sealing it with huge stones, paved it over and built above it the "mastaba" with its fore-court and passage, and perhaps a second chamber (which we did not find) for offerings; and after some ceremony filled in this, too, the passage with mud bricks, the court with mixed soil full of ancient pottery,

great stones, then a layer of hard clay, then clean, fine soil and a layer of mud brick to top it all, making a flat floor over the now shallower pit. On the floor was then built a new building, corresponding roughly to that below and leaving a narrow space between its walls and the pit's sides; the old passage was reproduced, above the "mastaba" was a chamber with no door and beside it a larger chamber whose roof was supported by wooden columns – the walls were low and the door so small that one could enter it only on hands and knees. Some kind of service presumably was celebrated, and then steps were erected in the passage, and men went up and removed the chamber roofs and flung in the mixed soil full of prehistoric pottery which they had found when they excavated the great pit; they made a layer of it about 18 inches thick and closed it down with bricks and a bed of clean clay. Surely they recognised that this mixed soil stood for the beginnings of the city's history; the dead king was no ephemeral creature of yesterday, but was divinely appointed from the beginning, and he lay by rights not in common earth, but under the ashes of Alalakh's remotest past.

Above this symbolic layer came course after course of bricks, rising to roof-level; the roof was replaced over the solid mass. Then the space around the building was filled with light brushwood, which was set on fire and a quick, fierce blaze purified the tomb. Thereafter bricks were laid round and over the building until it was buried 10 feet deep, and the bricks were but 5 feet below ground-level; then on them another building was set up and in its turn duly burned; its walls were trimmed flat, its interior filled with mud brick and round it was set concrete to serve as foundations for the walls of the Chapel Royal, the building above ground wherein stood the statue of Yarim-Lim, the fourth and last building required by the ritual of a king's burying.

1948

In this year there was another important article on Eridu, by Seton Lloyd; the excavations of the Karum of Kanes, a remarkable Assyrian trading centre in Hittite Anatolia; and of the Toltec site of Xochicalco in Mexico.

1949–50

This was the period when archaeology was really getting under way again, as the extracts show; but other major items published included more news of the fascinating Assyrian trading post in Anatolia, the Karum of Kanes; and the rich gold treasure of Ziwiye, found in Persian Azerbaijan.

May 14, 1949

FOUND AT LAST:
A bi-lingual key to the previously undecipherable Hittite hieroglyphic inscriptions

By Professor H. Th. Bossert, Director of the Department for Near-Eastern Studies, at the University of Istanbul

When in the year 1908 Winckler and Macridy uncovered the Hittite state archives of Boğazköy (Central Anatolia), with their thousands of legible clay tablets in cuneiform writing, the problem of the decipherment of the Hittite hieroglyphic script seemed to have come nearer to its solution. It was to be hoped that among the different languages represented in the Boğazköy archives the one known up to now as written in hieroglyphics should be found in cuneiform script. This seemed all the more probable, as a great number of seal impressions on clay, bearing legends in the Hittite hieroglyphic script, came to light. Their discovery led to the conclusion that, as far as it was not identical with the cuneiform Hittite, the hieroglyphic Hittite had to be considered a language co-existing with the former and equalling it in importance. . . . It was only in the years of 1929–47 that Meriggi, Hrozný, Gelb, Forrer and myself succeeded, by using new methods, in determining the reading values of the most common hieroglyphic signs. The fact that this language could now be read to some extent did not mean, however, that it could be translated, especially as it could not be identified with any of the Boğazköy languages. There was thus not much more left to do at this stage, than to hope for the future discovery of extensive bi-lingual records.

It was in the spring of 1946 that, while I was exploring the region together with Dr. Halet Cambel, Assistant Professor of Archaeology at the University of Istanbul, we discovered in the mountains bordering the Cilician Plain a fortified hill with a king's statue covered all over with old-Phoenician writing and fragments of sculptures and inscriptions in old-Phoenician as

badly damaged by a later Roman settlement. The Karatepe citadel is surrounded by a city-wall, fortified by rectangular towers projecting at almost regular intervals. The stronghold is accessible by two main entrance buildings, situated to the north and to the south, respectively, both of which have been excavated. The architectural plan of these buildings

148 Two reliefs from the right-hand side of the entrance corridor

well as in Hittite hieroglyphic writing, lying all around. The co-existence of these two writing systems, discovered for the first time on one and the same site, was the chief factor in the decision of the author to dig at Karatepe realised one year later. . . .

The results obtained up to now can be summarised as follows: two late Hittite fortresses on the Karatepe and the Domuztepe lie opposite one another, on both sides of the Ceyhan River, the ancient Pyramos. The larger and better-preserved stronghold is the one on Karatepe, while the one on Domuztepe has been

is essentially identical: a long corridor, flanked by towers and decorated on both sides by inscribed and sculptured panels, leads up to the main entrance-gate, flanked on either side by lateral recesses, equally decorated by inscribed and sculptured slabs *(Figure 148)*. . . .

What is sensational about the whole thing is, that in both entrance buildings the panels on the left-hand side bear inscriptions in old-Phoenician, the right-hand ones, however, inscriptions in Hittite hieroglyphic script. The study of the texts has shown, moreover, that they are not of different content, but that we are here in the presence of a bi-lingual record, *i.e.*, a text written in two different languages. For the very first time we have here the possibility of penetrating into the hieroglyphic Hittite language by way of the legible and translatable old-Phoenician text. The considerable length of the inscriptions should make it possible, moreover, to delve into the grammatical and lexicographical details of this new language, which has turned out to be of Indo-European character. In connection with this, the hope that before long it will be possible on the basis of the Karatepe inscriptions to translate the other Hittite hieroglyphic texts, seems fully justified. A very rich material that up to now could not be utilised will therefore be at our disposal for the study of Anatolian and Syrian history, for a period that is known to-day only to a very small extent.

It might interest the reader to hear something about the content of the Karatepe inscriptions. We are told that the stronghold was built by Asitawandas, King of the Danuna, and that he named the fort after himself: Asitawanda. The King claims to be of the dynasty of Mopsos. He belonged, therefore, to that famous family, known to us from Greek legends, but whom we did not know to be of non-Greek origin up to now. According to the Greek legends, Mopsos was the founder of numerous cities in Cilicia and Pamphilia. Asitawandas tells us of the time of his own reign, but he relates rather events of a peaceful than of a military nature. Again and again he insists on the fact that the time of his reign had been a time of happiness and well-being for his people, the Danuna. His father was probably Awarikus, mentioned as Uriki in the Assyrian texts. If this holds true, the reign of Asitawandas must have been before 730 B.C. He was therefore probably the last king before his country became an Assyrian province, around 725–715 B.C. As Karatepe has been settled in only one period, *i.e.*, the time before 730 B.C., all the finds belong to the same era, which archaeologically is of great significance. All in all, it is probably not an overstatement to say that the Karatepe finds can, from the philological as well as from the archaeological point of view, be ranked as a scientific event of first-rate importance.

July 16, 1949

FINDING THE EARLIEST REALISTIC PORTRAIT IN THE HISTORY OF MAN

By Professor Dorothy Garrod, Disney Professor of Archaeology, University of Cambridge

Recent excavations in a prehistoric rock-shelter at Angles-sur-l'Anglin, in the Vienne Department of Central France, have brought to light a remarkable series of limestone blocks, sculptured, engraved and painted by Magdalenian man. These excavations, which are being carried out by Mlle. Suzanne de Saint-Mathurin and myself, with the aid of a grant from the Viking Fund, are still at an early stage, and we have great hope of further discoveries.

The rock-shelter known as Cave à Louis Taillebourg (named from its owner, according to local custom) lies at the foot of limestone cliffs in the thickly-wooded valley of the River Anglin, a mile away from the little mediaeval town of Angles. . . .

By the end of the season it had become clear that the site was not a small cave, as Rousseau had thought, but a great rock-shelter, filled to the roof with earth and stones, extending along the foot of the cliffs to a distance whose limit has not yet been determined. The archaeological horizon, with its charcoal and burnt food remains, was covered by an overburden of fallen rock, due to a partial collapse of the shelter roof which took place after its occupation by Magdalenian man. This made digging a very laborious affair, as a disproportionate amount of time had to be given to removing the rocks in order to uncover even a small area of prehistoric hearth. In spite of this, by the end of September we had obtained a large number of flint tools, together with spearheads fashioned of reindeer antler, pierced shells and teeth, which must have formed part of necklaces, and pendants carved in bone and ivory. . . .

The most astonishing finds, however, were still to come. In the Easter vacation of 1949 we spent a fortnight at Angles carrying out work which was meant to be preparatory to the dig planned for this summer. Our first task was to remove a heap of stones thrown out by M. Rousseau which hampered the approach to the shelter. . . . Within the first half-hour we came upon a magnificent sculptured block showing life-size and in high relief the head and neck of a young ibex, certainly one of the most beautiful and appealing works of this kind yet found in any Palaeolithic site. We were gazing at this with delight when our workman, Edouard Gornay, called out that he had a stone showing traces of paint. This was removed with great precaution, and we saw that under a coating of earth there were not only patches of black paint but an engraved ellipse which looked like an eye; a few seconds later we realised with amazement that a human profile was sculptured on the edge of the block *(Plate 35, p. 224)*. Gornay at once fetched a bucket of water from the river, and we gently washed away the earth until there was revealed the head and shoulders of a Magdalenian hunter, carried out in a combination of painting, engraving and sculpture – the first life-size realistic portrait of a man of the Old Stone Age. After this, a block showing in very high relief the chest and fore-legs of an animal, probably a horse, came as an anti-climax, though it was interesting because made by the same pecking technique as the bison's hoof discovered *in situ* the previous summer. This was the end of sensational discoveries, though the rest of the dump yielded a number of engraved stones of exactly the same type as those already found in the Magdalenian horizon.

July 16, 1949

THE BONAMPAK MURALS

By Edward Bacon

The site of these paintings was found in early 1946 by Mr. Healey while he was making (for the United Fruit Company) a film record of the Maya, past and present. . . . After his first report and a further reconnaissance, an expedition was undertaken in the winter of 1947, financed by the United Fruit Company and directed by the Carnegie Institution of Washington. The major project of the expedition was the recording of the paintings, which was done both photographically and by the two artists, Señor Antonio Tejeda (of the Institution) and Señor Augustin Villagra (of the Mexican National Institute of Anthropology and History). . . . By various methods, and with the assistance of photography, infra-red, ultra-violet and colour, these vital transcriptions have been made. The transcription of Room I has been completed. It is generally taken to show two stages in the same ceremony, the upper panels comprising the preparation *(Plate 31, p. 220)*, the lower the ceremony itself *(Plate 32, p. 221)*. In the

149 The temple where the Bonampak murals were found

right-hand triangular section, three dignitaries seated on a daïs are probably discussing the ceremony to come; in the two panels to the left, white-robed notables are joined in vivacious discussion, while, on a small daïs, a servant is carrying a child, either taking it away or holding it up to see what is going on. It has been suggested that the child is going to be sacrificed; but such sacrifices were rare among the Maya and indeed, only three representations of Maya sacrifices are known – two, carved on stone, at Piedras Negras, and the one, painted, in the lower mural shown. In the extreme right, however, the three principal personages of the ceremony are being garbed with huge head and back structures of green quetzal feathers, the head-dress of which is a large water-lily nibbled by a leaping white fish – the water lily is *par excellence* the attribute of gods of the surface and interior of the earth. At the extreme right are several men in animated discussion and below are a number of servants preparing jaguar skins, which are worn only by persons of importance. In the long section below (with the blue background) is portrayed the ceremony itself. The three chief characters, with their green quetzal-feather accoutrements and their fish and water-lily head-dresses, can be seen in the centre. To the right is a group of thirteen characters, who appear to be taking part in the ceremony. Two of them carry parasols, some are wearing jaguar skins, and all appear to be talking together or arguing, one with another. The group on the other side of the three central figures is of the greatest interest. At the extreme left is a youth blowing what appears to be an ocarina; to the right of him are two trumpeters – long trumpets like these are believed to have been used by the Maya in the Oxtun dance; then follow a group of men in fantastic masks, which will be discussed later; then a cluster of men beating on turtle carapaces with pronged sticks, rather like catapult sticks; then a drummer, beating on a tall drum of the *huehuetl* (or upright) type; and lastly, five men with pairs of rattles, which appear to be gourds full of dried seeds and mounted on handles. The group of masked men are believed to be a band of dancers who are waiting to take their part in the ceremony. They are all garbed as deities of the surface or interior of the earth and are decked with vegetation, including the recurrent water-lily *motif* (sometimes stylised, sometimes portrayed naturalistically, and sometimes with the leaping fish, in one case gold-coloured). According to Mexican belief, the earth rested on the back of a great crocodile, which floated on a vast expanse of water; and this crocodile is not infrequently bedecked with water-lilies. One of the masked dancers has a crocodile mask on his head, and another is dressed to represent a crab or lobster with huge claws. On the right of the group is the old god of the interior of the earth, with a water-lily on top of his head, and the *tun* glyph carried under one arm. The left-most masked figure has a symbol "T" in his eye, which usually signifies the rain and storm gods. Most of the musicians have shell ornaments, which are usually characteristic of the gods of music and dancing. In the topmost panels of this room are seven masks of gods, full face and in profile, which have been identified from the "X" and "flattened U" symbols as being connected with the deities of the soil. Here and there throughout the murals and in the long strip dividing the two stages of the ceremony are

groups of glyphs. The long strip once recorded a date, probably that of the temple's dedication, but certain key glyphs are so badly defaced that it cannot be deciphered with certainty. There is little doubt, however, that the inscription was made during the great period of Maya art, between 730 and 810 A.D., as a date found elsewhere at Bonampak is read as 785 A.D. (in Christian chronology), and so shows that the place was in occupation at this era. The glyphs dotted here and there about the frescoes have not been deciphered, but are probably titles or may describe the functions of the persons portrayed. Another picture from Room II of the temple has not yet been completely examined, but the transcription of this particular picture has no doubt been hurried forward on account of the truly remarkable feature which it presents. This is a reclining figure in the centre foreground, which displays a knowledge of perspective, previously unknown among the Maya, and arguing a tradition of artistic sophistication, comparable with the early Italian masters. The exact nature of the scene portrayed is not yet known, but it has been suggested that it represents a scene of sacrifice. The different levels may be the steps of a pyramid on which the appointed victims, including the reclining figure and the figure with blood dripping from the hands, are kneeling or lying. The head at the bottom would appear to have been decapitated. The standing figures are obviously persons of importance, as is shown by their jaguar-skin garments. Some wear jaguar-head head-dresses, and one seems to carry a jade jaguar mask on his chest. Two of the head-dresses appear to carry symbolic vegetation, which may connect the scene with the earth ceremonies portrayed in the other fresco illustrated. The green plumes of one head-dress and those shown in other ceremonial objects may very well be quetzal feathers.... Even with what we already have, however, nothing approaching these paintings in skill or composition, freedom of execution, or brilliance of colouring has come to light in any Maya research.

May 27, 1950

NEW LIGHT ON THE INDUS CIVILISATION:
The Mohenjo-Daro granary

By Dr. R. E. Mortimer Wheeler, Archaeological Adviser to the Pakistan Government and Director of the Mohenjo-Daro Excavations

Like the sister-city of Harappa, Mohenjo-Daro falls into two parts: the Upper City, or citadel, and the much larger Lower City at its feet. The latter was laid out in large rectangular blocks on a grid-plan, with straight main streets 30 feet or more in width. On its western fringe rose the citadel, now eaten by the Indus floods into an archipelago of mounds, with crowded buildings raised on an artificial platform of mud and mud-brick to a height of 20 to 40 feet above the plain. At the highest (northern) point a Buddhist shrine and monastery of the second century A.D. are a landmark for miles across the flat countryside, but almost all the buildings round about it are earlier in date by 2000 years or more. Amongst them were included some of the principal religious and administrative buildings of the city, and the citadel was doubtless the headquarters of an autocratic priestly administration of a type well known in the ancient civilisations further west. Two pillared halls, one of them with five aisles, a collegiate building, and a Great Bath or tank of the kind still used for ritual purposes in the Indo-Pakistan sub-continent, add details to the picture. And now, as the result of digging during the past two months, can be added a large and imposing granary *(Figure 150)* adjoining the Great Bath on the western fringe of the citadel. Until a few weeks ago, this granary was concealed beneath a brick-strewn mound, 30 feet high, which gave no sign of its contents. But in the process of trenching its outer side in search of possible fortifications, the excavators came upon a high, sloping brick wall which at first appeared to be the expected curtain-wall and may, in fact, have served incidentally as a

local shield to the citadel. Its primary purpose, however, was of a very different order. It turned out to be a part of the lofty podium of a granary some 150 by 75 feet on plan and later enlarged. The podium rose to a height of 25 feet and had been pierced at the top by ventilation passages, above which the actual storehouse had been built of timber. Along the northern side of the podium was a loading platform about half its height, also with a sloping external wall, save where, near its outer or western end, it included a brick-paved alcove with a vertical inner wall, up which the supplies of grain could be hauled as they were brought in from the fields by bullock-wagon. The whole podium is in a remarkable state of preservation, standing in part to its original height. And structurally it shows an unusual feature of considerable interest. The external walls had been laced with timbers, some at right-angles to the face, some parallel to the face in the interior of the masonry, and some placed superficially as horizontal bonds. The decay of these timbers had in several places led to local collapses of the brickwork, and it is unlikely that this form of building construction was long in vogue. . . . In date, the granary was prior to the Great Bath, the main drain of which cut through its north-eastern corner, but the granary-annexe was proved contemporary with the Bath, thus combining with it to represent an epoch of maximum civic development. Immediately to the south of the granary were the remains of a large contemporary staircase leading from the level of the plain up to the platform of the citadel, with a well at its foot. The large granary, set prominently amongst the official buildings of the citadel, is a significant addition to the buildings of the city. It reminds us of the array of twelve small granaries with a similar aggregate capacity marshalled with other buildings in a cantonment under the shadow of the Harappa citadel, and implies a regulated system of grain-supply under the close control of the city authority. In the economy of the period, it may be supposed to have fulfilled some of the functions of the State Bank and Revenue authority at the present day, and was doubtless sustained by a regulated scale of tribute. It is yet another witness to the high measure of centralisation which is represented to us at every turn in the remains of the city. Whilst the work on the granary was in progress, a supplementary excavation uncovered a group of massive defensive brick bastions still preserved to a height of over 10 feet at the south-eastern corner of the citadel. They were built with or into the mud-brick structure of the citadel platform, and the earliest of them, probably contemporary with the Great Granary, shared with it the use of timber-lacing. If, as now appears, the buildings fringing the citadel were not continuously of a military character, they were, so far as they are known, at least defensible and were supplemented in the

fashion now indicated by specifically military strong-points. Incidentally, on a parapet-walk linking two of the bastions lay ninety-eight

150 The central granary of the Indus Valley city of Mohenjo-Daro

six-ounce slingstones of burnt clay, and many others were found round the perimeter of the citadel.

July 22, 1950

EXCAVATING THE GREAT PALACE OF ASSURNASIRPAL THE SECOND

By M. E. L. Mallowan, M.A., D.Litt., F.S.A., Professor of Western Asiatic Archaeology at the Institute of Archaeology, University of London, and Director of the British School of Archaeology in Iraq

Nimrud, which lies on the east bank of the River Tigris, about 20 miles south of Mosul, in Iraq, was known in ancient times as Kalah. Together with Nineveh and Assur, it was one of the three great Assyrian capital cities from which a succession of powerful monarchs built up a

great Empire. The special importance of Nimrud was its establishment as a military base where a large part of the Assyrian army was stationed, trained and recruited. . . .

The credit of being the first to reveal to the world the importance of Nimrud belongs to the celebrated archaeologist and diplomatist Sir Henry Layard, who made extensive excavations on the site between 1845 and 1851. . . .

The soundings made in 1949 were largely confined to the eastern sector of the mound, where traces of several formidable mud-brick buildings of the eighth and seventh centuries B.C. were exposed. It had been impossible for the early workers to disengage these walls from the soil, because a century ago the technique of digging mud-brick had not yet been mastered, and besides, they had been sufficiently rewarded by unearthing the sculptured stone

151 Ivory bull found in Assurnasirpal's palace

façades of the kings' palaces in the western sector of the mound. But a new discovery, full of promise for the future, emerged as the first result of our soundings. In the south-eastern sector, opposite one of the main gates in the citadel, we lighted on an imposing building with heavy mud-brick walls partly faced with burnt-brick, which had been the administrative offices of the Assyrian governors in the eighth century B.C. In one corner of that building was the archive office, and a collection of about 150 clay tablets which ranged in date from 808–727 B.C. These documents, which were inscribed in the Assyrian cuneiform script, consisted for the most part of contracts, sales of land and loans of various commodities which included slaves, cattle, cereals and metal; gold, silver and lead

were also mentioned. The tablets were dated by the name of the *limmu*, a high official appointed by the king for each year of his reign, and exact year dates could therefore be assigned to a considerable quantity of palace pottery, seals, jewellery, metal and architecture which were associated with this discovery. . . . Two beautiful objects emerged from the soil during the same season (1949). The first was a delicately-modelled ivory figure of a cow, which had once been represented suckling its calf, the head turned back to lick its tail. This little masterpiece, now in the Iraq Museum, Baghdad, was discovered in a room where Layard had found a wonderful collection of ivories, some of which date from the ninth century B.C.: this exquisite fragment had been overlooked by his workmen and lay in an undug patch of soil just as it had been abandoned 2600 years ago. The second object of outstanding interest and beauty was a translucent cylinder seal of mauve chalcedony, marvellously engraved with a mythological scene in which semi-divine bull-men carry the sun in its journey across the sky; this piece was probably made in the eighth century B.C., perhaps during the reign of King Sargon, a period at which the art of seal-cutting reached its climax in Assyria. (*Professor Mallowan, when discussing a group of rooms in the southern, or domestic, wing of Assurnasirpal, writes:*) But the principal treasure recovered from these rooms was a series of ivories which had once been used as inlay for caskets, boxes and the Royal furniture. These splendid pieces, which had been made by the most skilled master-craftsmen in the Near East, from Phoenicia and Syria as well as Mesopotamia, are still a delight to the eye; they clearly foreshadowed the making of the chryselephantine statuary which was to be so much admired by the Greeks three centuries later, in Athens. There was abundant evidence that many of these pieces had been part ivory, part gold. . . . Not less astonishing than their beauty and vigorous character is the size of some of these pieces. Two of the ivories, a fragment of a lion, with tail curling over the rump, and a bull (*Figure 151*), are perhaps the largest specimens of the kind ever recovered from ancient Western Asia. By a remarkable stroke of good fortune, we discovered on the floor of one of the ivory rooms an inscribed clay docket dated by the name of an Assyrian *limmu* official known to have held office in the year 715 B.C. This invaluable piece of dating evidence can only mean that some of these objects were still in use as late as that date, though it is generally supposed that many of the Nimrud ivories were made over a century and a half earlier, in the reign of Assurnasirpal II. In the light of this evidence the problem of the date at which these ivories were made will require further consideration. . . . Among the ivories are a few fragments of gold, and it is clear that the majority of the work was chryselephantine –

that is to say, of ivory inlaid or overlaid with gold. Perhaps the finest example of the combination is the much-mutilated goddess head, with which part of the overlying gold was found, and in this the rendering of the parallel strands of hair on the ivory head can be seen exactly reproduced on the gold foil which had surmounted it. The head in this case is bound with a triple fillet and decorated with twelve-petalled rosettes. Pendant from the fillet is an open reticulated pattern of strip gold overlaying the ivory and forming spiral curls. The eyebrows were probably also once encrusted with gold. The bull was found in a bed of clay and débris and a clay docket was found beside it inscribed and bearing a date of about 715 B.C.; and it would appear that about that time the palace was sacked by vandalistic enemy.

July 29, 1950

THE TREASURES OF ASSURNASIRPAL THE SECOND

By M. E. L. Mallowan, M.A., D.Litt., F.S.A., Professor of Western Asiatic Archaeology at the Institute of Archaeology, University of London, and Director of the British School of Archaeology in Iraq

A fresh attack on the north-west Palace of Assurnasirpal, where Layard had met with such astonishing success, produced the season's major discoveries. Here the expedition had before it two objectives: first, to go back to some of the chambers in the Palace which Layard had previously excavated and reburied; secondly, to break new ground at the south end of the Palace, where Layard had abandoned his excavations, for here we judged that there must lie an unexcavated wing of this famous building. In both directions, our prognostications that further monumental discoveries awaited us proved to be correct.

The unknown southern wing of the Palace was found to have been separated from the

northern by a broad passage-way several times relevelled by King Assurnasirpal and his successors, paved with burnt-brick, and lined with great inscribed gypsum slabs and sculptures in low-relief. . . .

. . . Not the least exciting discovery in the southern wing of the Palace were three perfect stone tablets, inscribed with the record of Assurnasirpal's campaigns; two of them had been reburied as an act of piety 160 years after they had been made, over the grave of a noblewoman who appears to have died in the reign of King Sargon. The same grave contained a lovely quartz seal pendant encased in gold and attached to a golden chain and a bronze safety-pin. . . .

In the northern wing of the Palace, where the expedition re-opened some of the chambers previously excavated by Layard, the results were no less spectacular. One of the rooms (O) was completely cleared; it was lined with great gypsum slabs inscribed with the "Standard" inscription of King Assurnasirpal; every block of the massive slabs in the stone pavement was similarly inscribed, as was the cushion-shaped stone threshold which led through a doorway into the passage beyond. There, still standing in position, in its pristine beauty, was one of a pair of gigantic winged genii standing on either side of a "heavenly tree". . . . Finally, at the extreme northern end of this vast Palace was a narrow entrance, this time flanked by two composite harnessed lionesses adjoined to the bodies of bearded human monsters. These giant stone guardians of the gate protected a narrow entrance only 6 feet wide and looked out on to a paved courtyard aligned with sculptured reliefs. Fallen on the pavement was a bull-man colossus which must weigh about 15 tons, a gypsum monster which once overtopped all the other statuary.

1951

A rich year; and other important articles concerned: in England, the discovery of a small but well-preserved Mithraic shrine at Carrawburgh on the Roman Wall, a gold torc found at Snettisham in Norfolk, and the famous Mesolithic fisher-hunter site at Starr Carr near Scarborough; work continued at the Karum of Kanes in Anatolia; the body of Tollund Man found preserved in a Jutland peat-bog; and Professor R. J. Braidwood's excavations at the "first farmers" site at Jarmo in Iraq. Starr Carr and the Carrawburgh Mithraic shrine were accompanied by reconstruction drawings by the late Alan Sorrell and although these were not the first of his to appear in the paper, they marked the real beginning of a period of years in which he took up the mantle of Amedeo Forestier and probably excelled him in bringing to vivid life for the general reader the discoveries of the field archaeologist.

March 31, 1951

THE MOST REMARKABLE DISCOVERY OF ROMAN PARADE ARMOUR EVER MADE

By Professor Gerhard Bersu, Hon. F.S.A., of Dublin and Frankfurt (Main)

During building operations at Straubing, in Bavaria (the Sorviodurum of the Peutinger Man), workmen came upon a heap of rusted iron tools at a depth of only one foot, and one man's pick struck a big bronze cauldron, mouth downwards in the earth. As the hole was quickly enlarged, there was great excitement when it was seen that the cauldron covered a mass of

152 Roman parade armour: the hoard of vizor masks, greaves, chamfrons, a big bronze cauldron and other objects

bronze objects, gilded and elaborately worked *(Figure 152)*. As the site is near the main building of a Roman villa, the Director of the Straubing Museum, Herr Josef Keim, was at once informed of what had happened. A young archaeologist, Dr. Hundt, also reached the spot at once, and together they were able to recover, in all probability, all the objects which had been hidden there – in all 116 items. The most important objects were those lying under the cauldron, the equipment from the "sports store" of a Roman cavalry formation. There were seven bronze vizor masks of helmets, the iron back part of a similar helmet, five greaves, six knee-caps, forming part of such greaves, seven chamfrons *(Figure 153)*, all superbly beaten from thin bronze plate, with repoussé and incised decorations, gilded and silvered on the surface. Many bear impressed inscriptions giving the names of former owners, with the letter "T" (for *turma*, or squadron) added. Some have several such inscriptions, indicating that the objects changed ownership; and some have inscriptions giving the name of the maker's workshop. All these objects are too brittle and thin to have been used in combat; and in fact we already know that such elaborate armour, made in central armouries, was used in sham fights, tournaments and similar displays by the cavalry of the Imperial Roman Army. . . .

The objects themselves convey much information that is new. The range of motifs represented on them throws light on the religious beliefs of the time, while the style and selection of the motifs suggest that we should look to the provinces of the lower Danube for the location of the privately owned workshops at which they were made; and, presumably, distributed or sold to the various units of the Imperial Armies stationed at strategic points along or behind the *limes*. The inscriptions show that they were taken by the owners with them when they changed garrisons, and that they were transmitted from owner to owner.

Two miles away from the site of the discovery lies the frontier post from which these objects most likely came. There was a permanent camp there, guarding the point where an important road leading north to Bohemia crossed the

153 Roman chamfron (or face armour for horses)

Danube. And here it is known was garrisoned a *cohors milliaria Canathenorum sagittariorum*, a unit originally recruited from Canatha, in Syria, which would include also the cavalry formations so necessary for scouting operations inside hostile territory.

July 28, 1951

THE TREASURES AND TRIUMPHS OF ASSUR-NASIR-PAL II

By M. E. L. Mallowan, M.A., D.Litt., F.S.A., Professor of Western Asiatic Archaeology at the Institute of Archaeology, University of London, and Director of the British School of Archaeology in Iraq

Nimrud, known to the Assyrians as Kalhu (Calah of the Old Testament), was between the beginning of the ninth and the end of the seventh century B.C. the most important military centre in the ancient Near East. King Assur-nasir-pal II (883–859 B.C.) spent the first five years of his reign in refortifying the city, and

154 Detail of stele *showing the portrait of King Assur-nasir-pal in full ceremonial dress*

during that time built the famous N.W. Palace which, as we now know, covers more than two acres of ground. . . .

In a recess of the courtyard outside the north entrance to the palace we made a discovery which will undoubtedly be of world-wide interest. This was a sandstone *stele*, 1½ metres high and just over 1 metre wide, standing in position on the pavement where it was intended to be seen by anyone entering the palace. On the upper part of the front face of this monument there was a panel *(Figure 154)* depicting the king himself fully robed, with his royal insignia, a long staff in his right hand and the royal mace in his left. He was carved in relief and represented as bearded, crowned with the king's mitre and armed with two daggers. Above him were the symbols of the principal Assyrian gods, Sin, Assur, Ishtar, Enlil, Adad, and the stars, the seven *sibilli*. On three sides of this imposing monument there is an inscription 154 lines in length, perfectly preserved. The king therein records the building of the palace, the names of the principal gods, the countries that he has conquered and the buildings that he has caused to be erected within the city, as well as the canals that he has dug. Most interesting is the account of the various kinds of trees that he has planted in the city, many of them imported from abroad. There follows a list of the temples, of the bronze, gold and different kinds of stone with which he has adorned them. There is a record of his lion and elephant hunts, and then comes a catalogue of the different kinds of animals and plants, flora and fauna within the city's boundaries. He concludes with an account of a great feast given to no fewer than 69,574 persons after the completion of his palace; for a period of ten days he caused them to be wined, dined and bathed, and thereafter to return to their homes with joy. This unique inscription, therefore, is a census of the city of Calah for the fifth year of the king's reign – that is, for the year 879 B.C.; it also enumerates the foreign notables who were in attendance on this occasion, and furnishes an inventory of the city's wealth. This monument was rightly judged to be of national importance to Iraq, and has been set up in the new museum at Mosul. . . .

One of the wells was remarkable for the excellence of its construction. It was built of burnt-bricks inscribed with the name of the king, and was 255 brick-courses deep. We dug it to a depth of 18 metres from the top, and there is now more than 4 metres of water in it. At the bottom of this well, preserved in the sludge, we found water-pots, an ivory figure of a stag, and a woman's comb, precisely similar in form to the combs which you can buy in the bazaars to-day. The sludge at the bottom of this well has had an extraordinary preservative effect; we found oak beams still in condition, and even traces of string. Next year we hope to pump the water out of the well and find yet more objects in the mud.

August 4, 1951

GEMS OF ASSYRIAN ART NEWLY EXCAVATED AT NIMRUD

By M. E. L. Mallowan, M.A., D.Litt., F.S.A., Professor of Western Asiatic Archaeology at the Institute of Archaeology, University of London, and Director of the British School of Archaeology in Iraq

The southern wing of the palace bore many traces of the damage which was done to it, most probably in the year 705 B.C., when a revolution appears to have occurred in Calah at the end of Sargon's reign. A large number of ivories, all of them fragmentary, were found in the débris overlying the floors, and they remained buried after the re-levelling of the building. Thereafter, a part of the palace was abandoned, though some of the rooms in the domestic wing were still in use in the seventh century. Apart from beads, pottery and amulets, the most interesting object recovered from this débris was an ivory figure of a sphinx standing erect, with its forelegs resting in foliage; this was found near the *stele*. Judging by the quantity of mutilated fragments which had survived the destruction, the palace must, in the ninth and eighth centuries B.C., have contained an enormously rich collection of ivory furniture, all of it carved and much of it overlaid with gold and encrusted with glass and semi-precious stones. This part of the building was composed of reception-rooms, living-rooms, bedrooms, bathrooms and lavatories, and an elaborate underground drainage system. The courtyards were open to the sky, and light was admitted from them to the surrounding rooms; in addition, it is probable that there were small, open windows high up in the walls, and these in the rainy season may have been blocked with brick, as is the practice in the countryside to-day. An interesting architectural discovery was a number of broad air-vents cut into the walls to admit fresh air from above. The shelf or ledge at the bottom of these vents was used as a cupboard, and water-pots were placed there to keep the water cool. . . .

But at this end of the mound the early diggers and the plunderers who succeeded them had left the ground covered with vast rubbish dumps which required machinery to move them. This

155 *The caryatid maidens excavated at Nimrud: (*left*) full face; (*right*) side view*

area was also promising because it contained the Nabu temple excavated by Rassam, and as Nabu was the god of writing, it is a legitimate deduction that the great library which Calah must once have housed may yet survive in this neighbourhood.

After the rubbish dumps had been removed from the surface, we were able to devote three weeks' work to the plot of ground where Loftus was known to have discovered the ivories. To descend down to the Assyrian floor-level proved to be a formidable operation, for in places the walls still stood to a height of 14 feet. This building we have named the "Burnt Palace", because it was destroyed by a violent fire, precisely when we do not yet know; I suspect at the end of the reign of Sargon in the year 705 B.C.

Our work in the "Burnt Palace" was confined to the re-excavation of seven rooms, most of which had only been partially cleared by Loftus. . . .

The various categories of ivories are too numerous to mention in detail. One enchanting object is a *pyxis*, or cylindrical ointment-box, carved with a scene representing a procession of male and female musicians playing the lyre, the cymbals and the pipes – all most delicately rendered. Most striking are the "caryatid figures" which include a pair of nude females *(Figure 155)* back to back, made of ivory and gold, their wigs and crowns still partly overlaid with gold foil and surmounted by floral capitals; one "caryatid column" was composed of a group of four maidens sensuously carved. Again, there is a remarkable ivory bull, perhaps one of a set, which originally ran around the edge of a circular tray and above it, the traces of a golden frieze, that is to say, gold foil beaten over an ivory strip which is engraved with a geometric guilloche design. Figures of males are less predominant, but one helmeted head, and another represented as wearing a beard are of a type hitherto unknown. No less skilfully rendered are the animal figures which include sphinxes, a pair of couchant calves and a *pyxis* lid depicting a grazing stag. The richest category of ivories consists of women's heads, most of them crowned, their physiognomy strikingly delineated. These seem to be Phoenician in type; a set of reliefs partly overlaid with gold, decorated with winged and hawk-headed figures sometimes surmounted by Egyptian crowns are Phoenician variations on Egyptian themes; many of these fragments have Phoenician signs carved on the back.

We do not yet know the date of this collection, but I suspect that it was not made before 800 B.C.

1952-53

As well as the articles quoted we also published during these years articles on the mosaics found at the Imperial Roman villa at Piazza Armerina in Sicily; a complex of excavations around Harran in southern Turkey, including the Temple of Sin and Sabian mosaics (with colour transcripts); work at Kouklia (Old Paphos) in Cyprus, with a reconstruction of the siege-mound; the early mastaba tomb of Uadji at Sakkara; and the startling cave-art of Monte Pellegrini, near Palermo, revealed as the result of war-time explosions, with its highly naturalistic ritual dancers.

March 15, 1952

THE MASTER SCULPTORS OF 12,000 YEARS AGO REVEALED:

Exciting "find" in a rock shelter in Vienne, France

By Professor Dorothy Garrod and Mademoiselle Suzanne de St.-Mathurin

It was clear that the occupation of the site had been brought to an end by a collapse of rock which made it uninhabitable to the prehistoric hunters, but preserved it for the archaeologist of the future. In this pile of stone were many fragments of sculpture, which revealed that the wall and roof had formerly carried a frieze in relief, with figures of horses, bisons, ibexes, chamois, and at least one human figure. This discovery presented us with the alarming prospect of trying to put together a huge jig-saw, of which the pieces varied from bits about the size of a matchbox to blocks weighing several tons. We therefore decided to try if there were not some part of the shelter where the sculptures had remained intact. A local sports-man, with tales of ferrets disappearing among the rocks had already suggested to us that the overhang stretched much farther downstream than appeared on the surface, and when we had forced our way through the brushwood along the face of the cliff, we found a spot where a natural archway was just visible above the surface soil. . . .

When we had raked out the small stones which had fallen in and almost completely blocked the top of the archway, we saw facing us, on the back wall of an alcove and just emerging from the vegetable earth, something which appeared to be a sculptured head; it was, in fact, the head of a horse. . . .

It was clear then, that at this end of the shelter, where there had been no collapse of the rock, the prehistoric hunters had lived on after the upstream end had been overwhelmed by débris, and that the remains of their habitation, piling up gradually against the wall of the shelter, had finally buried the sculptured figures left by their predecessors.

The finding of the horse changed the whole plan of our dig. Leaving the first trench for the time being, we decided to push upstream against the cliff face, uncovering the frieze section by section, until we came back to the great fall of rock from which we had started. This plan has brought results even greater than we had hoped. Immediately beyond the first horse was a second one, less well-preserved, but important because the attitude, with bared teeth and head lowered to graze, gives the clue to the true position of the horses' heads found among the fragments in the first trench. Next came the most remarkable group so far uncovered – three women life-size, depicted from the waist downward *(Figure 156)*. The first, three-quarter face, is surprisingly graceful, with long, slender legs fading out at the ankle, the feet apparently

156 Three nude female figures depicted from the waist downward in rock shelter in Vienne, France

having never been carved. The second, nearly full-face, is in higher relief, but the legs have broken away at the thighs, spoiling a line which must originally have been as graceful as that of the first. On the roof of the shelter, immediately above this figure, a triangular face with slanting eyes can be faintly seen, but it is so awkwardly

placed in relation to the body – much too low down, and to one side – that we find it impossible to admit that it belongs to it. The third woman is completely full-face, but flat and stylised. Behind her can faintly be seen the rather worn profile of a small bison, and a second bison, on the same scale, is superimposed on her legs from just above the knees. When we first found this scene we supposed these super-positions to be part of a deliberate design, but we now think it possible that the female figure was carved after the bisons, as part of a completely independent group which took no account of the first, just as one painting is done over another in caves like Altamira and Font-de-Gaume.

After the three women came a group of ibexes, also life-size, of which two are specially fine; a male animal facing downstream in an attitude of vigorous alertness, and below him, a female, beautifully carved in very high relief, who is cantering upstream preceded by a young kid, on whom she seems to keep a watchful eye. The head of the male is very much spoilt by the action of the vegetable soil, and by daylight is hardly visible, but at night it springs into relief when a lamp is placed so as to light it very obliquely. Facing this figure is another, very clumsily done, and probably in part refashioned. The head, which is completely disfigured by humic acid, is turned back to look downstream. In front of the kid is another male, not yet sufficiently disengaged for photography. This seems to be an old beast, stumbling forward on to its knees. The scene, then, shows a herd of ibexes, of which the weaker members are running from danger while the vigorous males stand guard. . . .

It is perhaps the finest thing of its kind yet discovered – longer and more varied than the frieze of horses in the Magdalenian shelter of Cap Blanc, near Les Eyzies, and more accomplished than the Solutrean sculptures of Le Roc de Sers, in the Charente – while nothing like the graceful, naturalistic life-size human figures is yet known in Palaeolithic art.

May 24, 1952

THE SUPERB ENKOMI CUP:
A 3300-year-old masterpiece of silver inlaid with gold and niello

Elsewhere Professor Schaeffer tells the story of his excavations at Enkomi, in Cyprus, during 1949 and 1950, and mentions in particular a number of intact burials of the early fourteenth century B.C. – i.e., the late Bronze Age, before the coming of the Sea People to Cyprus. One of

157 The bull-head cup of Enkomi as it was when discovered

these graves appears to have belonged to a family of priests, and has yielded a number of exceptionally fine treasures, chief of which is the cup illustrated. Beside the elbow of one of the male skeletons in the grave were a couple of bowls, one within the other, and both covered with a heavy, lumpy, green corrosion *(Figure 157)*. They were both assumed to be bronze, but they were despatched for cleaning and restoration to the British Museum laboratory, which is directed by Dr. Plenderleith. Under X-rays, the larger of the bowls appeared as a plain metal vessel, but in the smaller, the pattern of a bull's head and floral motifs appeared with startling clarity. By means of a complicated treatment the bowl or cup was cleaned and the whole brilliant design *(Figure 158)* emerged in almost pristine beauty – six bulls' heads round the rim, a series of linked rosettes round the base, a number of flower-head designs interspersed, and a pattern

of dots round the upper rim – the whole carried out in gold (of slightly varying tone) and niello (a black metallic compound) inlaid in silver. This cup is now on exhibition at the British Museum, and will remain there on loan until August, when it will be returned to the Cyprus Antiquities Department. Both in shape and design it is remarkably like the Dendra Cup of the same period, discovered between the wars in the Peloponnese by the Swedish archaeologist, Professor Persson, although the Dendra Cup has a lining of gold; and both are remarkable also, not only for their beauty, but for their use of niello, which is generally assumed to have been used for the first time in the Roman period, some 1300 or 1400 years later than these two cups. The larger bowl in which the Enkomi cup lay was also discovered to be of silver, but very thin, and covered and eroded so heavily with corrosion leached out from the copper alloyed in the silver as to be impossible to clean.

158 Two views of the bull-head cup of Enkomi cleaned and restored

August 16, 1952

IVORIES OF UNSURPASSED MAGNIFICENCE

By Professor M. E. L. Mallowan, D.Litt., F.S.A., Professor of Western Asiatic Archaeology at the Institute of Archaeology, University of London, and Director of the British School of Archaeology in Iraq

This year the Expedition's persistence was rewarded by historical and archaeological discoveries of supreme importance. With the assistance of hydraulic apparatus we were able to reach the bottom of a deep well built by King Assur-nasir-pal II, 883–859 B.C., at which we had begun work in the previous season. This well was lined with burnt-brick inscribed with the king's name, and was 83 feet 6 inches in depth. There were 330 courses of brickwork in all. Water-level was reached at just over 67 feet, and from here down to the lowest course we entered a belt of rich sludge of the consistency of wet plaster of Paris, and clean as a fine China-clay. This was due to the fact that the earth at that depth had been cleaned and refined by the rise and fall of the water table during the flood season for over 2600 years, and the soil thus cleaned had provided a protective coating for various kinds of perishable objects which would otherwise have disintegrated completely. Here were found thick coils of old rope which at first we thought our workmen had accidentally dropped into the well, but that the rope was actually Assyrian was proved by the fact that in this same belt of sludge we found nearly 100 clay vases, many of their necks still tightly bound. . . .

Many of the small incidental finds in the well were no less interesting; they included such things ˙ as shell beads, buttons and various ornaments, but none of them could compare in beauty with the marvellous ivories still preserved in their original colour, the finest of their kind ever discovered. The first masterpiece is the head of a maiden, 6½ inches high – a Mona Lisa of 2600 years ago *(Figure 159)*. It was indeed a thrilling moment when we saw this lady emerge from the deep waters of the well

where she had lain immersed in mud for more than 2600 years. Carefully we wiped away the dirt from her face, her hair and her crown. What we beheld was a thing of beauty still radiant with life. The warm brown tones of the natural ivory set against the dark black tresses of hair that framed the head combined with the soft, rounded curves of the face to give an extraordinary impression of life. The slightly parted lips appeared to have a light reddish tint; the black pupils of the eyes were encased in dark lids; the crown, fillets and stand were of a rather darker brown than the face. Originally crown and base must have been decorated with ivory studs, of which only one remained. Full use was made of the graining of the ivory, which showed to advantage on the crown, while the cheeks were cleverly contrived to display a concentric graining where they were fullest. Large lumps of sludge which had turned to the consistency of a cement had imprisoned the head from the back and at the sides, and thus prevented a number of vertical cracks from causing the face to disintegrate. It was, in fact, this fortunate circumstance which had saved for us what may be deemed to be at once the largest and the finest carved ivory head that has ever been found in the ancient Near East. We cannot be certain of the exact time at which this head was made, but for various reasons a date of about 720 B.C. is probably not far off the mark. . . .

Two other ivories, both of them chryselephantine, found in the same well were again supreme examples of the ivory carver's art and their conservation provided us with many moments of anxiety. The better-preserved of these two decorative objects is now in the Iraq Museum, Baghdad; the second, a duplicate, but with the base slightly damaged belongs to the School and is now in London. . . .

Each of the two brilliantly made miniatures *(Plate 33, p. 222)* is just over 4 inches in height: incredible lightness of touch and technical ingenuity have gone to the making of these two ivories, and the work has been crowned by the sensitive understanding of a great artist. The scene consists of a lioness in the act of killing an Ethiopian, who leans backwards, arms to the ground, head bent as far as it can go while

in alternate directions left and right to give the impression of motion before the wind. The blue lotus flower consists of lapis lazuli incrustation, and the alternating red of polished, dome-shaped carnelians serrated at the base to engage with the teeth of the gilt ivory calyces. The delicate operation of cleaning this ornament was entrusted to the skilled hands of Dr. H. J. Plenderleith, a part of whose technical report we have been allowed to quote here. "The miraculous preservation of this superb object

159 Ivories of unsurpassed magnificence: a Mona Lisa of 2600 years ago

the neck is proffered to the beast. This is the moment immediately before death, and one may wonder if the Ethiopian is not enjoying the ecstasy of sacrifice, for there is no sign of agony on his perfectly-drawn features. Only a great ivory master could have carved so small a head with such consummate skill. No less striking than the centrepiece is the background to this dramatic scene, which takes place in a meadow of blue and red lotus flowers, their stems leaning

after a sojourn of over 2000 years in a well, was evidently due to the accretions of a fine clay that built up around the specimen, protecting it from mechanical damage and from violent change in humidity and temperature. The deep cracks in the ivory seen in an X-ray photograph had their origin at the back, or external side, of the tusk, and by good fortune were scarcely apparent on the decorated side. That the object survived the ordeal of excavation without disintegration is due solely to the care expended in controlling humidity during this crucial time so that the change to museum conditions was accomplished with the minimum of strain. . . ."

The gleaming golden loin-cloth of the Ethiopian, closely moulded to his body, the golden spikelets of his hair, and a little incrustation on the arms provided an effective contrast to the powerfully carved lioness, whose left foreleg held her victim in the embrace of death. The upper arm and both wrists were once decorated with coloured incrustations, either lapis or carnelian. . . .

We may also guess that one and the same artist made both the "Lady at the Well" and these two plaques, if only for the reason that we have the feeling of a great individual temperament as well as an unrivalled craftsman's genius

latent in all of them. Technically, too, we may note that the little concentric circles of graining on the Ethiopian's shoulder are matched by the similarly selected graining on the lady's cheek. Whoever made the plaques was inspired by the high accomplishments of Egyptian art, but this artist was no Egyptian: he was probably a man from Mesopotamia, or maybe from Syria, a master-worker for the king who must rank among the great craftsmen of all times. . . .

Amongst the variegated assortment of objects associated with the ivories in the well there is little that pleases more than the miniature bronze models of dogs, standing, walking, sitting, with curly tails cocked over their backs; they are lively creatures full of character, clearly the domestic breeds favoured by the Palace at the time.

September 27, 1952

THE OVERLORDS OF MYCENAE BEFORE THE DAYS OF AGAMEMNON

By Dr. J. Papadimitriou, Leader of the Greek Archaeological Society's excavations during 1952

I was fortunate enough this year to excavate in Mycenae a second Grave Circle, containing royal graves, at a distance of 160 metres (175 yards) to the west of the Lions' Gate. These graves date from almost the same period as those which Schliemann discovered some seventy-six years ago within the citadel. . . .

The new Grave Circle we are now excavating has a diameter of about 27 metres (29½ yards); in that it is similar to Schliemann's circle in the citadel. The wall of our Circle, however, is much thicker, 1·55 metres (5 feet 1 inch), and is built of large, roughly-hewn blocks of limestone. Chronologically it belongs to the same period as the graves it encloses, while the Circle within the citadel was built of slabs of *poros* stone nearly 200 years after the closing of the

graves it encloses. The newly-discovered Grave Circle and its graves are contemporary and with some assurance could be placed around 1600 B.C., towards the end of the so-called Middle Helladic Period. . . .

It seems that the new Grave Circle encloses twice as many, and maybe even more, graves than the old Circle of the citadel. In the northern half alone, which has been only partially excavated, so far we have ascertained the existence of eight or nine graves, of which four have been completely excavated. There can be no doubt that graves exist in the southern section of the Circle, and these will be investigated in the future. . . .

The graves we are excavating belong to the type known as shaft graves: they are, in other words, rectangular shafts of varied dimensions cut in the conglomerate, but they are not always constructed in the same manner. For instance, grave B, with which we began our excavations this year, is a shaft 2·80 metres (9 feet 2¼ inches) in length and 2·15 metres (7 feet ⅝ inch) in width. But at a depth of 1·15 metres (3 feet 9¼ inches) the shaft becomes narrower, because along its two long sides a shelf is formed on which the beams of the roof of the grave were based. The shelf is carried around the short sides by a wall made of sun-dried brick. The floor was covered with pebbles on which a single body was laid. This grave was not so very rich. It contained seven complete vases; four of these were goblets of yellow Minyan, two hydriai with beautiful painted decoration, and a single plain amphora. *In situ* and on the skeleton were found two gold bracelets, a dagger of bronze, and a ribbon-like ornament of electrum, an alloy of gold and silver. Grave T proved more interesting, both for its construction and its richer contents. . . . This grave contained four skeletons, of which one, nearly in the centre, has the legs apart and the hands in a position of one stretched on a sofa perhaps; the other two, along the eastern and southern sides, are laid so as to face the centre of the grave. The fourth skeleton is seen below the skeleton lying along the eastern side of the

grave, and it is probable that at the north-western corner there exists another, fifth, skeleton, or its bones, below the many funeral gifts which were found in that corner and which have not been extracted as yet. . . . Nine clay vases with painted decoration were found on the floor of the grave; of these the most interesting and beautiful is the jug bearing a painted decoration of spirals and oak-leaves. That vase, belonging to a period at least fifty years later than that of the other vases, let us say to about 1550 B.C., proves that the grave was used for a long time, and that the last burial was committed to it at the beginning of the Mycenaean Age. Beside the various skeletons were found their individual gifts, among which are fourteen bronze swords, daggers and other weapons, some of which bear incised decoration; sword pommels, three alabaster and one ivory; some bronze and silver vases; two gold cups; one gold diadem; sundry gold head ornaments and a mask of electrum that was not found in its original position. All these gifts, I think, indicate the high position of the dead of this rich grave. And we must consider it as a certainty that these skeletons belong to a royal Greek tribe which established itself at Mycenae and built a strong State at an earlier period than that to which our heroes of the Trojan War belong.

June 13, 1953

THE BURIAL OF A CELTIC PRINCESS

By René Joffroy, Director of the Excavations at Vix and Curator of the Museum of Chatillon-sur-Seine

The discovery of a princely tomb of the first Iron Age in the north of the Côte d'Or Department, at Vix, near Chatillon-sur-Seine, is a remarkable archaeological event, both on account of the importance of the furnishings brought to light, and because it is possible to establish a relation between this tomb and the

important *oppidum* of Mont Lassois, which dominates the actual village of Vix. This *oppidum*, which was discovered in 1930, is being systematically dug and each campaign brings to light a number of new "documents" for the study of the civilisation of the Late Hallstatt era. . . .

160 Detail of the frieze of the great crater of Vix

Hitherto, the whereabouts of the necropolis had escaped me; but in January 1953, during methodical prospecting of the fields below the *oppidum*, I discovered a very rich tomb. . . . The methodical excavation of the tomb, considerably hindered by atmospheric conditions and the presence of standing water, lasted rather more than a month.

We first found, in the north-west corner, an enormous *crater* of bronze with voluted handles decorated with the bust of a gorgon, whose arms rested on snake-shaped legs *(Plate 34, p. 223)*. Small snakes also coil round the shoulders. The weight of each handle is 45 kilogrammes (99 pounds). All round the neck of the *crater* runs a frieze of *appliqué* reliefs composed of four horses attached to a chariot driven by a charioteer and followed by a *hoplite* or heavy-armed soldier *(Figure 160)*. The style and preservation of

these motifs are remarkable, and it is noteworthy that the eight groups of horses are all in different attitudes.

The lid of the *crater*, which has two handles ending in palmettes, has at its centre a conical boss surmounted by a very beautiful female statue 0·19 metres (7½ inches) high, of a very pure line *(Figure 161)*. It is in a style entirely different from that of the motifs which decorate the neck of the vessel.

On the lid of the vase had been laid a silver *patera* with a boss of gold, unadorned, and two Greek cups, one black and plain, the other of an Attic fabric, with black figures showing two scenes of combat between foot-soldiers.

On the soil of the tomb against the foot of the vase, lay a wine-jug, with a trefoil spout and a palmetted handle comparable with Etruscan specimens and those found in certain chariot tombs of the Marne, notably that at the Meillet Gorge.

Beside the west wall of the tomb, one above the other, were two bronze basins with straight handles whose attachment plaques were decorated with palmettes. These had been placed one inside the other. They had as neighbour a large *lebes*, or washing-basin, 0·56 metres (1 foot 10 inches) in diameter, also set against this wall.

Along the opposite wall had been set the four wheels of the chariot, dismounted from it. . . . Of the chariot itself there remain only the metal adornments. The body, that of a woman of about thirty, had been set inside the chariot, laid on the back, with the bust slightly raised. The

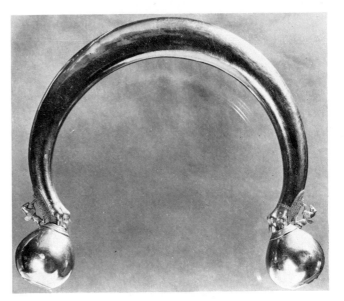

162 Diadem of gold found still around the brows of a Celtic princess buried at Vix

161 Bronze goddess which crowned the lid of the great crater *of Vix*

head, which had tumbled out of position, still carried a magnificent diadem of gold weighing 495 grams (*circa* 17½ ounces avoirdupois). This jewel is formed of an extended arc, each end of which consists of a lion's paw resting on an orb delicately decorated with motifs in repoussé. Resting on each orb is a little winged horse of particularly careful work, itself resting on a pedestal of filigree. This is the first time that a Hallstattian chariot tomb in France or Germany

has furnished a gold jewel of non-indigenous manufacture *(Figure 162)*.

The neck had been adorned with a torque of tubular bronze, covered with a leather thong twisted in a spiral. This object had fallen and was found at the level of the pelvis. At the level of the breast I collected a necklace of seven beads of amber (of which three had a diameter of over 1½ inches) and four beads of hard polished stone and seven brooches – two of iron, five of bronze. . . .

Such were the extremely rich furnishings of this tomb. It is simple to state that they comprise two well-distinguished series – one consisting of objects of indigenous manufacture, bracelets, torques, anklets, brooches, chariot; the other of imported objects, the *crater*, bowls, washing-basin, wine-jug, pottery cups. One or other of these series lead one to date the tomb to the extreme end of the Hallstatt Period, about 500 B.C. The origin of the imported objects seems pretty complex at first sight. The *crater* evokes, although much larger, those found in the necropolis of Trebenischte, in Yugoslavia. It seems to be of Greek manufacture. The pottery cups also are Greek, but the wine-jug and the bowls must be attributed to Etruscan workshops.

July 11, 1953

THE WORLD'S OLDEST PERSIAN CARPET:
New discoveries from the Scythian tombs of Pazyryk

The Pazyryk burial-mounds, or *kurgans*, were first observed by their excavator, S. I. Rudenko, in 1924, when he led a reconnaissance on behalf of the ethnographical section of the Russian Museum. The group of five large and several smaller stone-heaped mounds is situated on the sloping side of the small Pazyryk Valley, near the junction of the Ulagan and Balyktyul rivers, in a lonely part of Southern Siberia, some 124 miles south-east of Biisk, and about 49 miles from the Outer Mongolian frontier, in the region now called Gorny Altai. . . .

These were excavated by expeditions in 1927, 1929 and, with the support of the Hermitage Museum, in 1947–49. The most recently excavated tomb is No. 5. . . .

Rudenko believes, on the convincing evidence of textiles imported from the Near East, that the fifth burial mound may be dated in the fifth century B.C. In common with the other burial mounds its covering cairn of small stones sheltered a timber-lined pit containing in its southern half a smaller burial chamber constructed (pre-fabricated, to judge from guide-marks) of dressed logs. The pits had in every case become filled with perennial ice. The excavators were able to melt the ice away with hot water, revealing embalmed corpses, clothing, textiles, saddles and bridles, objects of leather and wool, all almost perfectly preserved. . . .

The burials reflect the customary conception of a material future state. In the burial chambers proper, surrounding the log coffins of the man and woman buried in each tomb, were found personal possessions of all kinds, for example, food in wooden dishes (these sometimes on small wooden tables with legs carved in the shape of lions); clothes and harness decorated in fantastic elaboration of animal motifs and patterns based on the lotus and palmette;

cushions, weapons, sometimes drums, and once, in the second burial-mound, a musical instrument "resembling the Assyrian harp". In the space in the north end of the pit between the wall and the internal burial chamber, were rows of horses, varying in different burials from seven to sixteen in number, all slain by a blow on the skull from an axe. With the horses in each pit was a cart, used, we presume, in the funeral cortège. The fifth mound contained in addition a light chariot of skilful construction, having wheels about 4 feet in diameter, with numerous slender spokes. Each burial chamber contained also a bundle of poles, convincingly interpreted by the excavator as the framework of a tent used for inhaling the intoxicating fumes of hemp. In the second burial-mound bronze vessels were placed under a six-legged stand of poles, to one of which a flask of hemp-seeds was attached.

The narcotic use of hemp and the rôle of carts and chariots in the funeral are in striking agreement with Herodotus' account of the Scyths of South Russia, who paraded a dead chieftain on a cart through his territory and among his subjects before he was buried, and then enjoyed a hemp bath. . . .

At Pazyryk the "animal-style" art of remote nomads is exemplified in wide variety: horses, eagles, falcons, cats, elks, deer, panthers, bird-griffins and lion-griffins, all drawn in the familiar vigorous convention. The finest examples of animal patterns found at Pazyryk, and among the best seen anywhere, are, in fact, the figures profusely tattooed on a male corpse from the second burial-mound. . . .

First in importance comes the patterned carpet of knotted sheared pile *(Figure 163)*. It was found in the saddlery buried with the horses of the fifth burial-mound, on one of which it had descended to serve as a saddle. It is 1·83 by 2 metres (6 feet by 6½ feet) and 2 millimetres

($\frac{5}{64}$ inch thick), and as the excavator assesses that there are 3600 knots per 10 square centimetres ($1\frac{1}{2}$ square inches), it is of fairly fine work. The design shows a border of griffins, then a procession of Persian cavaliers alternately riding and leading their horses. They wear the characteristic Persian head-dress, the ends of which were folded round the mouth and the peak of which fell sideways; for the only Persian permitted to have an upright peak was the Great King. Next comes a row of spotted stags, then griffins, and a sort of quatrefoil pattern derived from Assyrian palmettes. Carpets were made and used in various centres of the Persian Empire, at Sardis, Babylon and elsewhere, quite certainly in continuance of a long Oriental tradition going back at least to Assyrian times. . . . They are mentioned by Greek writers, who regarded them as Oriental luxuries. Their word (*tapétes*) still survives into modern times in French. Nevertheless, before these excavations not the smallest fragment of these carpets from the ancient East survived. It is not possible to say where this splendid piece was made, nor, until a detailed publication of it appears in which the knotting technique is described, to consider in what relation it stands to later

traditions of carpet-making. One is tempted, however, to suggest that it may have been made

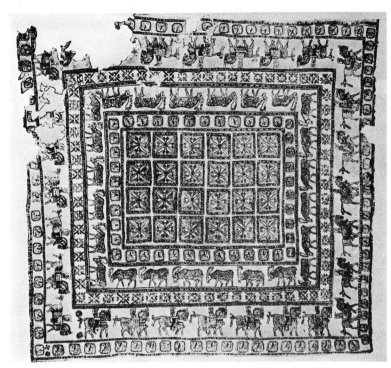

163 The world's oldest Persian carpet preserved in ice for 2400 years at Pazyryk

in Sardis, where, according to Xenophon, a Royal factory manufactured carpets for the exclusive use of the Persian King.

August 29, 1953

THE PYRAMID TOMB OF A PRINCE OF PALENQUE

By Dr. Alberto Ruz, Director of Research at Palenque, in Yucatan, Mexico

I began excavating and on the next day – May 20, 1949 – there appeared that stone which, in Mayan buildings, is always used to close up a vault. . . . A few days later I found a step, and then more and more steps. What had been found was an interior staircase descending into the pyramid and which for a reason which we then did not know, had been made impracticable by a filling of large stones and clay.

Four spells of work – each two-and-a-half months long – were needed before we were able to clear the filling from this mysterious staircase. After a flight of 45 steps, we reached a landing with a U-turn. There followed another flight, of 21 steps, leading to a corridor, whose level is more or less the same as that on which the pyramid was built – *i.e.*, some 22 metres under the temple flooring. In the vaulting of the landing two narrow galleries open out and allow air and a little light to enter from a near-by courtyard. . . .

And, on July 13, 1952, after demolishing a solid obstruction some metres thick, made of stone and lime – this was very hard and the wet lime burnt the hands of the workmen – there appeared on one side of the corridor a triangular slab, 2 metres high, set vertically to block an entrance. At the foot of this slab, in a rudimentary stone cist, there lay, mixed together, the largely-destroyed skeletons of six young

procession round the walls *(Plate 38, p. 322)*. The high vaulting was reinforced by great stone transoms, of dark colour with yellowish veins, giving an impression of polished wood.

Almost the whole crypt was occupied by a colossal monument, which we then supposed to be a ceremonial altar, composed of a stone of more than 8 square metres, resting on an enormous monolith of 6 cubic metres, supported in its turn by six great blocks of chiselled stone. All these elements carried beautiful reliefs.

Finest of all for its unsurpassable execution

164 The temple of the inscriptions at Palenque, whose pyramid contained a royal burial

persons, of whom one at least was a female.

At noon on the 15th of the same month we opened the entrance, displacing the stone enough for a man to pass through sideways. It was a moment of indescribable emotion for me when I slipped behind the stone and found myself in an enormous crypt which seemed to have been cut out of the rock – or rather, out of the ice, thanks to the curtain of stalactites and the chalcite veiling deposited on the walls by the infiltration of rainwater during the centuries. This increased the marvellous quality of the spectacle and gave it a fairy-tale aspect. Great figures of priests modelled in stucco a little larger than life-size formed an impressive

and perfect state of preservation was the great stone covering the whole and bearing on its four sides some hieroglyphic inscriptions with thirteen abbreviated dates corresponding to the beginning of the seventh century A.D., while its upper face shows a symbolic scene surrounded by astronomical signs. . . .

I then had the base bored horizontally at two of the corners; and it was not long before one of the drills reached a hollow space. I introduced a wire through the narrow aperture and, on withdrawing it, I saw that some particles of red paint were adhering to it. . . . The particles of cinnabar adhering to the wire inserted into the centre of the enormous stone block was unquestionable evidence of burial: and our supposed ceremonial altar must therefore be an extraordinary sepulchre. . . .

This was not the first time during my career as an archaeologist that a tomb had been discovered, but no occasion has been so impressive as this. In the vermilion-coloured walls and base of the cavity which served as a coffin, the sight of the human remains – complete, although the bones were damaged – covered with jade jewels for the most part, was most impressive. It was possible to judge the form of the body which had been laid in this "tailored" sarcophagus; and the jewels added a certain amount of life, both from the sparkle of the jade and because they were so well "placed" and because their form suggested the volume and contour of the flesh which originally covered the skeleton. It was easy also to imagine the high rank of the personage who could aspire to a mausoleum of such impressive richness.

We were struck by his stature, greater than that of the average Mayan of to-day; and by the fact that his teeth were not filed or provided with incrustations of pyrites or jade, since that practice (like that of artificially deforming the cranium) was usual in individuals of the higher social ranks. The state of destruction of the skull did not allow us to establish precisely whether or not it had been deformed. In the end, we decided that the personage might have been of non-Mayan origin, though it is clear that he ended in being one of the kings of Palenque. . . .

As shown in some reliefs, he was wearing a diadem made from tiny discs of jade and his hair was divided into separate strands by means of small jade tubes of appropriate shape; and we discovered a small jade plate of extraordinary quality cut in the shape of the head of Zotz, the vampire god of the underworld, and this may have been a final part of the diadem. Around the neck were visible various threads of a collar composed of jade beads in many forms – spheres, cylinders, tri-lobed beads, floral buds, open flowers, pumpkins, melons, and a snake's head. The ear-plugs were composed of various

elements, which together made up a curious flower. From a square jade plate with engraved petals, a tube, also of jade, projected and this ended in a flower-shaped bead; while on the back of the square plate (which carries a hieroglyphic inscription) a circular plug was fitted. All these elements would be united by a thread and it would seem that there hung as a counterpoise to them, behind the broad part of the ear, a marvellous artificial pearl, formed by uniting two perfectly-cut pieces of mother-of-pearl, polished and adjusted to give the impression of a pearl of fabulous size (36 millimetres). Over the breast lay a pectoral formed of nine concentric rings of twenty-one tubular beads in each. Round each wrist was a bracelet of 200 jade beads, and on each finger of both hands a great ring of jade. We found these still fixed on the phalanges, and one of the rings was carved in the form of a crouching man, with a delicate head of perfect Mayan profile. In the right hand he held a great jade bead of cubical form, and in the left, another, but this one spherical, the two being perhaps symbols of his rank or magical elements for his journey to another world. Near his feet we found another two great jade beads, one of them hollow and provided with two plugs in the shape of flowers. A jade idol of precious workmanship stood near the left foot and is probably a representation of the sun god. Another little figure of the same material must have been sewn above the breech-clout. From the mouth cavity we extracted a beautiful dark jade bead, which, according to the funeral rites of the Mayans, was placed there so that the dead person should have the means to obtain sustenance in the life beyond the tomb. At the moment of burial, the personage wore over his face a magnificent mask made of jade mosaic, the eyes being of shell, with each iris of obsidian, with the pupil marked in black behind *(Plate 39, p. 323)*. Of the hundreds of fragments, some remained on the face, adhering to the teeth and the forehead, but the greater part were lying on the left side of the head, clearly as the result of the mask's slipping off during the burial. The corpse must have been set in the sarcophagus entirely wrapped in a shroud painted red, and the same cinnabar colour adhered to the bones, the jewels and the bottom of the sarcophagus when the cloth and the flesh decomposed. The mask was fitted directly on the dead man's face, the fragments being stuck in a thin coating of stucco, the remains of which fitted to the human face. Nevertheless, the mask had to be prepared beforehand and may perhaps have been kept on a stucco head. It is perfectly possible that its main traits, realistic as they are, represent more or less those of the actual dead man.

October 17, 1953

JERICHO: MANKIND'S EARLIEST WALLED TOWN

By Kathleen M. Kenyon, D.Litt., F.S.A., Director of the British School of Archaeology in Jerusalem

The very great antiquity of the settlement at Jericho was first discovered by Professor Garstang, of Liverpool University, in 1935, and the present expedition has considerably extended the scope of his discoveries. It was in the Near East that early man, who had previously lived a precarious existence as a hunter and food-gatherer, first began to experiment in agriculture and stock-breeding, which alone made settled life possible. Such experiments are of very great interest to us, for from these beginnings all our modern civilisation is derived. The discoveries at Jericho suggest that here was one of the places in which settlement first took place, at a date which may be about 5000 B.C.

Professor Garstang reached the level of the very early occupation at the north-east end of the mound. The present excavations have discovered similar buildings at a distance of about 400 feet away, in the centre of the west side. The houses are solidly built of hand-made bricks, on which the maker had impressed his thumbs in a herring-bone pattern to provide a keying for the mortar. Doorways are wide, rooms are rectangular and of comfortable size. Floors and walls are covered with a fine, highly-burnished plaster, so hard that even to-day it can be scrubbed with water to restore its freshness. Such architecture is in no way primitive. Yet the period is so early that the method of making pottery, one of the first inventions of settled man, had not yet been discovered, and utensils were still of stone, presumably supplemented by perishable materials such as skin and wood. This very rapid development of an advanced architecture indicates how quickly settled life must have sprung up at Jericho, presumably since the abundant water supply assured the success of the early experiments in agriculture.

Evidence is just beginning to appear of the first stages in the growth of architecture. Bed-rock has so far only been reached in a very small area. Here, the first buildings were of curvi-linear plan, probably representing the translation into mud-brick of the temporary shelters and tents of the nomadic predecessors of the first settlers *(Figure 165)*.

The evidence suggests that development from this stage to that of the more advanced architecture was rapid. More interesting still is the evidence of the development of these early settlers into a true community. Over the débris of the early houses was built a massive wall. Only a short length of this wall has so far been

165 The walls of Jericho and (left) curved buildings imitating tents

traced, for it lies at a depth of about 25 feet from the surface, but it has every appearance of being an enclosure wall, and may well be the town wall of the earliest inhabitants. Jericho can thus claim to be by far the oldest town in the world. Such a wall can only have been constructed by an organised community, for its building, with stones up to 4 feet by 3 feet across the face, transported from the mountains a mile or so away, was a formidable undertaking.

The most remarkable discovery concerning the progress of these early people came at the very end of the second season's work *(Plate 40, p. 324)*. A portion of a skull was visible in the edge of one of the areas excavated, lying beneath one of the typical plastered floors. When it was cleared, it was found to have modelled on it in plaster an amazingly lifelike representation of the features. Moreover, when it was removed, in the cavity behind two more were visible. Three more appeared behind these, and yet a seventh behind them. They lay in a tumbled heap, discarded when a new house was built, and some were damaged by this rough treatment. But they are well enough preserved to give us a vivid impression of the artistic powers of this astonishing people. The contours of the faces are delicately rounded, the features small and fine, with the detail of the nostrils, ears, eyelids and mouths faithfully executed. The tops of the skulls are left uncovered, but one has on it broad bands of dark paint, possibly representing a head-dress. The eyes are inset with shells, in one case cowries, the rest with rounded shells, always in two segments, with a vertical slit to represent the pupils. One feels as one looks at them that one really is looking at the faces of men who died 7000 years ago.

These heads are the earliest known examples of naturalistic plastic representation of the human features which can be claimed as the direct ancestors of modern art. The great art of the Palaeolithic period has no direct descendant. But from the art of Neolithic Jericho the tradition descends through ancient Sumer and Egypt to the art of the Greeks and thence to modern Europe.

1954-55

These also were rich years, as the extracts show, with the highlights falling on Minoan and Mycenaean discoveries, the Pazyryk fabrics, and, in London itself, the discovery of the Walbrook Mithraeum. But other items included the resumption of work at Ras Shamra (Ugarit) in Syria, with the discovery of ivory bed-head panels; the first report of the intact funerary boat of Cheops, beside the Great Pyramid; and the excavation of the Eleusis necropolis, with Mycenaean and later tombs and the finding of a huge proto-Attic vase.

January 16, 1954

THE PALACE OF HOMER'S NESTOR

By Professor Carl Blegen, of the University of Cincinnati

The work at the palace, which was made possible through the generous financial support of Professor and Mrs. W. T. Semple, has already in two campaigns uncovered a considerable area in the central and south-western parts of the building. . . .

The principal apartment, or megaron, which follows the characteristic mainland or Mycenaean plan, comprises four elements: a narrow court on which the structure fronts, an entrance portico with a two-columned façade, behind the latter a vestibule, and, finally, a great hall or throne room.

The court, roughly 7 metres (7½ yards) deep and more than 11 metres (12 yards) wide, was bordered on the south-east by a wall, built of squared blocks laid in ashlar style. There were probably window-openings in the wall to provide light and air to a set of rooms beyond to the south-east. The court, which had a stucco floor, was accessible from the south-west or the north-east, perhaps from both directions; but these areas have not yet been excavated.

The portico, a little more than 11 metres (12 yards) wide and about 4 metres (4½ yards) deep, was finished in good style. The walls at the sides and rear had at the bottom a dado of well-cut stone, above which were found carbonised

166 The palace of Homer's Nestor: looking across the throne room (with circular hearth) to the pantries, a courtyard and a large hall of state

remains of massive horizontal beams. Symmetrically placed in the façade were stone bases for two columns. The latter, almost surely made of wood, had perished; but it was clear that they had been set in place before the stucco floor was laid. At the rear of the portico a broad central doorway opened into the vestibule; it was probably closed by hangings rather than by an actual door, as there are no traces of pivot-holes in the threshold. At the right, beside the doorway, is a low, rectangular platform made of stucco. Whether it served as a place for a seat or as a stand for a sentry or a servant has not been determined.

The vestibule, about 4·60 metres (5 yards) deep, occupied the full width of the megaron. Its floor of stucco was greatly damaged by the fire that destroyed the building; but where preserved it has a smooth surface, which retains traces of painted decoration arranged in rectangular panels. The walls on all sides were coated with fine plaster, which bore brightly-coloured frescoes. Hundreds of fallen fragments were salvaged. It is likely that human figures were represented, but much work of cleaning, joining and restoring will be necessary before the subjects of the composition can be recognised. A small doorway led from the vestibule to the north-east, where no digging has yet been undertaken. A large doorway provided entrance to the throne room to the north-west; and beside this opening, at the right, is another stucco platform, similar to that in the portico.

The throne room *(Figure 166)*, 12·88 metres (14 yards) long and 11·20 metres (12½ yards) wide, is of approximately the same size as its counterpart at Mycenae. Though it has suffered some damage here and there, the stucco floor is relatively well preserved. It was marked off by paired incised lines into squares that usually measure about 1·07 metres (3 feet 6 inches) on a side. Each bore painted decoration in varied colours. Abstract linear motives prevail, but in one instance, in front of the throne, is a large, semi-realistic octopus. In the centre of the room is a raised hearth, 4·02 metres (13 feet 2¼ inches) in diameter, made of stucco and rising in a stepped profile above the floor. Its vertical outer edge was decorated with a symbolic flame pattern, probably painted in red and black; a narrow step above bears solid triangles, apparently done in the same two colours. On top a broad, flat border surrounding the central place for the fire bears a continuous band of running spirals, which seem originally to have been painted in at least four colours, red, yellow, blue and black.

Four wooden columns, placed with rough, but not exact, symmetry, supported the ceiling and roof of the room. The columns which were all destroyed in the fire, were set in position, each on a stone base, before the floor was laid; and in the contiguous stucco are well preserved the impressions of the lower ends of the shafts. Each had thirty-two shallow flutings comparable in design to those of the classical Doric order. Beside the westernmost column stood a circular table of offerings made of stucco. Two or three small votive pots were found upon it.

Against the north-eastern wall, opposite the hearth, the place for the throne is indicated by a rectangular gap in the floor. The throne itself is missing. Whether made of stone, stucco or wood, it was installed before the floor was laid. Beside the royal seat, to the north-west, close to the wall of the room, is a shallow, basin-like depression in the floor. A narrow channel leads north-westward some 2 metres (6 feet 7 inches) to a second similar hollow. This was perhaps an arrangement designed to permit the king to pour libations without rising from his throne. . . .

The walls of the throne room were built of stone, with a framework of many upright and horizontal and transverse timbers. The surface was coated with fine plaster, which was decorated with gaily-painted frescoes. . . .

Beyond the wall delimiting the court is another quarter of the palace in which administrative records were kept. Here, in 1939, was discovered the archives room, a small, earth-floored chamber, bordered on three sides by a broad clay bench or shelf. On this latter lay some 200 inscribed clay tablets, while 400 more were found heaped up in confusion on the floor as they had evidently fallen. In 1952 a second chamber was exposed to the south-east of the first. It was connected with the archives room by a doorway that was used perhaps as an annex for overflow storage of records. Lying in heaps on its earth floor were more than 300 further tablets.

They all bear writing in what was called by Sir Arthur Evans the Minoan Linear B form of script. The eighty or more characters, each standing for a syllable rather than a letter, were incised with a sharp-pointed implement while the clay was soft. The tablets hardened as they dried, and were apparently never properly baked except by accident. The documents seem to be bookkeeping accounts, dealing in methodical entries with human beings, animals and commodities, using a decimal scale of numbers, and employing several standardised systems of weights and measures. The texts have not yet been read and understood, but recent researches have made it seem probable that the language is an early form of Greek.

Plate 36 *A felt wall-hanging from the fifth tomb at Pazyryk*

Plate 37 *Sphinx figure in a felt wall-hanging preserved in ice at Pazyryk*

Plate 39 *Jade death-mask found in the royal tomb in the heart of the pyramid temple of the inscriptions at Palenque*

Plate 40 *Moulded skull as it was found in Jericho, mankind's earliest walled town*

Plate 41 opposite *Elaborate gold* amphora *from Panagurishte in southern central Bulgaria*

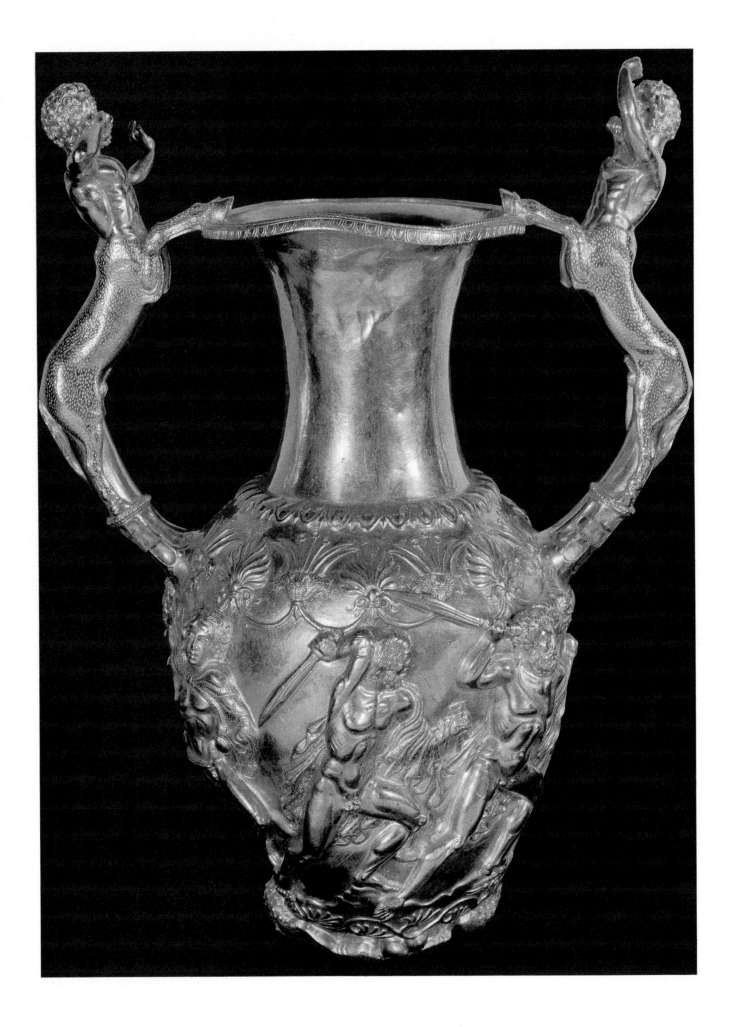

Plate 42   The Piazza Armerina Mosaics: detail from the Chase

Plate 43 The Piazza Armerina Mosaics: detail from the Big Game Hunt

*Plate 44   The Piazza Armerina Mosaics: detail from the Ten Girls showing three of the large-
eyed, scantily-dressed girls, one with a discus, another with dumb-bells*

February 27, 1954

THE NEWLY-EXCAVATED GRAVE CIRCLE OF MYCENAE

By Dr. J. Papadimitriou, Ephor of Antiquities of Attica and the Argolid, and Director of the Excavations

In my last article I gave a report of the first conclusions and results of the excavations at the time when the work had not then been finished. By the end of the summer of 1952 two other graves, which we named *Delta* and *Epsilon*, had been found, and last summer eleven others were also excavated. . . .

The *Delta* grave was very rich and three bodies were found in it. Near them were two bronze swords, and other bronze weapons and clay vases. One of the swords has a pommel of ivory and a gold handle with spiral decorations and four sculptured heads, two of bulls and two of lions, which join the handle to the bronze blade. On each side of the blade a series of griffins is engraved. The floor of this grave was also covered with the usual layer of pebbles, and in the north-west corner of it a bronze bowl and seventeen arrowheads of red stone were found. . . .

During the last days of the excavations we uncovered the richest of all the graves which have been found up to now in the new grave circle, similar in luxury to the Schliemann graves. It is the grave *Omicron*, the excavation of which was very tiring and expensive and has demanded much time and exceptional care. . . .

It was necessary to divert the road and the water-course in order to open this grave, but our fatigue was rewarded by the exceptionally rich gifts, of which some were of rock crystal. For this reason we have called it "the Crystal Grave". It contained two skeletons, one of which was packed at the west side of the grave without any offering. The other was in the centre in an extended position, and belonged to a young woman. More than thirty clay vases with various designs were found around the four sides and on the roof of the grave. Near the body of the second skeleton in the centre we have found the most precious offerings of all the graves which have been excavated in the new circle. First, at the north side, near three clay vases, a rock crystal bowl in the shape of a duck, carved with great skill, having the head with the neck gracefully bent as the handle of the bowl and its tail as the lip. No similar work of art has ever been found on the Greek mainland or in Crete. Only in Egypt or in Asia Minor can we find perhaps similar precious vases. It is amazing how the artist obtained this unusually large piece of crystal (15 centimetres – $5\frac{7}{8}$ inches), and was able to carve it in such a marvellous way. Near it was a bronze pin with a crystal head, two other bronze pins with crystal heads were also found, one on each shoulder of the skeleton, and presumably intended to hold a heavy robe, perhaps of flax. Another pin of silver, with a gold head, was near the right shoulder, and on the breast three necklaces, two made of various precious stones such as amethysts and cornelians, the other of amber beads. There were also two fine gold bracelets made of repeated spiral circles, two ear-clips of gold and a beautiful gold necklace of birdlike beads. Near the girl's head lay two large diadems of gold with embossed designs, and on one of these an ivory plate which was probably used to hold the diadems on the head. The richness and value of these finds prove the grave belonged to a person of high class, to a young princess of the powerful and wealthy Royal families of Homer's "Golden Mycenae."

March 6, 1954

PRE-HOMERIC MYCENAE

By Dr. J. Papadimitriou, Ephor of Antiquities of Attica and the Argolid, and Director of the Excavations

The excavation of last summer began at the end of July and finished at the end of September; eight large graves and three smaller ones being excavated.

Of these newly-found graves, the site of grave *Nu* had already been suspected during the excavations of the year before. . . . The skeleton belonged to a tall man about 1·80 metres (5 feet 10⅞ inches), an illustrious warrior, as the rich and strong weapons found near him prove. Two long bronze swords with ivory pommels, a beautiful bronze dagger, a bronze lance and other bronze weapons were found near the two skeletons. One of the bodies had a gold collar around the neck; and near the other skeleton, at the west side of the grave, were some gold ornaments and a gold cup with relief designs. Two bronze vases, another one of alabaster, and four clay vases were also found at the south side, and on the roof eight other vases had been placed, decorated with beautiful matt painting.

To the east of grave *Nu* another one, *Iota*, was uncovered, 2·65 by 1·40 metres (8 feet 8⅛ inches by 4 feet 7⅛ inches) in dimension. In this grave two male skeletons were found, and I have gathered from this and other examples that it was characteristic that the men were buried apart from the women and the children. Only in the graves of the men gold or silver cups were found, because only the men used these for drinking and for libations. A bronze sword with an ivory pommel, a bronze knife with a handle of rock crystal and a bronze lance constituted the equipment of the body. Big clay vases, two armlets, another gold ornament for a belt and a silver cup were also in the grave. . . .

Two other graves, *Xi* and *Omicron*, were richer, and *Xi* (1·96 by 1·38 metres – 6 feet 5⅛ inches by 4 feet 6¾ inches) belonged to a little girl of no more than two years of age. The skeleton was almost in the centre of the grave and was provided with beautiful jewellery which appeared *in situ* as they had been on the body of this unlucky child, and made a charming impression; around the head was a diadem of double gold leaves joined in a gold bandelet, one pair of earrings near the ears, and two gold rings for the hair at the temples to hold the tresses together. A gold ring on the left hand, a gold baby's rattle, a necklace of small, precious stones with a faience amulet in the centre, as well as many small fine clay vases were beside the remains. In the north-west corner of the grave the bones of another skeleton were packed without offerings and, outside the grave, not far to the west, a skeleton of another child in a strongly flexed position was uncovered. It is therefore probable that this skeleton, near which four small clay vases were found, as well as the other in the north-west corner of the grave, belonged to the companions and playmates of this rich and noble young girl of grave *Xi*.

167 Remains of the Roman Mithraic temple in London

October 2, 1954

MODERN LONDON DISCOVERS ROMAN LONDON

Rarely can an archaeological discovery have given rise to so much public interest as that aroused in London by the uncovering of the remains of the Roman Mithraic temple at Walbrook, near the Mansion House *(Figure 167)*. A fourteen-storey block of offices is to be built on the site, but the contractors, at an estimated cost to themselves of about £2000 a week, agreed to hold up the work for about a fortnight in order that further excavation and an archaeological survey might be completed. It was announced on September 20 that the excavation would be open to the public between 5.30 p.m. and 6.30 p.m. each day that week, but the numbers who arrived exceeded all expectations. Each day large queues formed hours before the site was due to open and many were unable to gain admission. On the first "public view" day the crowd of sightseers was estimated to number some 10,000; on the next day it had grown to 15,000 and at dusk between 3000 and 4000 people had to be turned away. High-level discussions about the possibility of preserving the remains of the temple have been held, but the conclusion reached was that to do so would be impracticable.

331

October 9, 1954

INVOKING THE PERSIAN SUN-GOD IN THE HEART OF SECOND-CENTURY LONDINIUM

At the time of writing the announcement has just been made that although the cost of preserving the newly discovered Temple of Mithras *in situ* had proved to be prohibitive, the owners of the Bucklersbury property on which it stands, the Legenland Property Company (whose chairman is Mr. A. V. Bridgland), announced their intention of dismantling the remains and re-erecting them in the forecourt of the eventual Bucklersbury House at their own expense. This generous act will ensure that this unique temple will be preserved for ever in optimum conditions within 80 yards of its original position. But these remains, complete though they are in plan, call for both knowledge and imagination to bring them to life, and to people them with worshippers. Our Artist, therefore, with Mr. Grimes' assistance, has reconstructed the interior of the temple and set the scene *(Figure 168)*. Its total length is 60 feet (from east to west) and its width 25 feet. It consists chiefly of a nave leading to an apsidal west end. There would stand, usually veiled in curtains, an elaborate relief of Mithras killing the bull. It seems certain that the first head found on the site was the head of Mithras in this relief, which would therefore be about 5 feet square. Before the relief and between flat pilasters stood the altar, raised above the nave level, and approached by wooden steps, and covered by a pillared tabernacle. On either side of the nave was a low wall, carrying seven pillars with a single ovolo moulding. On this wall ran a low sleeper wall, built round the bases of the columns, which carried beams which formed the floor of the two aisles. Towards the east end of the nave stood, facing each other, relief shrines of Cautes and Cautopates (Life and Death or Light and Darkness). Part of the Cautopates relief (with down-turned torch) has been found and is shown on the left. At the feet of other columns stood small altars, it is presumed. The temple would be dark and cavelike – the small clerestory windows were for ventilation rather than illumination – and during the ceremony, two initiates of the ranks of Leo (Lion) and Corax (Raven) hold torches, while Pater (the Father) invokes the god at the altar.

October 9, 1954

LONDON'S UNIQUE MITHRAS TEMPLE

By W. F. Grimes, M.A., V.-P.S.A., F.M.A., Director of the London Museum, Hon. Director of Excavations for the Roman and Mediaeval London Excavation Council

As such buildings go, the Walbrook temple is fairly large, with an overall length of some 60 feet and a width of about 25 feet. Not only is the circuit of its walls almost completely preserved, but within the building most of the floor-deposits are untouched. . . .

The setting is in itself of some interest. In early Roman times – that is, in the second half of the first century A.D. – the immediate area was a broad hollow, evidently part of the valley of the Roman version of the Walbrook stream, which has long been accepted as rising somewhere to

168 Invoking the Persian sun-god in second-century Londinium. A vivid reconstruction by A. Sorrell

the north and flowing to the Thames through the city to divide the Roman walled area into two approximately equal parts. . . .

Conditions were not identical on both sides of the valley. On the west there was much artificial building-up of the surface, with extensive use of timber structures, including revetments for the stream itself. On the east (where the general level was slightly lower) there seems to have been a semi-natural accumulation of silt and peaty layers to a depth of 5 or 6 feet. . . . These deposits seem in due course to have been succeeded by some "dumping" on the site, and the temple was erected in this artificial material, with the rounded wall of its apse or sanctuary about 20 feet to the east of the stream. . . .

The temple is well built, its chief material being Kentish ragstone, with levelling or bonding courses of tile. A feature of its con-struction is the massive character of the west end, with a square buttress on the crest of the apse and massive semi-circular buttresses flanking it. There is some suggestion, yet to be confirmed, that some or all of these buttresses are afterthoughts added at an early stage while the building was being erected. In any case, their presence is indicative of the unstable nature of the surrounding ground. . . .

The nave, 11 feet wide, runs the length of the building, from the entrance to the opening of the apse, the floor of which was raised high above those of the body of the temple as first designed. The nave is flanked by sleeper walls, which not only carried stone columns separat-ing it from the side aisles, but also supported and revetted the floors of the aisles. Timber had been extensively used in the aisle floors which, with or without movable furniture, served as benches upon which the worshippers reclined.

333

A feature of the sleeper walls is the concrete (*opus signinum*) settings upon which the pillars were erected; there were seven in all, spaced approximately 6 feet apart, their diameters varying between 18 and 20 inches.

This description of a columned hall with sunk central nave, raised side-aisles and elaborate apse applies to the temple as it would have appeared in the early years of its existence.... In any case, as time went on various structural

169 Marble head of the Egyptian corn god, Serapis, found in the London temple of Mithras

The floor of the semi-circular sanctuary was raised nearly 3 feet above the original floor of the nave. Here would have stood the chief group (depicting Mithras slaying the sacrificial bull) to which the head already found probably belongs. . . .

changes were made, the details of which will only be settled after prolonged study of all the evidence.

Amongst such changes were the steady raising of the general floor level, so that the last floor in the nave is some 3 feet above the first; alterations in the arrangements for the side-aisles, with at one stage the insertion of low walls between the pillars, presumably to support a new set of benches; a series of modifications of the layout of altars and other features in front of the apse, one of which led to the elimination of the timber-lined well. All this carries the story down into the fourth century: the last recognisable structural change was the insertion of a stone block in a hole dug through the last floor of the temple, to serve as a base for the last altar, which, now lost, must have occupied the centrepoint of the apse. Amongst the timbers of a rough frame supporting the block were several finds, including a bronze coin of the early part of the reign of Constantine the Great (307–337 A.D.), which derives additional interest from the fact that it was minted in London. But by this time the temple must have

become a shadow of its former self: already some parts of its equipment of sacred images had been buried beneath its later floors in circumstances which are still obscure. Its interior, too, had been drastically remodelled, and it must have been re-roofed: the floor of the nave was now level with that of the apse; the stone columns had been removed – a fragment of one had been used to patch a hole near the south-east angle of the building – and had either been replaced by an arrangement of timbers or had given way to a simple chamber with no distinction between nave and aisles. Building débris on the last floor shows that it must have been allowed to fall into disuse at a time when it was still more or less isolated in its marshy surroundings – a time when already the last years of the Roman occupation must have been approaching.

January 1, 1955

THE WORLD'S OLDEST CARPET, AND OTHER FABRICS PRESERVED IN PERPETUAL ICE

By R. D. Barnett, F.S.A., Deputy Keeper in the Department of Egyptian and Assyrian Antiquities, British Museum, and W. Watson, Assistant Keeper in the Department of Oriental Antiquities, British Museum

Whereas fur and leather were the materials preferred for clothing, felt and textiles were preferred for horse-cloths and wall-hangings. Two gaily-coloured horse-cloths of felt appliqué, illustrate the local taste in scale-patterns and in whirligigs derived from a pattern of stags' antlers. The felt was almost as compact as the best modern felt, and the appliqués were sewn on with woollen thread made from the finest down of the local fleeces. Felt appliqué strips were used as wall-hangings of the tombs (these imitate log cabins), and in several cases closely copy Persian and Assyrian patterns and textiles. The extraordinary felt hanging *(Plate 36, p. 321)* with the repeated scene of the horseman

and deity (or judge?) is in a class by itself. We suggested in our earlier article [p. 312] that the seated figure might represent a tribe whom the Greek historian Herodotus called the bald-headed Argippaeans, saying that they lived under trees, acted as judges and offered asylum to fugitives. Both these naturalistic scenes and the fantastic sphinx *(Plate 37, p. 321)* from the same hanging seem influenced by ancient Near Eastern art. Yet their style, exotic and fanciful, is more like that of puppets from some ancestor of the Turkish shadow-play than anything else. Whether they can be classed as Scythian art or are the work of some hitherto unknown group, remains to be decided.

As for textiles, good examples of local workmanship consist of woollen *kilim*-type weavings from Mound II. One apparently imported item, however, is the decorated carpet, the significance of which was pointed out in the earlier article, this being the earliest surviving pile carpet known. This piece undoubtedly takes pride of place among the remarkable finds of Pazyryk. As was said before, it is sheared pile and was made on a loom, with a selvedge at the bottom. It contains 36 knots per square centimetre, totalling some 1,250,000 knots in all, and representing, the excavator has computed, one-and-a-half year's work for one person. Can we go further in speculating on its origin? The knots of the pile are of the two-warp kind, and are separated by triple floating wefts. The late Mr. Lewis Edwards (*cf.* "The Legacy of Persia", p. 233) believed that this knot, as found in mediaeval and recent carpets, represents the Turkish tradition of carpet-weaving as distinct from the Persian. If this is true, it might be argued that the employment of the Turkish or Ghiordes knot in the Pazyryk carpet might indicate that it was made in the Altai, the homeland of the Turks. But even so, the Achaemenid horsemen depicted on it can only have been copied from a Persian carpet. Is it perhaps equally possible that the two-warp knot was also known to, and used by, the ancient Persians? Whether local or imported, the Pazyryk carpet is impressive evidence of contact between the Altai and the Near East.

March 5, 1955

THE CRATER OF VIX

By M. René Joffroy, Discoverer of the crater *of Vix, Curator of the Museum of Chatillon-sur-Seine*

The discovery at Vix (Côte d'Or) in January 1953 of a chariot burial of the first Iron Age, accompanied with funeral furnishings of extraordinary richness, was an archaeological event of considerable importance. The restoration of the objects found being now completed, the study of the principal objects can now be conveniently undertaken. The essential piece is the gigantic bronze *crater*, whose exact dimensions (with lid and statue) are: weight, 208 kilogrammes (4 hundredweight 11 pounds); height, 1·64 metres (5 feet $4\frac{5}{8}$ inches); diameter at the opening, 1 metre (3 feet $3\frac{3}{8}$ inches). This vase, the largest that antiquity has bequeathed to us, is remarkably well-preserved and has a beautiful *patina*. The frieze is made up of twenty-three appliqué reliefs, fixed on by means of rivets. On the reverse of the reliefs and on the neck of the *crater* are inscribed Greek letters or craftsman's symbols, to act as mounting marks. The lid is notable for being hollow and pierced with a number of holes in a rose design; and it suggests a sort of strainer. The statuette which surmounts the lid lacked its right hand when first discovered, but this was later found during the sifting of the soil which filled the *crater*. Where was this *crater* made? Some archaeologists have wished to see in it a product of the workshops of Etruria. It is, however, nothing of the kind and it must be attributed to the Greek world – more precisely Laconia, as the stylistic characters witness. It is, however, very probable that it was made not at Sparta itself but rather at a Laconian colony in Magna Graecia, Tarentum. It would seem that the objects found at Vix – that is to say the *crater*, the Greek cups, the *oinochoe* and the Etruscan bowls – reached the site by way of northern Italy, the passes of the

Alps, the Great St. Bernard, the Swiss plateau and the Jura, since this route is signposted by a sufficient number of characteristic finds, whereas the valleys of the Rhône and the Saône have furnished nothing of the kind. Another important question has been put: why did such precious objects come to this relatively poor corner of Burgundy? Since in those days the Chatillonais possessed only a little iron, whence did the inhabitants of the Celtic town of Vix derive their wealth? The explanation must be sought in the geographical position of the place and the tin trade. Aristotle at this time speaks of the tin which was sought in the distant Cassiterides and which would have to be brought by way of the Seine – which is navigable only as far as Vix. The *oppidum* of Vix, the terminal-point of the water transport and the beginning of the land transport, must have been a vast market at this junction of two great commercial streams, the one bringing British tin, the other Italo-Greek products; and the Celtic princes who held the town must have been able to enrich themselves considerably, thanks to this traffic. Now the colossal dimensions of the *crater* recall those of an analogous *crater* which Herodotus mentions and which was sent by the Lacedaemonians to Croesus. The Vix *crater* was perhaps also a kind of diplomatic present from Greek merchants desirous of access to the tin trade. The Vix discoveries have brought new material for the study of a problem which is hardly touched on in Greek literature – the problem of the penetration of Greek influences in the Celtic world.

November 26, 1955

THE PIAZZA ARMERINA MOSAICS

By Dr. Gino Vinicio Gentili, Director of the Excavations since 1950

The excavation of the Roman villa at Piazza Armerina, in Sicily, has revealed an extraordinary number of large mosaic surfaces decorated for the most part with figure subjects. The mosaics are, in fact, *pictures* which one can admire as they lie there before one. . . . It seems to me important to summarise and bring up to date the subject of the most important mosaics discovered during the last two years. . . . Among the realistic mosaics (which are the most important) we may note a group of pictures showing, in my opinion, the famous family of the Emperor Herculius Maximianus, the owner of the villa. After these the most important pictures are: the great scene of the chariot race of the four-horse chariots of the four factions; a torchlight race (reduced to fragments); and the mosaic of "The Chase" *(Plate 42, p. 326)*. In this bright, lively, naturalistic picture we can see plainly, as in "The Big Game Hunt", of which I shall speak later, that taste for presenting anecdote and episode in pictures which is a characteristic of the African mosaic school and almost certainly of the Carthaginian school – to which the Villa's mosaic pavements are to be attributed. In this picture, scenes of bird-catching and hunting in the countryside are shown. It is a picture of real life as lived in the neighbourhood of the villa during the last years of the third century A.D.: from the setting-out of the hunters, the pursuit of deer on horseback towards prepared nets, the capture of a hairy wild boar and the carrying of it back, tied to a pole, while lively dogs bound around, to the hunting of thrushes, both with birdlime and by hawks. Among these various episodes the hunting of the hare has an especial naturalness. In a bush at the foot of a tree which gives the scene a Hellenistic look, the hare, portrayed with the greatest realism, hides, worn out by the pursuit of the horsemen. It has tried to escape, but the horseman reining-in his sorrel is at hand and ready to strike with a two-pronged spear. In the central part of the painting are two episodes which naturally round-off the chase: a sacrifice to Diana; and an open-air picnic, in which the chief huntsmen are reclining on couches in a semi-circle before a round table on which lies a fat roasted chicken – overhead an awning is spread in the branches of the trees and the resting horses paw the ground. The same anecdotal character . . . is found in "The Big Game Hunt", which has a broader scope and a superb realisation of impressive scenes *(Plate 43, p. 327)*. Starting from the two ends, there is a succession of fights between animals, lion hunts, wild boar hunts and the capturing alive of wild beasts, such as the taking of the tiger-cubs from a cave by a horseman who rides off towards a boat, or the trapping of a panther in an open cage in which a kid has been tied as a bait; and the mysterious picture of a mythical griffin seizing a cage in which a man is imprisoned. In addition to the scenes of trapping, animals are shown being brought back alive, either in carriages of various kinds or being pulled along by their captors. The same Emperor Maximianus, accompanied by two bodyguards, is also present in the mosaic – symbolically, according to l'Orange, who was the first student of the mosaics to make this proposed identification. To round off these incidents there is the representation of the embarkation of the captured animals in two large, oared sailing vessels, moored in the centre of the composition in a sea

full of fish and enlivened with glistening faience tesserae. The captured wild beasts were evidently destined for the *venationes*, the spectacular wild-beast shows in the amphitheatre which were so dear to the taste of the Romans of the Imperial era. . . . The mosaic of the ten girls *(Plate 44, p. 328)* is completely different, both in subject and style, from the earlier mosaics of the age of the Tetrarchs. This mosaic caused considerable interest from the fact that it showed the girls in a most scanty dress, a mere band at the bosom and hips, precisely like the "bikini" of to-day. The girls are shown taking part not in those aquatic performances which in the later Imperial times were staged in swimming-baths built in the *orchestra* floor of theatres, but rather in a display of physical exercises, a competition perhaps staged after bathing on the lawn of the gymnasium of the *thermae*, with victory marked by the wreath and palm which the cloaked judge awards to the winner. Various interpretations can be given to the scene; and, with reference to the style and iconography, we may remark on the excessive lengthening of the bodies and their slender build, the three-dimensional impression being achieved by soft, shaded modelling. In harmony with this is a certain delicacy of the facial features, and, especially noticeable, the abnormal enlargement of the eyes, which become the dominant features of the whole face – a peculiarity which makes its appearance in the age of Constantine (fourth century A.D.) and reaches its peak in the sophisticated art of Honorius and Theodosia (beginning of the fifth century A.D.).

1956–57

Rich years again, with Professor Mallowan's discoveries at Nimrud in northern Iraq beginning to dominate the scene. But as well as the articles from which extracts have been made, there were many important discoveries published including: Professor Blegen's work at Pylos; Professor Yadin's at Hazor in northern Galilee; Dr. Kathleen Kenyon's at Jericho; and Professor Bernabo Brea's findings of the gold treasure (of Trojan type) at Poliochni in Lemnos.

November 10, 1956

THE GRAVE OF A PRINCELY CHILD AT GORDION

By Rodney S. Young, Ph.D., Field Director of the University of Pennsylvania Museum's expedition at Gordion

Phrygian burials in the eighth century were usually made in large oblong chambers of wood built in deep pits cut below ground-level. After the body and the offerings had been placed in the tomb, it was covered with a timber roof which, in turn, was covered by a large heap of stones; over this, earth was piled to make the tumulus. Given a tomb of this sort buried beneath a large mound, the best way of locating it seemed to be by means of a light portable oil-drilling rig. The drill can easily detect the stone-pile over the grave, yet there is no danger of the bit penetrating through the stones to do damage inside the tomb. Accordingly, the University Museum expedition acquired a suitable drilling rig and in the autumn of 1955 proceeded with the work, thus employing a new technique in archaeological work. Before the Great Tumulus was attacked, practice sessions were held on two of the smaller mounds. In each case the method proved successful; one tomb was located and dug, the second located and left to be dug the following spring. The apparatus was then moved to the Great Tumulus and several borings were made, but time did not suffice to complete the work and locate the grave before cold weather set in.

In the case of Tumulus P, a mound about 40 feet in height standing close to the Great Tumulus at the south-east, the results were more successful than could have been hoped. Not only were the position and limits of the mass of stones over the grave located – an oval mass with greatest dimensions about 45 by 56 feet – but the exact position of the wooden chamber itself was found. This was due to the collapse in ancient times of the wooden roof of the chamber. When the roof caved in, all the stones above poured down into the chamber, filling it; but the clay of the tumulus itself was sufficiently cohesive so that it did not collapse. The result was a dome-shaped hollow, over the grave, 3 to 4 feet high between the bottom of the clay and the top of the fallen stones. In four borings the presence of this cavity was detected from the sudden dropping of the drill before it struck the fallen stones below the hollow. . . .

At a depth of about 33 feet the hollow above the grave chamber was reached. . . .

The furnishings of the tomb were in varying states of preservation, some badly broken or crushed by the collapse of the roof and the inrush of stones, others, which had been protected by beam-ends fallen aslant, in perfect condition. Near the centre of the room a large bronze cauldron standing on an iron tripod had been crushed in the collapse. Inside it, however, was found a large number of small wooden objects, some in a remarkable state of preservation. Among the finest of these are a lion and a lion attacking a bull, which measure only about 3 inches in height and 4 in length; but despite their small size all details are meticulously rendered, including the wrinkles in the turning neck of the bull and the finely engraved hair of the lions' manes. More crudely carved, but more appealing, is a winged horse eating; he stands foursquare and uses one wing, bent forward, to hold the object he is devouring *(Figure 170)*. The contents of the cauldron included not only animals but also small

overall with geometric decoration, including a sort of feather pattern on the breasts. Of the same fabric and style is a large, round-mouthed jug decorated on the body with lions and bulls in panels, and on the neck with deer and antelope. This is the finest example yet found of the Phrygian painted ware of the late eighth century. Equally fine in its way is a black-polished jug in the shape of a goat, with horns and tail curved back to make handles at either side of a filling hole on top, and an opening in the mouth for pouring. . . . The north-west corner of the room was occupied by a bed, of which three legs were found still in place. Its width must have been about $3\frac{1}{2}$ feet, and its length

170 A winged horse (found in the child's tomb at Gordion) using one wing to hold the object it is eating

implements of wood – tiny saucers with openwork handles, a box with engraved decoration, a dipper, and several spoons, one of which is still unbroken, though its bowl has warped and curled inward.

Along the south side of the chamber were found many vases, painted or of finely-polished black ware, and many vessels of bronze. The most original of the painted vases are a pair made in the shape of geese, which were filled through openings in their backs and emptied by pouring through their bills. These are covered

about $7\frac{1}{2}$ feet. Many of the low bowls which presumably had contained food offerings had been placed underneath. At the centre of the bed-area lay a bronze belt, and within its circle was a large bronze fibula with fragments of several more. These were the personal adornments of the dead; there can, therefore, be no doubt that the body had been laid on the bed, used as a bier, especially since no traces of a coffin were found. The belt, of bronze so thin that it must have been completely flexible, was fastened by an elaborate clasp. . . . The belt itself, not quite 3 inches wide, is covered at the front with fine engraved designs, mostly variations on a complicated meander pattern. Its length, however, and the lengths of two similar belts found in the area of the bed, is only about 20 inches; evidently it was intended to be worn by a small child. Measurement of village children around the waist showed that 20 inches was the average circumference of four-year-olds; and Professor Senyürek's report on the teeth (the only human bones found in the tomb) attributed them to a child four to five years old. The burial, then, was that of a small child; its elaborateness and richness indicate that the child must surely have been of princely family.

November 17, 1956

"KING MIDAS' KITCHEN"

By Rodney S. Young, Ph.D., Field Director of the University of Pennsylvania Museum's expedition to Gordion

Since this original material was available, it was decided to rebuild the Phrygian wall with its own blocks, and the task was entrusted to a local country mason. The tools and methods used must approximate closely to those of the original builders in the ninth or eighth century B.C. In addition to a primitive hoist for lifting the heavy blocks, the only tools used were pick and crow-bar, sledge-hammer and mason's hammer, levelling string and measuring stick – all simple implements known to have been in use in primitive times.

The massive defences of the town, however, seem to have failed of their purpose. All the buildings within had been destroyed by a great conflagration which took place early in the seventh century B.C., probably in consequence of a raid of the Kimmerians, who were devastating Asia Minor at that time. The destruction of the city is dated by the masses of pottery found in an area nicknamed "King Midas' Kitchen" from the objects of domestic use found in it: loom-weights and whorls, cooking-pots and grinding-stones for making flour. One vessel of finer ware found in the "kitchen" is a tall spouted jug, probably of local fabric and decorated with deer, lions and birds in panels as well as with various conventional geometric motives. . . .

One building of this period was completely uncovered – a house built of crude brick reinforced by wooden posts and horizontal beams set into the brickwork. The wooden reinforcement had added fuel to the flames and the heat had become so intense that the lime plaster on the walls had in places liquefied and run down; it is now a vitrified greenish substance. The house consisted of two large rooms, each with a circular hearth of fine stucco at the centre. The smaller north room opened through two doorways to an extensive stone-paved court within the gate. It was itself paved with a floor of pebble mosaic, now in poor condition, but in which various geometric motives may be discerned in dark red and dark blue pebbles on a white ground. . . .

All around the outside, to east, south and west, ran a bench set against the wall, perhaps to accommodate people waiting to see the potentate who resided within. In any case, these people whiled away their time by scratching pictures on the stone wall faces of the building. A few of the stones bearing pictures (we called them "doodle stones") were still in place in the wall. More, however, were found fallen and broken; they give us contemporary, though crude, pictures of the eighth-century Phrygian

341

scene. One small piece is precious, because it shows two little houses of a kind that must have been normal in Phrygian Gordion, and they have double-pitched roofs. Another shows two pairs of boxers. On others are shown warriors fighting, all kinds of animals, and birds, including a crested species which may represent the hoopoe, common in present-day Anatolia. This decoration of the building was informal and certainly unplanned.

November 24, 1956

POTTERY FROM THE EARLIEST PHAISTOS PALACE

In our issues of September 29 and October 6 Professor Doro Levi described the results of the Italian excavations at Phaistos, in Crete, during the 1955 season. This was an extremely successful season – from the actual early structures revealed, the remarkable pottery discovered, and the new light thrown on the dating of the earlier phases of the Minoan civilisation. From the aesthetic and human aspects, however, the most striking of these is the pottery. The great wine *crater* and its companion *oinochoe*, the basket-shaped vase and the three-handled jug with the scallop shell reliefs – these were all found on the level of the earliest Phaistos palace. Professor Levi describes the huge *crater* as "one of the most magnificent and original of all Minoan vases . . . brilliantly painted with a chequerboard pattern and a coral pattern, the shoulder and pedestal being decorated with white, free-standing lilies, while chains of white rings were hanging from hooks along the lip." The *oinochoe*, or wine jug, is obviously by the same hand; and, as Professor Levi writes: "Evidently *craters* for mixing wine, placed in the corner of the banquet-room with jugs for drawing wine from them and pouring it into the cups, were present in the Minoan dining-rooms some fifteen centuries before the same usage was general in classical Greece."

The wine jug with scallop reliefs is obviously of the same period and general style, though in much more restrained taste. The basket-shaped vase is very interesting and unusual, and one of its most interesting features is its lustrous surface. The other four pots are of well-known shapes and styles with the exception of that which we describe as being "in the style of a *jardinière*", which is decorated in the manner of the large fruit-stand which we reproduced in our October 6 issue. The two *pithoi* are storage jars and are decorated *à la barbotine, i.e.,* with knobs, and with patterns derived from ropes or nets; and are reminiscent, on a smaller scale, of the giant *pithoi* of Knossos. The bridge-spouted jar is a beautiful example of a familiar type. All these last four are of the type known as "Middle Minoan". But Minoan dating is no longer as certain as it seemed to be and Professor Levi has written "the finds of our last season confirm that revolution in our ideas about Minoan antiquities which our researches of the last few years have foreshadowed: namely, the dating of the beginning of the palatial Minoan (the Middle Minoan, but at the same time also the so-called Early Minoan) to about 2000 B.C.; the immediate link between this and the preceding Neolithic age; and the discovery at the same moment of writing and the beginning of linear script."

April 6, 1957

AN UNPLUNDERED TOMB AT NESTOR'S PYLOS

By Professor Sp. Marinatos, Head of the Antiquities Department, Ministry of Education, Athens

A small but almost intact *tholos* tomb has been discovered and excavated near Myrsinochorion, about an hour-and-a-half to the north-east of the palace. The excavations lasted from August to October, 1956, and were financed, as in previous years, by the Archaeological Society of Athens.

The site, about 15 minutes to the north of the village mentioned above, is the summit of a ridge called Rutsi. A small *tholos* tomb was already known there and it was expected that it would have been plundered. This tomb – Tomb I – was fairly well preserved and only the upper part of the *tholos* was missing. . . . Tomb I had been plundered again and again. . . .

The second – and unplundered – sister-*tholos* was discovered about 65½ feet (20 metres) to the south-west. . . .

The tomb was in rather bad condition. Indeed there was no sign of it beyond the fact that some tombs of the earliest Christian era lay between the two *tholoi*. The actual beehive superstructure is preserved only in the southern part and to a height not much more than 3 feet. The northern part collapsed in ancient times, perhaps some sixty or seventy years after its construction, and it is this accident we must thank for the precious discoveries. The tomb was abandoned forever and the funeral goods of those who had already been buried escaped the robbers, who always seem to have plundered later burials. . . . The body on the floor was a well-built man in the prime of life, with all his magnificent teeth preserved; and he had been laid upon a rush mat or perhaps a thick blanket painted blue and red. The right foot lay on the left and both hands lay to the right side. Except

for a two-pronged bronze object which may be a fire-hook, the *paratoro* (*i.e.*, *spalathron*) of the Pylos tablets, all the dead man's property was found on his right side. It consisted of about ten swords and daggers (some gold-riveted), a great spearhead, a mirror with an ivory handle, a leather object, possibly the sheath of his sword, two cylinder seals, one Mycenaean and one Asiatic, about a dozen other gems of carnelian, agate, sardonyx and lapis lazuli, a gold bead-seal and about a dozen vases. Everything was in bad condition (except the gems, of course) owing to the collapse of the *tholos*. . . .

Shaft II was the main burial place of the tomb. It was covered with heavy slabs, on which stood, upside down, a great jar with octopus and seascape decoration. The upper dead person was still distinguishable, but three and perhaps four more skulls indicate that, in all, five persons were buried in this shaft. Only the property of the uppermost burial was still *in situ* and this was magnificent. Near the left hand on a sort of platform lay a superb inlaid dagger. The blade was decorated with nautiluses, alternately in silver and gold, swimming among sea creatures in gold, silver and *niello*. Nearby thirteen gold buttons in a characteristic position belonged, no doubt, to the leather or felt belt of the dagger. A shell cameo from Knossos shows a dagger with a belt and this belt has little dots indicating just such buttons. Beside the same hand of the dead man was a small mirror and with it a bronze dagger with three gold rivets and a gold ring to the hilt. Another heap of gold rivets surely belonged to its leather sheath. In the right armpit of the dead man was found, almost perpendicularly laid, a second inlaid dagger, the hilt of pure gold, the blade decorated with cat-like animals in a rocky and wooded landscape, again in gold, silver and *niello (Plate 45, opposite)*. A few other objects in bronze belonged perhaps to the same man. Huge neck-laces of amber lay round the neck of this man, as they did round the man on the floor of the tomb. No fewer than fifty-four beads, the central ones about 2 inches (5 centimetres) in diameter, belonged to the dead man of the shaft grave and these were still in their original position. A few others had rolled a little distance away. The

other finds in the shaft belonged to the earlier dead. Owing to plundering in ancient times they were not numerous, though no less precious. They include: a little silver goblet and frag-ments of a larger one; several gold leaves; a little gold spoon; some gems, among which was a wonderful gold-mounted sardonyx and a pre-cious solid gold bead bearing in fine, almost microscopic engraving the capture of a bull. The net, the tree and the bull-fighter remind us of the famous gold cup from Vaphio, which is of the same period.

November 23, 1957

"FORT SHALMANESER"

By M. E. L. Mallowan, D.Lit., F.B.A., F.S.A., Field Director of the Expedition and Professor of Western Asiatic Archaeology in the University of London

Whilst walking round the outer town towards the beginning of the season I was attracted to some high-lying ground which with its undulat-ing outlines obviously concealed a building contained within heavy walls. As luck would have it we noticed, at a point not far from a gap which seemed to indicate a gate, an inscribed brick of Shalmaneser III (859–824 B.C). From that moment we resolved that at the first opportunity we should move half of our workmen to this rich-looking cover which we named in anticipation "Fort Shalmaneser". So promising were our first efforts in this direc-tion that we soon felt constrained to move all the rest of our men and make a supreme effort to reveal the ground plan of what we knew must be an Assyrian building of exceptionally large dimensions. . . . In fact, the building was clearly designed to hold the food and drink required for the sustenance of officials and citizens employed in the Royal household. The magazine S.W.6, for example, contained four rows of huge terracotta jars with a narrow gangway between

them, and tablets associated with them showed that this wine cellar was at one time set aside for the provisioning of the king's male Kassite choir, specially selected singers from the Persian hills. Their ration, about a quart a day, was no doubt appropriate to their artistry.

November 30, 1957

In several of the rooms the ivories were distributed over a wide area of ground, em-bedded in heavily-packed fallen mud-brick. . . .

Outstanding amongst the carvings are the panels mostly discovered at the south end of room S.W.7. They lay in some confusion, and only fell into the position in which they were found after a part of the wall had collapsed. . . .

Other ivories no less spectacular were discovered in room S.W.37, where the east entrance was literally packed with fragments; in

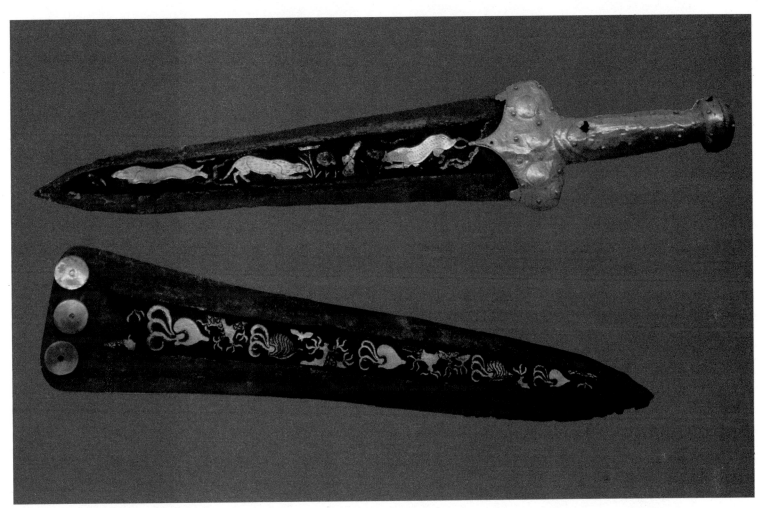

Plate 45 Inlaid leopard dagger with gold hilt from the tomb at Pylos

Plate 46 An extraordinary pot in the form of a seated woman with inlaid obsidian eyes from Hacilar I

346

Plate 47 opposite *Mycenaean rhyton from ancient Kition (modern Larnaca) in Cyprus*

Plate 49 Catal Huyuk: "owl-faced" sculpture of a kneeling goddess with small breasts, hands on her stomach

Plate 50 Elaborate and well-preserved mosaic found in Room 3 of the Roman Palace at Fishbourne

Plate 51 Catal Huyuk wall-painting: the hunt of the red bull

Plate 52 Stone head from Lepenski Vir: modelling follows the intrinsic shape of the river boulder but is given pronounced expressive features

171 Ivory from "Fort Shalmaneser" of a god or prince plucking the flowering lotus

seventh century B.C. have been a repository for treasures then ancient which had been discarded from the more modern palaces of kings, who had rejected ancient and often damaged carvings for more up-to-date material. Indeed, there can be little doubt that many of these objects were made nearly two centuries before the last Assyrian occupation of the fort, a building not designed either for residence or for the display of *objets d'art*.

Perhaps the most arresting feature of these ivories is the frequently repeated design of the sacred tree, which appears in the guise of an imaginary tree of life, buds, fruit, flowers and leaves growing out of the branches of a solid trunk. Who is the vigorously-drawn striding male, bearded, curly-headed, barefoot, yet clad in an elaborate linen garment, tugging at the branch and fruit? *(Figure 171)*. Is he a god, king or prince, hero or priest? Who is the four-winged lady with her strange hair style and her long trailing skirt? She perhaps we may with more confidence affirm is some magical, prophylactic personage, the Syrian counterpart, may be, of the winged Assyrian figures who protect the King.

Who are the splendidly enthroned ladies elaborately clad, yet barefoot, touching the bread and wine which is set before them as a feast on a bull-footed, cross-legged table which nestles in the arm of the sacred lotus tree? Goddess or queen, priestess or princess? We cannot be certain about the answers to any of these questions. But the repeated rendering of trees and flowers, associated sometimes with beings in human guise, at other times with animals, oryx, deer *(Figure 172)*, and lion, who peer out from a kind of lattice-work of foliage, inevitably suggest a cult of trees and of vegetation. It seems, therefore, not improbable that these sets of figures may in some way be connected with various forms of worship, especially popular in Syria, yet attested already between Tigris and Euphrates in the Third Millennium B.C., concerned with the seasonal renewing of life as manifested in the world of

the narrow gateway S.W.2, deliberately cast aside in the final panic of invasion; in S.W.12, and in N.W.15, where many were found lying on the floor. Their distribution leads me to the conclusion that "Fort Shalmaneser" may in the

172 Ivory from "Fort Shalmaneser" of a browsing stag in open work

vegetation. Such cults were personified for agricultural and pastoral peoples by gods with names such as Tammuz and Ishtar, where the male died and was resurrected by his consort. The Syrian Spring festival of Adonis is a late manifestation of that cult, and similarly in Egypt, Isis, often accompanied by the lotus, and Osiris, were a reflection of Phoenician and Syrian religions so well exemplified by the literature of Ugarit, for example, with its illustration of the life-and-death struggle in which Aleyn Baal, Mot, and the goddess Anat are the principal actors.

Indeed, the Old Testament itself, with passages in Isaiah and in the Song of Solomon, provides the best commentaries to some of these ivories.

December 7, 1957

THE TREASURES OF "FORT SHALMANESER"

The principal discovery of the season has been the excavation of a hitherto undisturbed site which has been given the name of "Fort Shalmaneser" and which has proved to be a repository of beautiful ivory carvings, which were stripped of their gold and left behind by the armies who utterly defeated the Assyrians in 612 B.C. . . .

More familiar are the many ivories depicting the courtesan, generally thought to be a Phoenician lady alluring passers-by from the window; cow suckling its calf in a meadow of golden lilies *(Figure 173)*; griffins, their wings still incrusted with bright blue frit and overlaid with gold; the kneeling boy Horus; another standing boy with golden hair; and a beautifully delineated sphinx, which was almost certainly captured spoil or tribute from the Syrian city of Arslan-tash, where similar figures have been found. The remarkable ram-headed sphinx wearing the Egyptian crown is also likely to have come from the same centre. Egyptian in

character, but almost certainly of Phoenician provenance, is the marvellous hawk-headed Horus with its shining golden wings and blue frit inlay. Many of the smaller pieces and the openwork panels are pieces which had once decorated the space between the rails and chairs. Here, in fact, we have the remnants of an ancient Assyrian Royal furniture repository, which must have provided the happiest of hunting-grounds for the Medes and Babylonians. . . .

The dramatic struggle for the last defence of Nimrud when the Assyrian army held the fort in 612 B.C. was well illustrated by finding many iron spearheads, daggers, and arrow-heads all along the line of the northern gateway and entrance hall. Large dumps of armour consisting of iron-plated corselets were thrown down into some of the abandoned rooms when the battle was over, and a single spent arrow with battered tongue which had hit its mark is a muted testimony to the end of Assyria.

173 Ivory from "Fort Shalmaneser" of a cow suckling its calf in a meadow of golden lilies

1958-59

As the extracts show, these were rich and exciting years; and articles of almost equal importance and interest included: the beginning of the excavations at Buhen, near Wadi Halfa in northern Sudan, where colossal Egyptian fortifications were revealed, eventually to be flooded as the result of the building of the High Dam; the finding of the famous Gold Bowl of Hasanlu in north-western Iran; a Maya city and necropolis uncovered by a British Museum expedition at Las Cuevas in British Honduras; Maya finds discovered by aqualung divers in the depths of Lake Amatitlan, Guatemala; and the curses of Esarhaddon, found at Nimrud on the world's largest cuneiform tablet. But the period closed with our exclusive reportage of the Dorak Treasure, probably the century's most controversial archaeological piece of news. This reputedly had been discovered just south of the Sea of Marmora, in two Royal burials, in a clandestine excavation, conducted, however, by a competent archaeologist. It was securely dated to the second half of the third millennium B.C. and was of the greatest richness and interest and appeared to belong to what is called the Yortan Culture. It had, however, been kept together, in private possession and in secret. Some years previously to our publication it had been shown to Mr. James Mellaart, then attached to the British School of Archaeology in Ankara, under pledges of secrecy and he was allowed to make a great number of detailed drawings of the innumerable items, which he coloured schematically, i.e. in such a way as to show the materials of which the objects were made – but on condition that he should not make these known or publish them until he should receive word that it was safe to do so. When this word came, he decided the treasure was of such interest and importance that in the interest of science it should be made known and his article accordingly appeared in The Illustrated London News *of November 28, 1959. Although this attracted a great deal of interest, it appeared, for some years at least, to have had no adverse effects, but in the end, at least to the Turkish authorities, it was held to be scandalous, and led to the extremely unfortunate effect of preventing Mr. Mellaart from continuing the extremely important excavations in Anatolia, which he had later begun at Haçilar and continued at Čatal Hüyük. These, especially those at the latter site, were of so important, indeed revolutionary a nature, that their discontinuance can only be regarded as a tragedy for Late Neolithic archaeology.*

February 8, 1958

TWO NEW STATUES OF DIANA OF THE EPHESIANS

By Dr. Franz Miltner, Professor of the University of Vienna and Director of the Excavations of the Austrian Institute of Archaeology at Ephesus

Near the vaulted passage the main road turns to the south, and at the bend is a drive leading up to the extensive Prytaneion (town-hall) district. Here we have excavated the large public altar, a work of the Hellenistic period; and a sanctuary of Hestia Boulaia, the goddess of the hearth who protected in particular the Boule, that is, the town council. The altar stood in a wide open hall, and on it a perpetual fire was tended by priests, the College of the Kouretes. Enclosed by a colonnade of Ionic columns, a statue of Artemis Ephesia, twice life-size, was found in 1956. The value of this statue is considerably enhanced by its impressive crown, in which the most famous temples of this ancient Anatolian goddess are depicted. The most precious object found in the Hestia sanctuary, however, was another statue of the same goddess in life-size (*Figure 174*). This was also found in 1956 in one of the western rooms of the Hestia sanctuary, that is to say, within the precinct of the Prytaneion. Sculptured in fine marble from the Greek islands, it is a masterpiece from an artist's workshop of the time of Hadrian (A.D. 117–138), and it occupies a particular position among the objects found during excavations in Ephesus: because it is the first image of the Ephesian Artemis found in Ephesus; because it is closer related than any other statue found to date to the image of the goddess in the great Temple of Artemis at Ephesus which was counted among the Seven Wonders of the World; and because its discovery marked the sixtieth anniversary of the Austrian Archaeological Institute's excavations in Ephesus.

The two statues of Artemis Ephesia, found in Ephesus during the current excavations of the Austrian Institute of Archaeology, are the first to be found in the city, but are examples of a type which was famous in antiquity. It will be recalled that St. Paul's unpopularity in Ephesus was due to the fear that he was ruining the business of the silversmiths who made images of the goddess. Artemis Ephesia has little in common with the chaste huntress of the Greeks and is indeed an Asiatic goddess, the "many-breasted Mother of Asia", who acquired the name Artemis because she was likewise a moon-goddess and a divinity of the woods and wild-beasts. The larger example is especially interesting on account of the crown which shows famous temples of the goddess above rows of gryphons and sphinxes. These latter are repeated in the panels of the skirt, where they are joined by bees. In the finer life-size marble the detail is even richer. In that statue the panel of the skirt shows lions, sphinxes and stags; there are lions on the upper arms; and the sphinxes are repeated on either side of the head. Below the massive necklace, the signs of the

174 Life-size statue of Diana of the Ephesians or Artemis Ephesia

zodiac appear in low relief. On the pedestal can be seen two groups of three cloven hoofs. These are the remains of what was certainly a pair of stags with one foot lifted, the usual supporters of the goddess. The small reticulated domes are less clear. In some representations of the goddess she is shown holding two elaborate staves, and these could perhaps be the bases of such staves; alternatively, in some Hadrianic coins (that is, of the same period), the goddess is shown between a pair of candelabra and perhaps the domes are candelabrum-pedestals.

357

May 17, 1958

THE TOMB OF A KING OF PHRYGIA DISCOVERED INTACT

By Rodney S. Young, Ph.D., Field Director of the University of Pennsylvania Museum's expedition at Gordion

The University Museum expedition was reluctant to attempt its exploration until a means could be devised for locating beforehand the position of the tomb beneath. This was ultimately done by the use of a light drill. A large number of borings showed the position and extent of the heap of stones customarily piled over a burial of Phrygian times. It lay at an average depth of 130 feet below the peak, just to the south-west of centre, and with a diameter of about 100 feet. . . . An open trench about 225 feet long was cut from the edge of the mound, and continued from its inner end by a tunnel of equal length, which brought us to the face of a stone enclosure wall around the tomb. This was built of roughly-dressed blocks of limestone to a height of eight courses, or about 9 feet, above the surface of hard-pan. The wooden tomb chamber lay about 6 feet inside the enclosure wall, the entire space between filled with stone rubble. The tomb itself was double, an inner chamber constructed of nicely fitted squared timbers, and an outer casing of round logs of juniper. These were piled one on top of the other to a height of nine or ten logs, held in place by the rubble filled in at either side. . . . As the chamber had no door or other means of entrance the burial must have been made from above before the roof was put in place. It was intended to be used only once, and for the burial of a single person – obviously an important one and probably a Phrygian king. After the burial had been made the roof was put on and more rubble piled over it; then finally the *tumulus* itself was heaped over that to a height of 130 feet or more. . . .

The chamber measured about 17 by 20 feet inside, with a north–south orientation. The walls were of squared timbers mortised together at the corners and so neatly fitted that many of the joints between are all but invisible; the tooling of the inner faces, barely visible, suggests a finishing with the adze before sanding. The floor, of squared timbers laid lengthwise, was bedded on a layer of rubble. Radiocarbon tests run on samples taken from the tomb walls have indicated an age of about 2700 years, suggesting that the timber for the tomb was cut in the second half of the eighth century B.C. . . .

The dead man had been laid on a four-poster bed beside the north wall of the chamber. The skeleton was found on its back, the legs extended, the arms along the sides, and the head toward the east. It lay on a coverlet of many layers of linen and woollen cloth of various colours. Bronze *fibulae* at shoulders, elbows, and wrists suggested a sleeved upper garment, while shreds of leather over the legs seemed to be the remains of a skirt decorated above the hem by a band of designs of bronze studs. The skeleton was identified as that of a male between sixty and sixty-five years old at the time of death, and of short stature – his height in life estimated at 5 feet 2 inches. This was probably a late-eighth-century Phrygian king who died and was buried before the kingdom was overthrown by the Cimmerians in the early seventh century.

The tomb was furnished with nine three-legged tables of wood, and two screens beside the east wall. Along the south wall were three large bronze cauldrons set on iron ring-stands; in these had been placed pottery vessels containing food and drink for the dead. One hundred and sixty-seven smaller bronze vessels had been placed in the tomb, those with handles evidently hung from rows of iron nails driven into the walls, and those without handles set in stacks on the tables. The iron nails had rusted through in

mane and the wool of the neck. Each of the other two cauldrons has four attachments for ring-handles. Of one all four attachments are in the form of sirens *(Figures 177, 178)*, human heads

175 A three-legged table, on the floor of the tomb, which collapsed under the weight of the bronze bowls

the course of time, and the wooden tables had collapsed *(Figure 175)* under the weight of their burdens, so that the floor of the tomb was found littered with the fallen bronzes. One of the tables, which had stood by the head of the bed, had borne a linen sack filled with 145 bronze *fibulae*, evidently the personal jewellery of the king. . . . Three of the bowls from the Gordion tomb bear inscriptions, not in the bronze itself but scratched on smears of beeswax applied to the rims close to the handles. The wax inscriptions are supplemented by a fourth, a *graffito* scratched on the wall of a black-polished pot. All of the inscriptions are in the Phrygian alphabet. They are brief and can not yet be read; but they prove that some at least of the Phrygians were not illiterate at the end of the eighth century. Two of the bronze vessels are bucket-handled cups, or *situlae*, in the form of animal heads – a ram, and a lion *(Figure 176)*. Both are of excellent workmanship, the eyes of white paste inlaid with black stone pupils, and with the very finest engraving for the hair of the

and shoulders with bird wings and tails, while the other has two normal sirens and two with square beards of Assyrian type. All of the sirens, and the two bearded heads, were cast in different moulds, and each has its own in-

176 Situla in the form of a snarling lion's head

dividuality. . . . The two wooden screens had been set beside the east wall of the tomb. Each was made up from a number of separate pieces fastened together by tongues fitted into sockets and held in place by pegs run through from the

177 The cauldron of the four sirens from a Phrygian burial

178 Detail of one of the four sirens

front. The front face was decorated, after it had been dowelled together, with elaborate inlaid designs which run across the almost invisible joints between the parts. The screens themselves are of light wood, probably boxwood, and the inlay of dark, probably yew. The designs are geometric, mostly variations on a complicated swastika motif, though the round medallions at the centre are filled with skilfully executed curvilinear decoration.

October 4, 1958
THE PROTON MAGNETOMETER
By Dr. M. J. Aitken, of the Oxford University Research Laboratory for Archaeology and the History of Art

The detector used is simply a bottle of water encircled by an electrical coil. The protons that form the nuclei of the hydrogen atoms contained in the water molecules gyrate at a speed which depends on the strength of the external magnetism in which the water is placed. Suppose these minute protons gyrate through 2000·0 revolutions each second over undisturbed ground. If now the bottle of water is placed over ground in which something magnetic is buried then the protons will go faster and for a slight disturbance this might be 2000·2 revolutions per second. Merely to detect the gyrations of the protons is a difficult task, let alone measure such minute differences in speed – particularly when there is the added handicap that the protons only gyrate for a few seconds at a time. Techniques more usually encountered in analogue computors and guided missiles are called in here and by using transistors (about 150 are needed) instead of conventional electronic valves the whole measuring apparatus has been compressed into the box, which weighs only 23 pounds. The electrical signal from the coil on the bottle is fed into this box by a light cable and the whole device – called a proton magnetometer – can if necessary be operated by one person. . . .

Why should these archaeological features cause a magnetic disturbance? Of course, on the rare occasion when an iron implement is associated with the remains, then the magnetism of this is very strong in itself – strong enough to be detected by a sensitive compass needle. But there was no metallic iron found in the Roman ditches at Dorchester which were originally cut into the gravel sub-strata and subsequently became filled with top-soil. It so happens, however, that the magnetic "susceptibility" of soil is higher than that of gravel – because of a higher (but still small) content of the same form of iron oxide – magnetite – which is responsible for the much stronger magnetism of lodestone. The resulting magnetic disturbance above the filled-in ditch was very weak and amounted to a change in magnetic strength of only 3 parts in 10,000. Nevertheless, because the proton magnetometer can detect changes one-tenth as small as this, it was possible to find the ditch. In the case of the filled-in pits on the Iron Age camp near Banbury the disturbance was very much stronger and this is attributed to an increase, resulting from chemical action due to the association of the soil-filling with human occupation, in the proportion of iron oxide in the magnetic state of magnetite.

The disturbance from a kiln is stronger still, and this is because after being heated to red heat the clay (again containing a small percentage of iron oxide) forming the walls of the kiln behaves as a weak permanent magnet when cool. . . .

One great virtue of the proton magnetometer over the resistivity method is that no probes have to be inserted into the ground and consequently the speed of operation is much greater – measurements can be made at the rate of 6 per minute. It is this rapid speed of ground coverage that will make the method of such inestimable value to the archaeologist, faced, as he so often is, with the laborious business of digging trial trenches before he can find the material on which to operate his paint-brush and trowel.

September 12, 1959

A MASTER-WORK OF EGYPTIAN MILITARY ARCHITECTURE OF 3900 YEARS AGO

By Walter B. Emery, Edwards Professor of Egyptology in the University of London and Director of the Excavations at Buhen

This plan and reconstruction *(Figure 179)* shows the fortress in its first or Middle Kingdom phase (1991–1786 B.C.). The drawing shows the west front, which had an overall length of about 188 yards, while the walls rose to a height of at least 30 feet, at the foot of which was a rock-cut dry ditch about 23 feet deep. When the fortifications were rebuilt during its second occupation they were at once simplified and strengthened. The massive west gate was cut back, the circular bastions were cut down and built over, the ditch was partly filled and converted into a sunk road, and the buttresses of the wall were made more massive. However, during this period outer defences consisting of a deep ditch and perimeter wall with a length of more than a mile were built; and a township grew up between the fortress and the outer defences. These have not yet been systematically excavated for they present an immense task.

361

179 Reconstruction drawing of the fortress of Buhen

September 12, 1959

THE FORTRESS OF BUHEN, AS IT WAS 4000 YEARS AGO

Specially drawn for The Illustrated London News *by Alan Sorrell, with the co-operation of Professor W. B. Emery. Plan by Professor Emery*

Last year Professor W. B. Emery described the first season's work he had done for the Egypt Exploration Society at Buhen, in the Sudan, on the Nile not far from Wadi Halfa. This consisted of uncovering about half of the west front of a large fortress, first built (on a most elaborate scale) in the Middle Kingdom, lost during the period of the Hyksos domination, and rebuilt on a somewhat different plan in the New Kingdom period of expansion; and these discoveries immediately revolutionised many of our previous ideas of Pharaonic military architecture. During the second season's digging (which began in October last) the whole of the west front (about 188 yards long) was uncovered and excavations were begun inside the walls. It is as a result of these excavations that Professor Emery has been able to make exact plans of both the Middle Kingdom and the much later New Kingdom façades and with his assistance Mr. Alan Sorrell has been able to make not only this large-scale reconstruction drawing but also drawings of the early West Gate and the later façade.

362

September 12, 1959

THE STORMING OF AN EGYPTIAN FORTRESS IN THE SUDAN SOME 3600 YEARS AGO:
The Great West Gate of Buhen

The imposing and massive gateway was perhaps the most outstanding feature of the Middle Kingdom fortifications of Buhen, on the Nile, near Wadi Halfa, which Professor W. B. Emery has uncovered in his second series of excavations conducted on behalf of the Egypt Exploration Society; however the gate was finally assaulted and captured *circa* 1675 B.C.

November 28, 1959

THE ROYAL TREASURE OF DORAK
By James Mellaart, Assistant Director, The British Institute of Archaeology, Ankara

A rich collection of objects derived from an unpublished excavation of two Royal Tombs of the Yorktan culture, undertaken at about the time of the Turco-Greek war, was rediscovered some years ago by the writer in private possession in Izmir. We are much obliged to the present owner for her permission to publish coloured reproductions of the objects and for the information from what remains of the original excavation records and from notes and old photographs, which has enabled us to reconstruct the approximate tomb lay-out.

A small cemetery consisting of two Royal cist graves and two *pithos* burials of servants was found high up on a hill slope near the village of Dorak, near the Sea of Marmora. A close investigation at the time showed that no other tombs were present in the immediate neighbourhood, and it appears, then, that this site was only used for the burial of a king in Tomb I, a king and queen in Tomb II and two servants of the Royal couple. . . .

Tomb I, the smaller of the two, contained the body of an adult stretched out on his back with his head to the east and feet to the west. . . .

Around the king's body were placed his funerary gifts: ceremonial arms, weapons, drinking vessels in precious metals, pottery and stone vessels, which may have contained food, and, most important of all, a piece of furniture, probably dismantled before being deposited in the tomb. . . .

On the king's right side lay a splendid sceptre with a pear-shaped fluted head of light-green stone and a diagonally fluted ivory handle with gold-capped ends, two black obsidian beakers, one smooth polished, the other vertically fluted, a vertically fluted *depas* (two-handled drinking cup) of gold, and a one-handled cup with *repoussé* design.

Near his right hand lay a dagger ($11\frac{3}{8}$ inches in length) with a carnelian pommel, silver blade and hilt covered with embossed gold sheet. Between the king and the south wall of the tomb lay a group of weapons: a lance with silver head and chased midrib, the long decayed wooden shaft being encased in alternate ribbed gold and plain silver tubular pieces of casing, a bronze (or copper) battle-axe of shaft-hole type, with plain gold-encased wooden handle, a flat axe of the same material and a pile of nine swords and daggers. . . .

The most remarkable object, however, in the tomb was a wooden chair or throne, probably dismantled when put in the tomb and unfortunately not restorable. It was plated with thick sheet gold; one of the surviving casings of the legs shows that it had animal feet. Strips of sheet gold bear in embossed Egyptian hieroglyphs the name and titles of the second king of the Fifth Dynasty, Sahure (2487–2473 B.C.). This piece of Egyptian furniture undoubtedly represents a Royal gift, and is the first piece of evidence of contact between the seafaring population of North-West Anatolia and Egypt in the Third Millennium B.C. . . .

The second and larger tomb . . . contained two burials: a king in the southern half of the tomb and his queen in the northern half, each accompanied by funerary gifts. . . . At the king's feet lay the skeleton of a dog, lovingly provided with its own stone bowl. . . .

The king's grave goods fall into the same categories as those found in the other tomb, and are on the same lavish scale, but the queen is provided with jewellery and toilet articles, objects naturally not occurring among the paraphernalia which accompanied the king's. The king was provided with a sceptre, the spherical head of which was made of pink-veined white marble. Its wooden handle was cased in gold sheet, ribbed and ornamented with gold granulation. Near it in front of the king lay a drinking cup of gold with a spirally-fluted body and granulated patterns on the neck.

A silver lance-head, like that in Tomb I, lay along the south wall of the tomb, its shaft decorated with alternate gold and silver tubular casings. Behind the king's head there lay four ceremonial battle-axes like those found at Troy. Other vessels of precious metal buried with the king included a gold jug with cutaway spout and embossed decoration and a smaller silver, half-corroded, two-handled *depas*, with horizontal ribbing. . . .

The queen's funerary offerings: In the north-western corner, in the queen's half of the tomb, there stood two wooden tables or trays supporting several pottery vessels, one of which contained a necklace of about twenty gold beads in the form of double-spirals, such as have been found at Ur, Troy, Poliochni and Brak. Near the neck of the skeleton were found other necklaces, consisting of carnelian, rock-crystal and gold beads, or of white marble and gold, or striped onyx, or of gold capped obsidian, and of rock-crystal beads. Below the queen's hips strips of silver and gold sheet were found, with holes along the edges for sewing on to garments, no longer preserved. Around the skull and partly slipped off, lay a badly corroded silver diadem with pendants, and behind the head were found four elaborate ear-pendants of Trojan type, made of silver. Around the wrist were found two silver bracelets, one piped with gold decorated with silver, and gold double-spirals and rosettes. Near them was found a bracelet made of silver wire with electrum rosettes and a gold bracelet, made of five wire loops, the outer ones plain, the inner ones twisted. In front of the queen lay a small sceptre with a peculiar knobbed amber head and silver-cased wooden handle, decorated like the king's sceptre, but in a bad state of preservation. . . .

The finest object deposited with the queen was, however, an ivory comb, worn in the hair, with a centre roundel framed by an open-work band, depicting two finely-carved wild goats or ibexes and two dolphins, the whole picked out in red and blue colour, and provided with a gold edge, carved rosettes and a carnelian rivet head surrounded by gold granulation.

With the exception of the piece of furniture from the Egyptian Old Kingdom none of the objects appear to be of foreign make, and the excellence of local craftsmen working for the ruler's court is nowhere more clearly shown than in a group of five statuettes, said to have been found in these tombs.

1960–61

The excavations at Nimrud are still continued; but recede a little in public interest compared with the new developments in Anatolia, with the first reports of Mellaart's first discoveries at Haçilar; and with the massively mounted Israeli explorations of caves overlooking the Dead Sea, with their discovery of fascinating documents relating to the Bar Kochba revolt of the first century A.D., and of Chalcolithic remains. Of important articles not quoted mention may be made of: continued excavations at Hasanlu, in Iran; Chalcolithic troglodyte communities near Beersheba and the face ossuaries of Azor, near Tel Aviv; excavations at Lothal, an important Indus Valley civilisation city; Leakey's discovery of a skull of Chellean man; the first Roman mosaics found at Fishbourne, near Chichester; and two Maya discoveries, at Aguateca, Guatemala and Xunantunich, British Honduras.

May 7, 1960

NEANDERTHAL MAN IN NORTHERN IRAQ

By Professor Ralph S. Solecki, of Columbia University, N.Y.

Three adult Neanderthal skeletons were found in 1957 in Shanidar Cave, northern Iraq, representing a very significant addition to human palaeontology. These finds, made by the Third Shanidar Expedition, will bring us closer to an understanding of this pre-*Homo sapiens* race. They apparently disappeared from the face of the earth about 40,000 years ago. The Shanidar skeletons are a welcome addition to our slim store of well-preserved and authenticated finds. Indeed, last season's work places Shanidar Cave among the more important Early Man sites. In western Asia, it is second only to the site of Mt. Carmel, in Palestine, in Upper

Pleistocene hominid remains. The skeletons are understandably an important addition to the already well-known later age archaeological treasures of the Republic of Iraq. . . .

The excavation, sunk in the centre of the floor area, was graduated down in steps to a total depth of 45 feet. . . . The Neanderthal skeletons lay in the oldest of the four major culture layers outlined, the Mousterian layer.

The first adult Neanderthal from Shanidar Cave, Shanidar I *(Figure 180)*, was missed by the excavation shaft of 1953 by the close margin of less than a foot and a half. During the latter season, an infant skeleton was recovered in the

180 The discovery of the Shanidar I skull of an arthritic one-armed Neanderthaler of about 46,000 years ago

same layer at a lower level, at about 26 feet. This find was studied in Baghdad by Dr. Muzaffer Senyürek, of Ankara University.

Shanidar I was found when it was decided to remove a threatening bulge of earth in the east wall of the excavation. The skull, which was uncovered first, was discovered at a depth of 14·5 feet in the top part of the Mousterian layer, its vault crushed under a stone. Dr. T. Dale Stewart, of the Smithsonian Institution, who later examined the remains in Baghdad, said that it was a male about forty years old. We were puzzled by the marked worn character of the upper and lower front teeth. The probable explanation of this was not learned until it was realised that the right arm and shoulder were never fully developed. Furthermore, according to Dr. Stewart, the same arm had been amputated at the elbow, an extremely early example of primitive surgery. The likelihood is that this individual used his teeth to supplement

his one good arm. We are reminded of the Eskimos, who used their teeth extensively in leather working.

This Neanderthal was not caught by the full force or weight of the rockfall. If he had, there would have been little to recover. He had fallen at full length, his left arm folded protectively across his chest. A low heap of portable-sized stones was found over his remains. It was presumably a cairn made by the survivors of the rockfall, or his kin. Thus, in death, he merited some respect. Burial rites were observed among this race elsewhere. . . . Shanidar I was probably not very handsome, even by Middle Palaeolithic standards. His features were asymmetric. The left side of his face and the upper part of his head bore extensive bony scar tissue. This pointed to some extreme disfigurement. . . .

Another adult (Shanidar III) was found just about 9 feet away from Shanidar I, towards the front of the cave. It lay at a slightly lower level, at a depth of 17·5 feet, in a small pocket of mixed earth and stones. This individual had been caught in a rockfall earlier than the one which killed Shanidar I. The upper part of his body had been smashed. Only a few scattered teeth evidenced his skull. His crushed and broken lower torso and parts of his lower limbs were all that remained relatively intact for field description.

Almost directly opposite these two Neanderthals in the west wall of the excavation was discovered the skull of the other Shanidar Neanderthal adult (Shanidar II). It was quite an accidental find, wholly unexpected. The discovery came about in the last days of excavation. In order to present a clean wall profile for final drawing and photography, I had ordered the wall be scraped clean its entire 60-foot length. Half-way in the process, the workman's trowel grated across two or three teeth at a depth of 23 feet. The unbelievable came true, and by a very close shave, we had recovered still another Neanderthal. He had been caught, like the others, under a rockfall. I estimate that this fatal accident happened at least 60,000 years ago.

February 11, 1961

STATUETTES FROM HACILAR

By James Mellaart, Assistant Director, The British Institute of Archaeology at Ankara

During the 1960 season of excavations, directed by the writer at the early site of Hacilar, in south-western Anatolia, several groups of clay statues came to light in the burnt settlement of Level VI, belonging to the Late Neolithic period, and dated by radiocarbon method to *circa* 5400±85 B.C. This find is of more than ordinary importance, both on account of its early age and for its preservation, variety and quality. . . . Nearly twenty figures are more or less complete with only a part missing and the total number restorable on paper is thirty-five. At least another twenty-five are represented by arms, legs or part of the torso *(Figure 181)*, but they add little to the picture. The naturalism of these small figures gives for the first time a good idea of what Late Neolithic women looked like. (There is not a single statue of a male by himself.) A number of the figures are scantily dressed and the prevailing nudity or semi-nudity does, in fact, suggest that Late Neolithic woman at Hacilar wore few or no clothes, at least in summer. . . .

These clay statues were found in private houses of the Level VI settlement. . . . Some were baked and finished, others were found in an unbaked condition either on the floor of the houses or fallen from the upper storey. The fact that many in House 5 were unbaked definitely proves that they were made locally. . . .

These statues exhibit a range of types: standing, seated, kneeling, squatting, lying down and enthroned, and all these types show a number of variations.

The largest figures are those of women standing with arms down the side and hands, schematically drawn, resting on the thighs. . . .

Another version of the standing goddess shows her with hands supporting the breasts. . . .

A number of others are shown dressed, one with an apron at the back only, the other with one in front, suspended from a belt. The articles of dress are shown in white paint. Other fragments show a long flowing garment such as the one painted on the statue of the lying-down goddess. Another wears "briefs" and the youthful figure of this small statue, with hair in

181 Upper part of Neolithic statuette from Hacilar

a plait coiled on top of her head, should be compared to a more mature figure with pronounced buttocks, wearing her hair in a bun at the back of her head. There can be no doubt that the one depicts the goddess as a young girl whereas the other portrays her as a mature woman. The difference in hair-style, buns for married (?) women and plaits for girls, has many modern parallels. It would appear that only young girls wore a brief-like garment, whereas married women went about either naked or dressed only in aprons or an ankle-long striped garment.

Another interesting standing figure shows a girl with plait, wearing a loin-cloth with a long strip hanging at the back and holding a pet under her left arm. The head of the animal is lost, but its paws and long tail strongly suggest that it was a young leopard. Leopards still exist in the Taurus Mountains and the long tail argues against the identification with a lion, nor can it have been a cat. . . . Seated figures are

182 Statuette from Neolithic Hacilar of a seated woman, holding a standing child to her breast

common. The most usual type shows the goddess seated in a typically feminine position with the legs to one side. . . . This type frequently depicts the goddess with a child, either seated on her lap, in the unfortunately very fragmentary statue, or with the child standing next to, and embracing, its mother *(Figure 182)*. . . .

Hardly less remarkable is the little group of a young woman and a youth. The young goddess is here shown in the embrace of the adolescent god, shown smaller than herself. Part of the statue is missing, including the goddess's arms, one of which rested on the boy-god's waist, as well as the upper part of his torso and head. The line of one arm and the hand of the other show him clasping her waist. The goddess's head is unusually fine and her torso shows that a young woman was portrayed. The scene is full of vitality without being in the least offensive to modern taste. . . . One group of statues remains to be discussed: that of the goddess enthroned. Two fine figures of this type were found, one unbaked but complete, the other baked but only partly preserved. The former shows a goddess holding a leopard cub to her bosom. She is depicted naked and seated upon what at first looked like a throne, but which, after cleaning, turned out to be a standing leopard, carefully modelled. The animal's long tail curls up the goddess's back. The whole group is of monumental quality in spite of its small size. The second figure shows a goddess holding her breasts. Her nose is broken and she wears her hair in an elaborate fashion, with tresses round the back of the head, surmounted by a bun. On her back are two tails symmetrically arranged with the tips ending on her shoulders. The animals to which they belonged are not preserved, but they probably were leopards as in the previous statue. The arrangement of the two tails and the traces left show that the goddess was seated, not on a single animal, but on two, placed side by side, thus presenting a more balanced view of the back with an animal head on either side. When complete this statue must have been as impressive as its counterpart.

April 8, 1961

TWO THOUSAND YEARS OF HACILAR

By James Mellaart, sometime Assistant Director of the British Institute of Archaeology at Ankara

Hacilar is the oldest site yet excavated on the Anatolian plateau, but already much earlier sites are known to await the archaeologist's pick.

The Hacilar mound – or rather, mounds, for one is superimposed on the other – is nowhere more than 15 feet high and the top is somewhat denuded. It contains no fewer than twenty building levels, even though at least three of these show the remains of houses preserved to a height of 5–6 feet. This apparent contradiction is explained by a continuous shifting of the centre of the settlement. . . .

The aceramic mound

The earliest inhabitants of the site of Hacilar built their mud-brick houses on stone foundations directly on virgin soil. Gradually a small mound grew up, containing at present not more than seven superimposed floors corresponding to building levels. Denudation and Late Neolithic building activities may have removed several others. The small settlement seems to have lived through a peaceful period, for there are no traces of burning and destruction and the site may have been deserted. Apart from the architectural remains, finds were exceedingly scanty and include only a few polished axes, fragments of stone bowls and some chert and obsidian blades, but no pottery and no clay figurines. Animal bones were few and badly splintered to extract the marrow. Straw was found, but no actual remains of cereals. Nevertheless, the fully settled character of the community, the presence of abundant straw on the floors and in the mud-brick and last but not least the carefully-constructed clay bins, hearths and ovens, suggest an early form of agriculture. . . .

Particularly interesting is an ancestor cult which involved the preservation of skulls, found propped up on stones in several instances on floors or on a corner of the hearth. Of skeletons no traces were found and nothing is therefore known of the burial custom of this period. This is the first occasion upon which a non-pottery Neolithic culture has been found in Anatolia, particularly so as the aceramic of Hacilar shares a number of important features with the pre-pottery Neolithic B culture of Jericho. Here we again find a skull cult, the total absence of pottery and the use of red burnished plaster floors, but the Jericho architecture in which they occur would seem to be far more sophisticated. What the date of this culture is at Hacilar is still unknown and a radiocarbon date is eagerly awaited, but in the meantime one may confidently assign it to the 7th Millennium B.C.

A great stratigraphical hiatus separates this period from the Late Neolithic. The newcomers who then settled at Hacilar, partly on virgin soil and partly on the earlier and deserted mound, arrived with a fully-developed and most sophisticated culture, that had no ancestors on the site. Not only did they make a fine burnished cream-coloured pottery, but attempts at painting were already made and the shapes of the pottery are rich and varied *(Plate 46, p. 346)*. They carved white marble bowls, fine vertical tubular jugs and bone tools, some with handles in the likeness of a human figure with a double-horned head-dress from Building Level IX. Clay figurines and ladles with handles in the form of animal heads also make their first appearance. Of the culture in its earliest phases little is known, and it is best represented by Building Level VI, which was destroyed in a conflagration, around 5400 B.C. Level VI marks the climax of Late Neolithic culture and art – the remarkable collection of small clay statues of the Anatolian Mother Goddess was the subject of a previous article. . . . The most characteristic product of the Early Chalcolithic

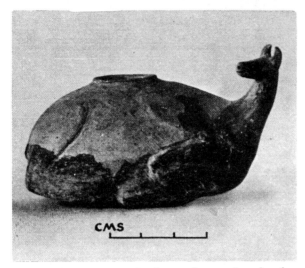

183 Animal vase in the form of a resting doe from Hacilar VI

Period, which attracted all the artistic talent of the community, was the pottery which occurs in two main wares, a monochrome red and brown, and sometimes porcelain-white, burnished ware and a red-on-cream painted ware, also burnished. It is difficult to exaggerate the superb quality of this pottery, which ranks among the finest pottery ever made in Anatolia. From Level IV onward, painted pottery formed about 50 per cent of the pottery; bulk and coarse ware is unknown. Except in Level I (about which presently), the patterns are predominantly non-linear. Geometric forms predominate from IV–IIa, and bizarre and fantastic patterns, already present in the earlier levels of the period, reach their climax in Building Level IIb. Many of these patterns appear to have had a textile origin and only few are stylised representations of animal heads. Common is an outstretched hand or arm, which may have been imbued with an apotropaic value against the evil eye. . . . Finally, at the end of the Early Chalcolithic Period, which may be dated to *circa* 4800 or 4750 B.C., the site was deserted. Newcomers introducing the much inferior Late Chalcolithic culture settled on a different site nearer the modern village.

December 2, 1961

THE COPPER TREASURE OF NAHAL MISHMAR

By Pessah Bar-adon

After a week of such surveying we began excavating one that had been inhabited: the "Scouts' Cave" (which later received the honorary name of "Treasure Cave" after an unexpected treasure was found there), on the southern bank of Nahal Mishmar. It is situated on a steep cliff-top, which reaches 886 feet·(270 metres) above the sea-level, and has a total height of 984 feet (300 metres). A first check revealed that the cave had not been visited by Beduin, apparently because of the difficult access. Therefore, and also because of the number of surface finds, including a human skull, Chalcolithic and Roman pottery sherds, fragments of glass vessels and remains of fabric, straw and wood, it was decided to examine this cave thoroughly *(Figure 184)*. . . .

The "Scouts' Cave" is a natural one, composed of two halls and some crevices in the south, south-west and north-west, parts of which are still filled up. . . .

The upper floor of stamped earth covered an earlier level of debris from the Chalcolithic period, up to 2 metres. . . .

184 *A new archaeological tool: mine detector at work in a cave*

Complete clay vessels and sherds were found, such as ladles, pots, jugs, bowls and basins. At least one of the small bowls was used as a lamp, as indicated by the soot-mark on the rim. Also found were pots with flaring rims and small pierced handles attached to the shoulder or body of the vessel; vessels with incised herring-bone decoration; thumb-indented ledge hand-les; rims of different types of hole-mouth jars; the upper part of a churn with a flaring concave neck and large pierced handles, together with other sections of the churn; spindle whorls of stone and pottery; a clay stopper; sticks of wood of various lengths, sharpened and scraped at their ends, various ornaments such as a round ivory disc, an ivory bead, tiny faience beads and a clay statuette of a sheep; remnants of textile and leather, including a sandal. Many remnants of animals were uncovered at this level, such as: ram (?), goats, mole, rabbit, various birds, fossil sea-snails, shells from the Mediterranean and the entire region. A large quantity of grain and other foodstuffs was found. The cereals are now being examined by Dr. D. Zaitschek, a Hebrew University botanist interested in prehistoric and archaeological botany. He has already arrived at the important conclusion that the wheat found in the cave is the "missing link" between the wild two-grained wheat (*Triticum dicoccoides*) discovered in this country fifty-five years ago by A. Aronson, and the primitive hard wheat species cultivated by the Arabs here for hundreds of years. . . . At a depth of about 6 feet

(2 metres), in the northern wall of the cave, the entrance to a niche was found, concealed by a smooth stone. When the stone was removed, there was revealed to us a veritable treasure, wrapped in matting, consisting of *circa* 430 objects of copper, including six beautifully-fashioned ivories (five objects with holes, and one box), six mace-heads made of haematite and one of limestone. The hoard includes items which can be identified, though not all can be named: copper mace-heads, work-tools such as chisels, axes, adzes and hammers, and pots with basket handles, sceptres, various "sticks", "crowns", "horns", standards *(Figure 185)*.

185 *A copper standard (or sceptre) from Nahal Mishmar*

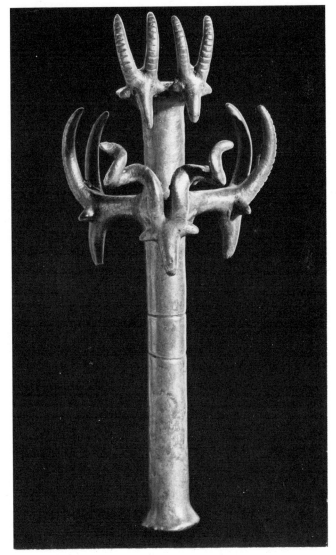

There is sculpture that can be described as abstract, as well as sculptures of animals such as deer, goats, antelopes, buffaloes, birds, in addition to decorative patterns and geometric designs. The artifacts are distinguished by extraordinary technical perfection and beauty, and reveal a very high standard of art and technology. Until the study of the finds is completed, including the Carbon 14 analysis and an analysis of the metal, some key items enable us to date the objects to the later part of the Chalcolithic period. Such items are mace-heads and work-tools which had been found in other excavations, for instance in Teleilat Ghassul, Beersheba, Metser, Beit Shean, and in the Chalcolithic level in the Seelim Valley; a small piece of holed ivory and a fragment of a stick, found earlier in Beersheba; and certain elements resembling features on the Chalcolithic ossuaries found in Hedera, Azor, Bnei-Brak and Tel Aviv. From these items it can be assumed that the entire contents of the hoard, including the unidentifiable objects, are homogeneous in character and that they all belong to the last part of the Chalcolithic period, bordering on Early Bronze Age.

1962–63

These were two rich years, as the extracts from finds from Guatemala, Marlik in Iran, Salamis in Cyprus, and, most important, Čatal Hüyük in Anatolia show. In addition Neolithic longbows were discovered in the peat in Somerset and reconstructed at Cambridge; a splendid treasure of Roman silver was found at Kaiseraugst, Switzerland; a Royal tomb was found in Nigeria; and a splendid Mycenaean rhyton at Larnaca in Cyprus (Plate 47, p. 347). Also in Cyprus a splendid group of Roman mosaics was found at New Paphos, while Professor Doro Levi continued his Minoan researches not only at Phaistos in Crete, but also on the Carian coast.

January 20, 1962

EXCAVATIONS AND RECONSTRUCTIONS AT TIKAL

By William R. Coe, Assistant Curator, American Section, The University Museum, University of Pennsylvania, Philadelphia; and Assistant Field Director in charge of Research, Tikal Project

Tikal, probably the greatest lowland Maya archaeological centre, lies 200-odd miles north of Guatemala City, in the midst of the heavily forested, limestone-based Department of Peten. The importance of the site has long been recognised. Its fabulous quality is only partly exemplified by its still undetermined size, by the plethora of standing "palaces" and "temples" –

186 The towering splendour of Temple I dominates the great plaza at Tikal

(Figure 186) the highest of the latter climbing over 200 feet in the air, as well as by the quantity of carved and plain stones, altars and *stelae (Figure 187)*. In 1956 the University Museum of the University of Pennsylvania inaugurated a long-term programme of excavations and collateral studies at this site with two primary objectives. The first aim was to elucidate, by whatever means were available, the details, trends and processes within and underlying the development of Tikal. Preliminary questions along the following lines were asked. To what extent had the sheer size

187 *The Mexican deity Tlaloc shown in a fragmentary* stela *from Tikal*

and magnitude of this single centre been contributory to lowland Maya cultural development as a whole? What factor or factors initiated occupation at Tikal, what caused the amazing cultural florescence of Tikal, and what were the causes of its eventual cessation as a "ceremonial centre"? Through excavations and inference could not the economic and demographic, as

well as political, components of Tikal eventually be specified? The second objective of the work – and one with the complete backing of the Guatemala Government – was the preservation of Tikal as a public archaeological monument. An airfield, scheduled flights, and a local inn have made the site an outstanding archaeological attraction for tourists in the Americas. No longer can a site be carefully excavated only to be abandoned to the jungle as a gutted ruin of pits and trenches. Restoration at Tikal has been costly but warranted by the public and private support given the Tikal Project for the combined aims of preservation and excavation.

Six seasons of work, varying from four to seven months in length, have been accomplished to date, with five more years of work immediately anticipated. These pages illustrate many of the aesthetically and scientifically interesting materials from these years of excavations. On the other hand, various ideas, largely tentative, regarding the evolution of Tikal are less easily presented. After six years of excavation and a fair amount of publication in the University Museum "Tikal Reports" series and other journals, it may well be asked what has been accomplished towards answering the questions that predisposed the work, as well as what are the questions which have arisen in the course of it.

One question that plagues Mesoamericanists centres on the widespread dissolution of Classic culture, of which Tikal was a major centre. The latest known carved and erected monument at Tikal was *Stela* 11, dated as 10.2.0.0.0 in the Maya system, or A.D. 869. Failure to erect such monuments subsequently appears to indicate the failure of the whole 600-year-old Classic hierarchic complex of priests, artisans, and traditions. The explanation of the collapse of priestly authority and thus the cessation of the directive force responsible for the recognised characteristics of Classic culture remains extremely problem-ridden. Work at Tikal has failed so far to reveal why that which had existed so long ceased to exist in such a seemingly sudden way. The late Pre-Classic and Classic occupations of the site cover at least a millennium, during which priestly power and peasant corn combined effectively to yield the monuments and calculations, the mundane and exotic artifacts, the thousand major and minor structures that we dig, mend and study. We do not yet know why it ended nor why it ended when it did.

Recent excavation at Tikal does, however, illuminate a most peculiar phase subsequent to the collapse just mentioned. This phase was "non-Classic" in that Classic standards had been relaxed and the remains of Classic culture were disturbed in one degree or another. The evidence for this phase is diverse and cannot be fully documented within the space of this article. In the area of the Great Plaza and the North Terrace about 40 percent of the seventy-four monuments located are not in their original, intended position: one early *stela* was found upside-down, another was fragmentary and set backwards, another had been set 90-degrees from normal, while others were erected more or less in accordance with Classic standards of positioning – but as fragments! In other instances early *stelae* were coupled with late altars, carved monuments with plain ones, and so on in various combinations. The top two-thirds of a plain Late Classic *stela* had been dragged roughly 100 metres from where it had been originally erected intact, and re-erected as a fragment in the Great Plaza; with it was set an altar formed from the lower part of the much earlier *Stela 2*, the top half of which occurs high up in the North Acropolis. Elsewhere at the site, the evidence demonstrates the removal from a Late Classic row of plain monuments of a presumably plain *stela* – to where is not known – and the abandonment of its plain altar, quite certainly after 9.18.0.0.0 (A.D. 790). It is hard to believe that disruption such as this would have occurred during Classic times when complete monuments were being carved and erected.

April 28, 1962

GOLD TREASURES OF MARLIK

By Dr. Ezat O. Negahban

Last year I began to plan an archaeological map of Iran for which a survey of the entire country will be required. Four months ago, as part of this survey, an archaeological team visited the Rahmatabad region of the Rudbar area. They inspected many mounds in this district, made surface collections, and in some of the mounds cut test trenches. Near the end of this survey we entered the Gohar Rud Valley and discovered a number of mounds situated on both sides of the river, including the five mounds on which interest is now concentrated. We cut a test trench on Marlik Tepe which, in the course of two days, yielded two small bronze figurines of cows, two cylinder seals and fourteen gold buttons. These finds indicated extremely rich remains in a mound that at first glance appears to be completely natural. Immediately, we realised the importance of the mound and saw that a serious and extended excavation was necessary. In less than a fortnight the formalities were completed and permission to excavate received. . . .

To date about two-thirds of the mound have been excavated, uncovering approximately twenty tombs, or rather, tomb chambers, for in only two of them have signs of human bones been found. In one chamber a badly-crushed skull was uncovered, and in another, fragments of chipped bone. The remaining chambers contained beautiful and varied burial objects, but no human bones.

The burial chambers are of four types. The first type consists of large, irregularly-shaped tombs fitted into the natural rock, which was utilised for walls whenever possible. The gaps in the natural rock were filled with pebbles and clay mortar. These tombs are as large as $16\frac{1}{2}$ feet (5 metres) by 10 feet (3 metres) and contained very rich remains. Apparently they are the burial chambers of Kings and warrior chieftains.

The second group are smaller, possibly 3 to $4\frac{1}{2}$ feet (1 to 1·5 metres) by $6\frac{1}{2}$ feet (2 metres), fairly rectangular in shape with one curved side and constructed of stone slabs and clay mortar. These tombs contained the richest and most beautiful objects, and it seems likely from their contents that they belonged to the queens and royal children. . . .

The third group of tombs are approximately 10 feet by 10 feet (3 by 3 metres), fairly rectangular in shape and constructed of cut stone and clay mortar. These were the most carefully constructed of all the tombs, but, to our surprise, did not contain rich or varied remains. . . .

The last group of tombs, of which two examples have been found, are small, approximately 3 by $6\frac{1}{2}$ feet (1 by 2 metres), and constructed of pebbles and clay mortar. The total contents of each of these tombs were a bit and a set of horse teeth, indicating the high value placed on horses and horsemanship by these people.

In these four types of graves equipment for daily use, for ceremonial and ritual use and for hunting and warfare, have been found, together with many decorative and documentary objects. These belong to a culture which, while it shows many unique characteristics, also can be compared to other contemporary cultures of the neighbouring countries of the Middle East.

However, the shapes of some of the pottery and bronze objects and the designs on the gold and silver, all show that it is basically a native art of this region. A beautiful grey spouted jar was inspired by the graceful stance of the crane which still can be seen along the riverside. The wild pomegranate, which flourishes here, was reproduced beautifully in the form of bronze bells and gold jewellery. A species of fir tree which covers much of this area is exactly reproduced on some of the gold vases. Some of the objects found in this excavation are still in use in the valleys of this region, such as the milking pot, ladles, cooking pots, bread hook, spindle, axes and sledgehammers, straight-edge razor and tweezers. The gold work is exceptionally fine and shows a wide variety of techniques. One of the most interesting and unusual of the techniques, however, is that in which the animal heads, which are hollow and made in one with the body of the vase, are extruded to a great extent, in the case of the vase with winged bulls to 2 centimetres. The vessel showing the most comparable technique to this work is the Kalar-dasht bowl (9th century B.C.), which has a design of lions with protruding heads. Here, however, the heads have been made separately and attached. On the legs of the Kalar-dasht lions are replicas of the swastika, which can also be seen on the hind leg of the lion on the gold-inlaid silver teapot. Among the most valuable objects found are a small gold statue of a king with separate crown and ear-rings and a tall vase of coloured stone mosaic. The jewellery uncovered includes necklaces, bracelets, ear-rings, nose pendants, forehead bands, rings, hair clips and pins. Necklaces have been found in red carnelian, gold, limestone, frit, gypsum and snail shell. Gold buttons ranging in size from $\frac{1}{2}$ to 6 inches (1·5 to 15 centimetres) in diameter, apparently for ceremonial use, have been found, together with bronze and frit buttons. *(See Plate 48, p. 348.)*

May 5, 1962

FURTHER FINDS FROM MARLIK

By Dr. Negahban

Since the archaeological remains of this mound constitute only one level, we are beginning to piece together a very well rounded picture of the material remains of this culture. However, the dating of it is hindered by the lack of stratification and writing to date. Consequently, until now, the dating is based mainly on a comparison of the objects of this culture with those of the neighbouring cultures, including the Assyrian, Mannaean, Scythian and others, which were fighting for supremacy in this region in the early 1st Millennium B.C. A few examples of this comparison may be found in the body of this note, the limits of which do not allow more detail to be given here. Many of the objects found were made as funerary objects to be placed in the grave. Some, however, show signs of use such as two bronze helmets found in the tomb of what was apparently a warrior chieftain on which indentations from a mace-head are clearly apparent. In other instances models of tools and equipment have been found such as the bronze model of a bow. The pottery is either grey or red, unpainted, and extremely well fired. Some of the pottery is burnished, such as the pottery humped bull. Pottery figurines of cows, deer, bear *(Figure 188)*, ram and of male and female human beings have been found. One of the most interesting is the red pottery figurine of a deer which shows a beautiful movement of the head. Pottery vessels have appeared identical with some found in Sialk B (early 1st Millenium B.C.). A large number of bronze vessels and weapons such as maceheads, swords, daggers, spearheads, arrowheads, helmets and cymbals, have been found, together with a great variety of small bronze figurines of deer, mountain goat, horse and cow. Larger figurines which have been uncovered include a cow mounted on four

wheels, stylised human figures and three statues of mountain goat. Numerous tools of bronze such as tweezers, awls, spools, needles, ear cleaners, buttons, bells, loops, horse bits together with many bronze ingots have also been unearthed. However, only two fragments of iron have so far been found, showing that iron

188 Begging for buns 3000 years ago: a pottery bear from Marlik

was newly introduced to this culture. So far the only writing found consists of one letter on a broken cylinder seal. We do not expect to find much trace of writing on the remainder of Marlik Tepe since it is a burial mound, but we are hopeful that in the excavation of the other mounds, some of which are residential, writing may be found. To date eleven cylinder seals have been found, made of stone, frit and gypsum, some edged with gold bands. Some of these are comparable to Assyrian, Babylonian and Mittanian cylinder seals, while others have entirely new designs which are probably native to this culture.

June 2, 1962

A "HOMERIC" BURIAL IN CYPRUS

By V. Karageorghis, Ph.D., F.S.A., of the Department of Antiquities, Cyprus

At a distance of a few yards from this tomb and not far from the tumulus, in a field, there was a small area never cultivated by the owner because of a few blocks of stone showing on the surface and hampering the plough. Here, obviously, we had another built tomb.

It became evident that it had already been entered by robbers, but even so it was decided that its investigation was worth undertaking. In fact, it soon proved that the stones appearing on the surface had been removed by the looters from the roof of the chamber in order to make a hole through which they entered it.

The tomb, which was found just below the cultivated soil, not more than 2 feet below the surface of the ground, consists of a rectangular chamber built of large, well-hewn blocks of hard limestone. Its floor is covered with slabs and its roof is run across by two enormous blocks of the same stone, measuring *circa* $11\frac{1}{2}$ feet by 4 feet 10 inches. Another large stone forms the lintel of the doorway. . . .

As already mentioned the chamber of the tomb where the dead were buried with all the gifts had been previously looted. . . . In a corner of the chamber near the entrance, lying right on the floor, we found a silver bowl, obviously never observed by the looters owing to the grey colour of its corroded surface. Though it has not yet been completely cleaned, one may well admire its finely-incised decoration at the inside, consisting of zones of winged sphinxes and floral motifs arranged round a large sphinx in the centre. There is a series of such silver bowls found in Cyprus which are all now in foreign museums. They are usually believed to be works of Phoenician art, such as those vases often mentioned by Homer as being the works of the Sidonians; recent research puts forward the theory that most of them were made by Phoenician artists working in Cyprus. This bowl, which is the first to be found in a safely dated context, is the first of its kind to be acquired by the Cyprus Museum.

The *dromos* of the tomb, measuring $29\frac{1}{2}$ feet by 20 feet and maximum height 10 feet, was filled with soil after the last burial in the chamber and had never been disturbed since then. Within the filling of the *dromos* and about 2 feet below the level of the cultivated soil, we found the skeleton of a human male *in situ*, with the head near to the entrance of the *dromos*; the body was lying stretched in a dorsal position with the head turned to the one side, the hands tied to each other and the legs close together. Remains of two other human skulls were found on a somewhat higher level together with a few skeletal remains. . . . The excavators rightly interpreted this phenomenon as evidence that sacrifices of human beings were performed in honour of the deceased. It has been suggested by various scholars that this practice was introduced to Cyprus by the Mycenaean colonists.

The rest of the *dromos* near the façade of the chamber was occupied by a chariot and the skeletal remains of two horses with their bronze front bands, blinkers and iron bits. One of the horses was lying on the ground flat on his side with bent forelegs and stretched hindlegs. On his head, still in their original place, were a large front band of bronze decorated in *repoussé* technique with lotus flowers and palmettes; two well-preserved bronze blinkers, perforated all round for fastening, protected the eyes of the horses. Next to this horse's head were the front band, blinkers and bits of a second horse, who evidently freed himself from the harness which remained near the yoke to which both animals were attached, and tried to escape the fate of the first horse after he had seen him falling down on the pyre of the sacrifice. He ran back into the corner which is formed by the façade of the chamber, and the right side of the *dromos*, fell on his hindlegs while from above they pelted him with stones which we have found all round him. . . . In the filling of the *dromos*, however, we have found large quantities of pottery, iron nails, horses' teeth and bones, all mixed up, suggesting that there was an earlier burial of horses and a chariot in the *dromos* together with large amphorae, as in the second burial. The filling of the *dromos* must have been carried out to make room for the last burial and thus the remains of the early burial covered up those of the second burial when the *dromos* was filled for the last time. Large amphorae have been made up from the sherds from the first burial found in the filling of the *dromos*, which date it to the period from 850 to 700 B.C. There is no doubt that the burial customs observed in this tomb and in the tomb excavated by Dr. Dikaios in 1957 are particularly important, in as much as they may compare admirably with burial customs described by Homer. In the twenty-third book of the "Iliad" we read that on the pyre of Patroclus, Achilles ". . . set two-handled jars of honey and oil . . . and four horses with high-arched necks . . . and twelve valiant sons of the great-souled Trojans slew he with the bronze. . . ." ("The Iliad", XXIII, 170–176, translation by A. T. Murray, the Loeb edition.) Such burial customs may have, as believed by many scholars, a Mycenaean origin. . . . We have, therefore, here a survival down to the 7th century B.C. of Mycenaean customs echoed in Homer but never found in tombs in Greece later than the Mycenaean period at least as far as our present evidence goes. This is not a strange phenomenon for Cyprus. In the Cypriote art of the same period we observe a survival or revival of Mycenaean elements, especially in vase-painting. And this happens at a time when Cyprus was under the political domination and the cultural influence of the Assyrians. One may interpret this phenomenon as the reaction of the Cypriots against Oriental domination – whether political or cultural – and their adherence to Mycenaean culture as the true foundation of their own culture. This explains the distinctly conservative character of the Cypriote culture in general throughout the first half of the 1st Millennium B.C.

June 9, 1962

FIRST EXCAVATIONS AT CATAL HUYUK

By James Mellaart, Director of the Catal Huyuk Excavations

The large double mound of Catal Huyuk lies 32¼ miles south-east of Konya, about 1 mile south of the village of Kucukkoy, on the banks of the Carsamba Cay.

The site was discovered during our survey of the Konya Plain in 1958, but it was not until the excavations at Hacilar were completed that investigations could be carried out at Catal Huyuk. . . .

In dealing with these early periods one has become accustomed to thinking in terms of peasant farmers living in villages, but first the discovery of pre-pottery Neolithic Jericho and now that of Catal Huyuk show that the development of towns and cities is of a much greater antiquity than one had previously thought. With its 32 acres, Neolithic Catal Huyuk is larger than any city of pre-Classical date in Cilicia or the whole of lowland Western Anatolia; it is twice the size of Troy VI or Old Smyrna, as large as most Anatolian Bronze Age cities, larger than the Phrygian capital and from three to four times the size of pre-pottery Jericho.

In the area excavated on the western slope of the mound, *i.e.*, facing the river, we have evidence for some ten successive building levels forming a deposit of 37½ feet (11·5 metres). . . . Party walls are unknown. The houses are arranged in blocks grouped round courts or along narrow lanes which form a system of communications between the open spaces. Where possible, access is gained from the courts or the narrow street, but those houses as are found in the middle of the blocks were entered through a shaft from the flat roof. These shafts originally, no doubt, contained wooden ladders, and in one well-preserved case there was a small plastered niche for a lamp. All houses would appear to have been one-storeyed and the roots were flat and made of compressed mud laid on beds of reeds. . . . From these types of tools and weapons one might infer that hunting played an important role in the life of the Neolithic inhabitants of Catal Huyuk, but it must be admitted that the weapons are just as effective for war, and the peaceful nature of Neolithic man is probably a figment of imagination. To the obsidian weapons we may add clay sling missiles, which occur in nearly every house; round clay balls, used as bolas (?), clubs, probably of wood, maces with finely-polished stone heads, traps and nets (shown in the frescoes). The efficiency of this equipment is shown not only on the frescoes but by the numerous bones of animals found in the settlement, which include now extinct wild cattle (with horn spread of up to 4 feet (1·20 metres), deer, boar, equids (wild ass ?), some carnivores, birds (stork ?), as well as the domesticable species of sheep/goat and dog. In a pit in level VIII was found a large collection of crude clay figurines of wild animals – boar, wild cattle, pig and deer (?) – showing intentional wounds made with pointed instruments – an interesting example of the old hunting magic which we find already in Upper Palaeolithic times. . . .

Particularly interesting are the stamp seals of baked clay. Whereas the earliest are round and small in size (level VI), the later examples are large and show a variety of shapes, including that of a human hand. They are decorated with fine geometric ornament in a pseudo-meander style. Spirals also occur. None of the designs is repeated and not more than a single seal is ever found in a house. Evidence for cults is rich at Catal Huyuk. We have already mentioned the burial customs, the hunting magic and the preservation of horns of wild cattle. A belief in a goddess of fertility and abundance is implied in the figurines, modelled in clay or carved in stone (alabaster, limestone and marble). . . . In terms of Near Eastern archaeology, Catal Huyuk O-IX would seem to be roughly contemporary with pre-pottery Neolithic B of Jericho, the culture which produced the plastered skulls and the plaster floor buildings and perhaps a little but not much later than the *floruit* of pre-pottery Jarmo. Compared to Europe, Catal Huyuk would be roughly contemporary with the middle of the Mesolithic period.

June 16, 1962

THE EARLIEST FRESCOES YET FOUND ON A MAN-MADE WALL

By James Mellaart, Director of the Catal Huyuk Excavations

Catal Huyuk's most spectacular contribution to Anatolian and Near Eastern archaeology in general, in 1961, lies in the discovery of its wall paintings, the earliest yet found on man-made walls. . . .

The frescoes are executed with a brush in a flat wash in dark or light red paint in the monochrome series, or in red, pink, white and black in the polychrome paintings. The background is of fine smoothed cream or pale pinkish-white plaster. The fine plaster itself is superimposed on a sandier and coarser mud plaster which covers the mud-brick walls. The colours are waterproof – *i.e.*, they did not run after rain. Upon exposure to the air the reds of the animals did not deteriorate, but that of the leopard-dancers gradually turned brownish. A fine pink, however, turned light grey within twenty minutes. . . .

In each case we are dealing with scenes; isolated groups or animals do not occur. The size of the figures and animals varies considerably; figures are normally about 8 to 10 inches (20 to 25 centimetres) in height, but some are nearly $15\frac{3}{4}$ inches (40 centimetres). Animals in the deer hunt are just over a foot in length but the great aurochs bull measures a full 6 feet. It is clear that we are not dealing with a miniature style. Geometric ornament is found only once.

The Frescoes of the Lower Shrine (building level IV)

Although less well-preserved, the wall paintings of the earlier building include a number of interesting figures. . . . On the north wall a scene in light red with additions in white and black shows a group of four men walking towards the left. A gap in the wall behind the last figure may have destroyed further figures. These figures approach a somewhat confused hunting scene which seems to depict a bear (?) falling into a net or trap. . . . At a later date, the pilaster had been covered in dark red paint. To the right of it, about 1 foot above the level of the bench, was found a small painting of a plump woman painted in white. Arms and head are lost but she is shown dressed in a whitish garment with black spots, probably leopard skin, exactly like a figurine found in the same building level. Two strings of red indicate a necklace or the hem of the dress and a red line likewise encircles each ankle.

Another small figure of a white woman without any signs of dress was found on the south side of an internal buttress. She is shown with raised arms and has an ample figure. More interesting is the long head and fine nose, such as we frequently find in the later shrine. . . .

The Frescoes of the Later Shrine

Here the emphasis is definitely on hunting, essentially a male pursuit, and the total absence of any representation of woman is therefore hardly surprising. . . .

The deer-hunt which measures in its present state about 5 feet by 2½ feet (1·5 metres by 0·75 metre) (originally it must have been 6½ feet [2 metres] long or more) is one of the liveliest frescoes discovered at Catal Huyuk. Executed in monochrome dark red on a creamy background, it shows a group of five men armed with bow and arrow, club and noose (?) attacking a herd of deer composed of three stags with magnificent antlers, at least one doe and two fawns. . . .

In the main chamber of the sanctuary the north wall carries the fresco of an enormous aurochs bull, 6 feet long and badly preserved and painted with no respect to the rib in the plaster, so that part of the animal is above it and part below. Horns are again shown in "twisted perspective", but the sheer size of the animal dominates the room with its strength. All round him we find a dozen pictures of men, in more than one coat of painting, some in a lively naturalistic style, others of inferior workmanship. With the exception of two strange beings, painted half-red, half-white ("harlequins"), the entire fresco is in red monochrome. At a certain point behind the bull the figures of men change direction and it is clear that they are pursuing another animal which is shown on the west wall of the room. . . .

The Leopard-Dancers' fresco

This fresco occupied the northern half of the east wall and consists of two unequal fragments separated by a large gap. The northern part, still about 3 feet long, is the best preserved and shows one of the most interesting scenes yet found at Catal Huyuk. In the earliest poly-chrome fresco we see no fewer than thirteen male figures, including two naked acrobats and two harlequins. The latter and a figure between them form a middle row and are shown a little larger than the rest of the figures. But for two figures in the bottom row, all are shown running towards the left, where round the corner on the north wall one finds the great bull fresco. Although stylistically different, it would be difficult to deny a connection. The dancers' fresco so obviously shows a ritual scene of hunters performing a leopard dance and the capture of a great aurochs, the main meat supply, would be an adequate cause. The gap between the two parts of this fresco is possibly large enough to have contained another, but smaller, stag and the four figures on the smaller fragment which again include a harlequin are also shown moving leftward. The whole scene is extremely lively and full of interest. The jumping figures are most remarkable; the man beating a drum is shown in accurate perspective. Heads are carefully drawn and many figures wear pendants suspended from the neck, drawn in white. Leopard skins (pink with black spots) and bonnets of the same material are worn by all except the acrobats. The armament consists of bows and clubs. One man holds a small animal (fox cub?). The fact that no harlequin's head is ever preserved is suspicious, but it may be a strange coincidence. Further evidence is needed before one attempts an explanation. . . . Similarities to the East Spanish Art at the other extreme of the Mediterranean, which is now also regarded as of post-glacial date, are evident and surprising. Are we at last getting some evidence in the Near East for the survival of Upper Palaeolithic art traditions? These and numerous other questions and problems may be raised to which as yet no answers can be given. What is clear, however, is that the Catal Huyuk excavations have raised a problem of more than merely regional importance.

January 26, 1963

CATAL HUYUK STONE SCULPTURES

By James Mellaart, Director of the Catal Huyuk Excavations

During the 1962 excavations at Catal Huyuk in the Konya Plain, Turkey, we cleared a building complex with about 35 to 40 rooms, belonging to Level VI (*i.e.*, *circa* 6500 B.C.). These rooms were grouped round a number of shrines or chapels, in the second of which we found a remarkable collection of 13 stone statues. Four others came from a room directly adjoining the shrine and a relief plaque was found in the fill nearby. This group of statues, the earliest yet found in Anatolia, differs considerably from those of the later levels on the site, both in material – the present series is in stone – whereas most of the later ones are in baked clay – and in artistic conception. I do not mean to say that we have no clay figures of this period – on the contrary, Level VI produced some fine ancestors for the later Catal and Hacilar [p. 367], (February 11, 1961) series as well as numerous crude "ex-voto" figurines which we found stuck into the walls of shrines, but the present series in stone shares few stylistic features with them. But for the fact that they are made of stone, they are as heterogeneous a collection as one could hope to find, and the absence of a consistent style as such is marked. Had these figures not been found in a closed stratigraphic context, no-one would have dated them all to the same period. There is, however, an important point to be borne in mind. Though covered by the fallen walls of the burnt structures of Level VI, these figures were evidently cult-statues and their old breaks and in some cases worn appearance *(Figure 189)* may indicate that some were already heirlooms of earlier days, whereas others were new and made during the period of our sixth building-level. . . .

Perhaps the weirdest and most awe-inspiring of all is a limestone concretion, probably a broken-off stalagmite from a cave, nearly eight inches high. Only the upper part of the figure has been carved into the resemblance of a human head with a nose, ears, chin and incised eyes and mouth. This only half-human figure invokes all the awe and fear of dimly lit caves and perhaps she was the "Lady of the Underworld", the Death aspect of the Goddess.

189 Catal Huyuk stone sculpture of young goddess with leopard-skin kerchief, standing beside a leopard. Broken and repaired in antiquity

Recognisably human, but no less forbidding is a fine marble figure, found in a room beyond the second shrine and possibly part of a group *(Plate 49, p. 349)*. It shows a kneeling goddess with small breasts and hands on her stomach. The absence of a mouth and the owl-like expression (the prototype of so many "owl-faced" figurines of the Bronze Age and of Homer's "owl-faced" Athene?) suggest to me,

190 Catal Huyuk: a twin goddess in white marble

shown above a clearly indicated belt. As so often with these statues, whether in stone or clay, the sculptor showed little interest in the lower extremities, but these figures are evidently meant to be seated. The composition of a twin goddess at this period is of great interest. . . .

Finally there is a most remarkable plaque in bold relief found in building rubbish below Level V buildings, but almost certainly to be attributed to Level VI.

This plaque, of greenish stone, is unfortunately badly battered so that most of the faces are almost, though not quite, obliterated. Two pairs of figures are shown without any indications of sex. The pair on the left might be male and female or mother and daughter, whereas the group on the right is certainly a woman holding a child, the head of which is lost. I am inclined to see in these two groups again Mother and Daughter and Mother and Child (probably male) but the possibility that the relief shows the sacred marriage on the left, is of course not excluded, and has a forerunner in a Natufian sculpture in the British Museum. The back of the plaque is not worked.

With these statues we have traced the art of sculpture in Anatolia back another thousand years before the remarkable late neolithic figures from Hacilar, but it is evident that the beginning of this tradition has not yet been reached. The lower thirty-five feet of deposits of the Catal mound – as yet untouched – are likely to produce more surprises in the years to come.

at least, the old Goddess. . . . A magnificent white marble statue of a seated young god: foreshadowing similar Early Cycladic figures by a mere 4000 years, calm and dignified, he is shown seated on a low stool, with his hands resting on the knees in a pose reminiscent of Egyptian sculpture of the Old Kingdom. . . .

One of the most remarkable figures shows a twin goddess in white marble *(Figure 190)*. Two heads with schematic rendering of nose and eyebrows, four breasts and two arms are

February 2, 1963

CATAL HUYUK SHRINES

By James Mellaart, Director of the Catal Huyuk Excavations

On the first day of the 1962 season we found the First Shrine directly east of a building which had produced the finest wall paintings found in

Level VI. On the west wall in bold relief there was the stylised figure of a goddess in the position of giving birth and below her,

191 North and west walls of the Second Shrine at Catal Huyuk

modelled in clay, was the head of a very large bull, mutilated, but still clearly recognisable. The hollow in the head showed that the face had been separately modelled, perhaps on a human skull like those of Jericho, but as the building had been cleared after the fire and had been replastered it was not found. . . .

On the east wall were first two bulls' heads modelled in clay (of which one survived); then between the two upright posts three bulls' heads, surmounted by two rows of women's breasts, the upper row set on a "beam", the lower underneath. Beyond the second posts there were traces of a ram's head, restored on analogy with the Third Shrine. All these had been replastered after the fire and when stripped of the plaster we found that the heads had been painted. The breasts hid a row of lower jaws of large boar or pig complete with huge tusks, the upper row set into a red painted "beam". Upon

removing these we found two earlier phases in which the sanctuary had had only painted decoration. . . .

The Second Shrine *(Figure 191)* shows a monumental group, 10 feet high, on the west wall. A squatting goddess with uplifted arms (collapsed but with only the head missing) surmounts a frame supported by three superimposed life-size bulls' heads modelled on the actual horns. A central column divides the frame into two equal halves and on it perches a small ram's head *(Figure 192)*. Deep niches are set into the wall on either side of this scene.

On the north wall the central post is supported by a large ram's head with four horns, a freak that occurs in nature. Beside it stood a little box for offerings or libations and to the right of it a "bull pillar", a pillar of mud brick incorporating the horn cores of a bull. These are common in all the shrines and also occur in houses and are probably the forerunner of the Minoan "horns of consecration". The central panel of the east wall shows a large bull's head with red painted muzzle projecting from the wall above a red painted niche which contained a few bone offerings. During several

192 In the Second Shrine at Catal Huyuk, three bulls' heads with horn corns in situ *and the ram's head above*

phases of the use of the building wall paintings of a schematic nature surrounded the bull's head. To its right a pair of heavy woman's breasts with open nipples were modelled in plaster and within each breast there was the skull of a griffon vulture, evidently already symbolising the belief of "in the midst of life there is death". In a hole below the platform in front of this panel lay a scattered pile of human bones – most unlike a normal burial, the significance of which still escapes us.

The Third Shrine, almost as well preserved as the Second, again bore a great scene on its west wall between two doorways, the northern one of which led into the shaft, whereas the

other gave access to a storeroom with eight grain bins. The upper part had collapsed, but even the heads had partly survived. It showed twin goddesses with two heads, two bodies but a single pair of arms and legs. From the northernmost body a large bull's head protruded which on its brow bore a smaller bull's head. Ears and muzzle were painted red and in one phase the large head bore the imprints of hands dipped in red paint, like those of the first and fourth shrines. A corner post bore a schematised bull's head and even the south wall had a panel decorated with a small ram's head. Three "bull pillars" stood on the edges of the platforms in front of the east wall. On the centre panel was a large bull's head, fallen, but found in front, whereas on either side there were further small heads: a bull's on the left (north); a ram's on the right, high above another red painted niche at ground level. The bench contained three more horn cores of bulls. The central part of the floor was covered with fine matting laid on strewn rushes.

Associated with this shrine are three houses, all with some wallpainting and two courtyards, but the greater part of the complex awaits excavation. One of these houses had a minute room entered by a typical porthole doorway near which were painted the hand of a child, dots made with the fingertips, the imprint of a child's foot and two superimposed hands, all in red. Another house bore a complicated geometrical pattern but the third was the most interesting. Here a panel bore a number of symbols: crosses, a double axe, a complicated cross painted in orange and manganese purple. A crystalline material had been added to the fatty paint to make it glitter. Between the two arms of the cross there were a few personages painted in red – a steatopygous woman, a seated archer, and two figures with raised arms and legs – the position of birth-giving – just as in our plaster reliefs in the shrines. Even the bench was altered and modified into the figure of a stylised bull's head with open muzzle, gaily painted, but lacking the ubiquitous horns.

February 9, 1963

CATAL HUYUK POTTERY AND TEXTILES

By James Mellaart, Director of the Catal Huyuk Excavations

In the 44 rooms excavated in Level VI were found a maximum of 45 pots, *i.e.* an average of about one pot per room! Actually of these 44 rooms only 16 produced any pottery, the largest number being seven pots in a shrine. It would have been easy to dig a trench through this complex without encountering any pottery at all. The greater number of the first pots at Catal Huyuk are cooking pots or bowls. They are black or brown in colour and provided with one, two or four lugs. There is one example of a jar with a basket handle and some have an oval mouth. Even this earliest pottery is thin and well-made and its technical proficiency shows that it must have some ancestry. All this suggests that pottery making must have started around 7000 B.C. in Anatolia and, as far as we can see, earlier than anywhere else in the Near East. . . .

It is particularly interesting that most of the Catal Huyuk pottery shapes can now be derived not from stone bowls, which are rare, but from wooden vessels and baskets. . . .

The technical competence displayed in their mats and baskets as well as the loom-weights, spindlewhorls, weaving needles etc., had by last year suggested that these people were familiar with weaving. The 1962 season confirmed this in a most spectacular way by the discovery of actual textiles in the burials of Level VI, the earliest yet known in the world. On the first day of the dig a patch of carbonised material appeared below the floor of a Level VI house and as this usually indicated vegetable matter, Dr. Hans Helbaek, our palaeoethno-botanist, took over the excavation of this area. Surrounded by remains of food he painstakingly and for a full month cleared a funeral deposit of at least eight individuals, whose dismembered bodies had been wrapped up in parcels of cloth, strapped into a bag or sack together with funeral gifts of food, wooden vessels, fur, beads, pendants, often with their thread preserved, traces of copper, etc. The textiles themselves, carbonised but otherwise well preserved, he was able to preserve and well over a hundred samples were sent to the Archaeological Museum at Ankara.

It is thought that the textiles were originally garments and the material is probably wool. No fewer than three different weaves could be distinguished; a relatively coarse one, a medium one with parts of the selvage and the fringe, and a fine shawl-like weave with a knotted fringe. Then there are straps and strings, including the remains of a "string-skirt", with the ends of each string enclosed in a small titulus of copper to weight it.

1964

An exceptionally rich year in which a great deal of space was devoted to a great number of fascinating discoveries (from which extracts are given) in: Čatal Hüyük, Kato Zakro in Crete, Fishbourne, Salamis in Cyprus, and Masada in Israel. In addition, other important articles covered: an important Neolithic site, parallel to Čatal Hüyük, at Nea Nikomedia, Macedonia; excavations at Ephesus and the discovery of huge apartment blocks there; excavations at Thebes in Greece, with the discovery of oriental seals and Linear-B tablets; more of the pottery from Marlik in Iran; and a Runic stick found in Greenland.

February 1, 1964

SHRINES AND IMAGES OF 9000 YEARS AGO

By James Mellaart, Director of the Chatal Huyuk Excavations

In the large sanctuary next door, the place of the goddess was taken by her animals, a pair of leopards *(Figure 193)*, flanked on either side by wooden posts, at one time painted red, or bearing a polychrome pattern in red, grey and cream. Of the two leopards, the fat left one is probably the female, the slender right one the male. They were found covered with white plaster – as usual – but underneath there were at least 40 layers of painting, though all very much the same.

In the upper painted layers, the leopards were a lemon yellow with black spots, black dotted outline and pink claws, tip of tails and a pink circle on the head (eyes, nose or rather mouth?). Further down they changed their spots into rosettes, painted in black on white with bright red claws. Below the animals was the normal red panel and on the platform in front of them lay a fine black stone statue of the mother goddess coated in grain. Six others lay in a pile associated with numerous concretions and broken off stalactites in the middle of the room, halfway between the hearth and the platform. . . .

Four great wall-panels in all, separated by wide gaps marking the place of vanished wooden posts and capitals – originally painted red – bore large plaster reliefs. Entering the sanctuary through a low doorway in the north wall, the worshipper saw on his right two panels on the west wall; first a large, tubby figure of the mother goddess, innumerable times re-plastered, accompanied by the symbol of her son, a bull's head. The arms were probably raised, and made separately, now only the sockets survive. The legs are even more battered and it is not certain that they moved upwards. In any case no scene of birth is shown. Several holes above the head either indicate the sockets for a headgear or pegs for the suspension of a cloth to cover the figure of the goddess from the profane. Beyond the central post, the second panel, pressed down and distorted by the weight of subsequent buildings, shows the cicatrices of an enormous bull's head with horns modelled in the plaster of the wall. High up towards the right the socket for another animal head is well preserved and to the left there may have been traces of a third. The third panel (around the corner on the south wall) shows the lively figure of a young deity with outstretched arms and legs associated with a projection at her left.

As the next panel carried the diagonal impression of the wooden ladder leading to the roof, no space was available for a relief here, and the sequence is therefore continued on the east wall. This shows another figure – with head in profile and hair flowing in the wind – in a state of motion or whirling. Traces of orange paint near the outstretched right arm may suggest that something was held in the hand, but this is not certain. Nor do we know what happened on the next panel, which has been destroyed down to the red border, frequently found over the main platform against the east wall, which on analogy with most other shrines of Levels VI and VII is devoted to schemes connected with death. Particularly important is the fact that, though not destroyed by fire, the heads of all figures have been defaced before the building was filled in; a deliberate act of desecration of the building, intended to rob the images of their magic power and avert any evil influence. This shrine is of great interest in that it appears to portray the current "pantheon", presided over by the mother goddess, her son and husband – male spirits of fertility symbolised by large and small bulls, and her (or their) daughter (or daughters?), the younger version of the goddess herself. The extraordinary concentration of

193   The large sanctuary: leopard relief

shrines, sanctuaries or cult rooms in the excavated area on the western slope as well as the building of sanctuary upon sanctuary through six building-levels demonstrates beyond any doubt that we are in the "temple-area".

February 8, 1964

SHRINES OF THE VULTURES AND THE VEILED GODDESS

By James Mellaart, Director of the Chatal Huyuk Excavations

In shrine VII. 21 next door we find the same group, breasts above ram's head, repeated in exactly the same position on the east wall, but on a much larger scale. The ram's head has horns and is painted, and from the heavy breasts above protruded the tusks and front teeth of an enormous wild boar. Over the central platform a bull's head, surrounded by three rams' heads rose above a row of six breasts and in the red panel below there was a niche, in front of which lay a human skull. Two others, one adult and one a child, lay on the edge of the corner

platform below a gruesome scene painted on the north wall. This showed a pair of vultures attacking a headless human corpse. The collapse of the wall has compressed the scene somewhat, but fortunately we have good parallels from a building to be described below. The association of the headless corpse in the painting and the actual human skulls needs no comment. Beyond a small post along the north wall enough survives of another vulture to show that the scene was repeated. Below the first scene panels of red and black alternated and these colours are

194 The veiled goddess of Chatal Huyuk: the goddess is pregnant and the focus of the figure is on the stomach

probably symbolic of life and death. Below the second vulture panel was found a complicated textile pattern consisting of red and black triangles, each with a white spot, separated by grooved lines, left white. A similar pattern ornamented the west wall, in the centre of which was found a painted bull's head with enormous horns of wild aurochs (a single horncore still measured three feet in length!). Below it lay another human skull and the imprint of a coiled basket. Although in an appalling state of preservation, this building, when intact, must have been one of the most impressive shrines of Chatal Huyuk and here for the first time do we find human remains still lying on the floors – as they were abandoned after some ancient rite. The magnificence of this building can only be conveyed in reconstructions.

In the later phases of the building so far described the east wall was blank and undecorated. All white plaster is suspicious at Chatal Huyuk especially so on east walls, and indeed,

below 4 centimetres, of white plaster (at least a hundred layers) some spectacular wall paintings were found. After more than a month of cleaning the entire scene was revealed starting from the door (and below the bull) on the north wall – running along the entire east wall, with a slight overlap onto the south wall. Seven vultures in all – three flying to the right and four to the left – are shown attacking six corpses, lying on their left sides (like the burials) in a contracted or extended position. All are headless and on one the short stump of the neck is shown. As the paint became very faint as it dried, the vultures proved difficult to record in black and white photography, especially those on the north wall. The interpretation of the scene offers numerous difficulties and though it would be easy to label it "The triumph of death", there is probably more involved. All burials found below these paintings were anatomically intact and no heads were missing, so there is no obvious connection there.

February 29, 1964

A NEW MAJOR MINOAN PALACE AT KATO ZAKRO

By Nikolaos Platon, Director of the Acropolis Museum, Athens, and Field Director of the Kato Zakro Excavations

An archaeological investigation has been conducted by the Archaeological Service at Athens, during the autumn of 1962 and that of 1963. It was carried out under my direction with the assistance of my wife and a team of young archaeologists. The investigation confirmed the hypothesis that an important palatial centre existed at Kato Zakro in the Siteia district on the eastern tip of Crete, and brought to light very important finds, some of which are unique and rival the finds of the great palaces of Knossos and Phaistos. . . . The Minoan town lies on a bay with a safe anchorage on the south-eastern tip of the island facing the east and the Nile Delta, a position clearly favourable for trade in importing raw materials and for exporting natural and manufactured products. It extended onto the slopes of the two opposing hills which surround a narrow but well-watered valley, at the seaward end of which the Palace was discovered. . . . Great success marked the discovery of the Palace which is the fourth in the series after the great Palaces of Knossos, Phaistos and Mallia and the first so far shown which has remained unplundered after the final catastrophe. This, it seems, took place suddenly, covering the whole city, at the end of the 16th century B.C. The catastrophe seems to have resulted from earthquakes of unique intensity accompanied by an extensive fire which burnt out most parts of the buildings. The great dressed stones of the façades were flung far apart and the upper storeys, mainly composed of large sun-dried bricks, fell to the ground, crushing under their weight the rooms below with all their wealth of objects. No disturbance took place in the Palace from that day to this. The destruction must

needs be synchronised with that which has been verified for most of the Minoan centres, about 1500 B.C. This followed, according to the prevalent theory of Professor Sp. Marinatos, the fearful eruption of the volcano of Thera (Santorin), and was accompanied by tidal waves

195 Minoan fruitstand vase from the palace of Kato Zakro

which swept the coasts of Crete. . . . Its position at the outlet of a narrow, well-watered valley between the two parts of the city on the opposing slopes was most convenient for commanding the routes, and controlling the whole city. Indeed, it would have been picturesque with its surrounding gardens. Today, orchards, banana and olive groves stretch out over the area. The main approach to the Palace was definitely from the seaward side, *i.e.* from the east, in which direction the main rooms face. The façade of great dressed stones uncovered on the south-west side had apparently been concealed in the last phase by the addition of a new industrial wing of which a small part has been excavated; this consisted of a small area with many openings round a court, a special section with a row of vats, a lavatory, and a plastered staircase leading to the upper floor. The arrangement of the main body of the Palace is labyrinthine, recalling in this the arrangement of the other Palaces. . . . From a treasury of an upper storey come four elephant tusks, apparently from the Syrian elephant, and six bronze ingots, precisely like the well-known talents from the Minoan villa of Hagia Triada near Phaistos. With them were found two dozen high-footed fruitstands *(Figure 195)*. In another room about 300 cups were discovered, together with a fine three-handled amphora decorated with very naturalistic octopuses. Two other rooms produced two small gold-riveted swords and a great bronze cauldron. Certain rooms had special magazines, built with mud-brick partitions. In one of these was discovered a tall circular stone table on a foot, apparently used in the adjacent room which was shown to be the shrine. This room had two benches, intended for the rites. Its use as a shrine was revealed by the discovery in it of 10 libation vases (rhytons) decorated with spirals and double axes and by the nature of the two adjacent rooms, one being a lustral basin of the type known from other Minoan palaces and villas, with a balustrade bearing a column, and steps descending to the bottom, whilst the other is the treasury of the shrine. It was, in fact, from these two compartments that there came the richest objects, constituting a treasure.

March 7, 1964

OBJECTS FROM KATO ZAKRO

By Nikolaos Platon, Director of the Acropolis Museum, Athens, and Field Director of the Kato Zakro Excavations

The objects in the Treasury were stored in chest-like compartments, nine in all, built of mud-brick around the chamber. The ritual character of most of the vessels is clear. There are vessels designed for libations or offerings, for the rite of "Holy Communion", for the adorning of the shrine, for its lighting, or else they are sacred emblems or symbols. The majority are brilliantly worked from various, mainly hard, stones such as basalt, diorite, porphyry, obsidian, alabaster, breccias, and variously coloured veined marbles. About 50 of these were collected, this due to the fact that the Palace had escaped pillage after its destruction. The Central Treasury of the Palace at Knossos produced only 17 such vases, the majority of which were very fragmentary. The Zakro vessels, however, are for the most part complete with handles, separate necks and rings. The rhytons are of conical or elongated oval shape; the finest is a unique vase of rock crystal with pulley-shaped neck, a handle of rock-crystal beads and a rim of fashioned crystal pieces and gilded faience. Three other rhytons were in the form of bulls' heads and of a lioness, the sacred animals of Minoan religion, and another is in the form of a large argonaut in faience. Amongst the finest vessels is a hemispherical one of basalt with carved vertical fluting, a fine ribbed rim and cylindrical handles with bronze attach-

196 A rhyton bull's head from Kato Zakro

veined marble and one of obsidian, the second known vase in this material, which is essentially volcanic glass; they have very elegant shapes with well-turned stem on circular base. One is quatrefoil, the other is horizontally fluted. Together with these vases were found three ritual hammers of veined marble. . . . The richest finds, however, were made in the light-well. Here was the other half of the carved rhyton and a stone rhyton in the form of a bull's head *(Figure 196)* similar to the famous rhyton from Knossos but smaller, yet of finer work-manship, especially of the curls which cover the greater part of the face. However, not all the parts were found and the horns were missing – which were perhaps of gilded wood – but sufficient was preserved for a restoration to be made in the Herakleion Museum workshops. The carved ovoid rhyton is of brilliant work-manship. It shows a mountain peak sanctuary, recognisable from the sacred horns placed upon it, the gate decorated with spirals and from the three altars beside it. Four small wild goats (*agrimi*) antithetically placed, are sitting at the top around what seems to be the aniconic form of the divinity, whilst two others are clambering up on to the rocks around the shrine with fine naturalistic movements. On the surface of the vase traces of gold leaf covering are preserved. The material is a grey stone with mica particles. This rhyton, which is the fourth stone vessel with relief scenes, is to be added to the three famous vases from Hagia Triada (The Harves-ter Vase, Boxer Vase and Chieftain Cup).

ments, and a most elegant jug of grey-white marble. An excellent handling of the material, especially the veined marbles, is to be observed of all these vessels.

Six high "Holy Communion" chalices or goblets derive particular significance from those represented on the well-known "Camp-Stool" Fresco from Knossos ("Libations Fresco") to which the "La Parisienne" fragment is known to belong. These chalices are of diorite, basalt,

May 9, 1964

IN THE DAWN OF RELIGION

By Mr. James Mellaart

The scene imagined takes place in a sanctuary of Chatal Huyuk VII, early in the 7th Millennium B.C. During one phase of a rite, probably funerary, a male skull is deposited in a basket below a huge bull's head, made of plaster, paint-ed and incorporating horns of an enormous wild bull (*Bos primigenius*), which is fixed on a post in the west wall of the shrine. Three priestesses, disguised as vultures – as in the wall-painting at the end of the room (north wall) – officiate while a fourth hooded figure of a woman, seated on the main platform, participates in her role of the man's wife or mother or that of the priestess directing the rite. Although the actual nature of the rite, the number of the participants, the effect desired, are of course imaginary, the existence of such rites in Neolithic Chatal Huyuk is beyond doubt. The funerary building and fittings, the costumes, etc., are all accounted for in the excavation. Rarely has so little been left to the imagination in an archaeological reconstruction of such a remote period. The sanctuary was built of mud-brick and plaster, roofed with wooden beams and matting, rush mats covered some of the platforms and a fire is lit on the hearth in the foreground. Entry to the building was gained through a porthole-like entrance, approached by steps in the far wall,

leading to a passage with stairs to the flat roof. Lighting was obtained through small square windows set high up in the west (and south) walls. Houses and shrines are alike in plan and structure but the latter are elaborately decorated with wall-paintings and reliefs, connected with the cult of fertility, ensuring the continuity of life in all its forms, both in this world and beyond the grave. Besides plain red and black panels, two others show elaborate textile-like designs (far corner) and a scene of vultures with human legs (disguised priestesses?) associated with a headless corpse on the north wall. Below it rest more human skulls, and on the east wall there is an elaborate group of bulls' heads, rams' heads, a row of breasts and a niche below, in front of which lies another skull. In the right foreground there is a horn-like shelf with a breast below from which protrudes the lower jaw of a gigantic wild boar, supported by a painted ram's head – a symbolic combination of life (ram, breasts) and death (boar).

June 27, 1964

THE ROMAN PALACE AT FISHBOURNE

By Barry Cunliffe, F.S.A., Director of the Excavations

The third season of excavations at Fishbourne has brought into focus for the first time the extent and elaboration of the great masonry building put up in about A.D. 75, which we must now unashamedly call a palace. In the first season, when the future of the site was unknown, part of the east wing and the eastern part of the north wing were rapidly explored by means of trial trenching. This was followed in the second year by a large-scale area excavation over the east wing to examine a most important series of timber buildings which lay beneath the floors of the masonry structure.

In the summer of 1963, secure in the

knowledge that the land now belonged to the Sussex Archaeological Trust, work began on the detailed examination of the unexplored parts of the great building. As a result of this work we now know that the masonry building occupied about six acres of land, on the north shore of an inlet from Chichester harbour, and consisted of a large central courtyard, some 250 feet by 320 feet, surrounded by a continuous colonnade beyond which were arranged the three wings of the building; the nature of the fourth (south) side is at present unknown. . . . In this area two new mosaics of the A.D. 75 phase were uncovered. Both bore black and white geometric designs and both were in rooms which had later served as workshops. In consequence they had been allowed to wear out and only later were patched roughly with areas of pink cement. In the centre part of the wing a large mosaic, part of which had been seen in 1961, was completely excavated. In spite of some damage, it was the best preserved of the early series of floors and its intricate, partly three-dimensional motifs demonstrate well the degree of sophistication which the owner of the house expected. . . .

The new mosaic in Room 3 *(Plate 50, p. 350)* was far more elaborate. It was made up of a central circular panel flanked by four semi-circles and four quarter circles set within a geometric surround. The centre circle depicts a cupid holding a trident and sitting astride a dolphin. The quality of its workmanship, though adequate, does not compare with the fabulous sea beasts with their remarkable vitality and poise which fill the half circles. An amusing sign of the mosaicist's originality appears in the tendril border along the top of the floor. Here he has broken the leaf of one of the tendrils and placed on it a small black bird. Although the building at this time contained elaborate floors, much of its architectural magnificence had been ruined by flues pouring smoke into the courtyard and by the complete demolition of the large courtyard in the east wing to make way for a bath building. At the beginning of the 3rd century steps were taken to restore some of the former splendours.

October 31, 1964

MASADA

By Professor Yigael Yadin of the Hebrew University, Jerusalem, and Director of the Excavation

We had to face enormous administrative problems. We pitched 40 tents for 200 members of the expedition west of Masada, where the ascent is easier, near the Roman General Silva's camp – and had to be satisfied with an inferior site since Silva had first choice and he chose well. Water, food and equipment had to be brought over long distances, through roadless desert terrain. Cable-ferries had to be built for lifting the equipment to the top of Masada. To the difficult conditions were added an uncommonly hard winter with heavy rains and storms. We had some compensation, however, in witnessing rare waterfalls in the desert, such as those which in ancient times fed Herod's great water reservoirs.

If we managed to pull through seven months of work, it was due to the enthusiasm of the thousands of volunteers from 28 countries, the youth movements of Israel and last, but not least, the help of the Israel Defence Forces. . . .

It is thanks to young amateur explorers from the *kibbutsim* of Israel that the palace was correctly identified in the early fifties as the extraordinary complex of buildings on the northern bluff of the rock beneath the casemate wall encircling the top of Masada. Now that we have excavated it completely, this three-tiered "hanging palace" can best be described as the villa-palace of Herod. It is built on the very edge of the precipice and is the only spot on Masada which enjoys both constant shade and shelter from the searing desert winds.

The living quarters proper were on the upper terrace. They consisted of only four rooms built on the two flanks of a covered portico; their floors were decorated with black and white mosaics of simple geometric patterns. Walls and ceilings were ornamented with frescoes and stuccos, some of them with floral designs. The northern part of this terrace once held a magnificent semi-circular colonnade. . . .

The centre terrace was for rest and leisure, boasting a circular pavilion and a covered colonnade to its south. In plan it very much resembles the type of buildings depicted on some of the frescoes of Pompeii and on the false façades of the rock-cut tombs of Petra, which may belong to the same period.

The bottom terrace is the best preserved and was the *pièce de resistance* of the whole edifice. Here we discovered the wall paintings – still in good condition – which adorned the lower parts of both the exterior and interior colonnades, surrounding the central square area, which may have been covered. The frescoes are not unlike other Herodian ones discovered in Caesarea, Samaria, Jericho, and Herodium, all of which aim to imitate a marble dado. On the very precipice on the eastern wing of this terrace, we found a small – but well built – bath complex, with its hypocaust and cold bath. . . .

The great public bath

A great surprise awaited us when west of the store-rooms we discovered a public bath, in the Roman style, one of the biggest of its kind ever found in the Holy Land, and definitely the best preserved (in comparison to those of Jericho and Herodium) with all its installations and lavish adornments. The walls of the hot (calidarium), tepid (tepidarium) and dressing (apodyterium) rooms were all covered with frescoes, and their floors were made of beautifully set black and white tiles, in *opus sectile*. . . .

The city wall and its last defenders

Our greatest surprise – and our most important finds – awaited us in the chambers of the fortress's casemate wall. This wall encircles Masada – except for the northern palace – and is about 1300 metres in length. Its casemates vary in length from 6 to about 30 metres.

When the Zealots captured Masada in A.D. 66

they used the many chambers in the wall as living quarters for themselves and their families – since the public buildings erected by Herod were unsuitable for such a purpose – averaging one to four families per room, according to its size. To these constructional casemates they added the necessary living appurtenances, such as stoves, shelves, basins, bins and partition walls. Here we discovered large quantities of domestic utensils as well as more than a thousand coins (bringing the total of coins found by us to 2000), amongst them a rare cache of 17 silver shekels of the Revolt ("Jerusalem the Holy – Shekel of Israel"), the first ever to be found in a stratified archaeological context. Amongst them even three shekels of the rare "year five", the last to be struck before the fall of the Temple in A.D. 70. Up to this discovery only six specimens were known of this year. . . .

The Synagogue (?) and the Ritual-bath (Miqveh)

Two interesting buildings – practically the only ones which were added by the Zealots to the Herodian buildings – were also found within the fortress wall, and both of them show, once more, that the defenders were very observant Jews. One is a rectangular hall with two rows of columns, to which the Zealots added mud benches in four rows, one on top of the other, on all sides, except in the west facing Jerusalem, where there is only one bench. The building is orientated towards Jerusalem, the entrance being from the east. It was here that we found an *ostracon* with the inscription "priestly tithe" as well as more than 20 clay oil lamps and many glass vessels. I believe it may have been a synagogue, built in the manner of the theatre-like assembly houses of the times. If I am right, then this is not only the earliest synagogue known, but the only one to survive from the times of the second temple.

The other is a chamber in the wall, turned into a ritual-bath (Miqveh) with its three basins or baths, supplied, as required by the *halakha* (the religious law), also by rainwater. Outside, the Zealots added a portico and dressing rooms. In one, scores of coins of the Revolt were found scattered on the floor, evidently entrance fees.

The discovery of the ritual-bath created a stir amongst the rabbis in Israel (it being the only Miqveh to survive from that period) and we were honoured by a visit of two of the greatest authorities on the subject. Their investigations confirmed our assumptions that the Miqveh was built strictly according to the meticulous rules of the *halakha.*

1965

In this year as well as the gold treasure found by Professor Marinatos near Pylos, we published articles on: Etruscan-Phoenician bilingual inscriptions found on gold sheets at Pyrgi in Italy; the re-opening of the Mohenjo-daro excavations; work at Iasos in Caria; and a Minoan tomb near Knossos.

December 4, 1965

A GOLD TREASURE FROM THE REALM OF NESTOR

By Dr. Spyridon Marinatos, Professor of Archaeology, University of Athens

Among the sites that have been found, the most prominent is that of Peristeria ("dove-hill") about 11 kilometres inland of the coastal town of Kyparissia in Triphylia. Soon after its discovery in 1960, Peristeria was identified as the most prominent centre of Mycenaean culture in the western Peloponnese, and thus comparable with Mycenae itself on the eastern side. . . .

Three *tholos* tombs were discovered inside the acropolis. The first of these is the most spacious and monumental vaulted tomb after the Treasuries of Atreus and Clytemnestra at Mycenae and the Treasury of Minyas at Orchomenos. Its inner diameter is over 12 metres, the façade is of ashlar masonry in *poros* stone, which must have been brought from a distant quarry and the door is 5·10 metres high and 2·39 metres wide. On its left doorjamb two incised Knossian masons' marks survive. . . .

Tomb two was a little inferior in size and in exterior appearance. Near it, to the west, a third and yet smaller tomb appeared. However – and this was a most curious feature – an imposing circular wall, almost exactly 2 metres thick, enclosed these two last tombs. It was not clear why this monumental wall should have been erected so near to the *tholos* tombs as to destroy them in part. There were several explanations possible. This year we decided to act on the most optimistic possible. Could we explain this wall as being an enclosure for older shaft graves, as was the case at Mycenae?

This year, therefore, we followed the semi-circular wall on its exterior side. The western extremity ends in a pointed corner and, inside it, to the left, appears the still surviving part of *tholos* three. . . . The floor consisted, partly and on the north side, of the local hard conglomerate rock and partly of hard earth. We decided to excavate beneath this floor and opened up two trenches in cross form.

Soon we began to find pieces of gold sheet, beads of semi-precious stones, and other objects – which encouraged us. Then, close to the south side of what may be described as an irregular shaft, 2·70 metres long and 80 to 90 centimetres wide, a gold bowl appeared, then a gold "diadem", and then a second goblet, the biggest of them all. Two days later gold goblet no. three appeared, standing by itself about 50 centimetres to the south of the rest of the treasure. In all, throughout the shaft a great deal of gold sheet and several gold objects were found. The stony ground underneath the treasure was covered with large pieces of gold sheet, as if a gold-covered wooden chest or basket or even a textile had contained the precious objects. . . .

A group of minor objects include: gold capsules partly filled with a blue material and fastened to a larger piece of gold sheet; seven cylindrical gold tubes fitted together which may be the guide tubes of composite necklaces consisting of several kinds of small beads; heart-shaped pieces of gold sheet impressed with rosettes and carrying suspension hooks; and impressed triton-shells. Such shells, either natural or imitated in several materials, served as ceremonial vases. Bird shapes were also found. One (with the beak missing) represents an eagle and is a divine being, as shown by the sacral spiral lock on the neck. Of the other bird there is no question of doubt. Much later it becomes that owl which is the symbol of Athene, but at this period it may be described as the typical bird of the Pylos excavations at Kako-vatos, the Palace of Englianos, and here. . . .

In one pleasant object, of which five examples were found, the wings of a butterfly, birds' heads, and the sacral ivy motif are amalgamated. This may be an emblem of the soul. In Greek the word for butterfly is *psyche*, which also means "soul". Similar fantastic creatures are found, though a little later in date, in clay sealings found at Zakro in Crete.

1966

This year was outstanding for three articles by James Mellaart on the frescoes and other finds at Čatal Hüyük

May 28, 1966

CHATAL HUYUK

By James Mellaart, B.A., F.S.A., Lecturer in Anatolian Archaeology in the University of London

The main aim of the 1965 expedition was to make a sounding into the deepest levels of the mound. . . .

To our great surprise we found pottery in every building-level right down to level XIII, so that no pre-pottery periods have yet been reached. This makes the Chatal Huyuk pottery the earliest in the Near East, as level XII must probably be dated to about 6800 B.C., plus or minus 100 years. There is no reason yet to assume that this is the earliest pottery at Chatal Huyuk and it is by no means unlikely that pottery was in use at this site from 7000 B.C. As the earliest pottery in Iran, found at Tepe Guran, probably belongs to about 6500 B.C., and that of south Syria and north Palestine is not earlier than about 6000 B.C., it looks as if pottery was first invented in Turkey, from where it spread to north Syria. This early pottery of Chatal Huyuk does not belong to the dark burnished group, but is a heavy cream-coloured ware, which only in level VII – about 6200 B.C. – gives way to the fine dark burnished wares that also extend to Syria. . . .

Also in the earliest phase there was a small panel of orange plaster with a circular mud-plastered hole in the centre set against the north wall. This is similar to a painted panel with a similar depression in the floor found in Hacilar Aceramic 2 (which is considerably earlier in date). It may have been a hole used for libations and at a depth of two feet below it was found the richly adorned cinnabar-stained body of a small girl, buried in a basket. Bracelets of beads, necklaces of apatite (blue and green), dentalium shells, and limestone with deer teeth and mother of pearl pendants were found with this burial. The hole in the orange plaster floor was too small for the insertion of the burial and this supports the idea that it was used for libations to the buried child.

Directly adjacent to this burial and overlying floor was a raised structure, a small platform about two feet long, one foot wide, and eight inches high, the eastern and southern sides of which had been painted in what appeared to be fantastic Hacilar patterns in red on cream, in three panels separated by polychrome bands in black and red on cream. . . .

The function of this painted platform was revealed when, at a depth three feet below it, we found one of the most remarkable ochre burials at Chatal Huyuk. In a shallow oval pit was placed the dismembered body of a woman in what seems to have been a seated position with detached head set on top of the body. She was buried with a mace – unique in female burials and evidently a sign of authority – and she was richly provided with necklaces, bracelets, rings of various stones, shell, deer teeth, and mother of pearl pendants. What was, however, the most remarkable feature was that this important personage was wrapped in fibres, probably matting, in which were deposited the skulls and legbones of a great number of common house mice (*Mus musculus*), the significance of which escapes one. It would appear that this shrine was constructed to commemorate the burials of a very important person – perhaps a chief priestess – and her daughter. Nothing similar has yet been found elsewhere.

June 4, 1966

THE LEOPARD SHRINES OF CHATAL HUYUK

By James Mellaart, B.A., F.S.A., Lecturer in Anatolian Archaeology in the University of London

A particularly fine shrine of level VII was found directly below the level VI leopard shrine found in 1963, and was better preserved. It was decorated with leopards in relief: a single one with a boldly modelled head on the east wall and a pair, probably male and female, on the north wall above two platforms. Their heads had been damaged by graves of level VI, and the top painted layer had not been covered with white plaster before the building was filled in. As expected these leopards were covered by a number of different painted layers – seven in all – of which only the earliest, in plain pink, bore no patterns. The others were painted in black on white with small touches of red for eyes, mouth, claws, and tips of the tails. The stylised decorations of the top layer on the leopards were rectangles containing St Andrew's crosses, those of the second from the top poorly preserved rosettes, the third open rosettes, the fourth rosettes with dots on leopards with black claws, the fifth reverted to coarsely painted squares with St Andrew crosses, and the sixth was decorated with lip patterns.

June 11, 1966

THE TEASING OF THE GREAT BEASTS

By James Mellaart, B.A., F.S.A., Lecturer in Anatolian Archaeology in the University of London

A hunting shrine decorated with lively pictures of dancers in leopard skins, figures of a large bull, and several red deer was found at level III of Chatal Huyuk during the first season of excavations in 1961. Nothing similar was found at the site until 1965, when, again by chance, a new wheelbarrow passage struck the north wall of a very similar building of level V, which dates from about 5850 B.C., or about a century earlier in date than level III.

It is the first shrine to be uncovered in this building-level and it was tolerably well preserved, in spite of numerous animal holes, roots, and silica concretions. It consisted of a main room about 18 feet square, with an antechamber which had a service hatch from the adjacent kitchen. Two long storerooms flanked its western side, beyond which lay a courtyard. Two bucrania or bull pillars originally stood on the edge of the eastern platforms of the main room, but they had been removed when the building was filled in. Apart from a spatula and a few bits of obsidian, no objects were found in this building, which was unburnt.

The wall-paintings, of which there was fortunately only a single layer, had been faced over with thick layers of white plaster, and they covered the greater part of all four walls – which is unusual – to a height of about 4 feet. The preservation was unequal, for whereas mineral pigments were used in painting the animals and some of the simpler figures, organic colours were used for most of the elaborately dressed figures, and upon exposure the flesh-coloured bodies turned brown and the pinks either turned grey or faded completely. It should be borne in mind that all wall-paintings at Chatal Huyuk are not frescoes but are painted in various colours without a medium on fine white mud, obtained from the bottom of the Pleistocene lake.

The subjects depicted are rich and varied, the draughtsmanship extremely lively and individualistic, and not less than five different hands may be observed. The subject of the paintings is ritual baiting of the main food animals by pulling their tongue or tail and by jumping on their back; and the importance of the animals is shown by their exaggerated size. Hunting scenes in the proper sense do not occur; no animal is killed or even wounded, even if the men are armed with bows, clubs, axes, or hunting nets. The hunters are dressed in festive costumes far more elaborate than those depicted in the level III shrine; they wear skins and bonnets of leopard skin, black goat skins or cattle skins with one, two, or three tails or black feathers – perhaps crane feathers – stuck onto leopard-skin tails. Several figures are bichrome like medieval pages, red and black, red and pink, black and white, or all black. Others are cream-coloured, but most are red or pink. Heads are most individualistic, especially in the bearded group around a stag on the west wall.

Women also occur; fat, with pendant breasts and black-painted arm-pits. There are even a few children portrayed and one large figure may represent a deity, presiding over what looks like a sexual scene. The animals include an enormous wild bull, two male red deer, a deer whose head was modelled in relief and is now lost, a fallow deer with broad antlers, four wild boar, one bear, a wolf, a pair of cranes, a pair of onagers, a frieze of wild asses (not horses), and several dogs. Finally there is a large damaged pink feline, without spots and therefore probably a lion.

The central figure is the enormous red bull (*Plate 51, p. 351*), placed as usual on the north wall and surrounded by hunters approaching from left and right. Below the bull there are many figures in red with a dog and a frieze of long-necked donkeys which continues onto the west wall. On the northern part of the west wall there are numerous figures, a fallow deer, and a recumbent deer in red outlined in orange and with a modelled head that is now lost. Below, a big wild boar with black outline, bristles, tail, and hoofs is cornered by two men holding nets. Beyond a wooden post on the west wall there is a further panel showing a red deer stag baited by a different group of bearded men in leopard and goat skins, drawn with great humour and naturalistic observation.

Returning to the north wall, east of the bull another post separates a further panel on the right, which shows a red deer stag baited by men, and, below, the teasing of a wild boar, once again approached from the right by a man holding a net. These scenes continue onto the east wall, divided into two registers. In the upper register there is another boar-baiting scene and in the lower one a bear is subjected to the same treatment. Further along the wall there is a procession of gaily dressed hunters in the upper register, whereas in the lower only their leopard skins survive. At the far end of the panel are a timid dog and a snarling wolf. Once again a wooden post intervenes. Beyond it in the upper panel is a scene of a group of men surrounding a feline, probably a lion, and this scene overlaps onto the south wall where another wild boar, a pair of black cranes, and a delightful group of two onagers is portrayed. Below this is an enigmatic scene – with, possibly, a deity; several figures, of which one is outstretched, two others hold their arms to shield their view – from the deity? – and one carrying a basket; and finally a lascivious female.

1967–70

In addition to the articles (quoted) by Dr. V. Karageorghis on his discoveries at Salamis in Cyprus, we published important pieces on Urartian discoveries near Lake Sevan in Russian Armenia; and a remarkable Persian silver gilt rhyton of Sassanian date, acquired by the Cleveland Museum of Art, Ohio.

November 18, 1967

KING NICOCREON'S CENOTAPH

By Dr. Vassos Karageorghis, Director of Antiquities of Cyprus

The tumulus was divided in equal segments and we started excavating from the top, removing the horizontal layers of the soil which formed the mound. . . .

But with our method of excavation, which admittedly demanded time and considerable expense, we could not miss a structure which was well off the centre of the rocky platform of the base, at the southern part. This structure, built entirely of sun-dried mud-bricks, has the form of a rectangular exedra, measuring 11·50 metres by 17 metres and is 1 metre high; it is surrounded on all four sides by a staircase of four steps, but in the middle of the western (short) side there is a ramp, which gives access to the flat top of the exedra. The steps all round the exedra and the vertical side walls of the ramp are covered with plaster imitating marble. . . .

Near the centre of the horizontal top of the exedra, where there were distinct traces of a large fire, there was a mound of rubble stone, about 2 metres high and 5·70 metres in diameter. All round this mound there were 16 holes in the mud-brick floor, symmetrically arranged in a quadrangle. The holes were rectangular, about 40 metres deep, and contained large pieces of semi-carbonised wood. The mound, which also contained pieces of charcoal, fragments of baked clay and large numbers of iron nails, covered a large pyre, surrounded by a boundary wall of stones. The

thick layer of ashes and charcoal contained a large number of objects, of which we mention the most important: more than 100 bottles in the form of alabastra, both in clay and alabaster. Those in clay were either gilded or painted in white, black, purple, and blue. There were also numerous beads of gilded clay, as well as myrtle leaves of gilded bronze. These evidently formed part of wreaths such as those which are usually found round early Hellenistic hydriae containing the incinerated remains of the dead. Traces of gold wreaths were also found, consisting of gold rosettes and leaves of gold. Most of these, however, were melted on the pyre and have been collected from its bottom in the form of drops. Apart from the large numbers of iron nails of various sizes there were also numerous iron arm-bands of shields, bearing an embossed decoration, mainly floral, and other attachments which may well belong to shields too. The body of the shields, obviously of leather and wood, must have perished on the pyre. There were also iron strigils, some of them gilded, as well as iron spearheads. From the ashes of the pyre as well as from the floor all round it were collected quantities of carbonised cereals, almonds, figs, and grapes. But perhaps the most important of all the finds on the pyre were the fragments of statues of unbaked clay which were hardened on the fire; these included five heads, almost life size, four of men and one of a woman. There were many more than five statues, however, of which various members of the bodies have been found, especially feet and arms. The torsos were not moulded, but draped, and were crudely shaped round wooden poles which have left their traces in the clay. In several cases iron nails were also found across the traces of the wooden poles, inside the baked clay; these were obviously used by the artist so that the clay could adhere easily and effectively to the wood. Two of the male heads represent rather elderly persons, with their individual facial characteristics clearly accentuated. The face is painted red and the hair black. The other two male heads *(Figure 197)* of young persons are idealised; they have all the characteristics of the style of the Greek sculptor Lysippos, a fact which helps to date the pyre to the end of the fourth century B.C. This date is also confirmed by the pottery and the small objects, e.g. the gilded wreaths and the painted alabastra, which recall comparable objects from Alexandria of the early Hellenistic period.

Systematic research under the exedra (entirely built of mud-bricks) did not bring to light any signs of a burial, neither a tomb nor any funerary urn. In fact there were no traces whatsoever of a skeleton, incinerated or inhumated. That the whole structure, on the other hand, with the tumulus and the offerings should be associated with a ceremony in honour of the dead cannot be doubted. The dead, moreover, considering the tumulus, the monumental exedra, and the rich offerings, could be identified only with a very important Salaminian, no doubt a king. Having in mind the more or less precise date indicated by the style of the statues, the end of the fourth century, we suggest that this tumulus may be associated with the last king of Salamis, Nicocreon, who committed suicide in 311 B.C. together with all the members of his family, and was buried under the burnt ruins of the palace, as Greek authors tell us. . . .

The Salaminians, in order to honour a brave king, or in order to expiate his soul out of fear

(as he had suffered a violent death), offered him a funerary pyre, which is due to the soul of mortals, together with all the honours and offerings which are due to a soldier-king. We suggest that the statues of clay, of which only a

197 One of the idealised young male heads found near King Nicocreon's funereal pyre

few fragments survived, were erected during the funerary ceremony round the pyre, possibly on 16 poles of which traces have been found round the pyre in holes. They probably represented the members of the royal family – hence the portrait heads – whose images could thus partake in the honours of the funerary rites. The pyre destroyed the wooden poles, the statues fell – some of the heads were flattened as they fell on the ground before being hardened by the fire. The whole was then piled up – including the statues and the offerings – and covered under a small mound of mud-bricks and rubble, and then by the tumulus, a monument for future generations, according to Homer.

December 16, 1967

UNIQUE IVORIES FROM CYPRUS

By Dr. Vassos Karageorghis

This chamber, lying within the limits of the royal necropolis of Salamis, with a monolith at its roof still visible above ground, had long been looted, but we excavated in front of its chamber. This is Tomb 79 in our register. We uncovered the monumental façade of the chamber and the large *dromos* in front of it, measuring about 13 metres in width and 20 metres in length. As in the other royal tombs of the same area of the necropolis, we found that the soil-filling of the *dromos*, which had never been touched by the looters, preserved an extraordinary wealth of objects.

Stratigraphic observation ascertained that the tomb was used twice at the very end of the eighth century B.C., within a very short period as we shall see below. During the first burial period, which was the richest, two chariots were sacrificed in honour of the dead: one was a four-horse chariot, and the other a hearse on which the body was transported to the tomb. The skeletons of the horses associated with these vehicles had already been disturbed when at the time of the second burial, shortly after the first, these were wheeled away to make room for the two vehicles of the second burial. Skeletons of horses used in the latter were found *in situ*.

The four-horse chariot was of wood, which decayed but left its impressions in the soil, and by careful excavation we have been able to rescue all the evidence about the detailed construction of the vehicle. The metallic parts, however, survived *in situ*. These include two magnificent lynch-pins, decorated at their lower part with a large bronze head of a sphinx, which is surmounted at the upper part by the bronze figure of a fully armed warrior. The latter was hollow and served also as a rattle. The warrior wears a crested helmet, a scaled cuirass decorated with inlaid blue glass, and is armed with a long sword hanging from a belt across his chest. The total length of these lynch-pins is 56 centimetres, and they may well be among the largest ever found. Obviously they were intended for the funerary ceremony and not for everyday use.

The hearse preserved on its four corners four bronze heads of lions and one in front, in the middle, all inserted in wooden beams which decayed.

Equally impressive were the bronzes which formed the gear of the six horses of the above vehicles. These had been piled up in a corner near the façade of the chamber at the time of the second burial. They included magnificent breastplates, with a rich embossed decoration of sphinxes, griffins, and other monsters, as well as gods and heroes of Oriental mythology; front bands, richly decorated with animal and human figures embossed on their entire surface, such as the winged God El, couchant lions, winged solar discs etc; blinkers decorated with animal figures, for instance sphinxes, striding over slaves in the well-known Egyptian fashion of the victorious king striding over his enemies; while some others were decorated with lions attacking bulls.

198 Ivory from Salamis showing the Egyptian god Heh

Four side-pendant ornaments for horses have been found, two of them decorated with crescent and disc ornaments, and the other two with complicated compositions of animals all round the nude figure of Ishtar, in the attitude of the *potnia theron* (the lady of the wild beasts). . . .

The bronzes associated with the chariots and horses of the second burial were less extrovert in their decoration. But the yokes of these chariots preserved their bronze standards *in situ*, and for the first time we are now able to identify the exact character of these flower-shaped banners or standards which we see in Oriental representations. These, no doubt, were also used to decorate a chariot solely during the funerary ceremony. . . .

The *dromos* of Tomb 79 has also produced a large number of ivory objects of unrivalled beauty, such as were never found in Cyprus before. We know how greatly ivory objects, especially furniture, were appreciated in the ancient world, and how much they were admired by Homer. Ivory furniture must have been some sort of a measure for people's wealth – "who lie upon beds of ivory". Such ivory furniture must have been made in one or more ateliers in Phoenicia and exported to the courts of the Near East.

Of the ivory objects from the *dromos* of Tomb 79 particular mention should be made of a throne of wood, dressed all over with thin ivory panels, dowelled on the wood. The total height of the throne is 90 centimetres, and its curved backrest is decorated at the inside with nineteen bands of ivory. They are alternately plain and covered with a guilloche pattern in two vertical rows, recalling in this respect the Homeric description of Penelope's throne with its spiral decoration. At the lower part of the back-rest, near the seat, there are two horizontal friezes of *anthemia*, applied on a plain plaque. The upper part of the back-rest had a broad ivory plaque, gilded with a very thin sheet of gold, on which one may still see embossed scale-patterns. We know that thrones decorated with ivory and gold were known also to the Mycenaeans, as they are often mentioned in the tablets of the Palaces of Pylos.

There must have been other pieces of ivory furniture in the *dromos*, of which only fragments survive. These included a bed, of which large bands of ivory and one leg survived. The leg terminates in the shape of a lion's hoof, with hollow sockets which contained blue glass for the claws. Gilded ivory flowers and blue glass encrustations also formed part of the decoration of the bed.

There were other panels of ivory, probably belonging to furniture or forming independent

decorative units, carved in relief or in open-work. The former included two panels consisting of smaller plaques, one decorated with antithetic sphinxes standing on either side of a flower motif, wearing gilded aprons, and the other decorated with figures of the god Heh with gilded trousers *(Figure 198)*, seated in front of a branch of a palm tree from which hangs the symbol *ankh*. The style of the carving is Egyptianising Phoenician, recalling in many respects the ivories from the palace of Nimrud. Other ivory panels carved in relief are decorated with flower motifs which are inlaid with blue glass.

There are two plaques carved in openwork. One represents a composite flower, meant to be seen from both sides, decorated with inlaid blue glass, and thin gold on the cloisons which contained the glass. The most exquisite, however, of all the ivories from this tomb is the second plaque *(Figure 199)*, with a winged sphinx wearing the two crowns of Egypt, decorated with blue and brown paste within gilded cloisons. Both sides of the plaque are carved, in a style which equals, if not surpasses, the best of the Nimrud ivories found by Professor Mallowan and recorded in *The Illustrated London News*.

199 Ivory from Salamis of a winged sphinx encrusted and worked on both sides

January 20, 1968

LEPENSKI VIR 7000 YEARS AGO

By Dr. Dragoslav Srejović

The prehistoric settlement at Lepenski Vir ("The Whirlpool of Lepena") is situated about 1½ kilometres from the point where the Boljetinska river flows into the Danube, or about 14½ kilometres up the Danube from Donji Milanovać. . . .

The natural outline of the site of the settlement is clearly indicated in the Iron Gate landscape. It is a steep amphitheatre-like recess on the bank, enclosed on the western side by high cliffs and cut off on the eastern side by the Danube. It is accessible only by a narrow passageway from the south, from the mouth of the Boljetinska river, where there is a stretch of level, fertile land. . . .

The cultural layer at Lepenski Vir, up to

3·5 metres thick at places, presents a very interesting picture. Within three distinctly separated cultural horizons, there is a series of superimposed remains of eight settlements with separate layouts, graves, and equipment. . . .

The earliest settlement is built on a hard base of limestone rocks covered with a thin layer of unstratified yellow sand deposited probably by wind. The basic layout of the original settlement was determined by the spatially limited U-shaped recess which descends steeply towards the Danube. . . .

It seems that towards the end of this cultural phase considerable climatic oscillations took place. It is probable that the level of the Danube also suddenly rose at that time, for the remains of the new settlement were found chiefly on the higher parts of the U-shaped recess, within a uniform deposit whose thickness varies from 0·30 to 0·50 metres (Lepenski Vir II). This later settlement does not exceed the boundaries of the older settlements, but its houses are considerably less numerous and spaced wider. The two latest habitation horizons, which form the top part of the cultural layer at the depth of between 1·15 and 0·30 metres (Lepenski Vir III a, b) overlie entirely the earlier settlements from Levels I and II, and even stretch beyond their south and north boundaries to include the whole strip of level ground along the bank of the Danube.

The particular significance of the discovery of the Lepenski Vir site proceeds from the fact that under the Early Neolithic settlements (Lepenski Vir III a, b) containing material of the well-known Starčevo-Körös-Criş culture, monuments have been discovered of a hitherto unknown culture and art: settlements built in a planned way (Lepenski Vir I, II) with impressive architectural remains and monumental stone sculptures. . . .

The material found within houses indicates that all the buildings had a double function – that is, they include both an area designated for the performance of magic and religious rites, and a working and dwelling area. The fireplace with the sculptures forms the core of the sacral area. This close connection between the sacral and dwelling areas and their integration into one architectural whole seems to suggest a close relationship between the higher forces and man, and even, in a certain sense, the equality of their powers.

The stereotyped trapezoid form of the house plans is in fact derived from the natural form of the U-shaped recess in which the settlement is situated. The lateral sides of the houses are almost parallel with the divergent wings of the recess. The longer, slightly curved parallel sides face the Danube and the shorter ones are dug in and wedged into the steep side of the hill. Each house is therefore harmoniously and organically integrated into the configuration of the terrain and emphasises its contours, transforming, as it were, its amorphous character into a neat architectural form. . . .

The sculptures found on the floors of the houses (54 in all) are permeated by the same rationalism tempered by a humanistic spirit. In the earliest sculptures the modelling remains always closed within the shape of the river boulder, which means that the artist alters the natural form only in so far as it does not interfere with its original appearance. . . .

The sculptures discovered in Lepenski Vir I and II can be divided into two groups according to their style and motifs; figural sculptures modelled in a naturalistic manner, sometimes with pronounced expressionistic features (*Plate 52, p. 352*), and sculptures which apparently represent only abstract arabesques. . . .

The austere, stereotyped forms of the Lepenski Vir architecture and sculpture show that their makers lived in social relationships which completely subjected the individual to the laws of the community, in the atmosphere of numerous taboos prescribed by custom or magic, and in complete economic dependence on the community.

February 3, 1968

LEPENSKI VIR

By Dr. Dragoslav Srejović

Settlements I and II were inhabited in a period of cold and dry Boreal climate, while those of IIIa and IIIb were built in the time of the warm Atlantic phase.

The buildings associated with horizons IIIa and IIIb have been only partly preserved. Stone is no longer the basic building material. In horizon IIIa there are underground dwellings which sometimes – in the level area along the bank of the Danube – descend to the floors of layer I houses *(Figure 200)*. The latest, IIIb settlement contains quadrangular huts of mud. Inside them, on the floor of beaten earth, there is frequently a stove with a U-shaped base of rubble and a dome of clay. Stone sculptures, distinguished by their decorative and monumental character in Lepenski Vir II, completely disappear, but the pottery shows a surprising wealth of forms and techniques of decoration. In addition to large *pithoi* for the storage of grain there appear spherical bowls, cups on a low foot, ball-shaped vessels without moulded bottom, *amphorae* with a cylindrical neck, large bowls and sacrificial vessels with a large recipient on a quadrangular perforated foot.

In addition to the burnished monochrome ware there appear vessels with rough external surface, or pottery decorated with impressions of fingers and nails, with incised geometric patterns, or with white (Phase IIIa) and, later (Phase IIIb), dark painted ornaments on red ground. Numerous polished stone axes, bone tools and pendants of clay, marble or bone complete the otherwise very rich equipment from these latest habitation levels. . . . It is impossible to account for the culture discovered at Lepenski Vir by these remote geographical and stylistic analogies. The basic forms of its architecture and sculpture are so exceptional that their significance at the present moment is but that of solitary messages which reveal only the strong and independent spirit of the early prehistoric Danubian culture.

200 Lepenski Vir: Phase IIIa grave dug down into Phase I

May 4, 1968

THE GREAT TUMULUS AT KNOWTH

By Dr. George Eogan

Around 3000 B.C. a sophisticated civilisation developed in the Iberian peninsula. These semi-urban people were metal users, they sometimes lived in well fortified towns, and buried their dead in chamber tombs outside the town walls. This passage-grave civilisation spread north-wards first of all to Brittany and then to Ireland, where in the east of the country a few miles inland, in the valley of the River Boyne in County Meath, we find one of its earliest and most striking manifestations. The Brugh na Boinne passage-grave cemetery is one of Europe's most notable groups of prehistoric megalithic tombs. Not only does it contain the three massive and internationally known sites of Dowth, Newgrange, and Knowth but these only form part of a large cemetery complex.

Knowth is situated at the western end of the cemetery and occupies the summit of a low hill around 200 feet above sea-level. Excavations started in 1962, and have been in progress each season since then. Their aim is to investigate an area of up to six and a half acres. To date almost two-thirds of the perimeter of the large tumulus and about two acres of the surrounding area have been investigated. There eleven smaller megalithic tombs have been discovered.

The large tumulus is almost circular in plan, it averages 100 yards in diameter and around 36 feet in maximum height. Excavation has established that very considerable care and planning went into its construction. The method used was to lay down in an ordered fashion layers of sod, clay, stones, and shale. Each layer was deposited in blanket-like fashion and its deposition was complete all over the site before the next one went on. From the edge each stratum thickens inwards. This composite mound is delimited by a series of kerb stones that are placed end to end. Some of these are up

to 6 feet in length and 4 feet in height. On the outer face most are highly decorated. The designs were applied by the pecking technique but sometimes incision was also used.

201 *Aerial photograph of the great tumulus tomb of Knowth*

In the main the motifs consist of concentric circles, both single and multiple gapped circles, triangles, zig-zags, and spirals. The art found on the kerb stones is strictly non-representational, and although the motifs keep recurring the artist or artists nevertheless varied the designs from stone to stone so that each is an individual work of art. Among the kerb stones there is one, on the west side, that is uniquely decorated with a series of concentric rectangles and a vertical line down the centre. Leading up to this stone from either side the kerbs become larger and are more elaborately decorated. In addition the line of the kerb swings inwards so as to leave the uniquely decorated member set in from what would have been a circle had not the kerbs changed course.

202 Stone with anthropomorphic design gives the impression of standing guard over the entrance to the burial chamber in the tumulus at Knowth

This is the kerb stone before the entrance to the tomb. Outside the entrance a combination of the incurving kerb on the inside and an arc of spaced stones on the outside forms a sort of elliptical-shaped area nearly 23 yards long. Within this area there are three semi-circular and one circular setting of small stones. The interior of the latter setting is paved with quartz.

The entrance to the tomb was discovered on the evening of July 11, 1967. It faces west and it is between 113 and 114 feet in total length, but

about 13 feet of the outermost portion of the passage has been destroyed. At a couple of points the side stones of the passage have fallen inwards, but otherwise the tomb is in a fairly good state of preservation. Indeed the fact that it was possible to enter the tomb straight away on discovery is proof of the constructional capabilities of the passage-grave builders. The tomb is built with orthostats and roofed over with lintels. The surviving orthostats number eighty-one – thirty-nine on the right (as one enters the tomb), forty-one on the left and the back stone. There are thirty-three cap stones. The present entrance to the tomb is around 2 feet in width and the same in height, but there is probably up to 2 feet of silt in the passage. From the entrance the passage increases in height and in the chamber it is about 7 feet high, and when the excavations are completed the actual height may well be more.

The passage is parallel-sided for most of its length, but at about two-thirds the way in it bends to the right. At the angle there is a slight bulge to the left and a short distance inwards a sill occurs. Around 8 feet beyond this point the passage widens out to form the chamber, but the widening is restricted to the left side. The inner part of the chamber is approximately square in plan. The outside of the square is formed by a

sill stone and between this and the back stone there is another but lower sill. Twenty-five of the orthostats and three cap stones are decorated, but in the main the decoration is confined to the chamber area. One decorated orthostat is worthy of special mention. This stands in the passage on the right-hand side just on the inside of the outer sill store. The stone bears an anthropomorphic design and gives the impression of a figure standing guard over the approaches to the inner sanctum *(Figure 202)*.

There is evidence for a deposit of cremated bone in the chamber area, but as excavations have not yet started within the tomb the extent of this, or of the grave deposit in general, is not yet known. Just outside the angle in the passage there is a stone basin, but this does not appear to be in its original position.

January 4, 1969

THE STRANGE IDOLS FROM MYCENAE

By Lord William Taylour

The primary object of the campaign was to dismantle a great baulk with a west-east axis purposely left unexcavated in earlier seasons; and secondly to clarify the plan of the site, particularly in regard to the earlier walls that had suffered heavily from a destruction in the latter part of the thirteenth century B.C. and which in the west part of the site lay at a great depth beneath the post-destruction walls. The second objective was only partly achieved because of spectacular finds that impeded the pace of excavation.

Partly underlying the great baulk, and near its east end, a small store room was uncovered. . . . Every available space of this room was filled to capacity with a variety of clay objects, except for a small area round the entrance in the south-east corner. Apart from tables of offerings, lamps, and pottery, there were tall figures with human

features, and snakes with heads raised, coiled up in a naturalistic manner, unlike anything found before on the Greek mainland.

A complete inventory at this stage is not possible, but on a rough calculation there are about sixteen figures and six snakes. Five of the larger figures are almost complete and one of the smaller ones. One snake is entirely undamaged, a larger one almost so. The large figures are about 60 centimetres (2 feet) tall. They have been made on the wheel, like pottery, and are therefore hollow, but the arms and features have been added separately. The large models have a hole in the crown of the head, and this may have been left for the purpose of inserting some instrument to model the features while the clay was yet soft; the protruding eyes and the prominent nose are specially notable in certain cases. On these same figures there are often tiny holes in the neck, on the chin, or under the arms. These were almost certainly necessary for the firing. They occur also on the snakes, both on the body and between the coils.

The larger figures and snakes are painted in monochrome, either red or black, but certain

203 *The most elegant of the strange idols of Mycenae*

areas of the face are left unpainted to allow the natural colour of the clay to show up, and the head of the smaller snake has a cross-hatched pattern. At least two of the smaller figures are decorated. A notable example is the elegant lady *(Figure 203)*. She is the only one that can lay some claim to beauty, or at least appeal – the others have a numinous but forbidding aspect. Her hair style, eyebrows, eyes, nostrils, and lips are painted, and her cheeks are coloured with a rosette pattern, but of greater importance is the decoration of her dress, painted in a style that in pottery would be dated to Late Helladic III A/III B, in other words, to the end of the fourteenth century B.C. And this would appear to be the date of the contents of this store room, which presumably are all contemporary.

All the figures reconstructed so far are those of women, with the exception of one that on account of the less prominent breasts is probably that of a man. In many cases the arms are missing, or have not yet been restored, but there is sufficient evidence to show that the right arm is usually raised and the left sometimes stretched forward. The general impression is that they are deities rather than worshippers. One figure has a unique posture. She appears to hold a pole (the upper part is missing) the base of which rests on her navel. It is possible that this incomplete object was a double axe, for a clay model of similar dimensions, interpreted as a stylised and crude form of the double axe, was found unbroken in the store room.

These idols are unique on the Greek mainland up to now. Similar and larger idols of about the same period have been found by Professor Marinatos at Gazi in Crete and there are the Minoan goddesses and attendants of the fifteenth century B.C. discovered by Professor Caskey on the island of Keos off the coast of Attica, but the Greek examples are only superficially related to these. As can be seen, each one has its own individuality. Each one is different in feature, in expression, even in hair style from the others. But the snakes *(Figure 204)* are unique. Snakes occur in close association with the goddess or in groups, particularly in Crete, but never, as it were, in their own right. . . .

The adjoining room to the west held even greater interest. The east wall to the south of the doorway was of mud brick. Its west face was decorated with a fresco, a large part of which was still in position – it has since been successfully removed. The fresco extends for a distance of just under 2 metres (6 feet) and in one place it is preserved to a height of 1 metre (39 inches). Against this wall and at right angles to it was built a platform of rubble and clay. The north face of this was also decorated with a fresco, of which the upper part is preserved. It shows a series of solid discs, alternately painted red and black, and above these three "horns of consecration". The wall fresco is divided into three panels with part of a human figure in each. The one to the north of the platform, and at the same level, is the best preserved. The upper half of a woman with elaborate headdress is depicted. In either hand she holds an object painted red that may be the sheaf of some cereal. The middle figure, above the platform, is also that of a woman. Only the lower half of her dress

survives but from the position of her feet she appears to face to the right (south). The third figure, the least well-preserved except for the dress, is that of a man, with the body painted

204 The best preserved of the unique snake idols of Mycenae

red. He is dressed, however, in woman's apparel – compare the "Campstool Fresco" from Knossos. His outline is not clear but he appears to be facing the middle figure, who is probably a goddess.

May 31, 1969

THE ANCIENT HEART OF HOLY IRELAND

By Dr. George Eogan

These events caused the resumption of work on the main mound, and a number of new cuttings were laid out. . . . A small hole began to appear on Tuesday, July 30, along the north baulk 3 to 4 feet below the surface. . . .

As work continued during the next couple of days the hole was becoming larger. Soon it was possible to establish that there was a passage below; the collapse of a lintel was responsible for the hole. By the evening of July 31 it was possible to drop down and when I did this I was

surprised to find that I was at the junction of an elaborate complex of passages, four in all. Three of these were constructed with dry-stone walling, so it seemed fairly certain that these were parts of *souterrains*, though the orthostats aroused my suspicion. However, as one was certainly dealing with a complex of *souterrains* and as these were roofed with large cap-stones similar to those found in the passage graves it was impossible to pass judgement on the orthostatically-lined passage. Just in from the hole some art was noticed on one of the orthostats, but yet there was the possibility that stones could have been taken from some of the "satellite" passage graves and re-used.

On the next day, August 1, it was decided to investigate the various passages and to sort out the pattern. It soon became clear that one of the dry-stone built passages was the entrance to the

205 Stone basin found in chieftain's tomb in Knowth

whole complex. Its mouth was blocked up. At a point around 3 yards in from the mouth a narrow passage led off to the right but soon it divided into two *souterrain* passages. One of these led north-westwards for a distance of 7 yards into a small chamber 2 yards in diameter. Leading out of this chamber at right angles to the entrance passage there was another passage. This may have served as an exit. The other *souterrain* passage would appear to have been built roughly on the line of the kerb-stones of the main mound. Its passage extends down-

wards and at the end there is a beehive-shaped chamber slightly over 5 feet in height. . . .

The orthostatically-lined passage was the last explored. The passage proved to be immensely long and then at its end was discovered a massive cruciform-shaped chamber. . . . The passage is aligned east-west and it is parallel-sided. For the last four or five yards before the chamber the orthostats have been pushed inwards, no doubt due to pressure of the mound, and these do not meet at the top.

But apart from this and a couple of other patches the passage is in a reasonably good state of preservation. Its sides are constructed with orthostats and it is roofed with lintels. In the main the lintels rest on the orthostats, except for the final five yards or so where dry-stone walling occurs so as to increase the height on both sides. A total of 73 orthostats survive, 36 on the left hand side and 37 on the right hand side. These are roofed with around 44 cap-stones. At the entrance the orthostatically lined passage is 2 feet 8 inches wide by around 3 feet 3 inches in height. For most of its length it retains approximately this height. At about 6 yards out from the chamber its height starts to increase rapidly, and at the junction with the passage it is 8 feet 6 inches in height.

The chamber consists of a central area with three recesses opening off it. It is formed with 21 orthostats. Some of these have shifted outwards slightly at the top but otherwise the chamber is well preserved. The central area tends to be circular, although this feature is not well pronounced. The chamber is nearly 11 yards in width and from the back of the end recess to the passage entrance it is a little over 6 yards long. The three recesses are similarly constructed: two side-stones, a back-stone, and a roof-stone. The sides and backs are heightened by the insertion of a block or blocks over the orthostats. . . .

A large stone basin occupies a central position in the recess *(Figure 205)*. It is circular at the mouth, where it is 4 feet in diameter. Both inside and outside are decorated. On the outside,

206 Reconstruction drawing by Alan Sorrell giving an impression of the ceremonies associated with the holiest part of the great mound

opposite the gap between the portal stones, there is a central motif that consists of three concentric circles with two flanking grooves on either side. There are seven horizontal grooves running around the body. The uppermost two are continuous, but the central motif interrupts the other grooves. These are again interrupted by vertical lines on each side. Some of the horizontal grooves are so deep that they give the impression that the ridges between them are standing out in relief.

In the interior of the basin a groove runs parallel to the edge and there is a circle in the centre. On two sides of this circle a series of "rays" with slightly expanded ends extend out from it. These are delimited on the outside by a groove. On the third (the outer) side of the central circle there is a motif consisting of four arcs which open on to the central circle. At the back the basin has been damaged and a portion is missing. Due to its large size, the presence of portal stones and the elaborately carved stone basin, the right-hand recess must have been the most important recess in the chamber.

The roof survives intact *(Figure 207)*. It is a magnificent example of a beehive-shaped roof produced by the corbelling technique, and standing to a height of up to 19 feet over the present surface. No excavations have been

207 The centre of the chamber rising in a corbelled beehive roof to the height of 19 feet

carried out within the chamber but there appears to be a considerable amount of silt-like material over the floor. There are a number of smallish boulders lying around on the surface.

January 10, 1970

IVORIES FROM MYCENAE

By Lord William Taylour

On entering the room and turning to the left one faces the fresco at the east end and the platform or altar in front of it. In the centre of the room is a long oval hearth with west–east axis, the north and south sides of which are bordered with large stones. At each end of it is a *pisé* construction plastered over with white clay. . . .

To the north of the hearth and right up against the north wall of the room was a *larnax*

or bath tub. It was complete but undecorated. Several broken pieces of pottery were found at the east end of it. Among them were a small krater or deep bowl, a kylix, and a jug.

But the most intriguing feature of this room was a long bench filling the whole length of the south side of it. About 1 metre (3 feet) high and 0·80 metre (2¾ feet) broad, it was built of earth and had a surface covering of long slabs in line and an outer border of large stones. When this bench was cut through it was found to contain a great quantity of complete pots, mostly at floor level: kylikes, stirrup jars, an alabastron, piriform jar, miniature jug, cup, ladle, etc. Other objects were also found, but an outstanding discovery was an ivory head, only slightly damaged, a little above floor level. It is carved in the round and has a diameter of *circa* 0·07 metre (3 inches). The craftsmanship is superb. . . .

Two features are difficult to explain: a hole in the crown of the head and the piercing of the ears. The holes in the neck were evidently intended for attachment to a body of different material, probably wood, but whether the complete figure was that of an idol or some royal person it is impossible to say.

In 1968 a much larger ivory – a couchant lion – was found behind (to the south of) the platform or altar in front of the fresco. The context at that time was not apparent, but it is now clear from its position that it also was buried, with a Minoan stone vase and an ivory sword pommel, within the long bench at its east end. The ivory has recently been restored. It has, unfortunately, suffered from its centuries-long confinement in the soil, but it is still a magnificent piece and displays the latent power with which it was endowed by the artist. Measuring *circa* 0·20 metre (8 inches) in length, it is one of the largest ivories ever fashioned by a Mycenaean craftsman. . . .

A door at the east end of the room of the fresco leads into the room of the ivories. On excavation this proved to be a corridor-sized room with a return to the south – in other words, an L-shaped room. The southern arm of this room was a shrine. A painted idol of clay on a low dais of roughly rectangular form with a north–south axis was found in the south-west corner of this annexe to the ivory room. The figure is somewhat similar to, and about the same size as, the attractive painted idol found in 1968, but the decoration is more formal and stylistically later, notably in the lozenges on the face and body. The apparent knob on the head of this female idol is a thick bunch of hair issuing from the crown and falling down to the waist at the back. As can be seen she is bejewelled with a necklace. . . .

When the floor of this small area was cleared, a variety of vases were uncovered: kylikes, a piriform jar, and several stirrup jars.

1971 onwards

The Illustrated London News *continues well into its second century of publication, and so does its link with archaeology. The articles which continue seem to the writer to be too recent for anthologising, and it is simpler, perhaps, to summarise what has been happening. There has been, of course, a great change. In May 1971, the paper went over from weekly to monthly publication and this inevitably brought on a number of other changes. The greatest loss was topicality; but there are other changes, not precisely definable, when a publication from being a weekly newspaper becomes a monthly magazine; but the principal one, as regards archaeology, is that the number of potential outlets for the subject drop from fifty-two to twelve. In fact, the change was not as drastic as this as, after some years of rather uncertain experiment, archaeology had settled down to a fairly regular fortnightly appearance, so that the effective change was from something like twenty-six to twelve. And it has continued at a steady twelve appearances a year since May 1971.*

A choice of highlights from this period includes: the resumption by the British Museum, under Norman Hammond, of the excavations at Mayan Lubaantun (in British Honduras, now called Belize) which Dr. Thomas Gann began many years before, and which the paper reported at the time; a number of activities in Israel, at Beersheba, the Old City of Jerusalem, Biblical Ziglag and at underwater sites near Acre; a new Neolithic site at Vlasać, in Yugoslavia; at Inamgaon, in Central India; at Shahdad, in Iran; a revelation of ancient Nepalese sculpture by Mary Slusser and G. Vajracarya; in Cyprus, the finding of 11,000 seal impressions of what was presumably a Ptolemaic Public Record Office at New Paphos, and the raising and preservation of a Hellenistic Greek merchant ship at Kyrenia; and a most important series of articles on Spanish and French rock paintings by the Belgian husband-and-wife team of Marcel and Lya Dams.

There have, too, been great changes in presentation in tune, perhaps, with the spirit and fashion of the age. There seems little doubt that the brilliant, rapidly moving and, now, coloured images of television have considerably altered periodical illustration technique. The television-viewer, it is argued, is easily bored by a group of black-and-white still photographs and can only be wooed with a tight selection of highly dramatic, or intensely personal or intrinsically beautiful pictures, or by gimmicky and trendy drawings. And so gone now are the old-style crowded pictorial pages of The Illustrated London News *archaeology, with pot upon pot, dagger upon dagger, flint upon flint and bone upon bone. Perhaps it is an advantage; even Sir Bruce Ingram used sometimes to say, "This is an uncommon 'boney' piece, isn't it?" But much also is lost. Television images pass without the possibility of recall (except in sporting events) and there is no possibility of study, comparison and second thought when there is only a fleeting image or at best only an arbitrary selection of pictures. Not everything reveals its nature at a first or fleeting glance; interest and beauty are rarely absolute, much more frequently relative and reveal themselves best in comparison and leisurely study.*

The Great Archaeologists
Biographical notes

Professor K. Absolon (1887–1960)
Czech. Was well known for many excavations in Moravia, especially in connection with the Stone Age mammoth-hunters and, more recently, at the Hallstatt site of Býči Skála.

Professor Carl William Blegen (1887–1971)
American. Educated at the University of Minnesota and Yale. Professor of Classical Archaeology, University of Cincinnati from 1927 to 1957. Best known for his exhaustive re-excavation of Troy and later, for his discovery of the Palace of Nestor at Pylos in the Peloponnese.

The Abbé Henri Breuil (1877–1961)
French. While a young man he discovered the Palaeolithic cave-paintings of Les Eyzies; with Cartailhac established the authenticity and nature of the Altamira cave-paintings, and became the world's leading authority on Palaeolithic art, constantly studying and recording examples in France, Spain, and, more recently, southern Africa.

Howard Carter (1874–1939)
Educated privately and principally as an artist. Went to Egypt at age of seventeen as assistant draughtsman on the staff of the Archaeological Survey of Egypt. Learnt excavation with Flinders Petrie in 1892, and was draughtsman with Naville for six years. After service with the Egyptian Inspectorate of Antiquities, was sent, in 1908, to superintend the excavations of Lord Carnarvon, which culminated in 1922 with the discovery of Tutankhamen's tomb.

Miss Amelia Ann Blanford Edwards (1831–92)
Novelist, journalist and Egyptologist. In the course of a successful literary career (during which she wrote for Dickens' *Household Words*) she visited Egypt in 1873–74, and this changed the whole course of her life. With R. Stuart Poole she started the Egypt Exploration Fund – of which they became joint secretaries in 1882. In 1889–90 she made a triumphal fund-raising tour of the Eastern United States. She left her Egyptian collections and a fund to found a chair of Egyptology to University College, London.

Sir Arthur (John) Evans (1851–1941)
Educated at Harrow and Brasenose College, Oxford. After travels and researches in the Balkans, he became, in 1884, Keeper of the Ashmolean Museum, Oxford, a post which he retained until 1908. In 1894 he acquired the site of Knossos and after the departure of the Turks from Crete he began excavating there in 1899 (with D. G. Hogarth) and from his many years of work there sprang the discovery of the Minoan civilisation.

419

Professor Dorothy Annie Elizabeth Garrod (1892–1968)
Educated privately and at Newnham College, Cambridge. Excavated many Palaeolithic sites in Gibraltar, Middle and Near East, and France. Best known for excavations on Mount Carmel and at Angles sur l'Anglin, France. Disney Professor of Archaeology, Cambridge, 1939–52.

John Garstang (1876–1956)
Educated at Blackburn Grammar School and Jesus College, Oxford. Joined Flinders Petrie in 1899 and excavated in Egypt, then at a Hittite site in Asia Minor, then again at Abydos, before the Meroe excavations (1909–14). Later he excavated in Palestine at Hazor and Jericho, and in Asia Minor at Mersin.

David George Hogarth (1862–1927)
Educated at Winchester and Magdalen College, Oxford. Excavated first in Cyprus and in Egypt (for the Egypt Exploration Fund) but his interests were classical and he became Director of the British School at Athens (1897–1900). Was with Evans in Crete where he excavated at the Dictaean Cave and Zakro. Later worked at Ephesus and Carchemish. Was Keeper of the Ashmolean Museum, Oxford from 1908 until his death in 1927. A prolific and lively writer.

Dame Kathleen (Mary) Kenyon (born 1906)
Educated at St. Paul's Girls School, London and Somerville College, Oxford. Has excavated at many sites in England, North Africa and Jordan. Best known for her revolutionary discoveries at Jericho. Director of the British School of Archaeology in Jerusalem, 1951–56. Principal of St. Hugh's College, Oxford, 1962–1973.

Sir Austen Henry Layard (1817–94)
The first and most famous of the archaeologists to uncover ancient Assyria. Of Huguenot descent. After travels in the East, became especially interested in northern Mesopotamia and the sites of Nineveh, Khorsabad and Nimrud – all, at different times, thought to be ancient Nineveh. Chief excavations at Nimrud, with patronage and support of Stratford Canning. Did no excavation after 1851 and entered politics.

Professor Doro Levi (born 1898)
Italian. Became Superintendant of Antiquities in 1933 and Professor of Archaeology and History of Classical Art at Cagliari University in 1935. Later Superintendent of Antiquities and Fine Arts in Sardinia. Succeeded Professor Federico Halbherr as the Director of the Italian excavations of the Minoan palace at Phaistos, and Hagia Triada in Crete. Also excavated in Caria, with a view to establishing the original homeland of the Minoans. Since 1947 Director of the Italian Archaeological School in Athens.

Sir Max (Edgar Lucien) Mallowan (born 1904)
Educated at Lancing and New College, Oxford. Fellow of All Souls, Oxford. Professor of Western Asiatic Archaeology, University of London 1947–62. Has excavated at various sites in Mesopotamia since 1925. Director of the British School of Archaeology in Iraq, 1947–61 and Chairman since 1966. Best known for the long series of excavations of the Assyrian capital at Nimrud.

Professor Spyridon Marinatos (1901–74)
Greek. Authority on Minoan and Mycenaean Greece. Best known for excavations in Crete, the western Peloponnese and Thera. Died, falling into his own excavation on Thera (Santorin).

Sir John (Hubert) Marshall (1876–1958)
Educated at Dulwich College and King's College, Cambridge. Started as an archaeologist with the British School at Athens and in Crete, but in 1902 became Director-General of Archaeology in India, remaining there until his

retirement in 1934. His principal work was concerned with Taxila and Mohenjo-daro and the discovery of the Indus Valley civilisation.

James Mellaart (born 1925)
While attached to the British School of Archaeology in Ankara he was shown the clandestinely excavated Dorak Treasure and allowed to draw it in detail. Later directed the revolutionary excavations at Haçilar and Čatal Hüyük in Anatolia.

Dr. Sylvanus Griswold Morley (1883–1948)
American. A leading authority on Mayan inscriptions. Connected with the Carnegie Institution in Washington from 1915, and in charge of the Chichen Itza project from 1924 to 1940.

Sir Charles (Thomas) Newton (1816–94)
After education at Shrewsbury School and Christ Church, Oxford, became vice-consul at Mytilene and acting consul at Rhodes, with a special watching interest for the British Museum. Thanks to his efforts, the famous antiquities of Halicarnassus, Cnidus and Branchidae were acquired for the Museum. In 1862 he became the first Keeper of Greek and Roman Antiquities at the British Museum and his keepership was marked by great acquisitions.

Dr. J. Papadimitriou (1904–75)
Greek. Director-General of Greek Antiquities in the post-war years. Best known for his discovery and excavation of the Second Grave Circle at Mycenae and of the Temple of Artemis at Brauron in Attica.

Sir (William Matthew) Flinders Petrie (1853–1942)
A great field-worker of prodigious industry. Excavated Tanis and Naukratis in the early days of the Egypt Exploration Fund, quarrelling with its directors in 1885, but resuming collaboration from 1896 to 1906. After 1926, he excavated in Palestine.

Hormuzd Rassam (1826–1910)
Born in Mosul, a Chaldean Christian of probably Assyrian origin, eventually a British subject. Started career as Assistant to Layard at Nimrud in 1845, but after 1851 excavated for the British Museum at various sites, including Nimrud, Kouyunjik, Assur and Balawat. Died in Hove.

Sir Henry Creswicke Rawlinson (1810–95)
Best known for his deciphering of cuneiform. After service in the East India Company's Army, reorganised the Persian Army and became interested in cuneiform inscriptions and Darius' great inscription at Behistun. Later excavated in Mesopotamia, while political agent and consul at Baghdad.

Professor Claude Frédéric Armand Schaeffer (born 1898)
French. Educated at the University of Strasbourg. Best known for the long series of excavations at Ras Shamra (Ugarit), Syria and Enkomi (Alasia), Cyprus. Captain of Corvette, Free French Naval Forces, London (1940–45).

Dr. Heinrich Schliemann (1822–90)
German. After acquiring a large fortune in Amsterdam and St. Petersburg, he was fired with a desire to "prove the truth of Homer" and carried out excavations at his own expense (and with the professional assistance of Dorpfeld) at Troy, Mycenae, Tiryns and Orchomenos. His success is world famous.

Alan John Bayard Wace (1879–1957)
Educated at Shrewsbury School and Pembroke College, Cambridge. Especially concerned with the modern excavations at Mycenae but also excavated at Sparta, Troy, Thessaly, etc. Director of the British School in Athens from 1914 to 1923 and Professor of Classical Archaeology at Cambridge from 1934 to 1944.

Sir (Robert Eric) Mortimer Wheeler (born 1890)

Directed many excavations in England (Colchester, St. Albans, Maiden Castle) and Wales (Caerleon and Carnarvon) and more recently in Pakistan and India. In 1944 he became Director-General of Archaeology in India. Served with distinction in both World Wars and widely known for his appearances on television.

J. T. Wood (1821–90)

Best known for his excavations at Ephesus from 1863 to 1874, partly done with his own resources, but with some support from the British Museum. He excavated the theatre and the odeum and in 1869 laid bare part of the two upper layers of the famous temple of Artemis – one of the original Seven Wonders of the World.

Sir (Charles) Leonard Woolley (1880–1960)

Educated at St. John's, Leatherhead and New College, Oxford. Worked at the Ashmolean Museum under Sir Arthur Evans. Excavated in Nubia, at Carchemish, Tell el Amarna and, then, in 1922 at Ur where he continued to work for thirteen years. He later excavated in Syria at the late Hittite site of Alalakh.

Yadin Yigael formerly Sukenik, and son of the famous Hebrew scholar of that name (born 1916)

After a distinguished career in the Israeli Forces, ending as Chief of Staff 1949–52, turned to archaeology. Now a professor at the Hebrew University, Jerusalem. Director of large-scale excavations at Hazor, Megiddo, the Dead Sea Caves and Masada.

Professor Rodney Young (born 1907)

American. Educated at Princeton and Columbia. Curator of the University Museum, University of Pennsylvania and later Professor of Classical Archaeology at the University of Pennsylvania. Director of the long and successful series of excavations at Phrygian Gordion.

Index

423

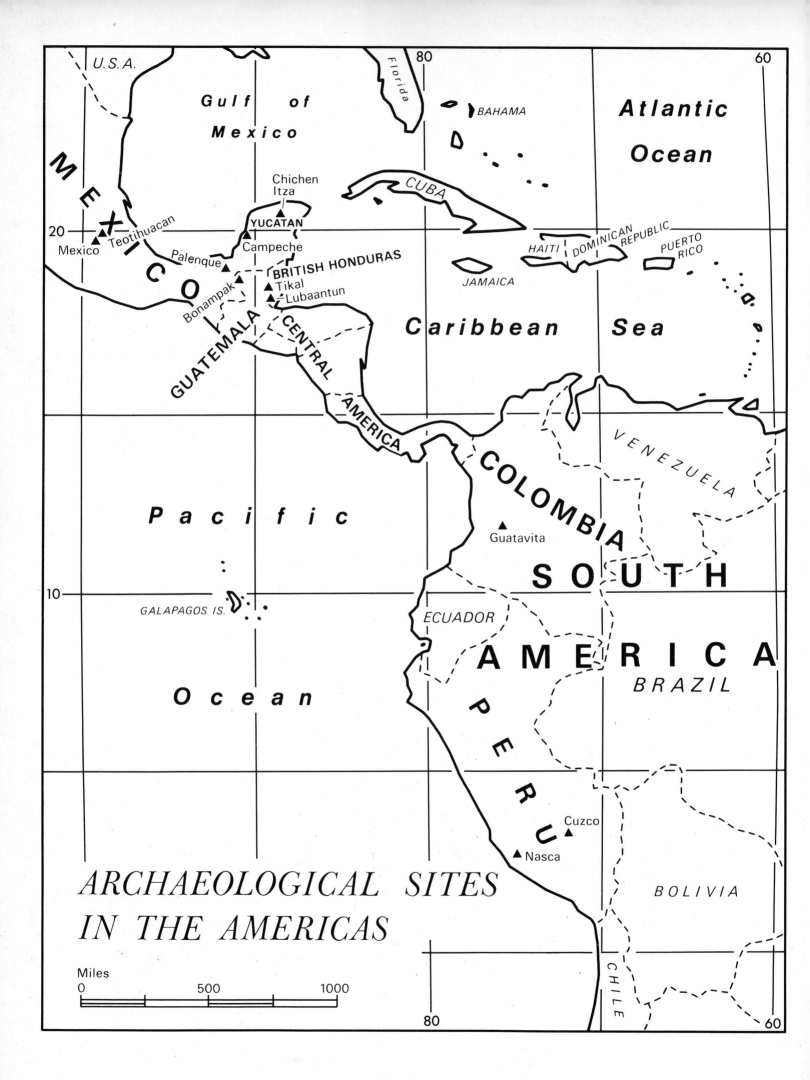

ARCHAEOLOGICAL SITES
IN THE AMERICAS